The African Color
Comparative Perspective

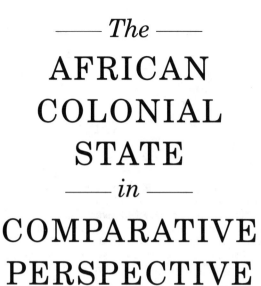

The AFRICAN COLONIAL STATE *in* COMPARATIVE PERSPECTIVE

Crawford Young

YALE UNIVERSITY PRESS

New Haven and London

Designed by Jill Breitbarth and set in New Century
Schoolbook type by Keystone Typesetting Inc.,
Orwigsburg, Pennsylvania.

Printed in the United States of America by
BookCrafters, Inc., Chelsea, Michigan.

Library of Congress Cataloging-in-Publication Data
Young, Crawford, 1931–
The African colonial state in comparative perspective /
Crawford Young.
p.   cm.
Includes bibliographical references (p.   ) and index.
ISBN 0-300-05802-0 (cloth: acid-free paper)
0-300-06879-4 (paper: acid-free paper)
1. Colonies—Africa—History. 2. Colonies—Africa—
Administration—History.   3. Africa—Politics and
government.   I. Title.
JV246.Y68   1994
325′.314′096—dc20   94-11020
                                                CIP

A catalogue record for this book is available from the
British Library.

The paper in this book meets the guidelines for
permanence and durability of the Committee on
Production Guidelines for Book Longevity of the Council on
Library Resources.

10   9   8   7   6   5   4   3   2

CONTENTS

TABLES

PREFACE

As a conscious project, this study dates from 1980 and has thus consumed a third of my professional years. Its roots extend back even further, to my first visit to Africa in 1956, in the twilight years of the colonial state. Vivid memories from my early contacts with Africa persist: the phenomenal enthusiasm surrounding the Tunisian charismatic hero Habib Bourguiba and his Neo-Destour Party in 1956, the intimidating fear the Belgian colonial state still inspired in young Congolese students in 1958. Attention was riveted on nationalist movements and the emergent architecture of the independent state, presumed to rest on new political foundations, transcending and repudiating the colonial order. I could not then have imagined the colonial state as an object of prolonged study.

Even two decades later in 1979, when an invitation came from the Institute for Advanced Study at Princeton to take part in a working group on comparative colonialism, my initial reaction was lukewarm. The building evidence of a profound crisis of polity, economy, and society was yet to congeal. My first effort to identify the nature of the state as a source of Africa's travail was in a 1978 essay, which focused on only three polities—Mobutu's Zaire, Amin's Uganda, and Acheampong's Ghana—as "perverted states," still seen as deviant cases tugged from the developmental pathway by singularly capricious and venal rulers.

My year of participation in the comparative colonialism research group at the Institute for Advanced Study during 1980 and 1981 coincided with a moment of spreading conviction that African development was at an impasse. Rather than a handful of "perverted states" that stood out as unhappy exceptions, a general pattern of decline took form, with only the exceptional cases—the small number of Botswanas or Tunisias—combining reasonable governance with satisfactory growth. The postcolonial sources of "perversion" were real enough, in the venal patrimonialism that characterized "life president" power management in many states, but there was more to the story than this. The intellectual exchange with distinguished Institute Fellows that year, whose regional specializations included India, Indonesia, Iraq, the Maghreb, Brazil, and Spanish America, persuaded me that the African colonial state was distinctive in important ways, which might provide some of the explanation for the crisis of the postcolonial state. I was then in the final stages of drafting with Thomas Turner the manuscript published in 1985 as *The Rise and Decline of the Zairian State* (University of Wisconsin Press). We abandoned the earlier conceptual apparatus informing that study and grafted state theory on it in its final revision. This represented an initial attempt at developing a conceptualization of "state" that could be applied to modes of colonial domination.

A research year at the Woodrow Wilson International Center for Scholars in Washington during 1983 and 1984 extended the scope of my inquiry and deepened my commitment to pursuing it as a major project. Fellows are expected to offer a paper at the end of their stay summarizing their findings; mine was a preliminary effort to delineate the major themes of this book. The paper was subsequently published in a volume edited by Donald Rothchild and Naomi Chazan, *The Precarious Balance: State and Society in Africa* (Westview Press, 1988). In this form it was widely distributed, and a number of invaluable critical commentaries were received.

My earlier periods of research in Zaire (1962, 1973–1975) and Uganda (1965–1966) had included extensive consultation of the basic documents of the colonial period and a number of interviews with former colonial administrators and agents, European and African. Before drafting my manuscript I wanted to benefit from one more field-research location, representative of a different colonial tradition, where I could draw on additional primary materials. A Fulbright lectureship at the University of Dakar, Senegal, during 1987 and 1988 presented this opportunity; the Senegalese national archives (formerly serving all of French West Africa) were an invaluable resource. My field research provided, I believe, a sufficient grounding in direct observation and primary materials, joined with coverage of secondary sources for the balance of the continent and other former colonial areas used for comparison.

Naturally this venture has not consumed all of my time during the past thirteen years, but throughout them it has loomed large, attracting benefactors and collaborators so numerous that it is not possible to acknowledge them all.

My most salient debts, however, require recognition, and I begin with those whose support made possible periods of full-time commitment to this research. The roster begins with the Institute of Advanced Study. My greatest debt is to Albert Hirschman, without whose invitation, encouragement, and stimulation the project would never have been undertaken. The Woodrow Wilson International Center for Scholars provided equally congenial surroundings and superb support, including an excellent research assistant, Brian Digre. The center's associate director at the time, Prosser Gifford, provided crucial encouragement and support. My lectureship year in Senegal was supported by the Fulbright Program. My teaching duties at the University of Dakar provided invaluable intellectual associations and left ample time for work at the Senegalese national archives, whose chief archivist, Saliou Mbaye, was unfailingly helpful, as were his colleagues. The staff at the American Cultural Center in Dakar, particularly Robert LaGamma and Helen Picard, were remarkably nurturant to the Fulbright contingent. The Graduate School Research Committee of the University of Wisconsin—Madison provided crucial supplementary support for the Institute for Advanced Study and Wilson Center years, and it helped make possible research time during 1988 and 1989, when most of the first draft was composed.

I sought critical readings of the initial Wilson Center paper and the later manuscript from a large number of scholars, who provided valuable correctives. I was particularly anxious to elicit reactions from African scholars; those who responded to my appeal include Mamadou Diouf and Boubacar Barry (Senegal), Ammar Bouhouche (Algeria), Bayo Luwal and Vincent Ekpu (Nigeria), and Bereket Selassie (Eritrea). Others who commented on the manuscript or its forerunner include Jan Vansina, Steve Stern, Michael Schatzberg, D. A. Low, Gretchen Bauer, Lucy Colvin Philips, Richard Joseph, Shaheen Mozzafar, and Atul Kohli. To all of these I extend my warmest thanks and the customary absolving of any responsibility for surviving deficiencies in the work.

A number of graduate students at the University of Wisconsin—Madison have helped at one stage or another, earning my warm appreciation. They include Andrew Sessions, Tasha Nathanson, Kristen Thomas, Timothy Longman, and Jennifer Owen. Louise Young gathered much of the statistical data; she and Emily Young, specialists in Japan and Latin America, respectively, were valuable critics on the comparative dimension. Elizabeth Diez ably performed the large task of preparing the index.

The catalogue of debts must be completed by a collective but no less heartfelt expression of gratitude to numerous others—Africans of many lands, colleagues, students, family—who in ways large and small have contributed to this undertaking.

Chapter One

BULA MATARI AND
THE CONTEMPORARY
AFRICAN CRISIS

We are not interested in the preservation of any of the structures of the colonial state. It is our opinion that it is necessary to totally destroy, to break, to reduce to ash all aspects of the colonial state in our country to make everything possible for our people.

The problem of the nature of the state created after independence is perhaps the secret of the failure of African independence.

—Amilcar Cabral, "The State in Africa"

BULA MATARI: THE ORIGINS

In 1879–1880 Henry Morton Stanley, an American in Leopoldian livery, forced a small army of porters bearing dismantled steamers over the tortuous terrain separating tidewater in the Zaire estuary from the vast pool of the Congo (Zaire) River above the rapids. Beyond lay the huge network of navigable waters along which the meager yet sufficient "tools of empire" projected the developing power of the colonial state in formation.[1] Stanley's logistical feat engendered mingled fear and admiration in the Kongo regions through which he passed, reflected in the nickname Bula Matari (he who crushes rocks) by which he became known.

Over time, as the new state on whose construction Stanley had surreptitiously embarked ceased to be his personal undertaking as Leopoldian emissary and burgeoned into an impersonal embodiment of oppressive European power, Bula Matari came to represent this intrusive alien authority more generally. The metaphor captured well the crushing, relentless force of the emerging colonial state in Africa. "For all Bakongo," wrote a Zairian sociologist, "the name of Bula Mata(r)i signified terror."[2]

European administrators found this semiotic imagery congenial, as it suggested the irresistible hegemony deemed necessary to performance of their guardian role. In the everyday informal discourse of rule, the prefectoral agents of Belgian colonial power widely employed the term as a synonym for "state"; a summons from Bula Matari was an order from the government. In the symbolism of Bula Matari the colonial state is stripped naked: the term did not apply to the layers of African intermediaries who in a number of settings partially concealed it from village view; it referred solely to the alien, white domination that was the energizing force in the superstructure of imperial hegemony.

Bula Matari as specific lexical rendering of the colonial state was particular to the Belgian realm. Yet its evocative imagery can be projected onto the much larger domain I explore: the African colonial state in its variant forms throughout the continent. In its ultimate teleology—the vocation of domination—are embedded the behavioral imperatives that marked its operation.

Bula Matari as a codeword for the superstructure of alien rule brings us back to Cabral's normative appeal in the epigraph above "to totally destroy, to break, to reduce to ash" the colonial state, to repay Bula Matari in his own metaphorical coin. The empirical Cabral sounds a more somber note than does his moral exhortation; the colonial state lives, absorbed into the structures of the independent polity. A state, once institutionalized, has a formidable capacity for its own reproduction across time and in the face of systematic efforts by new regimes to uproot prior forms and build new blueprints. Residues of Czarist Russia and the Middle Kingdom remained within the state socialist forms constructed by revolutionary design in the Soviet Union and China. Nationalist revolution in Africa had less sweeping goals, and thus by silent incorporation it retained more of the operational code of its defeated enemy in the postcolonial polity. In metamorphosis the caterpillar becomes butterfly without losing its inner essences.

THE CRISIS OF THE POSTCOLONIAL STATE

Some will find Cabral's categorical pronouncement of the "failure" of the African state too sweeping: not in all places, one might demur, not in all ways. For those states whose disarray and decay were most striking at the beginning of the 1990s—the Sudan, Somalia, Zaire, Mozambique—the label fits reasonably as a global judgment, although even here on close inspection some positive elements might be discerned. For the most capably ruled states—Botswana and Mauritius stand out—the progress we once believed immanent in modern historical process has occurred and been widely shared with civil society.[3] But for most African states the 1970s and 1980s were years of disappointment and often decline; by the 1980s the term *crisis* had achieved general currency as a description of the African condition.

2

African independence in the 1960s coincided with a time of immense self-confidence in the world at large. In the West the prolonged postwar prosperity was at its apogee; Keynesian theory had conquered the business cycle, and Western Europe had recovered from the ravages of World War II. In the Soviet Union Nikita Khrushchev was promising to bury capitalism and to surge triumphantly into full communism by 1980. China's "great leap forward" then under way was not recognized as a lethal catastrophe until many years later. With hubris resonating throughout the world and exhilaration at the unanticipated swiftness of African independence, the high optimism that attended the transfer of power is not surprising. An influential pan-African assembly of intellectuals at Ibadan in 1959 reflected the general mood: supreme confidence in the capacity of the intelligentsia to lead new nations through socialist policies to social justice; "to throw off the imperialist yoke, and end discrimination and the exploitation of man by man"; to gain "freedom, and respect for the dignity of the black man."[4]

A few discordant voices were heard from the outset. In the exquisite polemics of Frantz Fanon are some memorable passages warning that a new ruling class drawn from the petty bourgeoisie might engross the benefits of independence.[5] The irascible French agronomist René Dumont warned in 1962 that Africa was off to a poor start.[6] But these were isolated views; a handful of Cassandras did not suffice to shake the robust confidence of the early years.

In the late 1960s some negative trends appeared, but they seemed confined to the political sphere: the Zaire rebellions, the Nigerian civil war, the spread of military coups, the rise of autocracy.[7] African economic performance remained respectable throughout the 1960s—ironically contributing to the magnitude of the current debt crisis; in the early 1970s the major international banks, lacking profitable outlets in the industrial world, turned to aggressive lending in Africa (as well as Latin America).[8] Not until the mid-1970s did a mood of pervasive pessimism begin to take hold.

New academic paradigms both shaped and reflected this gradual transformation of perspectives. The "dependency theory" imported from Latin America replaced the visions of inevitable progress fostered by the assorted approaches collectively labeled "modernization theory," ascendant in the 1960s; Africa was seen as doomed to inevitable "underdevelopment," whose engine was world capitalism.[9] A fresh wave of neo-Marxist scholarship rediscovered the state, often with the help of Althusserian structuralism, and found it to be the simple instrument of a variously defined but uniformly avaricious dominant class (the metropolitan bourgeoisie, bureaucratic bourgeoisie, petty bourgeoisie, among others). The state was no longer the custodian of liberation and development but the instrument of extraction and exploitation.[10]

By the end of the 1970s a sense of alarm had percolated into the economic realm. The Nigerian director of the United Nations Economic Commission for Africa (ECA), Adebayo Adedeji, wrote in 1979, "How have we come to this sorry state of affairs in the post-independence years which seemed at the beginning to have held so much promise?"[11] A report prepared for the 1979 Organization of African Unity (OAU) summit in Monrovia offered the dispiriting conclusion that "Africa . . . is unable to point to any significant growth rate or satisfactory index of general well-being."[12] The deepening pessimism led to the preparation of two key documents, at the initiative of the African leadership: the Lagos Plan of Action, reflecting OAU thinking, and the World Bank report drafted under the leadership of Elliot Berg.[13] The contrasting demonology of these rival reports (the ravages of the world economy, for the OAU; African state policy and performance, for the World Bank) framed the intensifying debate on the African development impasse; the common ground in both was the severity of the economic crisis afflicting the continent. The gentle and understated cadences of Jacob Ajayi epitomize the transformed perspectives: "The optimism of development plans of the 1960s has given way to increasing frustration in the 1970s and disillusionment in the 1980s. The general lament is that this is not what was expected from independence."[14]

Throughout the 1980s a drumfire of disheartening statistics deepened the apprehensions. The African external debt, insignificant in 1970, had ballooned to well over $200 billion by the beginning of the 1990s. In proportion to the scale of the economies, it extracted an even heavier ransom than the better publicized Latin American debt. Before the late 1970s only Ghana had ever had recourse to an International Monetary Fund (IMF) stabilization program; in the 1980s most IMF clients were African. Per-capita income continued to decline, in many countries to below 1960 levels.[15] Carl Eicher, in an influential article, demonstrated that Africa was the only major world region to experience declining per-capita food production after 1960.[16]

The state found itself the object of growing opprobrium. The Zairian bishops declared in an angry 1981 pastoral letter that the state had degenerated into "organized pillage for the profit of the foreigner and his intermediaries." Michael Crowder, while pointing to the colonial origins of state autocracy, exorbitant extraction, violence, and personal despo-

4

tism, notes that "Nigerians of all classes have developed a deep cynicism about their leaders, both civilian and military, and certainly have little faith in the liberal economy and mixed economy that were the legacy of their colonial rulers."[17] Naomi Chazan echoes these views in her Ghana monograph:

> By the early 1980s it was apparent that Ghana had forfeited its elementary ability to maintain internal or external order and to hold sway over its population. Although its existence as a *de jure* political entity on the international scene was unquestionable, these outward manifestations did raise doubts as to its *de facto* viability. The Ghanian state thus seemed to be on the brink of becoming less distinctive and relevant. Indeed, some kind of disengagement from the state was taking place . . . an emotional, economic, social, and political detachment from the state element.[18]

Carl Rosberg and Robert Jackson question the "empirical" existence of the state in many instances, arguing that it is sustained above all by its juridical status in the international realm.[19] John Ayoade characterizes postcolonial state evolution as a regressive trajectory from "Mother Theresa" state to a bedridden, comatose, and now virtually expired condition.[20]

Achille Mbembe, in a penetrating analysis, characterizes the African state as driven by a *principe autoritaire,* whose citizens flee into an astonishing assortment of religious and other shelters: "Bref, l'indigène recourt, comme à l'époque coloniale, a toutes les ressources de ce qu'il faut bien appeler sa *capacité historique à l'indiscipline. . . . Partout, la délinquance d'Etat a produit une culture de débrouillardise et de sauve-qui-peut et un déclin de l'identité citoyenne."*[21]

Jean-Françoise Bayart, in his magistral summation of the African state, echoes Mbembe: "The under-remuneration of agricultural labor, the brutality of the territorial administration, of the chiefs and of the armed bands which control the countryside constitute . . . reasons for . . . desertion as the sole pertinent response to the arbitrary action and wasteful consumption of the state . . . exit [by the subjects] . . . continues to sap civic space, to constrain the process of accumulation of power and wealth, and to render predation easier than exploitation."[22]

A mordant critique of the postcolonial polity pervaded African literature. The biting satire of the weekly cartoons in *West Africa* mirrored such despairing novels as *The Beautyful Ones Are Not Yet Born*[23] and *Petals of Blood.*[24] One of the most powerful bards of nationalist liberation, Okot p'Bitek, records his despondency in his final work: "The walls of hopelessness surround me completely," with "no windows to let in the air of hope!"[25]

Dominer pour servir, wrote Belgium's most distinguished imperial proconsul, Pierre Ryckmans, in an unintentionally ironic *plaidoyer* for a reformed colonial state, whose postcolonial successor dominated too much and served too little.[26] It was, in the words of Patrick Chabal, "both overdeveloped and soft. It was overdeveloped because it was erected, artificially, on the foundations of the colonial state. It did not grow organically from within civil society. It was soft because, although in theory all-powerful, it scarcely had the administrative or political means of its dominance."[27] Its hegemonical aspirations were costly in more than one sense. Spiraling state consumption was reflected in the extraordinary degree to which governments came to dominate the employment markets. By 1980 public-sector employment accounted for 50 to 55 percent of all nonagricultural jobs, compared to 36 percent in Asia, 27 percent in Latin America, and 24 percent in Organization for Economic Cooperation and Development countries.[28] The Egyptian bureaucracy, which had long guaranteed employment to a hundred thousand university graduates a year, quadrupled in size between 1952 and 1970.[29] Relative to per-capita GDP, central-government wages were high: a ratio of six to one in Africa, twice the Asian and Latin American figures, and almost four times those of OECD countries.[30] State expenditure levels, as fractions of GDP, also rose inexorably, until forced into retreat by structural adjustment programs in the 1980s. In 1967 the average fraction of GDP consumed by the African state was less than 15 percent.[31] By 1982 it was more than 30 percent in several countries.

The tale told by these figures goes beyond their simple magnitude. In many cases this phase of rapid state expansion coincided with a drop in the state's apparent capacities. In global comparative terms, an exceptionally high fraction of state outlays was devoted simply to compensating the bureaucracy. Further, there was a little noted but important distortion in national-income accounts; because government expenditure enters GOP calculations at factor cost, a dilation of the state payroll is measured as if it were economic "growth"; in this way, the real level of deterioration was greater than stagnant GDP figures might suggest.

A phenomenal parastatalization of the economy had occurred in states of all ideological orientation. Zambia had 134 parastatal enterprises by 1970, the Ivory Coast nearly a hundred by the late 1970s, Nigeria approximately 250 by 1973; Zaire by 1975 had vested most of its economy in public enterprises.[32] In Tanzania 75 percent of the medium and large enterprises were parastatals in the early 1980s.[33] The ubiquity of the parastatal led Sudanese African Development Bank economist Lual Deng to characterize the African state as a "policed economy," with comprehensive administrative rationing its most salient (and negative) feature.[34]

The state security apparatus contributed as well to hypertrophy. In 1989 an estimated 20 percent of the $230 billion African external debt was incurred for armaments. Until the mid-1980s African arms expenditures were high relative to those of other regions; during the 1970s they rose faster than anywhere else.[35]

The hegemonical ambitions of the state were imposing, measured in its "policed economy," the scale of its apparatus, and the weight of its consumption. But its quantitative expansion was not matched by qualitative improvement in services to civil society. Educational systems and health networks expanded numerically but often deteriorated in performance. The parastatal sector became the target of the gallows humor that helps make everyday survival bearable: NEPA (Nigerian Electrical Power Authority) was rendered "Never Electric Power Again"; the Zairian Office des Routes was better known as "Office des Trous." The option for radical quantitative expansion carried an unanticipated trade-off in qualitative decline.

As the African crisis deepened in the 1980s, so did the contrast between Africa's aggregate developmental performance and that of most other third world regions. The emergent phenomenon of the "newly industrializing country" (NIC) stood in particular counterpoint to African trends. The increasingly sharp discrepancies in outcome in different spheres of what had been conceptually globalized as the third world punctured the credibility of such explanatory frameworks as "dependency theory," which postulated uniformly operating determinants on a world scale. By the 1980s the specificity of regional patterns within the world political economy came to dominate the problematics. The NIC heartland of East and Southeast Asia towered over the others—although only two decades before, the international development community had regarded South Korea as hopelessly corrupt and singularly unpromising; the Pearson Commission report had concluded that it "seemed doomed to permanent dependence on foreign aid with *no possibility* of achieving a high growth rate from its own resources. Critics could point to almost every abuse in the catalogue. There was serious corruption, there was inflation, the aid dialogue was most acrimonious, and exports of the country's own products were low."[36]

No other third world area could match the Pacific Rim, but the severity of the crisis in Africa compared to other regions was underlined both in repeated World Bank reports and in Economic Commission for Africa documents. India—which a quarter century earlier seemed destined to absorb the globe's grain surpluses—became self-sufficient in food and found ways to manage the world's most complex cultural pluralism through constitutional governance and open political competition. The Middle East, although dominated by an array of autocracies (theocratic, monarchical, or military), survived its endemic regional conflicts with a modicum of prosperity (partly through an informal secondary distribution of the oil windfall to such nonoil states as Yemen, Jordan, and Syria). Latin America was severely damaged by its debt crisis in the 1980s but nonetheless enjoyed a strong trend toward political democratization. Here and there were polities afflicted with decay or even disintegration: Afghanistan, Burma, Haiti. But the pattern of regionwide decline of the political economy was particular to Africa.

IN SEARCH OF EXPLANATION

The quest for explanation leads one down a number of pathways. Natural calamities have struck much of the continent with distressing regularity, above all the prolonged droughts in the Sahel zones in the first half of the 1970s, then in the early 1980s both there and in much of southern Africa. Some observers argue that the African physical environment is more unfavorable than any other.[37] The dialectics of colonial partition and decolonization spawned a proliferation of sovereign units— fifty-two in 1990, many small and weak (thirteen had fewer than a million people, and only thirteen had populations of more than ten million; a mere four had a GDP as high as Hong Kong's). Population growth—about 3 percent since independence—produces huge younger generations to educate and employ, growing pressure on historically abundant land, and the necessity for relatively high growth rates to avert a per-capita decline. By some projections, a country like Nigeria will have a population of four hundred million by 2030 if present trends continue. No continent has suffered more from the AIDS epidemic that became visible in the 1980s; by the turn of the century, countries like Tanzania and Uganda will have well over 10 percent of their population HIV positive, and a wide swath of eastern and central Africa faces a comparable threat.

Although the terms of international trade were very favorable to Africa in the 1950s, and reasonably so in the 1960s, the pattern changed during the 1970s and by the 1980s had become heavily unfavorable for most African states.[38] The debt issue became serious at the same time, and by the late 1980s outflows in debt repayments exceeded aid inflows and new credit. External investment had all but ceased, private and public financial institutions offered little but debt reschedulings with costly charges, and aid levels stagnated. Even the most moderate African leaders, such as Félix Houphouët-Boigny, spoke bitterly of the relentless pressure on African states to slash their expenditures and shrink their institutional infrastructures.

Political calamities too have played their part in African distress. Such singularly capricious tyrannies as those of Idi Amin of Uganda, Francisco Macias Nguema of Equatorial Guinea, and Jean-Bedel Bokassa of the Central African Republic wreaked havoc with their countries. Persistent regional conflicts in northwest, northeast, and southern Africa triggered spiraling arms races, unleashed refugee flows that made the continent home to half the globe's displaced populations, and put many rural communities at the mercy of marauding armed bands. Above all, the deliberate South African strategy of aggressive destabilization during the 1980s took a terrible toll on vulnerable neighboring states, especially Mozambique and Angola; Hanlon makes a convincing case that between 1980 and 1984 the South African riposte to what its security establishment labeled a "total Communist onslaught" produced a hundred thousand deaths and a million refugees and cost the region $10 billion.[39] More recent estimates run as high as $60 billion.

Thus, the various contemporary pathways supply important elements to understanding the African crisis: core-periphery interactions in the world political economy, political logic and class dynamics of the postcolonial polity, angered gods of climate and environment. Yet one broad trail leads us backward to the historic determinants that have molded the contemporary state and shaped its behavioral imperatives. The colonial system created the African states in most instances; only a handful have a more distant ancestry, and even fewer have decisive institutional continuities with a precolonial past. The vertebral thesis of this book is that a retrospective examination of the African colonial state can illuminate some of the frailties of its postcolonial successor and perhaps even suggest avenues of escape from its more burdensome legacies.[40]

The colonial state in Africa lasted in most instances less than a century—a mere moment in historical time. Yet it totally reordered political space, societal hierarchies and cleavages, and modes of economic production. Its territorial grid—whose final contours congealed only in the dynamics of decolonization—determined the state units that gained sovereignty and came to form the present system of African polities. The logic of its persistence and reproduction was by the time of independence deeply embedded in its mechanisms of internal guidance.

Our task, then, is to decode the operative logic of the African colonial state. The first step is to locate our analysis in the unfolding and recently reinvigorated debate on the nature of the state, and to suggest how this master concept might be given usable form. The notion of "state" usually includes the attribute of sovereignty as one of its defining characteristics: a state is a normatively autonomous entity within a broader international community of similar units. The colonial state, as species, lacks this crucial trait. One therefore needs to demonstrate the applicability of a theoretical discourse derived from a genus that has additional chromosomes. Some observers dispute that the concept of state can be applied to the colonial dependency; my third chapter examines the particularity of the African colonial state, argues in brief for its inclusion in the state genus, and locates its origins within the broader spread of Western imperialism.

The incorporation of Africa into colonial space was a continental phenomenon; the dialectics of partition in the last quarter of the nineteenth century operated from "the Cape to Cairo." We thus take the entire continent as geographical referent, while at once acknowledging the importance of regional variations. In particular, the white-settler zones of southern Africa and the Arab tier of states whose historicity was never wholly extinguished on the northern rim stand somewhat apart from most sub-Saharan polities. Nonetheless, I believe that there are enough common patterns in the construction of colonial states to justify a common analytical framework for all. I hope to suggest overarching patterns as well as ranges of variation within them.

The political scientist who emigrates to the past, fleeing momentarily the tyranny of the present that permeates our discipline, encounters in this brazen trespass elementary issues of historiography. Conceptual capture of the past inevitably requires its periodization. Any venture confining the infinite complexity of historical process to a handful of temporal demarcations has its disabilities, but for our purposes a three-fold division of the colonial epoch is serviceable. The first period extended from the (variable) moment of conquest until World War I; during this stage the dominant objective was to construct an apparatus of domination that would transform military (sometimes political) subordination into permanent rule. The second phase, covering the interwar years, was an era of consolidation. The superstructure of colonial domination was institutionalized, rationalized, and routinized. This second period had two rather distinct economic phases: the relative prosperity and economic expansion of the 1920s, and the acute depression of the 1930s. The third and final period entailed the gradual realization by the managers of the African colonial state that it could not indefinitely persist as a formal construct of alien rule; growing African nationalism forced reluctant metropolitan acceptance of transfer of sovereignty and formal decolonization.

By the 1980s the plight of the African state seemed distinctly worse than that of other world regions formerly subject to imperial rule. If the African colonial state bore the pathologies of the contemporary polity, at least in part, then comparative examination of its counterparts in other zones of the once-colonized world should reveal significant contrasts. This requires difficult comparisons across historical time; the colonial state in the Americas was ascendant from the sixteenth to the eighteenth centuries, well before the European presence in Africa was anything other than a few coastal outposts. Nonetheless, I believe that the comparison helps draw attention to dimensions of Africa's colonial state legacy that have been detrimental to the postcolonial polity.

In conclusion I suggest some ways in which the legacy of the colonial state remains deeply embedded within its postcolonial successor. Not only the state: the forms taken by the civil societies that crystallized in the postwar years to challenge European rule, examined in chapter 7, bore the imprint of Bula Matari in unsuspected ways. The opening epigraph drawn from Cabral, composed before Africa's past two dismal decades, is a prescient acknowledgment of the contemporary weight of the colonial state legacy.

This study, like its subject, has external origins. It began with an invitation from Albert Hirschman to join a working group on comparative colonialism at the Institute for Advanced Study in Princeton during 1980 and 1981. Only gradually did that first stimulus awaken the ambition to undertake a work of this scope. The gathering gloom concerning the immediate prospects of the African polity was powerful reinforcement. A sustained inquiry (then nearing completion) into the contemporary state in Zaire deepened the conviction that a grasp of the constraining legacy of the colonial state was crucial to any understanding of present dilemmas.[41] In beginning our Zairian study in 1973, our assumption was that, although voice (to borrow from the Hirschman triptych of exit, voice, or loyalty) might be subdued by the expansive hegemonical project of the Mobutu regime, loyalty was assured. By the time we concluded our research, exit was unmistakably the preferred option of civil society,[42] which found in the public order no means for constraining the three vices of passion—ferocity, avarice, and ambition—identified by Giambattista Vico two centuries ago as the destructive energizing forces in any society that the enlightened state had to tame.[43]

Thus, the journey to Princeton took us much farther than we initially imagined. Doubtless Hirschman's "hiding hand" played an indispensable part, by concealing during the early stages the magnitude of the task until it was too late to abandon it.[44] Whether the inquest vindicates the Cabral call for a total destruction of the colonial state, I leave for the reader to judge; what is certain is that large residues of the African colonial state are everywhere present. The topic of this book is historical; its purposes are contemporary.

Chapter Two

ON THE STATE

> The modern state is a compulsory association which organizes domination. It has been successful in seeking to monopolize the legitimate use of physical force as a means of domination within a territory.
>
> —*Max Weber,* "Politics as a Vocation"

> The executive of the modern State is but a committee for managing the common affairs of the whole bourgeoisie.
>
> —*Karl Marx,* The Communist Manifesto

> The word [state] commonly denotes no class of objects that can be identified exactly, and for the same reason it signifies no list of attributes which bears the sanction of common usage.
>
> —*George Sabine,* Encyclopedia of the Social Sciences

IN SEARCH OF THE STATE

The state is the lead actor in the analysis that follows. Accordingly, this macrohistorical personage requires full introduction. The anatomy of the "master noun of political discourse," as Clifford Geertz appropriately labels it,[1] occupies this chapter; in the next, I turn more specifically to the subsidiary species of the state genus, the colonial polity.

The state as analytical quarry is an elusive and complex prey. In part, our conceptual grasp arises by perhaps unconscious empiricism through inductive contemplation of the political entities in the modern world which have borne that name. Also, states are known through the rich body of normative discourse that has accompanied their evolution over the past 2,500 years. The major paradigms that shape contemporary intellectual patterns of cognition supply contrastive vocabulary, categories, and metaphors for incorporating state into our field of conceptual vision.

State, after a lengthy period of virtual occultation as a recognized actor, has returned to center stage with a vengeance in the past decade. We are far removed from the epoch when, with behavioral revolution at its apogee, such influential theorists as David Easton urged us to banish the very word in favor of function-laden "systems."[2] Those, such as Theda Skocpol, who led the campaign to "bring the state back in" may now savor the ultimate triumph of discovering their paradigms used as a foil for new antitheses.[3] While stopping short of the contrary injunction to "take the state back out," the insurgents have recalled the innumerable exit routes and channels of response of civil society to challenge an abusive ascendancy of unmitigated state-centric theory.[4]

The return of the state, whatever its excesses, was long overdue. As an agency of domination, which in Weber's view is its defining feature, the state constitutes and bounds a civil society. As a purposive instrument, pursuing collective goals, the state aggregates, however imperfectly, rational choice.[5] As a resource consumer, the contemporary state almost everywhere preempts at least 20 percent of GNP (in advanced welfare states and state socialist polities, well over half). As an economic manager, even when buffeted by the new winds of liberalism in the 1980s, the state wields extensive powers. As an international actor, an armed participant in the anarchical order of world politics, it decisively shapes the global system. And, most crucial for our purposes, the state initiated, designed, and imposed the colonial order.

The object of this chapter is to extract from history and theory a concept of state as actor that will facilitate our inquest into the African colonial state. No comprehensive treatise on the state is intended, only a clarification of the notions I use in this book.[6] To identify the critical elements defining a state, and the behavioral imperatives that shape its action, I turn first to this "master noun" as an empirical historical entity and theoretical object. In setting the conceptual stage, we need to consider some problematic dimensions of state theory: structure versus human agency as historical demiurge; state as unitary rational actor versus structural complexity and institutional fragmentation of the polity; interpenetration and interaction between state and civil society; possibly contrastive logics of state, regime, and ruler.

The state as a human construction originated more than six thousand years ago; if we take as a minimal definition the existence of permanent institutions of rule, then for at least three millennia most of humanity has dwelt in their shadow.[7] State forms have been invented in a number of times and places, and distinct varieties have evolved—among them patrimonial monarchies,[8] the Islamic state,[9] the Buddhist polity in south Asia,[10] the Sino-Confucian kingdom,[11] the Indic state (or, in its Geertzian representation, the "theater state"),[12] the far-flung empire state,[13] the city-state, the feudal state. Africa had an especially rich endowment of state forms before they were submerged by the territorial grid of colonialism: the quasi-feudal monarchy of Ethiopia, the Mameluke states of the Nile valley, monarchies of various descriptions (divine, Islamic, conciliar, among others), military-conquest states, mercantile polities, jihad theocracies, as well as many interstices where societal organization operated without benefit or burden of state institutions.[14]

Remarkably, this extraordinary historical diversity virtually disappears when one contemplates state as political discourse. One form of state tradition in particular has decisively molded our perceptions of "stateness": the "modern state" as it evolved in Europe from the fifteenth century and then spread, through imperial expansion and response to it, to the rest of the globe. Oakeshott describes well the emergence of the notion of state—a lexical referent to political phenomena that can be traced back no farther than the sixteenth century:[15]

> The somewhat novel associations of human beings which came to be called modern states, emerged slowly, prefigured in earlier European history. . . . They were the outcomes of conquest, the extinction of palatine independencies in feudal realms, the consolidation of fiefs, purchases, the marriage settlements of rulers, multiple treaties, rebellion and secession. . . . Each was a piece of inhabited territory with a government, land (often ill-defined), people (often miscellaneous) and a ruling authority (usually in the course of recognition). . . . But although the differences . . . were large and have never been extinguished, they came to be recognized as versions of, or as approximations to, an emergent ideal character.[16]

THE MODERN STATE

In its initial form, the early modern state was absolutist. The emergence of unmistakably hegemonical institutions giving older monarchies an entirely new ascendancy over society is intimately associated with the recognition of state as a concept.[17] Rulers created standing armies and professional bureaucracies; royal writ and law penetrated the territory; flows of revenue beyond the circumscribed income from royal estates secured the treasuries. The philosophers of absolutism—Machiavelli, Bodin, Hobbes—supplied a normative text through which the early modern state achieved recognition and claimed legitimation.[18] In time, coalescent and increasingly structured civil societies sought—fought for—voice and through constitutional devices imposed institutionalized limits on state power.[19] As constitutional democracy became a normative model, the scope and mission of the state expanded, especially after the generalization of the welfare state.

A degree of bifurcation occurred between the Anglo-American state (especially Britain) and the Franco-Prussian continental state (especially France), as empirical models. The construction of the absolutist state, resolutely undertaken by the Tudors, as well as their Spanish, French, Prussian, Austro-Hungarian, Swedish, and Russian counterparts, was aborted in mid-seventeenth-century England by the religious, social, and regional forces that cost Charles I his head and by 1688 had laid the groundwork for parliamentary supremacy. The precocious constraints on absolutism in Britain, and the parallel emergence of a relatively stateless form of colonial polity in the New World, engendered a distinctive state tradition whose institutional core weighed less heavily on civil society than was the case in the prefectoral Franco-Prussian model. The latter model was of crucial influence on the Continent; as Nettl says in his seminal 1968 article, "It is the French state, and idea of state, that provide the basic European model—even though the philosophical and intellectual tradition of ideas about the state reached the fullness of universality and precision in German hands from the beginning of the nineteenth century onward."[20]

The dominance the European form holds over intellectual images of the state derives from its forcible imposition or defensive imitation through the globalization of imperialism, its strategic position at the core of the contemporary world system of states, and its virtually exclusive place in the field of vision of moral philosophers and contemporary theorists. Beginning with the Portuguese footfalls in 1415 in Ceuta and Melilla on the Moroccan coast, a gradually accelerating dynamic of European overseas expansion developed. Only a handful of relatively large (China, Iran, Japan), unusually isolated (Nepal), or very diplomatically skilled and geopolitically fortunate (Thailand, Ethiopia) polities escaped imperial subjugation. For most of this huge swath of territory—all of the Americas, most of Africa and the Middle East—political space was entirely redefined; in Asia some historically existing units were preserved, but even here profound structural and normative alterations in the state occurred, incorporating the European model. In states that escaped the imperial yoke, survival required a conscious state reconstruction largely based on European images and ideologies. Thus, both colonialism and resistance to it yielded diffusion of a notion of stateness whose lineage lay in the European core.

In a different way, the core state model acquired universal currency through its constitutive role in the development of an international system of states and the associated emergence of a law of nations. The contemporary system of states, the first to achieve universality although other regional systems preceded it, is conventionally dated from the Treaty of Westphalia in 1648. This European assemblage laid down some of the cornerstones of the international state system: the sovereign equality of states and a set of formalized rules governing their intercourse.[21] At this juncture the state system was exclusively European; only gradually, during the eighteenth century, was the first non-Christian state, the Ottoman Empire, partially incorporated. Although polities in the Western Hemisphere were easily brought within the Westphalian frame, only in the twentieth century were non-Western states like Japan and China accorded full standing.

Elsewhere, the colonized world was incorporated into the Europe-centered system of states as a dependent appendage. At the core of the system an institutionalized set of norms gradually took shape. Some of the concepts that gained standing within this international normative order, such as sovereignty and self-determination, became crucial instruments in the struggle for liberation from colonial subjugation. With independence, new states took their place in a global system of states whose juridical precepts—defining the nature of the state as international legal person—had evolved from the Westphalian system.[22] If law is the language of the state, then the new sovereign subjects of international law became at the same time subject to the complex of received meanings that played a decisive constitutive role in their very identity as independent states.

From the classic political philosophers to contemporary social theorists, the overwhelming object of Western conceptual reflection has been the liberal constitutional (or, if one prefers, capitalist) state. Other intellectual traditions—Chinese, Indian, Islamic—contain rich bodies of systematic reflection on the state, situated within its own cultural space (by, for example, Mencius and Confucius, Kautilya and Ibn Khaldun). But the insularity and hubris of the Western intellectual world prevented a full assimilation of their perspectives into the corpus of Euro-American knowledge, and the comprehensive political and economic domination of the Western world assured its ascendancy in the epistemological realm as well.

In short, all the main theoretical trails led to the same handful of contemporary polities—Britain, the United States, France, West Germany, Sweden—as the empirical source for conceptual reflection on the state in its exemplary form. Certainly other forms of state enjoy analytical recognition; the bureaucratic authoritarian state, for example, is given elegant exposition by Guillermo O'Donnell.[23] The Bolshevik Revolution in 1917 brought a wholly new and once widely diffused polity type, state socialism, now in terminal decay. The authors of the 1979 Iranian Revolution resolutely undertook a resurrection of the Islamic state, with the ambition of making it an exemplary model. State socialism and Islam as a political dynamic have both engendered a vast and rich monographic literature. But in one way or another core state theory perceives all of these variants as deviant, whether by pathological flaw (the totalitarian state), by temporal sequence (the underdeveloped state), or by classification as exotic other (the Islamic state as "orientalism").

The state that has been ushered back in is thus in part a set of attributes abstracted from a delimited empirical universe. But there is also a transcendental dimension, something inextinguishably Hegelian, to the state. This elusive element, "the unity of the universal and subjective will . . . present within the state, in its laws and in its universal and rational properties," points to state as idea, as something beyond what may be deduced from its visible empirical forms. "The divine principle in the state is the Idea made manifest on earth," adds Hegel, in identifying the state as the manifestation of a world historical spirit.[24] The notion of state has evolved in an ongoing dialectic between its institutional manifestation and its abstracted theoretical existence. The real and the ideal are conjoined in permanent tension and continuous synthesis. In contrast to such other master concepts in contemporary paradigms as world capitalist system, bourgeoisie, or system adaptation and maintenance functions, state is a living reality and not simply an abstract analytical category. The world capitalist system is an imagined actor, which achieves historical agency only through anthropomorphic empowerment by the theorist. States make war and peace, reward and punish their citizens, and engage in innumerable other material acts. And yet states are also theoretical subjects, conceptually metamorphosed into abstracted and symbolized entities. "Being in part constitutive of political activity and of the state itself," writes Dyson, "the idea of the state is connected in an intimate, complex and internal way with that conduct, shaped by and shaping it, manipulated by and imprisoning the political actor whose political world is defined in its terms."[25]

THE STATE AS CONCEPT

The reappearance of state as idea was perhaps the most momentous theoretical event in political science during the 1980s. The curious marginalization of state as concept during the first quarter century after World War II remains an oddity, and it illustrates the occasional disjunctures between the empirical and ideal realms. During this historical moment the modal Western state experienced a dramatic expansion in scale, driven by the institutionalization of both the welfare and the garrison states. Yet theory, in its behavioral mood, abandoned the state for the individual and the group. The radical challenge that emerged in the 1960s was at first drawn toward paradigms—neo-Marxism and dependency—which likewise saw states as ultimately derivative and secondary phenomena.[26]

Central to the notion of state as idea, rising above its visible institutional machinery, is the Machiavellian discovery of a reason embedded within it. The classic exegesis of Machiavelli by Friedrich Meinecke opens with reason of state (the logic that governs state action):

> Whatever the circumstances the business of ruling is . . . always carried out in accordance with the principles of *raison d'état*. *Raison d'état* may be deflected or hindered by real or imaginary obstacles, but it is part and parcel of ruling. It is not realized, however, as a principle and an idea until a particular stage of development has been reached; namely when the State has become strong enough to break down those obstacles, and to lay down its own unqualified right to existence in the face of all other vital forces.[27]

The modern state indisputably meets this qualification. In its original Machiavellian sense, *raison d'état* essentially sprang from the desire to accumulate and maintain power. The ultimate objective of the state is to ensure its own reproduction through time. By the seventeenth century the core state system had sufficient ascendancy over other societal forces to acquire a purposive steering mechanism, analytically distinct from the specific human agents and institutional apparatus that applied state reason. In the evocative imagery of Michael Mann, society was effectively "caged" in the territorial grid of the state system.[28]

At the Machiavellian moment when the emergent modern state struggled for dominance, power alone could perhaps be perceived as the energizing element in state reason. But as states achieved relative security in their hegemonical role, raison d'état became a more complex calculus, incorporating other elements instrumental to its authority; mercantilism soon became more central to statecraft than the more elemental survival-oriented cunning prescribed by Machiavelli. According to its classic student, Eli Heckscher, mercantilism offered a logic of unification: "Its adversary was the medieval combination of universalism and particularism, and its first object was to make the state's purposes decisive in a uniform economic sphere and to make all economic activity subservient to considerations corresponding to the requirements of the state and to the state's domain regarded as uniform in nature."[29] Assurance of resources remained central to state reason, even as the particular devices of mercantilism in the seventeenth and eighteenth centuries were left behind. When during the nineteenth century civil society in the core state system imposed constitutional restraints on the previously absolutist state, sustaining the legitimacy of its authority entered state calculus. In its fullest form, raison d'état is presented by Hegel as the actualization of a universalized reason. As summarized by Anthony Giddens, in Hegelian thought "the modern state embodies reason, not by absorbing civil society but by guarding certain of the universal qualities upon which it is predicated. The state is [in Hegel's words] 'the Universal that has expressed its actual rationality,' representing 'the identity of the general and the particular will'."[30] As the deliberative, reflective element, suggest Bertrand Badie and Pierre Birnbaum, "the essential function of the state is to think."[31]

Thus, over time reason of state moved far beyond the pristine power-driven equation of its first formulation. In imputing to the state as idea the capacity for optimizing choice, the notion of a polity as a rational actor emerges. Here we encounter the Weberian concept of the modern state as a legal-rational organism, whose institutions are impersonal, rule-bound, purposive, competent hierarchies that maintain "domination by virtue of 'legality,' by virtue of the belief in the validity of legal statute and functional 'competence' based on rationality created *rules*."[32] We also find some junction between state theory and the idiom of rational-choice models and "new institutionalism," as projected upon the state as a collective actor.[33] State actors apply iterated decision rules to recurrent tasks, combined with a calculation of consequences grounded in constraints of time and resources, scripted routines, and pressures from interested social groups.[34]

If the state as idea becomes an impersonal organism, then an inherent authority must reside within it. This property, crystallized as the doctrine of sovereignty, was first given philosophic statement by Bodin, in whose sweeping formulation it was "high, perpetual, and absolute."[35] Sovereignty embodies the theoretical unity and indivisibility of the state and is expressed through its authoritative commands, or law. In its Hobbesian gloss, sovereignty became a hypothetically limitless reservoir of authority. In its Rousseavian metamorphosis, this intrinsic font of authority was transferred to the people. Yet through the collectivization of people as a nation and the personalization of the state as the nation-state, hyphenated embodiment of civil society, the Hegelian synthesis reinvested polity with sovereignty. So also did the Austinian doctrines of jurisprudence, which argued that positive law could only exist in conjunction with a determinate locus of power, an underived authority.[36] Through the covenant of constitutionalism, the "high, perpetual, and absolute" qualities of sovereignty are circumscribed for the state as a domestic actor, although not as an international person. Even for the constitutionally domesticated *état de droit* the notion of sovereignty remains more than the "bloodless legal fiction" to which Watkins finds it reduced by democratic governance of the exemplary modern state.[37]

The state as sovereign acquires the clothing of power and the vocation of domination. Many theorists would follow Andrew Vincent, if summoned to a one-phrase definition, in identifying the state as "a public power above both ruler and ruled which provides order and continuity to the polity."[38] Power, in the useful conceptualization of Giddens, "is regarded as generated in and through the reproduction of structures of domination." This structuration of power, bracketing time and space, rests on both material (allocative) and ideological (authoritative) resources.[39]

State as idea is a mere mental category, but in the quotidian sense the structuration of its power is visible through its formal institutions, in a normative sense incorporating the Weberian notions of rational division of function, competence through professionalization and specialization, and hierarchy. The abstract power of the state attains concrete form in its standing code of commands, or law. Rule-based behavior lies at the heart of state rationality and the stable order created for civil society. Or, in Foucault's terms, "the state consists in the codification of a whole number of power relations which render its functioning possible."[40] Here the notion of codification is enlarged to include not just formal rules but also regularized practices and customary prescriptions, which serve as an informal complement to statutory law.

In many respects the idea of the state emerges with particular clarity in its role as a member of an international system. It is this dimension of the state that Skocpol and her associates capture in conceptualizing the state as "Janus-faced," inward looking in its institutional congeries of administering and policing apparatuses but externally focused in its security obsessions. "Analysts," they write, "must take account of the embeddedness of nations in changing transnational relations, such as wars and interstate alliances or balances of power, market flows and the international economic division of labor, and patterns of intellectual communication or cultural modelling across national boundaries."[41] Gianfranco Poggi, pursuing a parallel dual concept of the state, suggests that, whereas the polity turned inward is governed by scarcity (and hence allocation), externally it is driven by danger (and thus defense). The anarchical nature of the international system of states compels a sharp distinction between "us" and "the other," an identification of potential foes who threaten the core state values of integrity and autonomy.[42] Nowhere in theoretical contemplation of the state does it appear more starkly as a unitary rational actor than in international-relations theory. Despite innumerable efforts to qualify or even abandon this image of the state as an international person, it stubbornly populates our concepts of global politics.[43]

The notion of the state, then, is constituted in part by induction from real units of world historical process, although in actuality the orbit of empirical vision is restricted to a small number of polities that achieve exemplary force through their visibility, location at an apex of prosperity and seeming social advance, and ethical properties presumed to inhere in their institutional arrangements (constitutional democracy). But the state as a concept, as Vincent argues, is also "a complex of ideas and values . . . dense in texture and diverse in interpretation."[44] It is, adds Timothy Mitchell, "a common ideological and cultural construct," occurring "as a subjective belief, incorporated in the thinking and action of individuals," but also "represented and reproduced in visible, everyday forms, such as the language of legal practice, the architecture of public buildings, the wearing of military uniforms, or the marking out and policing of frontiers."[45]

The very complexity of the notion of the state compels due recognition of its problematic aspects. The peril of reification, present in any sustained reflection upon a given theoretical object, is a clear and present danger, perhaps even an ineluctable artifact of analytical language. State theory, to begin with, tends to constitute the polity as a unitary actor. Weber himself, in characterizing state institutions as a product of collective rationality, hastens to add that he traffics in a mere ideal type. The most cursory observation of that set of states from which the theoretical notion derives confirms the chasm that separates the unitary-actor model from empirical fact. The organizational theory that fosters viewing the state as a firm applies with equal force to the numerous agencies into which it is divided; each ministry, branch of government, public corporation, or local jurisdiction has its own sliver of raison d'état, buttered with an organizational logic of its own. Constitutionalism in some of its guises deliberately divides the institutional apparatus, by using branches of government to check and balance each other, or dispersing power areally through federal doctrines. An état de droit invariably insulates the judiciary with a wall of autonomy, to ensure that public law stands above some readings of raison d'état.

LIMITS OF STATE THEORY

Certainly a due recognition of the institutional complexity and fragmentation of the state played its part in the decline of the concept; political system as central idea was more readily unpacked into its structural components, with subsystem autonomy and differentiation being the defining features of modernity in the hands of structural-functional analysts. In the field of international relations, the influential threefold typology of state behavior by Graham Allison, adding the terms *bureaucratic politics* and *organizational process* to the conventional term *rational actor,* demonstrates the qualifications that a polity's complexity imposes on understandings of its behavior.[46] When polities are in disarray or decline, in addition to widespread institutional fragmentation there is the degeneration of overlayers of monitoring and coordination, as well as decay in the central capacity to apply raison d'état. Schatzberg, in his splendid inquest into the Zairian state, is led to define it "as a congeries of organized repositories of administrative, coercive, and ideological power subject to, and engaged in, an ongoing process of power accumulation characterized by uneven ascension and uneven decline."[47] Fragments of state authority become instruments of predation among dispersed structural segments and individual actors.

A second problematic dimension of state theory reflects the broader tension between structure and human agency in diverse modes of conceptualization.[48] A state as an abstract entity cannot act; only the human agents that staff its apparatus can do so. Giddens provides a helpful statement of this issue: "All human action is carried on by knowledgeable agents who both construct the social world through their action, but yet whose action is also conditioned or constrained by the very world of their creation," echoing Marx's aphorism that men make history, if not entirely as they choose. It is through knowledgeable human agents that states apply reason, transcend the immediacy of sensory experience; although states have impersonal systems of storing information, their human servants' remembrance of the past and purposive sense of the future greatly enlarge the experiential base of polity action. State norms, professional role definition, and bureaucratic hierarchies constrain, although they do not totally determine, the behavior of human agents.[49] State reason implants itself into the decision-making upper layer of public servants, who come to share an "official mind," while retaining a possible range of variation in the individual application of its postulates and logic to particular policy choices.

A third risk in state theory is detaching polity from population. A state exists in a dynamic interaction with the human community over which it exercises rule. Mitchell, in an influential article, argues that analysis of the state needs to dissolve the boundary between state and society to be efficacious. "The state," he writes, "should not be taken as a free-standing entity, whether an agent, instrument, organization or structure, located apart from and opposed to another entity called society," although the "distinction between state and society should nevertheless be taken seriously, as the defining characteristics of the modern political order."[50] When we turn to Bula Matari, it will become evident why the African colonial state stands in contradiction to the Mitchell analysis and must be seen as a free-standing entity; for the contemporary liberal state or the postcolonial African state, his injunction to blur the boundary becomes pertinent. This collectivity of state and society, constituted by its common incorporation within the territorial boundaries and hence sovereign jurisdiction of the state, acts and reacts in complex patterns. "The state," suggests Philip Cerny, "in and through its own process of structuration, itself produces, or is a key factor in producing, the 'society' itself."[51] Its interests and preferences, as aggregated by various intermediary agencies (associations, political parties, interest groups, among others), press upon the state and weigh—perhaps heavily—in the logic of state action. Its major cleavages (class, cultural pluralism, interest) find reflection within the state apparatus itself, and not only within the representative structures of government. If state apparatuses, as Poulantzas argues, "are never anything other than the materialization and condensation of class relations,"[52] the same reasoning applies to divisions of race, religion, ethnicity, gender, and interest. At bottom, a civil society is infinitely more complex than its collective representation as a corporate whole governed by and acting upon a state. Ultimately, society dissolves into myriad individuals joined in a cellular structure of households and branching into kinship affinities, workplace associations, and social roles, before nesting into the broader structural cleavages that unite its segments and crisscross the collectivity.

State and civil society are thus indissolubly bound in an unfolding relationship of conflict and cooperation. The state by its very nature seeks to rule, to uphold its domination over civil society as indispensable to performing its role. In the exercise of rule, constant application of coercion devalues its currency; the state seeks pathways to domination that rest on authority rather than force, that preserve and enhance its legitimacy. By marching to the drum of raison d'état, it will nurture its autonomy. Civil society in its component elements can secure collective goods only through the state; thus its behavior is in part cooperative. The subjects of state rule, be they individuals or diversely defined groups, are collectivized in an active civil society through citizenship. In the words of one of its leading students, citizenship "requires a bond of a different kind [other than kinship], a direct sense of community membership based on loyalty to a civilization which is a common possession. It is a loyalty of free men endowed with rights and protected by a common law."[53] Deference and loyalty, spun into affective doctrines by the ideological representation of state as nation, assure the state routine obedience and ultimate emotional support.

But recognition of the legitimacy of the state is interlaced with undercurrents of conflict. Civil society is vigilant as well as deferential. The inherent tendency of the state to accumulate power engenders resistance and a constant struggle to enforce limits on state prerogatives. Civil society, like the state, values autonomy. The political slogan "get the government off our backs" of the Ronald Reagan years captures a perennial disposition of civil society, expressed well in African terms by Mbembe's observation about the "historical capacity of Africans for indiscipline."[54] Civil society simultaneously pursues exit, voice, and loyalty at any historical moment; what may vary over time is the valence of each of these factors. The state constitutes, dominates, and rules civil society, which in turn penetrates the state and imprints its collective personality and major cleavages. Civil society, in the sovereign embrace of the state, acts out an unending prisoner's dilemma with shifting combinations of cooperation and defection.[55]

DEFINING THE STATE: ATTRIBUTES

From the foregoing, we are compelled to conclude that conceptual capture of the state is arduous. No single, well-turned phrase will suffice. The most satisfying definition I have encountered, by Dyson, triumphs by its comprehensiveness, if not its verbal economy:

> Besides referring to an entity or actor in the arena of international politics, state is a highly generalizing, integrating and legitimating concept that identifies the leading values of the political community with reference to which authority is to be exercised; emphasizes the distinctive character and unity of the "public power" compared with civil society; focuses on the need for depersonalization of that power; finds its embodiment in one or more institutions and one or more public purposes which thereby acquire a special ethos and prestige and an association with the public interest or general welfare; and

produces a socio-cultural awareness of (and sometimes dissociation from) the unique and superior nature of the state itself. . . . The idea of the state is dedicated to the value of reason, placed at the service of a set of public norms that are to be guaranteed against violation by individuals who are attempting to satisfy egoistic wants. Its grandeur as an institution lies in its authority, but equally power (though not a good in itself) is a necessary basis of its action.[56]

This passage contains a number of the aspects of state I wish to explore. Two overall dimensions deserve our attention. First, the state as a conceptual object may be captured through an identification of its most crucial attributes. Second, and of particular importance for the analysis that follows, the state as a macrohistorical actor may be grasped in terms of a half-dozen behavioral imperatives that guide its action.

Territory

To begin with the most fundamental trait, the state is a territorial entity. Rule is exercised over a spatial domain; in the Giddens aphorism, a state "brackets space and time."[57] The territorial dimension of stateness has been defined with particular sharpness in the modern era following the emergence of a global system of states with precise boundary demarcations. Iconographically, the territorial personality of the modern state finds expression in the ubiquitous national maps with frontiers etched in bold lines. Physical artifacts—boundary markers, even fences—represent territorial limits; at all points of passage, the frontier is personified by the array of uniformed state agents policing the entry and exit of living and inanimate objects, with the flags emblematic of the state assertively placed at the limits of its zone of authority.

Although states have always had spatial domains, in some historical epochs their demarcation was fluid. Well-defined at its center, a state's territory often fluctuated at the periphery. For the city-state, from the Greek polis to the Italian or Hanseatic Renaissance polity, only the urban nexus mattered. For such far-flung empire states as Rome or China, defensive walls or lines of outposts (the Roman *limes*) were constructed to keep out nomadic intruders. For many kingdoms, a core zone of royal rule was surrounded by an outer sphere of looser, tributary relationships.

The rise of the Westphalian system of states over time transformed territoriality into a rigid grid of demarcation. Beginning with the extravagant papal bull of 1493 partitioning the "Indies" between Spain and

Portugal, a global territorialization of the state initiated by imperial expansion culminated at the start of the twentieth century in the universal imposition of defined boundaries on all land surfaces save the ice cap of the antipodes. The territoriality of states became a bedrock postulate of international jurisprudence; one of its leading scholars writes: "The mission and purpose of traditional international law has been the delimitation of the exercise of sovereign power on a territorial basis. No rule is clearer than the precept that no State may lawfully attempt to exercise its sovereignty within the territory of another."[58]

Population

A second and classical attribute of the state is population. As I noted in my discussion of civil society, rule is exercised over an ensemble of human subjects resident within the state's sphere of territorial jurisdiction. The sharp distinction between polity and population emerges only in philosophical reflection upon the modern state. The political thought of antiquity does not perceive a clear difference between the polis and the minority of its populace (free adult males) that it joined in civic association. Perhaps this reflected the weakly articulated institutional superstructure of the state per se. Subsequently, the state as a theoretical object was long concealed in the person of the ruler, lost in the honeycomb of personal, contractual relationships characteristic of high feudalism, or submerged in doctrines of universal Christian (*res publica christiana*) or Islamic (*umma*) community. The rise of the absolutist state created clearly differentiated institutions of rule and imbued subject status with visible meaning.

The population of a state is not only subordinated to its rule but also organized into a formal set of statuses stipulated by the polity. Male and female, husband and wife, adult and minor, citizen and alien, free and slave, sane and insane, at large and incarcerated: these categorizations may exist independently as ideological representations in society, but they are also formal legal classifications carrying rights and encumberments. A state that loses its population (or its territory) ceases to exist; in the precolonial African state, one of the most potent checks on the power of the ruler was the threat that segments of the population would simply flee beyond reach.

Sovereignty

A third attribute of the state is sovereignty, which I mentioned earlier. In its essence, the idea of sovereignty vests a final and absolute authority in

27

the state, derived, in various post-Rousseauian versions, from its role as the authoritative agent of civil society.

Claims by rulers to absolute power of course extend back into the mists of time. In a number of cases, the authority of the ruler—coercive and normative—was sufficient to construct such colossal monuments as the Egyptian pyramids, the temples of the Meso-American and Andean states, the water-management systems of the great hydraulic states. But the specific theory of sovereignty is a critical innovation in state theory, supplied in the 1576 definition by Bodin: "Sovereignty is that absolute and perpetual power vested in a commonwealth which in Latin is termed *majestas.*"[59] Two key developments in the rise of the modern state gave full force to the idea of sovereignty: penetration and secularization. In older large-scale state constructions, power was directly exercised only at the center, and for delimited purposes: making war, raising revenue, public works related to the ideological (temples) or economic (canals, roads, and caravanserai) reproduction of the state. At the community level, lineage, clan, or feudality regulated social life. The rise of the early modern absolutist state saw the extension of regulative authority by the royal bureaucracy down to local levels, and the enforcement of the king's law in all corners of the kingdom.

Prior to the enunciation of the secular doctrine of unrestricted state authority, monarchical power was subject to the higher law of God, or a natural law, interpreted and exercised through the Church, the theological jurisprudence of *shari'a,* or diverse priesthoods. The doctrine of sovereignty, which detaches the notion of ultimate authority from any transcendental moorings, was an extraordinary extension of the idea of the state. In the words of de Jouvenal, "history records the actual erection of this boundless and unregulated Sovereignty of today, of which our ancestors had no conception. . . . That any human will whatsoever possessed an unlimited right to command the actions of subjects and change the relationships between them—that, for a whole thousand years, was something which was not only not believed but not even imagined."[60]

Sovereignty has two faces: external, constituting the state as an international legal person, and internal, asserting unlimited theoretical dominion over its subjects. The external dimension is in doctrinal terms particularly vast; whether sovereignty is believed to inhere in the state as such or to derive from civil society, with respect to the international system of states the claim to unlimited intrinsic independence is the same. Within this system, the state by metamorphosis becomes a single international legal person and thus equal to every other similar entity.

The incorporation of the idea of sovereign equality of states into the law of nations in the twentieth century, formally sanctified in the United Nations charter,[61] doubtless helps explain why the contemporary theory of the sovereign state has found such a remarkably large export market. As James Mayall observes, the Western doctrine of sovereignty has won "universal and enthusiastic acceptance" by investing a newly independent nation with formal equality of international standing and empowering it normatively, with "an authority, supreme by virtue of its power, uncluttered by any mythological explanations of its mandate and beyond which there could be no appeal."[62] The state as an external actor, adds Charles de Visscher in his classical treatise on international law, as "historical center of national exclusivism, . . . by its mere existence conduces to the intransigent assertion of sovereignty."[63]

There are, of course, important empirical limits to the practical exercise of external sovereignty. Power remains the most important currency of international affairs, and most states are usually in no position to enforce their will against the opposition of others. For individual states the growing economic interdependencies generate ever-greater constraints on the exercise of external sovereignty. Smaller and weaker units are subject to diverse coercive pressures from stronger actors. A court of world opinion also exerts some constraint in the contemporary world; the institutionalization of human-rights monitoring, for example, can, through the sanction of international scorn and shame, weigh upon state exercise of its sovereignty. The growing web of international law provides some curbs as well, even though there is no ultimate sanction-wielding global mechanism of enforcing its general jurisdiction. The paradox of international law noted by one distinguished jurist bespeaks the continued vigor of the external aspect of the sovereignty doctrine: the "stronger parts" of the law of nations, "assured of regular observation in the practice of States, relate to questions that have no bearing upon truly vital problems," while the "weaker parts, consisting merely of formal prescriptions, concern the use of armed force and the choice of peace and war between peoples."[64]

Sovereignty, internally viewed, refers to the amplitude of state authority over subjects. "A scientific theory of the State," writes Hans Kelsen, "is not in a position to establish a natural limit to the competence of the State in relation to its subjects. Nothing in the nature of the State or the individuals prevents the national legal order from regulating any subject matter in any field of social life, from restricting the freedom of the individual to any degree."[65] The positivist jurisprudence of Kelsen is in dispute, but his statement of the full meaning of domestic sovereignty is beyond reproach. There are no limits on state action intrinsic to the doctrine of domestic sovereignty. Land without an owner belongs to the state; property without an heir escheats to the state. A helpless individual is a ward of the state. The state may conscript labor for its projects or personnel for its armies. The possessions of the individual are subject to taxation; behavior is open to regulation through law.

Domestic sovereignty, in the modal contemporary state, does indeed have important limits. These are inscribed above all in the covenant between state and civil society embodied in a constitution. By legal compact, substantial limits are placed upon state power. A state is rendered subordinate to its own public law; a degree of autonomy is guaranteed to civil society through the interdiction of state action that intrudes on defined individual and group rights—although states regularly test these curbs on their behavior. Accountability and responsiveness of the state to civil society are prescribed through representative institutions. Public power is tamed by its dispersal among several branches of government. The state and civil society thus become full partners in the exercise of sovereignty; in such circumstances, the limitless, total, indivisible power embedded in the doctrine is domesticated. In the contemporary world, however, although nearly all states have formal constitutions, far fewer have fully institutionalized constitutionalism; here sovereignty remains a lethal instrument for the ruler. In the colonial polity no real état de droit existed to restrain its domination of subject society.

A colonial state, like all other states, is circumscribed in deploying its residual powers of sovereignty by its practical capacities. Authority sustainable in abstract jurisprudence is of little value without the ability to enforce it in a given domain. The absolute power that the domestic face of sovereignty theory might allow is never in practice attainable; the theory is no less important as a reservoir of claims that support expanding the frontiers of actual rule.

Power

Power itself is a fourth attribute of the state. In the unconscious text of everyday expression, the word *power* is indeed a freely exchangeable synonym for *state,* especially in its international role. Its French variant, *le pouvoir,* even more explicitly refers both to the state (or regime) and to the capacity to alter the behavior of another.

The aggregation and accumulation of power is inherent in the state. In the Weber quotation that opens this chapter, the successful assertion by the state of a legitimate monopoly of coercive force is its defining feature. Through their armed forces for external defense and their policing apparatus for internal law enforcement and control, states equip themselves to realize the core value of security. Even in the extreme nineteenth-century liberal laissez-faire model of the state, where all other functions are abandoned to the market, the night-watchman role remains; presumably armed with a club, the minimalist state still thwarts predators. In the empirical state of all recent centuries, its security forces—the quintessence of its power—have consumed an important portion of its resources.

The power of the state lies partly in its authority—its capacity to secure habitual obedience and deference through legitimacy, custom, or fear. It may be observed in what Giddens calls the state's different "containers": surveillance and information storage capacity, assembly of specialized human skills in organizational structures, and sanctioning ability through its instruments of violence and punishment.[66] An unfolding calculus of the relative power of state actors is a driving vector of international politics.

Law

A fifth characteristic of the state is its status as a legal domain, through which its power is systematized, congealed, and expressed. In the colorful text of Kelsen, "The power of the State is the power organized by positive law—is the power of law. . . . Speaking of the power of the State, one usually thinks of prisons and electric chairs, machine guns and cannons. But one should not forget that these are all dead things which become instruments of power only when used by human beings, and that human beings are generally moved to use them for a given purpose only by commands they regard as norms."[67] Elsewhere, Kelsen writes that law is to the state as gold to King Midas; everything touched by the state is transformed into law.[68]

The legal order may be embodied in a purely customary body of social rules; if these are interpreted and applied through permanent institutions of rule, they play the role of law. The major acts of assembling and systemizing such rules—codifications of law—are momentous acts of statecraft, whether by Hamurabi, Justinian, or Bonaparte. The rise of the modern state was intimately associated with the extension of a single body of law, and unified judicial system, to all nooks and crannies of the realm. For the colonial state, law was a major field of contest in the initial struggle for hegemony, as the colonizers imposed their law in spheres critical to state security and economic action and asserted supervisory rights over customary law in other spheres.

Law is crucial to the bonding of the state and civil society. Public law defines the relationships between the two and sets rules to which the state itself is subject. The criminal code establishes boundaries of acceptable behavior. Civil law brings a wide array of private transactions under state regulation, creating in the process rights in property. A host of subsidiary administrative rules complete the finely spun web of law in which civil society is enmeshed.

The State as Nation

A sixth attribute defining the modern state is its momentous marriage with the idea of nationalism.[69] The warm, vibrant, profoundly emotive notion of nation invests the more arid, abstract, jurisprudential concept of state with a capacity for eliciting passionate attachment to it by civil society. Nation evokes an image of civil society as a natural community, with a vocation of unity and an embodiment in a state—the nation politically organized, with its Hegelian echoes.[70]

Nation is a recent accretion to the idea of the state. While precursors can be found, the notion emerges with clarity and force at the time of the French Revolution, combining such concepts as popular sovereignty, an organic view of the human collectivity constituted by common culture and language, and—subsequently—the doctrine of self-determination. This potent amalgam acquired intellectual force through its incorporation into the political thought of such philosophers as Herder and Hegel, and its assimilation into the ideologies of German and Italian unification movements and a host of self-determination movements rattling the multinational empires of Austria-Hungary, Russia, and Ottoman Turkey. After roaming around various language families and racial categories in search of vast regrouping missions (pan-Slav, Turanian, Arab, and African), the idea of nation combined with the right of self-determination to supply an ideology for anticolonial revolt in the third world. This highly efficacious combat weapon eventually won its battle for liberation from imperial subjugation; the idea of nation was then appropriated by the postcolonial state as a key component in its ideology of legitimation.

Today the concept of nation is universally absorbed into state doctrine, although in a sense quite different from its pristine meaning of a natural cultural community. The contemporary reasoning flows backward; the populace under the sovereign authority of a given state, whose territorial integrity is held sacrosanct, has a natural vocation of unification, if not necessarily a common cultural identity.[71] In conventional discourse the words *nation* and *state* are joined by a hyphen or used interchangeably, as if synonymous.

The State as an International Actor

Seventh, a state is an international actor, which pursuant to its external sovereignty asserts its independence of all other such units. In the anarchical yet patterned world system of states,[72] the sovereign polity pursues its interests and seeks self-calculated quantums of security. As a juridical person it is constituted by public international law; as a political person it is identified by the algorithms of power (military strength, resource base, economic capacity); as an ideological person it is classified by its alignment and orientations in global politics.

In enacting its external role the state must ensure its survival and preserve its independence in a violent arena. Force has been a driving factor in the international system of states; in the formative period of the modern state, from the sixteenth century to the eighteenth, warfare was frequent—almost continuous—for long stretches. More recently, wars occur less often but are of much greater scale. Of the roughly 475 autonomous political entities that disappeared in Europe between 1500 and 1950, most were extinguished through violence.[73] Warfare and preparation for it are consuming preoccupations of states; the urgent necessity to secure revenue for these purposes has been a major factor propelling state expansion and was the most important single factor in early modern state-building.[74]

The presence of the alien "other" in the world beyond the frontiers participates in the definition of the national identity of the state. It is in the international arena that reason of state operates most explicitly; state interest is national, implying a closer conjunction between the state and civil society than may obtain in the domestic sphere.[75] Here as well the state more closely approximates the unitary rational-actor model than in its internal behavior.

The State as Idea

The eighth attribute, elusive yet critical, is the state as idea. Here we encounter the ensemble of affective orientations, images, and expectations imprinted in the mind of its subjects. In the tangled perceptions of civil society, the state is benefactor and oppressor, hero and villain. Few wholly escape the seductive force of the idea of nation; elements of patriotism resonate, even if interlaid with more negative sentiments. There is likely to be a generalized set of beliefs concerning the normal spheres of activity of the state. At the most basic level, the state is expected to assure prosperity and to protect civil society from its enemies, whether foreign aggressors or domestic perturbers of the public order. Sustained failure to achieve these ends calls into question the fitness of the incumbent set of human agents directing the apparatus of rule.

States tackle the task of transforming their mundane reality into symbolic splendor with remarkable ingenuity. In the monumental architecture of their capital cities, states affix the signature of power.[76] These often magnificent structures evoke awe and admiration and encode the core values of the polity: the evocation of classical Greece with its democratic overtones in the United States capitol building; the opulent splendor of the absolutist monarchy in the Palace of Versailles; the remote majesty of Imperial China in the Forbidden City of Beijing; the despotic power of the state in the fortress towers of the Kremlin. The iconography of the state is ubiquitous, visually expressed in its flag, postage stamps, coins, and currency; in textual form in its anthems, pledges of allegiance, oaths of office. In theatrical projection, the state represents itself in resplendent ceremonial: inaugurations and coronations, parades displaying its military might, rituals of national commemoration.

In the critical perspective of Murray Edelman, the whole policy process of the state is best understood as a mere performance, "constructing the political spectacle" in order to conceal the patterns of inequality and exploitation that the state upholds through its power.[77] In some variants, the very ontology of the state pivots around its ritual, through which it images a more perfect cosmic order, of which it is the earthly reflection, as what Geertz calls a theater state, "in which kings and princes were the impresarios, the priests the directors, and the peasants the supporting cast, stage crew, and audience. The stupendous cremations, tooth filings, temple dedications, pilgrimages, and blood sacrifices, mobilizing hundreds and even thousands of people and great quantities of wealth, were not means to political ends: they were the ends themselves, they were what the state was for . . . mass ritual was not a device to shore up the state, but rather the state . . . was a device for the enactment of mass ritual."[78]

One might well adduce further attributes of a state; for my purposes, this portrait of the polity will suffice. What remains to be examined is the set of determinants that guide state action; one must answer Goran Therborn's evocative interrogation, "What does the ruling class do when it rules?" while substituting "state" for "ruling class" as the prime theoretical actor.[79] Conceptual recognition of the agent is not enough; it must be set in motion, and regularities governing its behavior identified.

THE STATE AS A HISTORICAL ACTOR

A state is both creature and agent of history. Embedded within its institutions is a memory, not simply a store of information but a transformation of this data into generalized images of the past as a narrative text. The past is a reservoir of instructive experience, a library of lessons. The present is but an evanescent moment in the passage to a future that the state struggles to control and shape. The state, in exercising its constrained autonomy, is a goal-driven, purposive agent of history. Perhaps predisposed to overvalue its omniscience, the state never fully masters the vector of chaos and complexity in macrohistorical process; that archetype of its hubris, the five-year plan, is always overtaken by events. In moments of crisis, the state is virtually overwhelmed by the exigencies of immediate survival, and its time horizon becomes foreshortened, almost to the morrow. But in normal phases a state embraces a longer vision of its future.

Reason of state is embodied in an operational code by means of which the instruction of the past is weighed, the dilemmas of the present examined, and the future aims selected. The essential elements of this state logic, I believe, can be summarized under a half-dozen headings. Differently weighted in varying circumstance, they constitute a teleology of the state as a historical agent.

Imperative 1: Hegemony

The roster of behavioral imperatives may begin with hegemony. All states are continuously engaged in a struggle to ensure the supremacy of their authority. Profoundly imbued with the notion of their own sovereignty, even if constitutionally circumscribed, states will not brook direct affronts from segments of society to their right to rule. No one, the adage goes, is above (or beyond the reach of) the law. Quiet, unavowed exit may be possible for elements of society; even civil disobedience—action that recognizes the law while disobeying it—may be tolerated. But if any group formally declares its refusal to acknowledge the domination of the state, a forceful riposte is certain to follow—unless the state is too derelict or disintegrated to apply it, as in the last days of the Soviet Union or in Somalia and Liberia at the beginning of the 1990s.[80]

Hegemony is sustained through the policing apparatuses whose professionalization is one of the hallmarks of the modern state.[81] Domination requires that the unruly be disciplined, the refractory punished.[82] The law—the will of the state codified into standing commands—supplies an armature of hegemony. An ideology of domination adds to the instrumentation of state ascendancy; hegemony comes in Gramscian clothing and is articulated as a normative doctrine. States employ "national histories" as a pedagogical device, transforming the past into a morality play. The self-representation of the state as a commanding hegemon enacts the illuminated frontispiece to the 1651 edition of Hobbes's *Leviathan:* the sovereign as a colossal giant towering over a geometrically ordered civil society, his body composed of the lilliputian figures of his subjects.[83]

Imperative 2: Autonomy

Autonomy is a second behavioral imperative. Like the idea of sovereignty, which it encodes, autonomy has two faces: external and internal. Externally, it embodies the drive for independence, the most elemental of survival instincts. No intrusion on the national domain can be tolerated, nor can another state be permitted to assert its jurisdiction within state territory. The quest for autonomy within the global system of states is perpetual, governing policy choices for states large and small.

With respect to civil society, the autonomy drive is twinned with hegemony. Society battles to impose its will on the state, and the lines of conflict are reproduced within the state apparatus. Reason of state can operate in pure form only with autonomy. State agents are disposed to perceive themselves as clairvoyant interpreters of the public interest, a notion given fruitful development by Eric Nordlinger. Although I differ from Nordlinger in his insistance that the state be defined solely in terms of the function of its human agents, his definition of the (internal) autonomy of the modern constitutional state is helpful:

> The state is autonomous to the extent that it translates its preferences into authoritative actions, the degree to which public policy conforms to the parallelogram of the public officials' resource-weighted preferences. State autonomy may be operationally defined in terms of the overall frequency with which state preferences coincide with authoritative actions and inactions, the proportion of preferences that do so, the average substantive differences between state preferences and authoritative actions, or some combination of the three.[84]

Imperative 3: Security

Security is a third imperative of the state, which is threatened by a Hobbesian world where life is "nasty, brutish, and short." Some form of national security council, whatever its title, is to be found at the institutional core of any state. For the contractarian school of political thought, the apprehension of disorder and insecurity in the hypothetical state of nature explains why civil society entered into compacts that formed states in the first instance. As Giddens reminds us, "virtually all modern states are 'First World' in one sense—they possess the material and organizational means of waging industrialized war."[85]

Public safety is a powerful motivating factor within the territory as well. The speed with which "crime" preoccupies civil society when any wave of social disorder or assaults on persons or property emerges is matched only by the alacrity with which political representatives embrace a restoration of security for neighborhood and hearth as electoral discourse. The surge of drug-related violence in many American cities during the 1980s, the fears of a dissolution of public order it triggered, and the state responses it evoked in accelerated prison construction and pledged expansion of police forces exemplify the security imperative at work.

Imperative 4: Legitimacy

Legitimation is a fourth component of the operational code of the state. Weber with good reason places patterns of legitimation at the core of his notion of the state; absent this property, the state is in a condition of extreme vulnerability. Hegemony is rendered credible by the visible possession of superior force. However, coercion may well be conceived of metaphorically as a gold reserve underpinning the currency of power. If constantly employed, the reserves are emptied in short order, and rapid devaluation of power itself soon follows.[86] Through investing its institutions with legitimate authority, the state seeks habitual acquiescence in and consent to its rule.

Legitimation is pursued in a number of ways. In ancient Rome, bread and circuses were crucial to sustaining public order: a grain dole organized by the state, and a series of extravagant spectacles—circuses, gladiatorial combat, games, banquets—endowed by private contributions from leading notables.[87] Ideology as an expression of the ultimate aims and final source of authority plays a critical role. Historically—and in some instances, in the Islamic world, still today—religion is intimately linked to legitimation; the state represents itself as the defender of a given faith and as upholding on earth the divine authority of a theological system. In the vanishing domain of state socialism, the state clothed its operation in Marxism-Leninism, justifying its behavior in terms of its congruence with this official dogma. The capitalist state advances liberal democracy, individual rights, and protection of property as its legitimating creed. The common theme is an interwoven corpus of ideas that provide a vision of the future and a yardstick for measuring the present. The state claim that its behavior is guided by a particular doctrine succeeds, of course, only if the ideas themselves retain a wide resonance within civil society; the accelerating decay of Marxism-Leninism confronts state-socialist polities with a profound crisis of legitimation.

Another avenue of legitimation is respectful conformity to canons of constitutional behavior. "Democracy" reappeared as a remarkably inspirational idea in the late 1980s, from the streets of Beijing to the wave of national conferences across Africa.[88] Regular observation of constitutional assurances of the political rights of civil society, and procedures persuading civil society that accountability and responsiveness exist, are time-tested instruments of legitimacy. Performance criteria enter as well; pervasive corruption or conspicuous incompetence in statecraft corrodes legitimacy. Apparent success in economic management, as measured in the master indicators of growth, inflation, and unemployment rates, supply an aura of effectiveness.

Imperative 5: Revenue

The revenue imperative is the bedrock postulate of state behavior. Levi exaggerates only a little in asserting that "the history of state revenue production is the history of the evolution of the state." The reason is simple enough: "revenue enhances the ability of rulers to elaborate the institutions of the state, to bring more people within the domain of those institutions, and to increase the number and variety of collective goods provided through the state."[89] The state is engaged in a ceaseless struggle with civil society to extract the resources necessary for performance of its other roles. Society does not readily part with its goods; states have always sought revenue sources that can be securely collected with minimal visibility. The Roman state in its expansive phase financed itself in large part by plunder, grain tribute from conquered provinces, and Spanish mines. Early modern states found taxation on external trade easiest to collect; lucrative monopolies on such basic commodities as salt and tobacco were other major sources, as was, for a time, the sale of public office. For Spain (especially in the sixteenth century), Portugal (mainly in the eighteenth), and the Netherlands (in the nineteenth), colonial empires yielded large and relatively painless state revenue flows, although this bounty was subject to wide fluctuation. Direct taxation always evokes resistance and evasion; it has generally been extended, in modern states, under cover of war needs.[90]

In short, the state, in pursuit of its revenue imperative, is cast in a predatory role. State agents are inevitably mindful of the transaction costs associated with a given revenue strategy: the political investment required to secure approval for a revenue source, implement collection, monitor compliance, and punish violators.[91] The trade-off between legitimacy and revenue is often direct, even if civil society values many of the public goods purchased with its extracted contributions. In the constitutional polity, the "no new tax" pledge on the hustings is indisputably effective. The state is beset by an endemic "fiscal crisis."[92]

Imperative 6: Accumulation

The final state imperative is accumulation, a determinant of state behavior that becomes clear only in the modern era. Mercantilism became absorbed into reason of state in the sixteenth century; from that point on, state managers could readily grasp the urgency of fostering expansion of the economic base, from which the state derived its revenue. Thus, the commitment to accumulation has become institutionalized as a constant; what has shifted over time is the recognized means of accomplishing this goal.

In the contemporary capitalist state, the investment decisions crucial to sustaining a dynamic of accumulation are in the hands of private actors. The delicate mission of the state is to sustain conditions in its economic management conducive to investment, while simultaneously pursuing revenue-consuming distribution policies indispensable to its legitimation. The trade-off between revenue and accumulation may be excruciating: if fiscal sources linked to private investment choices are taxed too heavily, the accumulation process may be damaged.

Accumulation as the central determinant of state behavior emerges in the German school of neo-Marxist state theory, especially the work of Claus Offe. The core of this argument, as captured by Martin Carnoy, holds:

> In order for resources to flow to the State, depending on sources
> that are now owned by the State, the State apparatus must promote the general accumulation process. It must do so in the face
> of threats that cause problems of accumulation, threats from compe-

tition among accumulating units, both domestically and internationally, and from the working class. The function of creating and sustaining conditions of accumulation means establishing control over these destructive possibilities and events.[93]

Adam Przeworski and Michael Wallerstein add that the constraints of the structural dependence of the state on its capacity to assure accumulation means that "the range of interests that governments find best for the interests they represent is narrowly circumscribed, whatever these interests may be . . . no government can simultaneously reduce profits and increase investment."[94]

For the many developing states, especially the African set, and for the state-socialist realm, the current dilemma of polity management in many ways hinges on the accumulation imperative. State socialism reached an outer limit in its capacity to sustain accumulation within the framework of the state model fashioned by Lenin and Stalin. The African state impasse is directly related to an incapacity to foster accumulation through the state, to find domestic private substitutes for the state, or to secure external finance other than to facilitate reimbursement of its gigantic debt.

The state as actor is thus introduced. These broadly defined determinants of state behavior do not of course lend themselves to precise measurement. They operate always in interaction; they usually compete rather than cumulate. No more is claimed for this conceptualization of state as actor than the capacity to organize our understandings and clarify our analysis.

STATE, REGIME, RULER

Before leaving the state as theory, one final distinction requires formulation: state versus regime and ruler. Although states are at times extinguished, usually through conquest or violence, sometimes through disintegration (the Soviet Union and Yugoslavia in 1991), they are generally permanent entities. Certainly the presumption of perennity permeates reason of state. Regime and ruler are less stable and have their own logics of reproduction, which may contrast with the state operational code in some respects.

By regime I understand a given political formula for the organization and exercise of state rule. Major revolutionary events—the Russian, Chinese, Cuban, French, Iranian revolutions—produced changes of regime; so also did many less dramatically charged events. The radical nationalist military group that overthrew King Farouk in Egypt in 1952, for example, went far beyond simply replacing the incumbents. The legitimating ideology and basic rules of the political game were altered in fundamental ways. Similar changes of regime, and not just ruler, occurred in Indonesia and Zaire in 1965; both new sets of state managers scrapped the previous institutional structures and supplied a new political discourse and structuration of power. Decolonization as well provided a systematic form of regime change throughout the third world. The analytical frontier between mere change of ruler, and succession of regimes, is not always clear. Nonetheless, there is some conceptual value in distinguishing them.

A regime develops a logic of its own, whose ultimate aim is the reproduction over time of its particular configuration of institutional arrangements and dominant ideas. Measures taken pursuant to a logic of regime are not necessarily congruent with state interests. For example, the command economy and collectivized agricultural system imposed by Stalin from 1929 on were arguably important to the realization of the model of state socialism devised by its founding fathers; it is much less evident that they were dictated by the interests of the Soviet state.

The ruler has yet a different logic: essentially, to remain in power. The time horizon for calculating the ruler's imperative is much shorter than for the state's. The ruler's position is inherently precarious; one may assassinate a ruler, but not a state or even a regime. There is great latitude for purely personal idiosyncrasies to enter the logic of ruler behavior; as one student of the ruler's imperative wrote, "The unknowns are so numerous that a ruler's choice of one course as against another depends in substantial part upon his own inner dispositions and his own conceptions of the reality with which he deals."[95] Thus, an Idi Amin is led by impulse and paranoia to policy choices that doubtless seemed to him crafty but were in effect profoundly destructive to the Ugandan state, and only functional to his survival in the short run.

In highly institutionalized constitutional polities, these distinctions have only modest value. Even if, as in the Levi and Nordlinger contributions to democratic state theory, stress is placed on state agents as enactors of state reason, they perform their roles believing themselves to be intelligent servants of reason of state.[96] The interests of regime and state become, under conditions of prolonged stability, indistinguishable; constitutional prescriptions in practice make almost impossible the indefinite perpetuation of a given ruler's term in office. In the volatile environment of contemporary Africa, however, these differences do matter. The anguish of such polities as Ghana, Ethiopia, Uganda, and Zaire, among others, lay in policy behavior by a given ruler, in terms of his reading of his survival requirements, which were at indisputable variance with choices that might have been determined by reason of state.

In the colonial state, which in its own way was a stable pattern of rule until its rapid decay in its last days, the regime did not really change once the colonial framework had been established. Although swashbuckling individuals weighed heavily in the original dynamics of colonial conquest and partition, and some unusual imperial proconsuls later left their mark, the formulation of colonial policy above all marched to the beat of a very special kind of reason of state.

— *Chapter Three* —

THE NATURE
AND GENESIS OF
THE COLONIAL STATE

If we hold the colonial state up to the mirror of "state" as portrayed in the preceding chapter, we find that the reflection is flawed. Of the defining attributes of stateness, three crucial elements are missing. Sovereignty was emphatically denied; this comprehensive, ultimate power was vested in the colonizing state, delegated to its agents of rule. The doctrine of nation, redolent with overtones of self-determination, was vigorously disputed by the proprietary powers until the eve of their departure. And the colonial state was not an actor in the international scene; at most, it was occasionally a stage hand. The question may arise as to whether the colonial polity merits the dignity of recognition as a state.

THE PARTICULAR FEATURES
OF THE COLONIAL STATE

Although I would affirm the colonial polity's standing as a state, the ambiguities are sufficient to require some exploration of the special characteristics of the colonial appendage as state. One may note that, when the process of European expansion overseas began in the fifteenth century, the idea of the modern state had yet to take form, and the very word was not yet in circulation. The three missing attributes of the colonial state—sovereignty, nation, external actor—had still to emerge as clear adjuncts to stateness for the European kingdoms that were poised to impose their dominion around the globe. Thus, the emergence of the colonial polity as a distinctive species of the state genus occurs as a process paralleling the development of the modern state.

As this dialectic unfolded, the colonial state gradually acquired a distinctive personality of its own—at different rates and in different ways in varying instances. At the very core of this process was its definition as alien other by the ruling power. Differentiated institutions of rule were erected, and separate legal classifications for the subject population instituted. This historical dynamic built upon differing state traditions among the colonizing powers, and thus the range of variation in the profile of the colonial state was considerable.

As full-fledged civil societies took form in Europe and struggled for empowerment, the distinction between metropolitan citizens and overseas subjects sharpened. The juridical personality of the colonial state was affected by the preservation of an older state under its rule, as in Morocco or Egypt. The composition of the dominated population was of crucial import in defining the colonial polity: indigenous, imported servile labor, or transplanted subjects of the crown. The common thread, in the later stages of imperial rule, was the conceptualization of the colonial territory as a juridically distinct sphere, clearly separate from the domestic realm. The essence of state construction was the institutionalization of agencies of domination that at once perpetuated rule and upheld the polity's categorization as other. At a final imperial moment, with the institution of the League of Nations mandate system, the specific personality of the colonial state became enshrined in international law, along with an (initially ineffectual) assertion that rule was exercised in trust for an indigenous civil society, whose interests were paramount.

In time, the subject populations internalized their classification as other, fused it to the emergent doctrines of nation and self-determination, and fashioned an ultimately invincible weapon of liberation. On the long road to escape from imperial rule, the maps of exit varied at different times and places. A recurrent temptation among some colonial subjects was to transcend otherness by claiming the full entitlements of citizenship in the realm. Eventually, however, almost everywhere the successful response to subjugation as colonial other was utilization of the political space and territorial personality of the colonial state to assert the right to complete its stateness by acquisition of sovereignty, nationality, and full membership in the international system of states.

In the early stages of the age of imperialism, then, the colonial state is a blurred object. Above all in Africa, whose continental space was restructured in colonial polities only in the final phases of globalized colonialism, the colonial state offers a sharply delineated analytical field. The European political systems at the moment of the partition of Africa were fully elaborated states, with technological, economic, and ideological resources far beyond those available in previous centuries. The experience and accumulated knowledge of extended periods of overseas domination—directly or through vicarious observation of neighboring powers—yielded a sophistication in the construction of an apparatus of domination often absent in earlier ventures. The distance of the other was enhanced by newly intense Darwinian notions of racial superiority that permeated the institutions and agents of rule. The comprehensive marginalization of the subject population (except in those few territories with substantial European settler populations) invested the African colonial state at its apogee with leviathan qualities. The image of the state as Bula Matari does not come so readily to mind in other colonial realms.

The high degree of hegemony and autonomy that the African colonial state enjoyed at its zenith makes it a particularly fit subject for analysis as actor. Because its behavior was relatively uninhibited by constraints imposed by subject society, the polity had unusual freedom to chart a course by reason of state. After the initial moment of conquest, the colonial state also acquired substantial autonomy from metropolitan oversight. The colonial elite that staffed its structures enjoyed broad latitude in applying the six imperatives of state behavior in the management of its destinies. Only in its final phases, when it was caught between an emergent civil society constituted by nationalism (which demanded liberation) and the metropolitan state (which reasserted its authority over the process of power transfer), did the African colonial state find itself progressively hamstrung.

THE EARLY ORIGINS OF THE COLONIAL STATE

To set Bula Matari in context, a backward step is needed to observe the crystallization of the notion of the colonial realm, and to note some of its variant patterns of genesis. I shall return in chapter 8 to a systematic comparison of colonial state rule and legacy elsewhere with the African form. Here I wish to illustrate the genetic relationship between the African colonial state and its predecessors, and to embellish the argument that the inner logic of colonial rule can be usefully grasped by viewing the state as an actor. At the same time, the stage is set for a return to this theme at the close of this volume, where I suggest that exceptional features of the African colonial state, arising from the exigencies of its own reproduction, produced a singularly difficult legacy for the postcolonial state.

In its original meaning, in the mists of antiquity, the word *colony* referred to a self-standing settlement of migrants from a Mediterranean city-state. The Phoenician and Greek worlds, turned toward the sea, scattered large numbers of such fragments from the Black Sea shores to the Straits of Gibraltar. In rare instances, such as Carthage, these offspring became large territorial states. Derivation was a basis for alliance, but the notion of colony connoted no accompanying institutions of domination. Autonomous political communities arose in the image of the mother polis, separate from rather than ruling over earlier populations. Settlement was the core element defining a colonial polity; indeed, this view persists even in treatises composed before the rise of the African colonial state in the twentieth century as most visible exemplar made subjugation its essence. If a territory is entirely populated by "aborigenes," reads one 1900 text, it is not a colony but a mere possession.[1]

Imperialism of an altogether different order, whose model and ideology supplied inspiration for aggressive states over many centuries into contemporary times, was pioneered by the Roman state. In its transformation from small city-state to world empire, Rome developed a comprehensive strategy for the metamorphosis of conquest into incorporation. Its modes of gaining territory included forcible conquest, but acquisition was often accomplished by guile and diplomacy.[2] New regions were frequently brought under Roman hegemony as client or tributary states; over time, the logic of Roman state construction brought full annexation and dissolution of partly autonomous structures.

What began as colonial other gradually dissolved into incorporated civil society, although residues of the distinctive Roman core persisted; the grain dole, however, was restricted to the bloated imperial capital.[3] Avenues of co-optation were opened to provincial elites.[4] Over time, entry into the equestrian order, and eventually elevation to senatorial status, became available, although unevenly and confined mainly to the inner provinces. Citizenship, a precise legal status, was gradually extended, especially as a reward for service, and then became more universalized in concept in A.D. 212. An increasingly uniform legal code, whose codification was undertaken by jurists in the third century and promulgated by Justinian in 533, provided an integrative common jurisprudence for the empire. In practice, the peoples of the empire's periphery remained in Roman eyes semibarbarians, too closely related to the uncouth hordes beyond the frontier.[5] But the European myth of Rome as incorporative polity, as suggesting a millennial model for perpetual propriety over colonial domains through distant absorption of the alien other into state and civil society, lived on into the second half of the twentieth century.

The Roman imperial pattern, with its faint echoes in the modern colonial era, stands in contrast to patterns of territorial expansion and incorporation in such vast empire-states as the Ummayad Caliphate in early Islam, the Ottoman state, and the Chinese Middle Kingdom. In the instance of Islamic state as empire, the core value of the faith militant provided an ideology of absorption through conversion. Membership in the community of Islam obliterated the otherness of conquered communities; forcible annexation of new lands enlarged Dar-al-Islam, rather than built an empire. The Ottoman state, which absorbed large nonconverting Christian and Jewish populations, devised a new stratagem of incorporation by providing religiocultural autonomy through the millet system to Christian sects and Jews, while upholding the suzerainty and religious monopoly of the Islamic state.[6] In self-concept and doctrine, it was thus a conquering but not a colonizing power.

The same can be said for the historical Chinese state. From the Han dynasty on, its institutional apparatus, cultural system, and communicative codes expanded with its frontiers. In its secular ooze and flow to the south, the Chinese state sinified and assimilated, but it did not develop colonial metaphors of rule, even with respect to its thousand-year ascendancy over Vietnam. The alien other was the barbarian beyond the walls; in an intermediate role was the orbit of tributary states in regular intercourse with the Middle Kingdom. For those brought fully within the Chinese zone of rule, its metaphors were incorporative.[7]

IRELAND AS A COLONIAL STATE

The rise of the modern colonial system was foreshadowed in different ways by two precursors, Ireland and Venice. Ireland is a striking deviant case within the European arena of state formation and serves as a laboratory for competing modes of domination, colonial and incorporative. In many respects Ireland should be considered the oldest colony of the modern era and the first instance of indigenous anticolonial nationalism compelling the imperial power to withdraw.

In the long period of formation and dissolution, expansion and contraction of emergent European states, incorporative metaphors predominated. Territorial acquisition brought the resident population into full association with the state. In Ireland, however, English rule from the first papal donation to Henry II in 1154 entailed repeated reassertions of English domination through new waves of alien agents and structures of domination, punctuated occasionally by moments when incorporative tides seem to run. The twelfth and thirteenth centuries saw a feudal mode of colonial subjugation, through the allocation of large fiefs to Anglo-Norman lords, with the crown represented by a lord lieutenant. This oligarchy was gradually localized, and Ireland became dangerously alien in religious terms when the Protestant Reformation failed to secure a real foothold there in the sixteenth century. Morbid English fears of papal armies in the service of their Catholic Majesties of Spain or France drove the English state in the sixteenth, seventeenth, and eighteenth centuries to fasten far more extensive superstructures of subordination: the confiscation of Catholic lands and their award to a new influx of English gentry; the vesting of political power in this "Protestant Ascendancy"; the settling of many thousands of Scottish and north-English farmers in confiscated Catholic lands in Ulster; penal and exclusionary laws aimed at Irish Catholics; the imposition of a standing army on Ireland.

The Protestant Ascendancy in its turn began to display independent impulses, acquiring almost full autonomy in 1782 in the wake of the American Revolution. New apprehensions of the security threat to Britain awakened by the Napoleonic Wars and the Wolf Tone rebellion in the 1790s brought full incorporation through the 1801 Act of Union. As a dissident zone of the domestic realm, Ireland was subjected to a new form of control, colonial in its inner logic, now exercised through an explicit English state administrative and policing apparatus rather than a superimposed social hierarchy. Even when fully incorporated within the British constitutional state the Irish remained a subversive other; they in turn increasingly rejected a status they perceived as colonial. Even after eight centuries of rule, so profoundly rooted in the British state and among Irish civil society was the perception that the linkage was essentially colonial that, in the end, only decolonization could bring to an end the permanent crisis in their relationship.[8]

VENICE AS A MARITIME EMPIRE

Venice of the late medieval period provided a model different from the Irish case of territorial domination of a differentiated population. From the thirteenth to the fifteenth centuries the rising mercantile power of Venice constructed a sea-borne empire in the Adriatic, Black, and eastern Mediterranean seas, an empire whose logic and structural features were embyronic representations of those soon to be constructed by the Portuguese and the Dutch. The Venetian core of this state, modest in

48

territorial dimensions but great in wealth and mercantile skills, sought a string of outposts athwart the main trade routes to the east through which it could assert its commercial dominance. Its coercive powers rested in its navy, which until the sixteenth-century ascendancy of the Ottoman Empire sufficed to protect its outposts and dominate the sea lanes. Except for its island base of Crete, Venice as colonizer exercised rule over only small numbers of people; the sinews of the state were trade, and the boundaries of hegemony were fixed by close calculation of commercial need and advantage. Resident mercantile agents, and the modest cadre of Venetian state delegates, had no real objectives other than maximal Venetian monopolization of trade. This greenhouse for the early germination of capitalism required a strong navy but no more than a skeletal colonial apparatus to protect its position.[9]

The genesis of the modern colonial state lay above all in the discovery of new trade routes to the East around Africa and the appearance of the Americas within the European field of vision and navigation. The maritime kingdoms on the western shore of Europe soon became engaged in an intense competition for exploitation of the new material opportunities thus revealed. Interlocking regional economies emerged to fuel this competition: spices and fineries from south and east Asia, bypassing the Muslim-controlled overland routes; precious metals from Meso-America and the Andes; sugar from the South American coast and the Antilles; slaves from Africa; pirate lairs everywhere. Vast new populations became available for Christian evangelization, unimpeded by the frustrating barrier that Islam created in contiguous zones. The eddying currents of the newly globalized rivalries, shaped by the differing physiognomies of the participating states, swirled around the coasts of Africa and Asia and over the Western hemisphere. In their wake emerged the first generation of modern colonial states. Colonizing structures took form, whose evolving nature and experience imprinted upon the European imperial mind an array of assumptions, premises, and principles of statecraft constituting the "policy knowledge" that was subsequently applied to the partition of Africa. An excursion through the major patterns in early colonial construction will help set the stage for the detailed scrutiny of Bula Matari that begins in the next chapter.

THE SEA-BORNE PORTUGUESE EMPIRE

In the first period, four main models took form: the Portuguese sea-borne empire, the Spanish conquest state, the Anglo-Dutch quasi-private mercantile corporation, and the chartered colonial plantation. The first of these, the Portuguese maritime polity, began with its outpost at Ceuta in 1415, motivated both by the anti-Muslim sentiment of the *reconquista* (the conquest of southern Spain), and the prospect of connecting directly to the trans-Saharan gold trade. It then continued with the series of African coastal voyages pushing ever closer to the Cape of Good Hope (rounded in 1488), with some coastal posts established in the initial hope of diverting the gold trade. The uninhabited island chains of the Azores, Madeira, and Cape Verde were added to the Portuguese realm and lightly settled.

The new vistas of extended dominion opened by the exploits of the Portuguese fleet prompted the quest for legitimation of proprietary claims. With res publica christiana still a living idea, and the papacy the sole supranational fount of authority, Prince Henry the Navigator solicited papal benediction for his regalian assertions. In three bulls issued from 1452 to 1456, the pope gave full satisfaction to his petitioner; the Portuguese monarch was authorized to attack, conquer, and subdue all Saracens and other "unbelievers" from Morocco to the Indies, to reduce them to slavery, to transfer their lands and properties to the crown, to have title to all maritime domains, and to enjoy a monopoly of navigation, trade, and fishing. For good measure, the Order of Christ, under the royal patronage of Prince Henry, received spiritual jurisdiction over all conquered domains.[10]

This extravagant colonial charter invested the small kingdom perched on the southwestern extremity of Europe with a global mission beyond its grasp, but in the century that followed a remarkably far-flung maritime realm was constructed. Although at its peak in the mid-sixteenth century it had a fleet of just three hundred ships and there were only ten thousand Portuguese and mulattoes from Mozambique to Macao, a loose-knit mercantile state emerged, based on domination of the Indian Ocean trading routes, and a nucleated string of outposts at key commercial intersections whose central base was Goa. Portuguese images of the dimensions of their empire are captured in a 1663 account by Jesuit Father Manuel Godinho, bemoaning its seventeenth-century decline:

The Lusitanian Indian Empire or State, which formerly dominated the whole of the East, and comprised eight thousand leagues of sovereignty, including twenty-nine provincial capital cities as well as many others of lesser note, and which gave the law to thirty-three tributary kingdoms, amazing the whole world with its vast extent, stupendous victories, thriving trade and immense riches, is now either through its own sins or else through the inevitable decay of great empires, reduced to so few lands and cities that one may well doubt whether that State was smaller at its very beginning than it is now at its end.[11]

This partly imagined empire could take form and subsist for a time because even its modest capabilities, in the absence of stronger predators, permitted effective domination of the Indian Ocean sailing routes and major entrepôts. It arose in a historical interstice, just before the rise of Ottoman Turkey, the resurrection of the Persian state by the Safavids, and the reconstruction of a powerful polity on the Indian subcontinent by the Moguls brought far more potent land rivals, and the aggressive entry of English and Dutch armed merchants challenged the sea-lanes. It survived as well because of the limitations of its territorial ambitions. It sought security for its outposts but ignored the more dangerous injunctions of the 1452–1456 bulls proposing subjugation and enslavement of "unbelievers" and confiscation of their lands.

The Portuguese empire in the Indies took shape before ideologies of colonial rule were at hand to mold its political organization. The inertial path was the reproduction overseas of the primary institutions of royal governance at home. A viceroyalty was erected at Goa, charged with surveillance of the extended network of outposts; naturally, its practical capacities were small and really effective only in the Indian coastal settlements, the largest single Portuguese concentration. Conceptually, however, it was perceived as a self-standing state linked directly to the Portuguese crown—the Estado de India. In a few major settlements— Goa, Macao, Bahia, Luanda—municipal councils on the Lisbon model were chartered, creating an institutional base for a nascent civil society composed of settled Portuguese, people of mixed ancestry, and some local inhabitants culturally incorporated into the Lusitanian world, usually through Christian conversion. The essentially precarious nature of the terra-firma outposts of the Portuguese sea-based colonial state is described well in a 1582 characterization of Macao by a Spanish observer:

The Portuguese of Macao are still nowadays without any weapons or gunpowder, or form of justice, having a Chinese mandarin who searches their houses to see if they have any arms or munitions. And because it is a regular town with about 500 houses and there is a Portuguese governor and a bishop therein, they pay every three years to the incoming viceroy of Canton about 100,000 ducats to avoid being expelled from the land, which he divides with the grandees of the household of the King of China. However, it is constantly affirmed by everyone that the king has no idea that there are any such Portuguese in his land.[12]

The revenue imperative was central to the expansive impulse of the Portuguese crown in the fifteenth century; returns from the royal estates in Portugal were far from sufficient to sustain the court expenses. The new trade outlets held the promise of added crown revenues through assertion of royal monopolies over key commodities, or rents obtained from the grant of monopoly licenses to merchants. The mercantile sector was also enlisted as partner in the risks and costs of expansion, through the participation of its own vessels and capital. The fiscal potential of these new sources was inevitably circumscribed by the limited regulatory capacities of the state projected over such vast distances. The merchants naturally maneuvered to divert from royal to private channels as much of the returns as possible. In turn, both the crown and the merchant community were unable to stem leakages in the network of monopolies through patterns of contraband trade by agents of the trading houses and the state, which developed in tandem with the empire in the Indies. In practice the forts and outposts strung along the coasts of Africa and the Indian Ocean had to sustain themselves by informal foraging; this imperial superstructure lacked regularized budgetary mechanisms of support. The whole apparatus fed on trading profits from a small number of luxury commodities serving a limited upper-class market; gold, spices, and later sugar.

Only in Brazil did an extensive land-based colonial state under Portuguese sovereignty emerge before the late nineteenth century. The Brazil image was to permeate the Portuguese colonial ideology when its African footholds in Angola and Mozambique became substantial interior occupations as the scramble for Africa gathered force. The political economy of colonial construction in Brazil had contours very different from those of the sea-borne Indies empire. A nominal claim dated from Pope Alexander VI's exorbitant bull of 1493, obtained by the Spanish crown to convert the Columbus footfall in what were believed to be the Indies into a vast claim over western lands and seas; the "Indies" were partitioned along a longitudinal axis running a hundred leagues west of Cape Verde. As elaborated by the 1494 Treaty of Tordesillas between Spain and Portugal, these "discovery"-rooted claims provided Portugal with a shadowy title to the Brazilian coast, which was reconnoitered only in 1500.

Initially, Portuguese action in Brazil followed the sea-borne imperial model of the African coast and the Indies. The coastal posts developed a modest trade in dyewood, which the Indian populations could be induced to cut by trinkets and tools; thus no direct control over their labor was at first needed. However, a security menace developed in the form of French poaching on their trade, which could not be repelled as in the Indian Ocean by patrolling the sea-lanes. Only Portuguese settlements along the coast could secure Lisbon's dominion, whose legal basis was furthermore challenged by French jurists, who contested papal authority to accord territorial proprietary rights and the validity of Portuguese-Spanish bilateral diplomacy. The contrastive principle of "effective occupation," which, as we shall see, played such a driving force in the early logic of the African colonial state, was introduced into imperial jurisprudence.

Thus forced into more active assertion of its claims, the Portuguese crown fell back on a medieval notion of territorial incorporation, which had seen service in the Atlantic islands of Madeira, the Azores, and Cape Verde: royal donation of land as feudal fiefdoms to gentry with a background of service to the crown. The Brazilian coast was assigned in fifteen captaincies to twelve "donatary captains," who received a hereditary delegation of royal jurisdiction and a cut in the royal tithes and rents in return for securing and settling these horizontal strips extending indefinitely inland.

The new mode of colonial dominion had far-reaching implications. To profit from their grants, the donatary captains required an auxiliary population of Portuguese settlers. Recruitment of settlers was difficult; there was little land pressure in Portugal, and those restless souls bent on expatriation and adventurous pursuit of riches had other choices in the Indies. Thus, a significant fraction was recruited from the convict population, a turbulent and often uncontrollable element. Further, the agricultural base envisaged by the donatary captains in the first instance was sugar, whose profitability had been demonstrated in Madeira and Sao Tome. This implied both engrossing land that Indian communities regarded as theirs and coercive incorporation of Indians as servile labor. A crisis in relations with Indians followed at once.

This in turn brought the superposition upon these patrimonial foundations of a rudimentary royal administration, beginning in 1549. The standing royal instructions to the new governors clearly reveal the logic triggering this move: defense of the settlements against Indian attack from within and French encroachment from abroad, and increase in the royal revenues (which the court believed the donatary captains were diverting). The security and revenue imperatives brought about the first rudiments of a distinctive colonial state: the need for assertion of hegemony over the Indian communities within reach of the coast compelled a search for definition of the alien other.

"Tupi social organization did not fit any of the categories the Portuguese could comprehend," writes Johnson; "hence the crown's confused hesitation in defining the status of the Indians."[13] Two contrary motivating forces operated. On the one hand, the medieval doctrine of the state as an agency for upholding and enlarging the Catholic community had a potent hold; the more contemporary jurisprudence of Vitoria imposed similar obligations of considerate treatment. In 1549 the Jesuits were given spiritual jurisdiction over the Indians and soon developed their evangelical strategy of creating separate Tupi communities under their direct control, designed as autonomous socioeconomic entities. On the other hand, sugar estates and mills could operate only with Indian slave labor; both the private profits of the plantation owners and the captaincy and crown revenues depended on this. A dual doctrine evolved to incorporate these contradictions: peaceful Indians who accepted conversion deserved royal protection as subjects, while rebellious Indians could be targeted for "just war" and violent enslavement. By the end of the sixteenth century, disease and exploitation had decimated the coastal Indian population; African slave imports—about whose status there was neither debate nor scruple—gradually eliminated the need for Indian labor on the sugar plantations.[14] The remaining Indians within the still coastal orbit of the emergent Brazilian colonial state were incorporated as legal minors; those resident on the Jesuit missions were wards of the Church. The Indian as other had retreated to the interior, subject to enserfment on the moving frontier but free in regions to which the colonial state had only a purely theoretical claim.

The Portuguese colonial edifice in Brazil thus developed along lines very different from the maritime Estado de India. A century after its creation, the population under its rule still numbered only about twenty-five thousand whites, fifteen thousand Africans, and eighteen thousand Indians.[15] In 1588 Brazil contributed no more than 2.5 percent of the crown's revenues, while the Estado de India provided as much as 26 percent.[16] But the basic structure of colonial Brazil—a complex interpenetration of patrimonial and bureaucratic elements—was clearly visible. A civil society capable of engaging the colonial state in a struggle for autonomy was also established, resulting in combat that continued and intensified as the eighteenth-century gold boom drove state and society toward the interior.[17] I shall return to this state in its final form in the penultimate chapter.

THE SPANISH COLONIAL STATE:
TERRITORIAL DOMINATION

The Spanish colonial state, in contrast to the others, was from its first beginnings a territorial rather than maritime construction. Spain itself as early imperial power had extraordinary qualities of stateness. Also, its Castilian core had been embarked upon the reconquista for the preceding three centuries, a dynamic that embedded within its doctrines and practices an experience of institutionalizing domination and incorporation of the alien other that deeply marked its colonial policies.

The reconquista and the colonial venture symbolically fuse in the 1492 date marking the end of the former and the beginning of the latter. The periodic surges southward and the accompanying acquisition of new Muslim and Jewish subjects posed a challenge to the statecraft of conquest very different from that elsewhere in late medieval Europe, where it sufficed to stitch a fabric of contractual relations with the nobility. But Moors and, by the fifteenth century, Jews were an unspeakable other, hostile adversaries in a holy war not yet extinguished and, parenthetically, holders of property ripe for expropriation. There could thus be no permanent solution through co-opting existing social hierarchies (though this was sometimes a temporary expedient); wholly new ones had to be imposed, and the subject population displaced or converted. The military orders of knights as beneficiaries of large expropriated estates, the institution of the *encomienda* as tributary grant of labor extraction rights over conquered populations in return for their protective management and Christianization, the Church and its orders as spiritual agents of social control: all these mechanisms of conquest emerged in the period immediately preceding Spanish expansion across the Atlantic.[18]

Also coincident with conquest in the Americas was a remarkable renovation and elaboration of the Spanish state, really created by the dynastic union of Castile and Aragon, consolidated in 1479 through the marriage of Ferdinand and Isabella. Building on the relatively centralized medieval tradition of the Castilian kingdom, with its more feudalized Aragon counterpart, the Spanish crown added many novel elements that foreshadowed the continental absolutist state. Ferdinand maneuvered his way into leadership of the military orders, and the crown gained control over parts of the immensely wealthy Church in Spain and full *patronato* over that in the Americas. To these quintessentially medieval stratagems of state-building were added the distinctly modern devices of the legal-rational bureaucracy. This new Spanish state was able to ground its rule doctrinally in the theories of a talented generation of legal philosophers and staff its departmentalized bureaucracy with lawyers with a vocation of state-building.[19] A measure of the dynamic of its expansion and institutionalization is the increase in crown revenues, from less than 900,000 reales in 1474 to 26 million in 1504, well before bullion from the Americas began to swell crown coffers.[20]

This precociously absolute Spanish state, barely formed, faced a colossal challenge in extending its dominion over the enormous territories allocated to Spain by Pope Alexander VI in return for the commitment to evangelization. In an extraordinary burst of imperial energy in the half-century that followed, some Spanish presence was established from northern Argentina and Chile to northern Mexico, and in the main islands of the Antilles. From the outset it was apparent that Spanish dominion was to impose itself on land and people, and not to follow the Portuguese model of the coastal trading outpost. The unprecedented challenge of absorbing these vast domains into a Spanish polity compelled a philosophic reformulation of the state. The kingdom enlarged by the new continents, notes a historian of Spanish renaissance thought, "did not fit into any known political system" and could not easily be contained within the categories of medieval constitutionalism alone.[21]

The establishment of empire proceeded in two distinct phases, the first leading dialectically to the second. Initially, the object was discovery and conquest; this was undertaken not by the crown directly but through a large cohort of individually organized expeditions. Chartered by the crown, they operated under the umbrella of legitimacy. The crown received for its blessing the royal fifth, a cut in any plunder, and new lands for its realm. The conquistador, as entrepreneur of conquest, raised the funds to finance the expedition from merchants and banking houses, and recruited its personnel. A successful conquest promised a share of the booty and claims on patrimonial compensation from the crown: honors and encomiendas. The spectacular success of some—the Cortes syndrome—lured an ample supply of others, financiers and aspirant conquistadores, into the venture. These private agents of conquest, operating under the flag of Spain and in the name of its monarchs, added to the five hundred thousand square kilometers of territory and seven million subjects in Iberian Spain some two million square kilometers and fifty million new subjects—before the demographic holocaust took hold. The tiny bands of Cortes and Pizarro subdued vast kingdoms; wherever settled, sedentary, politically organized Indian communities were encountered, the agents of conquest prevailed. The very success of conquest compelled Spain to invent a colonial state.[22]

In both Mexico and Peru the large Indian conquest states (Aztec and Inca) had only recently been established, opening opportunities for alliance with discontented segments of these empires. Spanish forces were too small to impose their rule by military means alone; a combination of force, negotiation, and alliance was required. Collaboration could be profitable for Indian elites, chiefs, and entrepreneurs; at the same time, the swift establishment of a colonial mining industry required forced delivery of laborers on a scale that often outstripped Spanish authority. By the latter part of the sixteenth century, an operative colonial state was in place; Steve Stern notes that the agents of Spanish domination had mastered "the organization of coercive, violent institutions and relations into power structures capable of implementing a grand design for economic development."[23]

The nature of this challenge to the political imagination of the crown was also transformed by the shift of its center from its initial Antilles bases to Mexico and Peru. Cortes set forth to subdue the Aztec state with 508 soldiers and 110 sailors in 1519; Pizarro decapitated the Inca Empire with 180 men and thirty horses in 1532. The acquisition of these vast domains, with their large, subordinated populations, huge stores of accumulated wealth, and quickly discovered silver mines, at once made their organization and exploitation the central determinant of Spain's Americas policy.

As a metropolitan superstructure, Spain created the Casa de Contratación (Board of Trade) in 1503, to monitor all commercial dealings with the Americas, and in 1524 the Council of the Indies, the first colonial ministry. In theory, all persons and goods departing for the New World required clearance. The lawyers and clerics who toiled for the Council of the Indies, in a little more than their first century, prepared no fewer than four hundred thousand decrees.[24] In the Americas the crown created two viceroyalties (Mexico and Peru), each under the command of a noble appointed for a delimited period serving as delegate of the king. The viceroyalty, of which there were then seven others in Europe (including Aragon, Catalonia, and Valencia in Iberia, and Sardinia, Sicily, and Naples in Italy), reproduced in the Americas the notion of a distinct crown realm under the authority of the monarchy. The Spanish realm was a federated conglomerate, joined at the summit by the rapidly bureaucratizing institutions of the crown, with no sharp conceptual distinction between the units in Europe and those in the Americas.

The viceroyalty was territorially subdivided into captaincies and other lesser units. It was paralleled by a separate and autonomous judicial structure, the Audiencia, which at times assumed political roles and served to monitor the viceroyalty. The Iberian town, with its corporate privileges and locally elected offices, provided an institutional base for settled Spanish population, under the watchful eye of appointed royal officials. The Church as well formed part of the institutional matrix of royal control.

The emergent colonial state apparatus, with its sophisticated array of partly competing and mutually monitoring hierarchies, was pulled in different directions by its various imperatives. Its first and fundamental task was to create a permanent framework of hegemony. This required, on the one hand, asserting royal authority over the conquistador class, rewarding it for its service yet blocking its crystallization into a hereditary landed nobility refractory to state authority, as had tended to happen in the reconquista Iberian south (and also the Canaries, brought within the Spanish orbit by feudal land donations the crown soon came to regret immediately prior to the Columbus voyage). On the other hand, a stable definition of state relationships to the Indian communities was indispensable.

Although many conquistadores were initially rewarded with encomiendas, the king was careful to deny them permanent hereditary status, and gradually to extinguish them. The crucial confrontation with the conquerer generation occurred in Peru when Francisco Pizarro's successors went into open revolt after publication of the 1542 New Laws of the Indies and killed the viceroy. A new viceroy with an armed force was dispatched; their success in arresting and executing Gonzalo Pizarro dramatized the ultimate supremacy of the crown. At the same time, effective control of the crown over its royal agents and civil society was always incomplete; the New Laws of the Indies, with their radical protective ambitions for the Indian populations, could never be widely enforced, and the colonial bureaucracy did not try: "I obey, but I do not comply" (*obedeizco pero no cumplo*) was the frequent response of royal agents faced with instructions they felt unwise to apply.

The Indian question became a crisis even before the Cortes and Pizarro conquests. Within two decades of the first Spanish settlement in Hispaniola, the Indian population had been decimated, and the first denunciations of Spanish abuse and mistreatment of Indians were reaching the court. The legitimacy of Spanish claims derived in part from the papal donation, itself linked to conversion and protection. Yet coercive extraction of Indian labor appeared to be fundamental to settler economic pursuits. In the succinct formulation of Lang, "where there were no Indians, there were no Spaniards."[25]

A running debate about the nature and rights of Indians continued throughout much of the sixteenth century. The conquistador faction that sought a license for unlimited exploitation argued that Indians lacked essential elements of humanity which would qualify them for subject status: practice of human sacrifice, purported sodomous proclivities, idolatry. They were thus destined by nature for enslavement. Others fell back on the "just war" doctrine, by which failure to comply with the *requieri-miento* (the proclamation summoning Indians to instant submission and conversion) permitted their seizure as slaves.[26] In a more nuanced form, as enunciated by the legal philosopher Juan Gines de Sepulveda, natural law vested rule in the wisest and most prudent of "higher races" and supplied a mandate to subjugate those who "require, by their own nature and in their own interests, to be placed under the authority of civilised and virtuous princes or nations."[27] Ranged on the other side was the intrepid Bartolomé de las Casas, a Dominican who for four decades tirelessly upheld the rights of the Indians and excoriated their oppressors. Indians were not only human subjects endowed with reason and capable of willing conversion but were also, in the eyes of many missionaries of the mendicant orders, unspoiled children of God through whom the early Church in its pristine purity might be resurrected. The swift apparent spiritual conquest of those within reach consolidated their recognition as subordinated subjects.

Although the crown generally repudiated Indian slavery, its disappearance was above all due to the appearance of African slaves for the Caribbean and coastal lowland sugar estates, and the development of other forms of coerced labor to supply the Mexican and Peruvian silver mines with Indian workers. Even though Indians became recognized as crown subjects, they were decimated in the first century of Spanish rule by an unprecedented demographic catastrophe (the introduction of new diseases; brutality of exploitation; despair). In Mexico their numbers fell from an estimated twenty-five million in 1519 to 2.65 million in 1568, and in Peru from nine million to 1.3 million from 1532 to 1570.[28] In Hispaniola a sizable Arawak population had virtually disappeared by the middle of the sixteenth century; over time, comparable indigenous population decimation occurred on the other Caribbean islands.[29]

In the crucial wealth-producing zones of Spanish empire, Peru and Mexico, the size and structuration of Indian societies required the collaboration of Indian intermediaries; Stern carefully documents how uneasy this relationship was during its first century in the former Inca realms.[30] Indians differed from Moors as crown subjects, in Spanish eyes, because they did not reject Christianity. They were viewed as perpetual minors from whom labor tribute had to be extracted without benefit of a Spanish army of occupation. The local judicial and policing structures, abetted by the Church, were the key operative mechanisms of local control. The surprising volume of peasant litigation found in both Mexico and Peru attests paradoxically, as Taylor suggests, "acceptance of the Crown as legitimate arbiter of peasant grievances and a direct link between peasant and king that deflected peasants from potential insurrection."[31]

Africans, for Spaniards as well as Portuguese, were of a different conceptual category. Black slaves began appearing in the Iberian Peninsula in some numbers by the thirteenth century from the trans-Saharan trade; by the fifteenth century the Portuguese African outposts added to the flow. The association of Africans with slave status—social death, in Orlando Patterson's evocative notion[32]—meant that from the outset they were perceived as a human category devoid of any civil standing.[33]

Coincident with the creation of the New World viceroyalties and the windfall revenues that came from the first appropriations of Aztec and Inca treasure was a phase of aggressive expansion in Europe. In 1519 Charles I managed to secure title to the crown of the Holy Roman Empire (as Charles V), and he waged relentless military campaigns financed by the Spanish treasury to transform this shadowy construct into a real state. Philip II later in the century was likewise embroiled in constant warfare, to sustain Spanish claims in the Netherlands and Italy and to combat Ottoman, French, and English designs. The war-driven expenditures required intense taxation pressures on Castile and the Italian possessions, as well as frequent large borrowings from German and Italian bankers. Despite its considerable revenues, Spain was often in acute financial distress during its century of expansion; thus, state policy toward the Indies was invariably revenue-driven in significant measure.[34] This meant in turn that the viceroyalties in the Americas when exercising their hegemony had to ensure that those productive activities yielding crown revenue went forward. Labor supply was the key factor; this meant guaranteeing Indian labor for the mines and African slaves for the plantations.

In translating these equations of state reason into institutional structures and policies on the ground, the Spanish colonial edifice acquired its particular profile. In fundamental concept, during the early phase, the western viceroyalties were new satrapies of the crown, not totally distinct colonial appendages. Indeed, the term *colony* was not used by, and would not have occurred to, the sixteenth-century scholastics who designed and managed the new state. Over time, its colonial specificity became more clear, as we shall see when we compare the Spanish colonial state with its African counterpart.

Another crucial aspect of Spanish empire construction needs to be noted here. Spain's European rivals took full, even exaggerated, measure of the flow of bullion from the New World, attributing Spanish power largely to this source. At first those equipped to enter maritime competition—initially, England, France, and (after its independence in the late sixteenth century) the Netherlands—sought a share of this wealth through authorized piracy and smuggling. By the end of the sixteenth century, projects were developing to create competing imperial realms in the Indies or the Americas, schemes that were stimulated in the minds of royal officials and the mercantile classes by the conviction that autonomous royal revenues and trading profits would reward colonial ventures.[35]

THE DUTCH MARITIME MERCANTILE EMPIRE

In pursuing the imperial temptation, the Dutch and English developed a wholly different model of colonial expansion. Both chartered merchant associations invested with sovereign attributes as the organizational weapon. A wholly mercantile logic propelled their enterprises; no crusading commitments encumbered the East India companies launched almost simultaneously on both sides of the North Sea.

The Netherlands as a state was not only newly born, at the end of the fifteenth century, after its costly struggle against Spanish rule but was also a singularly jerry-built structure associating the seven Dutch-speaking, mainly Protestant provinces.[36] The merchant houses in the main trading towns, mostly turned toward the sea, were the dominant social force; the States-General, the deliberative assembly bringing together the delegates of this essentially bourgeois republic, elected a Stadtholder, but it lacked the centralizing institutions of royal absolutism ascendant in most European polities of the time. Thus, its vesting its colonial venture in a merchant association mirrored the inner nature of the embryonic Dutch state.

The Dutch East India Company at its birth in 1602 had a highly targeted goal: to capture the spice trade, then mainly in nutmeg, mace, cloves, pepper, and cinnamon. The original charter authorized company agents to "take suitable measures" if their trading partners in the Indies caused them to be "deceived or treated badly." This innocent clause was the wedge through which commerce was leveraged into conquest. In the words of a student of the birth of the company,

By this clause, the Company was authorized to make treaties with foreign potentates in the name of the States General, to establish forts, and to appoint governors and judges to maintain law and order. Although this was for the express purpose of creating stable conditions for trading, it actually authorized the Company to take the law into its own hands. When contracts were repeatedly broken, it was inevitable that such authority would establish a basis for territorial conquest.[37]

The nature of its mandate indeed shaped the company's operation, and brought about its metamorphosis from trading association into agency of territorial rule. To secure its profits in a risky and volatile market, there were natural inducements to move beyond mere exchange relationships into physical control of the source. This occurred first, with particularly devastating results, in the Ambonese and Moluccan islands of eastern Indonesia. Facing weak local polities, the company was able to enforce its own prices and coerce deliveries. In Java—quickly to become the core of the Dutch East Indies—stronger states were encountered, but a foothold was soon gained, with a nuclear stronghold at Djakarta (then Batavia). The armed company acquired territorial control, exercised through existing rulers, over much of the island and footholds throughout the archipelago (where exportable produce was found). However, the outer limits of this form of mercantile exploitation were eventually reached; the company as proxy colonizer was in decline by the eighteenth century and bankrupt on the eve of the Napoleonic Wars. The Dutch East Indies became a real colonial state, highly profitable to the Netherlands, only after the Napoleonic interlude of British domination.

EARLY BRITISH EMPIRE: COMPANIES AND PLANTATIONS

In the British case, the model for expansion was supplied by the royally chartered merchant adventurer associations created for the Levantine and Baltic trade and for exploration of a northern route to the Indies in the mid-sixteenth century. These associations permitted a pooling of risks and such protection as state patronage provided. The merchants were driven by private motives of accumulation; the participation of the crown as sovereign sponsor in part gave satisfaction to a socially important class, but it also responded to reason of state: the prospect that this enterprise, privately financed, would yield through customs and other rents significant public revenue independent of parliamentary assent.

The 1599 petition of the merchant collective asked that "Royal assent and licence to be granted unto them, that they, of their own Adventures, costs and charges, as well for the honour of this our realm of England as for the increase of our navigation and advancement of trade of merchandise . . . might adventure and set forth one or more voyage . . . to the East Indies." In granting the charter the following year, the queen constituted the associated merchants as "a body Corporate and Politic in deed and in name."[38] In the first instance, the body politic referred solely to the federated merchants, but yet the model of the Estado de India was at hand. Some 250 years were to pass from the landing of the first fleet of East India Company vessels and the proclamation of Queen Victoria as empress of India in 1858. By imperceptible degrees, the trading association became the jewel in the imperial crown.

In its early days the East India Company was a feeble entrant to the south Asian stage. Its first delegate to the Mogul court cut a sorry figure in comparison with the ostentation and wealth of Emperor Akbar, who regarded England as a remote and impoverished land of shepherds and fishermen.[39] Permission to establish the first trading post at Surat cast the company in the role of tributary supplicant to the Mogul state.

Built into this mercantile venture, however, was a hidden logic of expansion and territorialization. Trade profitability required permanent warehouses, or "factories"; a vessel entering port in transit lacked leverage on price bargaining, because its stay was necessarily limited, and it could not afford to return empty. Although the Portuguese had established many of their sixteenth-century entrepôt strongholds by force, the East India Company was not initially in a position to do so; permission for a factory was at first negotiated. Once established, and stocked with trade goods, protection was required—the rudiments of what grew into an army. Around the warehouse grew up a permanent community, whose daily needs had to be provided, and whose conflicts be resolved—an embryonic apparatus of public order. By osmosis, the factory tended to acquire a security perimeter of surrounding territory, drawn under its jurisdiction. The merchant directors of this venture were of no mind to dilute company profitability by meeting from its commercial revenues the growing costs of its quasi-state operations; factory managers became fiscal hunters.

By 1647 the East India Company had twenty-three factories and ninety employees. In 1685 a company agent openly articulated a sovereignty claim for the first time, with respect to the six-mile-long and one-mile-deep Madras strip. Governor Sir Josiah Child ordered company agents staffing this post to reject the suzerainty claims of the local ruler, adding that "if nevertheless he pretend to any dominion over your city, you may, when you are in good condition, tell him in plain terms that we own him for our good friend, all and confederate, and sovereign and lord paramount of all that country, excepting the small territory belonging to Madras of which we claim the sovereignty and will maintain and defend against all persons and govern by our own laws, without any appeal to any prince or potentate whatsoever, except our Sovereign Lord the King."[40]

As the company became a territorial sovereign, it also became a military power. When Charles II was presented with Bombay as a marriage dowry for his Portuguese bride, Queen Henrietta, he sent four companies of British troops. When he gave Bombay to the company in 1668, the British contingent became company soldiers. By the middle of the eighteenth century, large numbers of Indian auxiliaries (*sepoys*) were being added to the small British core. In 1746 the French demonstrated that a small European-officered Indian force, applying European military doctrine, could defeat Indian armies many times larger. The explosive phase of the company's transformation from mercantile agency to territorial sovereign followed almost at once, elbowing aside the French competition and successively reconfiguring Indian states as company clients.[41]

By stealth, a mercantile company by the logic of its own reproduction had indeed become a body politic, whose public character compelled recognition. Britain, as Low suggests, discovered it had in commercial disguise an Indian empire, and was forced to decide what to do with it.[42] The formal assertion of British state control came through the three great parliamentary acts of 1773, 1784, and 1793, which invested the company with the personality of a state. Administration of hegemony, management of the land revenue, and imposition of a legal order became its missions; company agents became quasi-public servants rather than mere commercial representatives. As Edmund Burke noted with respect to the 1793 India Act, the political edifice in India "did not seem to be merely a Company formed for the extension of British commerce but in reality a delegation of the whole power and sovereignty of this Kingdom sent into the East."[43]

The pathway to colonial state formation in India, and its long disguise in the clothing of a mercantile corporation, had important implications. The matter of the status with respect to the crown of the swelling numbers of Indians within the ambit of company control never arose until the nineteenth century; a company has clients, not subjects or citizens. Empirical modes of domination evolved that later deeply marked colonial state construction in Africa. In India, however, they emerged only gradually and were not filtered through a prism of conscious state-building theory. A minimalist overlayer of actual British rule—the thousand or so British agents of the Indian Civil Service at the center—might be seen as incorporating the bottom-line mentality of the commercial firm: a sufficient quotient of hegemony to nurture a positive balance, rather than hegemony as an intrinsic good in the pure logic of the state.

A final model of early colonial state formation is found in the English North American and Caribbean settlements. In this instance a civil society was implanted, which came to play a crucial part in state formation. Early in their development a bifurcation occurred. In the Caribbean the emergence of the sugar-plantation economy, bringing in its wake large majorities of African slaves, instilled the haunting fear of servile insurrection in the settler community, and thus the need for the security guarantee from the colonizer.[44] In North America, colonial civil society was able to construct an institutional armature entrenching its autonomy, which the British state was subsequently unable to dismantle.

The planting of the "western plantations," advocated by late Elizabethans, occurred in a context quite different from the Indies. English involvement began with plunder and piracy, under royal license; John Hawkins and Francis Drake were decorated for their exploits (only in the eighteenth century were pirates hanged rather than knighted). Bases for preying upon Spanish trade were valuable; Spanish strength came from its New World domains. The lure of possibly matching Spanish discoveries of precious metals, the developing mercantilist notions that wealth and hence state power were rooted in control of trade, and the attraction of such strategic resources as naval stores and dried fish predisposed the state to view favorably initiatives for settlement. Also, the idea emerged that welling up on the margins of civil society were inconvenient population groups who might be more useful servants of the crown at some distance. In the words of the tireless pamphleteer Hakluyt on behalf of a "western planting," these surplus souls were "many thousands of idle persons within this realme, which, havinge no way to be sett on work, be either mutinous and seeke and often fall to pilferings and thevings and other lewdness, whereby all the prisons of the lande are daily pestred and stuffed full of them."[45] Among these were the crystallizing religious refractories whose Puritan doctrines were straining the limits of Anglican convention. Thus, there were many reasons for establishment of North American and Caribbean settlements; however, the crown lacked the will and resources to carry these out on its own, or to direct the process.

The formula employed drew from the same model of the chartered corporation that inspired the East India Company, but with the crucial difference that the delegated quasi-sovereign rights and privileges in practice devolved upon the settlers. The fifty-six London merchant firms and 659 individuals who were awarded the Virginia Company franchise in 1606 extracted crucial legislative and judicial powers in their character, which provided that they "shall and may have full Power and Authority to ordain and make such Laws and Ordinances, for the Good and Welfare of the said Plantation, as to them from Time to Time, shall be thought requisite and meet."[46] Further, the settler community was constituted as a civil society by charter: "All and every the Persons, being our Subjects, which shall dwell and inhabit within every and any of the said several Colonies and Plantations, and every of their children . . . shall have and enjoy all Liberties, Franchises and Immunities within any of our Dominions . . . as if they had been abiding and born within this our Realm of England."[47]

Although the original charter was revoked in 1624 and Virginia became a royal colony in 1641, the quasi-sovereign powers had in good part slipped into the hands of local assemblies that had sprung up. The "rights of Englishmen" came to be perceived as the entitlement to have all laws voted by their assemblies, which were the overseas analogy to Parliament. A concomitant logic led to the eighteenth-century conviction that Parliament had no right to enact fiscal or other legislation applicable to the domestic affairs of the colonies.[48] The royal governors had little means of imposing their will as crown delegates, neither a territorial administration, nor a judiciary under their control, nor a security apparatus other than the local militia. The hollowness of their power finds eloquent iconographic expression in the symbolic claim to coercive force in the vestibule to the Williamsburg governor's palace: a circle of muskets in the ceiling display, which stood in lieu of any real intimidating capacity of the colonial state.

The Massachusetts Bay Colony charter, granted to those bent on constructing a novel "shining city upon the hill" beyond the reach of state-supported religious orthodoxy, gave rise to an even more extended pattern of settler autonomy, rendered the more troublesome when its promoters profited from a flaw in the drafting of the charter to remove it and the governing body it prescribed beyond seas in 1629. Fragments that fell from the Massachusetts venture—Connecticut and Rhode Island—were even more radical in their autonomy, lacking provision for a royal governor. Above all, the moral threads of innate loyalty to the crown of England sustained the connection; until the 1760s this fabric remained sufficiently sturdy to prevent the autonomous dispositions rooted in colonial civil society from even contemplating the step beyond.

The nature of relationships with native American populations likewise shaped the contours of institutional linkages with the crown. In these formative stages, nothing drove the settlements toward a policy of conquest. There were no compact, politically organized Indian polities that could be overcome only by conquest. Areas for settlement could be acquired by a combination of negotiation and alliance with some Indian communities against their rivals and competitors.[49] Although frictions and skirmishes were frequent enough, in the early stages they did not pose a security issue beyond the capacity of local militia. The Iroquois confederacy, for example, perhaps the strongest native American military force in the seventeenth century, could muster only limited numbers: by the estimate of a Jesuit father in 1660, barely about two thousand men. In those northern colonies where the fur trade became an economic lynchpin, political domination was not necessary to profitable commerce—indeed, it was inimical to it.[50] Some evangelical impulses may be identified, but spiritual conquest was not at the core of colonial teleology.

Further, Indian labor was not indispensable to the colonial political economy, as in Spanish America and early Brazil. Desultory ventures to capture Indian workers did occur in the southern sphere when tobacco emerged in the late 1620s as a profitable but labor-consuming crop. The initial assumption in Virginia was that Indians would be freely incorporated with English indentured servants as a labor force on tobacco farms, bringing native Americans to "humane civilitie and to a setled and quiet government."[51] With the easy option of evasion and retreat, involuntary Indian plantation labor was soon shown to be beyond reach. In its place an indentured white work force alone cultivated the tobacco plantations, progressively and swiftly replaced by African slaves in the labor-intensive agrarian zones from the Chesapeake southward. For all these reasons, the native American remained not just an alien other but a human category entirely external to colonial state formation in the English colonies. Racism first germinated in the settler mind as intense anti-Indian sentiment, an exclusionary view quickly extended to Africans as they became numerous by the late seventeenth century.[52]

The energies of religious construction were directed inward, among the settlers themselves. Even where the Church of England was established, as in Virginia, it was wholly unable to play the implicit secular role as a parallel hierarchy of social control matching that in the metropole; in 1662 there were a mere ten Anglican clergy serving forty-five parishes.[53] In the words of an influential study of the Church in America,

> Far removed from the status-giving context of an ordered church life and dependent upon what support they could enlist among the laity both for the formation and the maintenance of the congregations they served, the only real authority the clergy possessed was the authority they could command by their powers of persuasion and the force of their example. Given these circumstances, it is scarcely surprising that the laity soon began to exercise a decisive voice in church affairs . . . lay vestries gained effective control by neglecting to present the clergy to the governor for permanent induction into office, thus retaining, as the Archbishop of Canterbury complained, the right to hire and fire them like "domestic servants."[54]

A final factor permitting the constitution of entrenched autonomous institutions in the American colonies was the growing political distraction in England. The first colonies were barely planted when the clouds of impending civil war began to darken the horizons. Indeed, colonial unrest in Ireland, and the felt need to raise supply funding for military repression, contributed to the summoning of the Long Parliament in 1641, which ultimately cost Charles I his crown and his head. New crises in the relations between crown and Parliament occurred during the Popish Plots from 1678 to 1682 and the short, contested reign (1685–1688) of the Catholic successor, James II. By the time a reconstructed British state was in a position to reconceive its apparatus of colonial control, the institutionalization of autonomy had proceeded too far to be systematically undone.

Hegemonical compulsions did emerge, however, with the Stuart Restoration in 1660. The first three Navigation Acts of 1660, 1663, and 1673 reflected a British determination to enforce control over colonial trade and its export staples, and to compel its flow through taxable channels. By the 1660s, the crown had a major stake in tobacco revenues, which constituted 25 percent of customs revenues and 5 percent of all state income.[55] Customs officials were posted in colonial ports from the 1670s on, less for collection than for surveillance, porous by its frequent venality. In 1676 a detachment of 1,100 British troops was used for the first time to repress a frontier uprising. Charles II undertook to circumscribe colonial assembly prerogatives in charter colonies and replace them with royal colonies where possible. In 1696 the Board of Trade was created as a specialized agency concerned with "colonial policy."

None of these measures, however, could alter the fundamental weakness of the infrastructure of metropolitan hegemony. When, in the wake of the successful but very costly Seven Years War (which incurred a war debt of 130 million pounds), Britain sought to establish permanent garrisons in the thirteen colonies, to impose direct taxation to pay for colonial defense, to reinforce the authority of royal governors and extend the jurisdiction of royal judges, and to assert a more comprehensive formal hegemony through the doctrine of parliamentary supremacy,[56] it faced a set of autonomous institutions, spearheaded by the colonial assemblies, that in the words of one insightful analyst "could levy taxes, raise armies, and issue currency. It was an established institution that held together the dominant interests of colonial society. The revolution in English America sustained and defended a basic, operating, legitimate institutional framework."[57]

The loss of the thirteen colonies was a searing lesson for Britain as a colonizing state. Thenceforward its colonial infrastructures—beginning in Canada—were much more attentively designed, and although the political formulas were diverse the structural requirements of hegemony were not in the future neglected by inadvertence. Subsequent colonial states in the British orbit were never again such sparse, ramshackle, largely stateless political creations.[58]

The English colonies in the Antilles began with an identical pattern but soon diverged. The first three—Barbados, Bermuda, and the Bahamas—followed the charter-company model, with the Barbadan planters quickly acquiring an ascendancy analogous to their counterparts on the North American mainland. In 1651 settler defiance provoked the dispatch of a military expedition by London. In 1664 the charter was revoked, and by 1700 British crown domination was secure. Decisive in this process was the shift from the initial smallholder to a sugar economy, from 1640 on, with a large African slave majority; by 1643 there were already 6,400 slaves, and by 1683 the few thousand settlers were submerged by the forty-seven thousand slaves. British ships and soldiers were crucial to their security, and a colonial state totally different from the North American model had taken form.[59] It was in the West Indies that the crown-colony juridical vessel for colonial rule was devised and developed.

Buccaneering remained an important supplementary activity through the seventeenth century. Indeed, Bermuda and especially the Bahamas, unsuitable for sugar, subsisted essentially through preying on the sealanes in one way or another. The addition of Jamaica to the British colonial sphere in 1655, by a Cromwellian plundering expedition, added the first island of substantial size to the Antilles holdings. Jamaica had been lightly held by a Spanish colonial population of only fifteen hundred. The dimensions of the island, the ample space it provided for pirate lairs, and the mountainous interior that sheltered growing Maroon communities of Africans escaped from slavery beckoned the erection of a more sturdy apparatus of colonial control. So also, by late in the seventeenth century, did the growing royal revenues from the 4.5 percent sugar levy, which by the middle quarter of the eighteenth century yielded four million pounds of West Indian revenue, four times as much as the primary domestic direct tax, the land impost.[60]

Before turning to a summation of the ideologies of empire that informed the scramble for Africa, a final observation on the pre-nineteenth-century imperial epoch is pertinent. The second half of the eighteenth century was marked by intense rivalry among the early colonizers, epitomized by the Seven Years War in mid-century. This global conflict, which raged from the Indies to the Americas, reflected a mercantilist conviction that national strength and wealth were tied to empire. Also, the second half of the eighteenth century was a period of intensive colonial state-building: the Pombal reforms in Brazil,[61] the introduction of a new hierarchy of royal officials, the intendants, in Spanish America,[62] the British efforts to strengthen colonial controls in North America and to transform the East India Company into full territorial rule under direct colonial control. Paradoxically, this more systematic and self-conscious reflection upon rationalized and securitized structures of colonial hegemony triggered the successful revolt of the thirteen colonies, as well as Spanish loss of most of its American holdings in the disorder of the Napoleonic Wars. Haiti, the most profitable Western Hemisphere colony in the late eighteenth century, demonstrated that, in favorable circumstances, successful servile insurrection was possible. These painful experiences strongly influenced subsequent imperial policy premises.[63]

LEGACIES OF THE EARLY IMPERIAL AGE

By the time the European powers lunged inward from their African coastal enclaves in the latter nineteenth century, doctrines of domination had matured over five centuries. Although some of those scrambling for a share in the partition—Belgium, Germany, Italy—had only been spectators to the game of overseas domination in the past, there was an accumulated set of concepts of subjugation and exemplary lessons in "colonial science" on which to draw. In the long imperial pause in the first part of the nineteenth century, major changes occurred in the nature of the European states; when the impulses of expansion were born again in the final quarter of the century, the armature of domination was of a different order.

Now embedded in the historical consciousness of the European state system was the idea of empire. Overseas holdings were a natural accoutrement of a strong state. They were proprietary domains of a national state, no longer simply crown appendages. The sovereign was the state, not just the monarchy. The medieval patterns of thought, still vibrant at the moment of first colonial conquest in the fifteenth century, had long since been effaced by modern ideologies of the state.

There was, in the wake of the Napoleonic Wars, a period of relative remission in European dispositions toward colonial expansion (although imperial occupation and conquest spread in Australasia, Oceania, the East Indies, and India). Except for the Antilles and Canada, the Americas were beyond serious reach of reconquest (although not of American imperial ambitions). The regions of Asia outside the imperial sphere were too strong to subdue (China and Japan) or too remote. And the African interior was protected by the limitations of European military and medical technologies. Also important was the displacement of mercantilism by free trade in the state doctrines of the naval hegemon during this passive interlude in the imperial age.

In the reason of states, as instructed by the pedagogy of the earlier period, overseas dominions held the possibility, although not the certainty, of significant returns—and not simply the psychic income supplied by contemplation of pink-shaded areas on the world map. At certain places and times, colonial holdings had generated major revenues for the colonizing power: the Antilles in the seventeenth and eighteenth centuries; Meso-America and the Andes, especially in the sixteenth and eighteenth centuries; the Portuguese Estado de India in the sixteenth century; Brazil in the eighteenth; and the Dutch East Indies in the nineteenth. These state returns were volatile and uncertain; they required production of precious minerals subject to royal monopolies or rent extraction, or high-value export commodities whose trade could be taxed. There was certain to be a recurrent struggle for appropriation of these rents with the mercantile private sector and emergent civil societies in the colonial holdings. But the lure of potential state gains was a permanent given, to be set against the costs and risks of colonial conquest.

These risks were essentially military. There were the costs of protecting the overseas domains, and the trade that held the potential of state and private profit, from rival predators. In addition, the subjugated populations and emergent civil societies had to be held in thrall. The former exigency required naval strength; the latter some form of colonial military instrument. In the best of circumstances—as in British India—perfection of a locally recruited and financed armed instrument might make colonial domestic security possible at negligible charge to the metropole. However, where self-conscious civil societies emerged, as in the Americas, colonial militias carried their own risks of uncertain control. Everywhere garrisoning large metropolitan military detachments was expensive, and difficult to charge to the colonial budgets. And naval forces were inevitably a metropolitan charge.

But civil expenditures falling on the imperial treasury were minimal in these early centuries of the colonial period. The earliest agents of conquest—the conquistador generation—were rewarded with the expectation of a share in the initial booty and land grants or tribute rights. In the venal hours of the baroque age, colonial offices were often sold rather than compensated by the crown—a fiscal art developed in its most elaborate form in eighteenth-century Spain. Delegation of sovereignty to private mercantile corporations—the British and Dutch East India companies—was another device. Until the final moments of the colonial era, metropolitan treasuries almost never permitted significant outlays from domestic resources for colonial civil administration. Even more alien was the notion of capital expenditure in colonial domains by the home treasury—indeed, "development" had not yet entered the teleology of the state.

The didactics of the colonial past carried another instructive lesson: colonies could be lost as well as gained. At first the only danger appeared to come from other aspirant colonizers; Spain, in the end, was able to consolidate its rule over only a fraction of its 1493 Alexandrine donation, while France lost most of its Canadian and Indian domains to Britain in the mid-eighteenth century. The wave of Western Hemisphere insurrection a few decades later showed that colonial civil societies or even slave colonies could shake off imperial links. Closer to home, the repeated episodes of Irish rebellion demonstrated that colonial control could not be safely entrusted to transplanted social hierarchies; a firm infrastructure of alien state control was indispensable to the reproduction of imperial domination. Even Adam Smith, the scourge of mercantilist theories, argued a security-driven reason of state dictating careful attentiveness to a well-designed overlayer of control:

> To propose that Great Britain should voluntarily give up all authority over her colonies, and leave them to elect their own magistrates, to enact their own laws, and to make peace and war as they might think proper, would be to propose such a measure as never was, and

never will be adopted, by any nation in the world. No nation ever voluntarily gave up the dominion of any province, how troublesome soever the revenue which it afforded might be in proportion to the expense which it occasioned. . . . Such sacrifices, though they might frequently be agreeable to the interests, are always mortifying to the pride of every nation, and what is perhaps of still greater consequence, they are always contrary to the private interest of the governing part of it, who would thereby be deprived of the disposal of many places of trust and profit, of many opportunities of acquiring wealth and distinction, which the possession of the most turbulent, and . . . the most unprofitable province seldom fails to afford.[64]

In the calculus of state power, empire was, in a diffuse way, a positive element in the equation. Not, of course, at any cost: barren tracts devoid of revenue potential requiring expensive garrisons and provisioning held no attraction. Domains whose returns were subject to diversion by free-riding rivals could also be a liability; as a 1698 tract, "Discourses on the Publick Revenues and the Trade of England," put the matter, "If a Breach in the Navigation-Act be conniv'd at, even our own Plantations may become more profitable to our Neighbours, than to us. . . . Colonies are a Strength to their Mother Kingdom, while they are under good Discipline, while they are strictly made to observe the Fundamental Laws of their Original Country, and while they are kept dependent on it."[65] But empire was believed to contribute to the wealth, and hence power, of nations. Its loss was seen as explanatory to the decline and enfeebled condition of such formerly lustrous imperial states as Spain and Portugal, and—on the other side—to the hegemonical standing in international politics and prosperity of Britain. To these components of state reason were added on the eve of African partition new metaphors of imperial expansion as expressive of state virility, as Darwinian theories of biological evolution found easy transfer into the political as well as the social sphere.

NEW ASPECTS OF EUROPEAN STATE POWER

The European state about to explode into the African interior in the late nineteenth century was far removed from the polity that began the imperial age five centuries before. The professionalization and specialization of its formal apparatus was far advanced. Uniformed forces included not just armies and navies but also gendarmes and police. Even as ideologically portrayed in Anglo-American liberal thought as the "night watchman," the nineteenth-century state had a scope of action and capacity of control—modes of rule seemingly natural and intrinsic to stateness—which vastly exceeded that of its early imperial ancestor. Instilled within its structures and agents of rule were conscious notions of the legal-rational order that Weberian reflection identified as the essence of the state, and purposive expansion of the "capabilities" for regulation, extraction, integration, and penetration of civil society that a later generation of structural-functional theorists were to discern as the core of state development.[66]

Further, the late colonizing state was conjoined in a constitutional pact with its civil society absent in the earlier phases. This had several implications for the final African colonial wave. With the metropolitan population now enjoying an array of participative entitlements and constitutional protections as "citizen," there was a dramatic sharpness in the status differential between colonial subject and colonizing civil society that had not existed at the time of the sixteenth-century Spanish debates over whether Indians were in a full sense human beings and thus subjects of the crown. Also, the legitimation imperative of the colonizer now included a requirement of justification of colonial conquest to a much larger audience than simply the merchant interests, clerics, and restless aristocrats who had been interested partners in an earlier age.

The jurisprudence of the state was likewise far more elaborate. Austinian doctrines of sovereignty put a new gloss on this potent doctrine, even if it were implicitly shared with civil society. The legal consequences of the supremacy of the state—transferable to the African domains without their metropolitan restrictions—were elaborated into what became formidable juridical conceptualization of the prerogatives of domination.

The state was now invested with the moral personality of nationhood. At the crucial moments of the scramble, when an infernal dialectic of European state rivalries contributed powerfully to driving forward the forces of partition, the passions of the national idea engaged important segments of civil society as a popular base for colonial aggression. The capacity of the national idea to invest with high moral purpose essentially sordid acts of filibustering adventure played its part in propelling the diverse agents of conquest. It provided the next generation of colonial agents with an effortless rationalization of the premise that alien domination of Africa was an end in itself.

Finally, the nascent professionalization of science in the nineteenth century stocked the imperial state with an inventory of technological capabilities that suddenly brought African conquest—physically impossible in earlier periods, even had it been desired—within the range of acceptable cost. In the military sphere, industrialized modes of warfare in Europe produced a decisive alteration in what Soviet theorists once delicately labeled "the correlation of forces."[67] The musket—with an effective range of less than a hundred yards, 30 percent failure to fire even in dry weather, a reloading time of one minute—was supplanted in European armament by breech-loading rifles and Gatling, then Maxim machine-guns. Although musketry was widely available to African armies, especially in West Africa where such weaponry had long been a commodity exchanged for slaves, the vastly enhanced firepower of the machine-gun was a European monopoly; unlike the musket, it could not be reproduced by African blacksmiths.

Steamboat technology—when coupled with iron construction, shallow-draft applications, and screw propellers—made African inland rivers arteries of conquest once it was perfected by the 1860s. The construction of the Indian railway network, which began in 1852, demonstrated how new transportation modes might not only create a security infrastructure but also fundamentally alter the cost structure of capitalist ventures far removed from the coast. Telegraphic communication—whose land applications were known by the 1820s—became an invaluable adjunct of imperial communications when sea cables were operational by the 1840s; West African cable connections were in place by 1885 as the hour of partition struck. Finally, startling advances in medical knowledge utterly transformed the terrifying mortality ratios for Europeans in Africa—which in the tropical regions in and of themselves were an absolute barrier to the institutionalization of conquest. Above all, the identification of the malaria vector in 1897, and the prior discovery of quinine as a suppressant, demolished the formidable malarial barrier to colonial subjugation of Africa.[68]

For all these reasons, the colonial encounter in Africa was to take on a distinctive cast. The idea of imperialism was already old, and empire in Africa built initially upon older notions of domination. But its historical conjuncture was very different. African societies were to encounter a colonial master equipped with doctrines of domination and capacities for the exercise of rule that went far beyond those available in earlier times and other places. African, for the colonial state, was in a far more systematic sense a subjugated other. More systematic theories of European racial superiority, laced with Darwinian ideas about evolutionary hierarchies of human societies, extended earlier views of African as a socially nonexistent other that were a doctrinal correlate of plantation slavery in the Americas. At the same time, the idea of progress, now at its zenith, and notions of African society as malleable clay in the hands of the colonizer, available for reshaping into new economic functions and social contours, suffused the colonial system. But mind the pennies: penurious treasury officials mounted guard at the portals of their counting rooms, to ensure that whatever African domains were added to the colonial estates were fiscally self-sufficient.

There now existed relatively well elaborated notions of how a colonial state should be organized, distilled from four centuries of imperial history. Newcomers to colonial empire, such as Belgium, Germany, and Italy, had clear models of rule on which to draw. Thus, the wide variety of colonial forms noted earlier in this chapter was reduced to a single basic form of overseas territorial domination, though with modest variations (to be explored in the next three chapters). A basic territorial grid of regional administration, staffed by Europeans, was indispensable. This required a coercive underpinning from a military force directly controlled by the colonial state; however, only a small cadre of European officers was needed, to train, discipline, and command forces whose basic ranks were filled with locally recruited (or conscripted) soldiers. Effective occupation could only be mediated through an array of collaborating indigenous intermediaries. A well-stocked library of imperial science was available to the agents of colonial conquest in Africa.

An important new factor confronting African colonial state construction was the official abolition of slave and other unfree labor in the nineteenth century. Profitable management of the colonial estates was bound to require mobilization of large amounts of labor at low levels of remuneration. Forcible conscription at the onset of the African colonial era was certainly permissible. The diverse forms of unfree labor that were so central to earlier colonial state forms in various regions could no longer be openly utilized.

Thus, the African colonial state to which we now turn was a far more distinctive polity than its predecessors were. Its institutions of rule and its subjugated human communities were both carefully defined as external to the metropolitan realm. Africans about to enter the sphere of sovereignty of European states encountered a status of distancing as subjects—in civil standing and racial categorization—far removed from that of the crown subjects of earlier centuries. An apparatus of rule emerged that, once consolidated, acquired an important degree of autonomy from its metropolitan sovereign and a high order of autonomy from its subject society. In its application of the imperatives of rule, it was ineluctably led to a set of policies and a texture of relationship with subject society portending the difficulties of adaptation that beset the African state today.

—— Chapter Four ——

CONSTRUCTING BULA MATARI

Article 2.... all vacant land must be considered as belonging to the State.

—Ordinance of 1 July 1885 regarding occupation of land,
Congo Free State

I will not conceal from you the fact that, in completing your efficiency report, I will base myself above all on the results you will have achieved in the collection of the head tax, which must be for each of you a constant preoccupation.

—Circular from governor-general to commandants
de cercle, *Afrique Equatoriale Française (AEF),* 1903

Day by day, we understand better that the real treasure from which we must profit in the colonies is not the natural riches, nor the open spaces, but the native races . . . it is the population which gives the force and the wealth of a country; the capital which we must develop, is man.

—Ivory Coast administrator, 1908

. . . loot like blazes. I want any quantity of marble stairs, marble pavings, iron railings, looking glasses and fittings, . . . doors, windows, furniture of all sorts.

—Lord Kitchener, instructions to Major Wingate in Khartoum, 1899

IMAGES OF BULA MATARI

Lord Kitchener, fresh from the smashing triumph over the crumbling Mahdist state at Omdurman in 1898, had just won designation as governor-general and *sirdar* (commander-in-chief) for the newly constituted "Anglo-Egyptian Sudan." Commanding an essentially Egyptian army with some British contingents, Kitchener directed the final assault on the Mahdist capital, slaughtering eleven thousand of their troops while losing only twenty British and twenty Egyptian soldiers.[1] He was to preside over the creation of a bizarre colonial polity that by strange alchemy during the fourteen years of Mahdist rule became transformed from Egyptian province into de facto British possession, lightly concealed under the contemptuously flouted provisions of a "condominium" jointly ruled by Britain and Egypt. In one of those deft acts of juridical legerdemain that fill the chronicles of colonial partition, Britain managed to invoke the participation of British troops as a lever inverting Egyptian claims of prior occupation into "the liability to provide the military and financial resources which enabled the British to rule the Sudan."[2]

77

Kitchener was determined to inscribe the signature of power on his rebuilt capital without delay by constructing a governor's palace projecting the force and majesty of the colonial state whose blueprint he was sketching.[3] His instructions differ from many other administrative circulars in this first phase of building a colonial state only in their brutal candor; state agents everywhere were driven by the logic of constructing institutions of domination with improvised resources. Kitchener's essentially limited and banal act of predation metaphorically expresses the broader drama of the colonial state in its initial period: simultaneously to create agencies of rule and to invent extractive devices imposing on the subordinated societies the cost of the unsolicited governance proposed for them.

Other images of Bula Matari emerge in the epigraphs to this chapter. On the very day of its proclamation, the proprietary imperial domain of King Leopold II of Belgium articulated through its first ordinance the scope of its theory of sovereignty. "Vacant land" was defined as all terrain not under African cultivation—that is, most of the land surface. At first, virtually the sole products of export value—wild rubber and ivory—were located on state land, and were therefore by preemption state goods. As Jean Stengers remarks, "As a consequence of this system, a trader might not buy ivory or wild rubber from the Africans without becoming a receiver of stolen goods—stolen, in effect, from the state."[4] Through the fiscal powers of the state, African labor was expropriated to collect and deliver these products to Congo Free State agents or the concessionary companies that exercised delegated sovereignty in its name. The naked pretensions of this Leopoldian imperium went farther and faster than most; yet the example reveals the formidable weapon contemporary doctrines of sovereignty supplied to a statelike entity neither limited in its claims by a civil society nor restrained in this instance by an ethos of civility, a superego operating on the official mind of the colonizing state.

The capacity of the embryonic colonial state fully to apply its doctrines of domination of course fell short of its ambitions for some time. Yet the special circumstances surrounding African partition made urgent the consolidation of a basic hegemony. The rapid creation of a fiscal base was crucial to the very survival of the nascent structure; administration in the first years essentially came down to tax collection. Governors flogged the territorial administrators in ways illustrated by the AEF memorandum; they in turn exerted relentless pressure on the African intermediaries held responsible for the actual collection.

The naive illusions of many partisans of colonial partition, sustained by the mendacious propaganda of the more swashbuckling agents of the scramble touting natural riches gasping for development in the African hinterland, were soon shattered. In most areas, existing production systems and immediately exploitable resources imposed severe limits on the management of accumulation. The control of African labor, channeling it into basic infrastructure and taxable activity, became the very core of colonial state construction, the hinge on which its logic turned. This realization, not always expressed so explicitly as by the Ivory Coast administrator cited, permeated reason of state in the process of constructing Bula Matari.

The task of this chapter is to decode the logic of African colonial state construction in the period between the sudden acceleration of a dialectic of partition, about 1875, and the outbreak of World War I, by which time its basic structure was in place. The basic patterns of rule and axiomatic premises that guided the official mind took form during this crucial period. Africa was constituted as a single, interacting colonial field in this phase; it is no accident that, in response, the continent found simultaneous collective definition in the protest ideology of pan-Africanism. The first Pan-African Congress, organized by an emergent intelligentsia of the African diaspora, took place in 1900, coincident with the closure of the frontier of partition.[5]

Although there were broad common themes in the process of colonial state construction, there were also significant variations. The environment of conquest was not always the same; African societies differed in their scope of political organization and their interstate relations at the moment of intrusion. The swift implantation of European settler communities in the Mahgreb, in southern and parts of eastern Africa, engendered a dynamic different from that in areas where the colonial state faced only a subordinated African society. Meeting the revenue imperative was more excruciating in some areas than in others, although everywhere a determinant factor shaping the personality of the colonial state. Zones where Islam was well implanted were subjected to cultural policies and stratagems of colonial security different from those in regions where customary religions held sway. The colonizing states, despite sharing many fundamental attitudes toward their newfound vocation of African domination and the societies on which they imposed their rule, also had some differences in their own historically shaped personalities as polities. Most fundamental was the contrast between Britain and the Continental states, which were more centralizing and comprehensive in their innate dispositions. Their own stored historical memories as imperial rulers likewise had some impact; Belgium, Italy, and Germany embarked on African colonial rule as states without history, and the superficial Spanish colonial ventures were in almost complete rupture with the earlier phase of expansion in Latin America and the Philippines.

AFRICA ON THE EVE OF PARTITION

In 1875 there were a handful of European beachheads in continental Africa, which became launching platforms for the assault on Africa that impended but that few would then have forecast. Algeria had already been established in 1830 as the core of the second French empire, after the first—save a few scattered islands—had been lost by the time of Napoleon. By 1875 Algeria had more than three hundred thousand European settlers, only about half of them French. There were also some painful lessons; the initial conquest—once decided on in earnest in 1840—had required more than a hundred thousand French troops, as did repression of a major uprising in the early 1870s. During this period the French had absorbed more than 150,000 military casualties, inflicted an estimated three hundred thousand on their Algerian subjects, and—between 1830 and 1900—expended in excess of five billion francs on creating a colonial realm in Algeria.[6]

In West Africa, there were sundry coastal outposts, some of which had begun to push inland. The French toehold on Senegal, which dated from 1626, began serious expansion inland in 1854 when General Louis Faidherbe was appointed governor with a mandate for conquest. From its St. Louis and Gorée bases, a sphere of hinterland domination began to take form up the Senegal valley and inland from Dakar, which then went into hibernation from 1864 to 1877.[7] Small mercantile outposts also existed at coastal points in what became Guinea, the Ivory Coast, and Dahomey, and a naval base at Libreville from 1839.

On the British side, a settlement in Sierre Leone dated from 1788, as a refuge for freed Africans from London and Nova Scotia. After two decades of fruitless effort to vest the operation of this small enclave in a chartered company, with some modest crown subsidy (67,000 pounds total from 1792 to 1807), in 1807 it became a colony. In about 1860 creeping annexations began, driven primarily by the desire to tax the trade flowing through adjoining areas to evade Sierra Leone customs.[8] British coastal forts in the Gold Coast, some of which dated from the seventeenth century, by imperceptible degrees acquired some loose hinterland jurisdiction in Fante areas, motivated largely by the security preoccupations engendered by the series of nineteenth-century wars with the powerful Ashanti state; in 1874 the coastal strip was formally proclaimed a colony.[9] The British slaving toehold in the Gambia estuary had two centuries of history, and Lagos island was annexed in 1861. After the rise of abolitionism drove slave trading to cover by the end of the eighteenth century, trade volumes were small, and there were repeated proposals in London to abandon the West African settlements, especially in the 1820s and again in the 1860s. The biggest single stumbling block to such disengagement was the depth of the entanglement in Sierra Leone, a key base for the British antislavery naval patrols until the 1860s.

Remnants of the sixteenth-century Portuguese sea-borne empire subsisted in the Bissau area, Mozambique, and especially Angola. The sheer scale of the slave-trading economy in Angola, the direct participation in it of the agencies of civil government, interlaced with a more formalized ideology of empire, made coastal Angola the shell of a colonial state, momentarily erected into an assimilationist vision of greater Portugal during the liberal period in the 1820s and 1830s. A distinctive pattern emerged linking the Portuguese coastal enclaves with hinterland African states through a moving slave frontier manned by Afro-Portuguese traders with enduring ties to the slave-supplying states of the interior. Periodic use of the coastal settlements as a dumping ground for convicts crowding the metropolitan dungeons imprinted a special character on coastal Angola, while the peculiar Afro-Portuguese institution of the *prazo* (autonomous estate) in the Zambezi valley marked the more slender colonial foothold in Mozambique.[10]

Another form of colonial state, which was to cast a long shadow northward, had taken hold on the southern tip of the continent. Beginning as a supply station for the Dutch East India Company in 1652, the Cape was settled by a small number of company servants, augmented by 150 or so French Huguenots fleeing the 1685 Edict of Nantes. By 1691 this European settlement numbered about a thousand; by the time of British occupation in 1795 it totaled somewhat more than ten thousand, whence virtually all the contemporary Afrikaner population descends. British intervention, at first a temporary measure to safeguard the Indian searoutes, was made permanent in the 1815 settlement of the dislocations of the Napoleonic Wars. In several waves, an English settled population entered the demographic equation, and new patterns of colonial state formation appeared. These included a growing web of frontier conflict with African communities, fueled by the emergence of "commandos," autonomous military formations poorly controlled by the state, which spearheaded aggressive outward expansion by the Boer communities and provoked increasingly serious warfare with African societies threatened by their encroachments.

This dynamic interpenetrated with the zone of warfare created by the formation from the 1820s of the Zulu military states and the eddying conquest polities set in motion by the *mfecane,* the Zulu wars of expansion. The Cape-based colonial state responded with a classic specimen of what Joseph Schumpeter characterized so well as imperial atavism: "the objectless disposition on the part of a state to unlimited forcible expansion."[11] Coastal Natal was annexed in 1842; the need for frontier security embedded in the reason of the Cape colonial state brought a steady expansion in its orbit of asserted jurisdiction. At the same time, a settler-dominated civil society won recognition, first through elective municipal institutions, then in 1852 through a Cape constitution creating representative institutions whose franchise was not explicitly racial, but whose provisions ensured white electoral domination.

The endless frontier skirmishing over white land claims, Boer indignation over the 1834 abolition of slavery in territory under British jurisdiction and the great Boer trek beyond crown authority that followed, the battles between settlers and missionary interests over the status of Africans, or those of partly African ancestry, congealed the racialist modes of thought that were to become so central to the doctrines of the South African state. Moshoeshoe's embattled Sotho state, created in defensive reaction against the menace of the mfecane and the relentless encroachment of the Boer states, was annexed by Britain in 1868 as a protectorate, creating a new kind of client African state under the colonial umbrella. Finally, the discovery of diamonds in 1867 foreshadowed a wholly new political economy for southern Africa, driven by the lure of precious minerals.[12]

Overall, then, on the eve of colonial partition, with the important exceptions of Algeria and the Cape, colonial footholds in Africa were superficial and precarious. Doctrines championing the "imperialism of free trade" and low-cost informal empire through coastally based zones of mercantile influence were predominant. Many of the coastal outposts paid tribute to local African rulers, subsisting by their sufferance. Occasionally, the European traders pushed for some inland assertion of colonial influence; for example, the Bordeaux trading houses becoming dominant in St. Louis in the 1850s lobbied in Paris for the appointment of Faidherbe as governor with a view to conquering the Senegal valley, on the grounds that the tolls being levied by African states (especially the Trarza and Brakna Moor emirates) were excessive. Not long after, these same groups were pushing for a halt to up-river military action because the disorders it provoked were too disruptive of commerce.[13]

More generally, such expansion of jurisdictional claims inland as did occur employed the nebulous notion of the protectorate, which at the

onset of the colonizing onslaught comported only the ambition to regu-
late (and tax) trade and the Europeans engaged in it, and did not include
any intent of interior administration of the African populations affected.
As Hargreaves notes, "The early partition treaties were essentially al-
locations of fiscal resources," motivated by a desire to enhance revenues
to support the coastal installations. For the most part, private European
traders and the African rulers with whom they dealt viewed these encroachments as diverting trade proceeds that would otherwise remain in
their hands.[14]

FACTORS PROPELLING THE SCRAMBLE

From 1875 to 1900, in an extraordinary moment of imperial enthusiasm,
a veritable collective intoxication of colonial expansionism set in. The
motivating factors triggering this dialectic of African conquest are not
the primary focus of my analysis, except insofar as they entered the
teleology of colonial state construction. But a few observations concerning the catalytic elements in this far-reaching reordering of political
space may help supply a context for my subsequent analysis of colonial
state construction. Single-factor explanations have fared poorly; the classic theses concerning imperialism by Hobson and Lenin, and those derivative from them, stressing capital-export exigencies or monopoly finance
capitalism, do not withstand close inspection.[15] A complex web of political, economic, and ideological factors spun in unfolding interaction with
the dynamic of events drove the partition forward.

The international system of states—the balance of power mechanism
erected by the European concert of states at Vienna, loosely managed by
Britain as relative hegemon—altered in ways that diminished its stability with the entry of unified Germany and Italy onto the world scene.
The security calculus of states became more complex, and their rivalries
more intense. Particularly when Germany and Italy entered the African
scene, from 1883 on, competition for African territorial aggrandizement
acquired a wholly new sharpness. Until this point, contests in Africa,
when they arose, essentially concerned Britain and France and could be
resolved by bilateral diplomacy. Once rivalry became many-sided, agree-
ments constraining it became much more difficult to achieve.

Germany and Italy were not the only new players. The unquenchable
colonial ambitions of King Leopold II of Belgium, despite the fact that his
adroit maneuvering for a share in the African partition took place without the support of his kingdom, contributed importantly to the chain
reaction. Leopold had long been persuaded that only a colonial hinter-

land could raise Belgium from the ranks of small and inconsequential polities governed by a provincial mercantile ethos into the more cosmopolitan ranks of significant world actors. He was also obsessed with the notion that colonies were storehouses of wealth awaiting the possessor, an obsession illustrated in a revealing letter he wrote in 1859, before ascending the throne, concerning Japan, one of many lands on which he cast a covetous eye: "In Japan there are incredible riches. The treasure of the Emperor is immense and *poorly guarded* [Leopold's stress]."[16] Leopold was an avid student of the 1861 text on colonial extraction by the appropriately surnamed English observer J. W. Money, *Java, or How to Manage a Colony,* documenting the substantial revenues the Netherlands derived from the East Indies during the "cultures policy" period in the middle of the nineteenth century. By 1876 the crafty monarch was at work, under the cover of a geographical association, acquiring signatures of African rulers in the Congo basin to treaties purportedly alienating their sovereignty to this Leopoldian innovation, a quasi-state as personal property of the king.

The Portuguese were driven into renewed activity by the specter of stronger powers starting to swell with new African possessions. The cherished memories of past grandeur embalmed in the residual overseas domains were in danger of disappearance unless Portugal somehow mustered the energies to participate in the scramble. Thus, a hexagonal pattern of chained interactions came into play.

As the European state system became less secure and stable, statesmen began to conflate colonial possessions with the equations of state power. After all, even during the imperial pause of the nineteenth century the prime hegemon, Britain, by one estimate, continued to expand its zone of imperial jurisdiction by a hundred thousand square miles per year during the 1815–1865 period.[17] As the industrial revolution became recognized, notions of strategic materials, such as vegetable oils for machinery lubricants, took form. Theories like those of Admiral Mahan on the pivotal role of sea power in national "strength" also nudged statecraft in the direction of global aggrandizement.

Economic factors played their part as well. Free-trade formulas in Africa increasingly eroded as expanding spheres of jurisdiction were used to disadvantage or even exclude merchants of other nationalities. Dispatches from French imperial missions penetrating inland in the 1870s and 1880s bristle with warnings about rival British commercial networks diverting trade to their enclaves; unnecessary to express is the strategic damage to French interests.[18] The emergence of a mass soap market raised the value of West African palm and peanut oil.[19] The Civil

War interruption of American cotton exports to British and other textile factories suggested the strategic value of an imperial source. The pressures in support of colonial expansion did not emanate from the most powerful segments of metropolitan capital, who were for some time skeptical about potential economic returns in Africa, and whose overseas energies were engaged in much more attractive ventures in North and South America, Russia, and to some extent India. But the trading houses established in the African coastal enclaves were the noisiest voice on the spot and had some channels of influence in the metropole—which were particularly effective in the absence of strong opposition from other capital groups (for example, the Bremen and Hamburg trading houses that agitated successfully for aggressive colonial expansion by Germany).

The emissaries of conquest were prodigal in their visions of the potential wealth of the territories they surveyed. In the report of Captain Joseph Gallieni, the humble savanna plain in the Niger valley was a treasure store awaiting Bula Matari to unlock it: "The terrain appears to be of uncommon fertility, and one is no longer astonished, in viewing it, at the renown the Niger valley enjoys among the natives for its riches. What a magnificent agricultural and commercial domain for a European nation which establishes its rule along this beautiful watercourse, and which brings into production not only this fruitful new land but also the immense metallurgical riches."[20]

Here and there Christian mission initiatives brought added momentum to the expansionary tide. The vast resurgence of evangelical fervor that gathered force in the West from the end of the eighteenth century came to focus on Africa as the largest field of unharvested souls, many of whom lay in the path of an expanding Islamic world. Although the mission movement inland preceded the flag in a number of areas in both east and west Africa, the security of their ventures was quickly found precarious. Thus, in Buganda, Malawi, western Nigeria, and even in the Congo basin missions at first clamored for extension of colonial jurisdiction and the protective cover it provided. Their interests were by no means identical with those of the colonial state, and particularly in the Congo Free State case the Protestant missions were the primary source of the revelations concerning the atrocities of the state-building phase.[21]

In indirect but important ways, the changing nature of state–civil society relations in Europe contributed to the expansionary impulses. The new class forces spawned by the industrial revolution sent regular tremors through the state apparatus and dominant social groups. Proletarian unrest, and the revolutionary ideologies through which it was articulated, little by little forced open the voting rolls. Radical and socialist parties emerged in turn, to capture the energies of these new constituencies. Public opinion, flowing into the openings of more democratic politics, became a more consequential factor in statecraft. Apprehensions of unmanageable social unrest suffused the environment of state behavior, particularly at moments of economic distress, such as the severe depression of the mid-1870s. The memories of 1848 and 1870 were still fresh. The coincidence of the final paroxysm of partition in Africa during the 1890s and the peaking of a wave of anarcho-terrorism in Europe merits notice.

The incorporation of these new social forces in the constitutional polities of Europe occurred largely through two processes: participative co-optation through democracy, and ideological capture by the deepening of nationalism. The former produced parliamentary formations that were frequently critical of the behavior of colonial states in formation but quickly came to accept their existence. The latter force became, by the 1890s, a formidable propellant to colonial aggrandizement. At a minimum, prudence and skepticism were for a time overwhelmed by the interactive chemistry of nationalist passions. Rather than a constraint on state risky aggrandizement in distant arenas, civil society often became during the scramble a force pushing toward adventure.[22]

A subsidiary theme was the perspective that new territories might serve as a vent for surplus populations or socially undesirable categories. This mirrored an earlier colonial idea that distant domains could transform the liability of convict populations into the asset of empire-building settlers, which had earlier operated in Australia, New Caledonia, Guyana, and Georgia. Only the Portuguese ever used Africa as a penal settlement. But the Italian thrust into Africa—"poor people's imperialism," for one analyst[23]—bore the imprint of official obsession with population-surplus dilemmas. The northern Italian elites who dominated the newly unified state found themselves suddenly confronted with dense and impoverished southern Italian populations, whose perceived backwardness was a social abscess that needed to be drained. Yet their massive emigration to the United States and Argentina between 1890 and 1905 was a hemorrhage of national strength, to be redirected to the "fourth shore" soon to be created in Libya and Italian East Africa. More generally, J. R. Seeley in his 1881 treatise on colonial expansion expressed the assumptions of the age in weaving together the notions of enlarging the imperial domain, nationalism, and emigration:

> The modern idea on the other hand—few of us know how modern it is, or how gradually it has been formed—is that the people of one

nation, speaking one language, ought in general to have one government. . . . But if the State is the Nation (not the Country, observe, but the Nation) then we see a sufficient ground for the universal usage of modern states, which has been to regard their emigrants not as going out of the State but as carrying the State with them . . . the organization of the modern State admits of unbounded territorial extension, while that of the ancient State did not. . . . The modern State, being already as large as a country, would bear to become larger.[24]

Cumulatively, this concatenation of predisposing factors bearing on the behavioral choices of the colonizing states gave a range of free play to forces in the periphery, which often supplied the specific catalyzing energy to partition. Once a dialectic of conquest was underway, it became intertwined with conflict patterns within Africa and the unending process of state formation and dissolution. The slave-trade era partially shifted commercial gravitational pulls from the trans-Saharan exchange toward the Atlantic; in its wake emerged an array of hinterland states rooted in human commerce, whose normal mode of production was warfare. In the nineteenth-century decades preceding the partition an ensemble of new conquest states emerged, linked to Khartoum or Zanzibar-based slave-trade networks, the sundry Ngoni military states spinning far into Central Africa from their Zulu nucleus, or the religious-renovation jihad states in inner West Africa. These recently created polities offered the same opportunities for intruding imperial agents as did the Aztec state for Cortes: imperfectly incorporated or oppressively subjugated populations, and ruling classes who misread the colonial contingents as allies of circumstance.

In other instances, long-standing polities were in the throes of intense civil strife and dislocation, offering armed factions eager for external alliances; the four Wolof states in Senegal, the Yoruba cultural zone, and Buganda all illustrate this pattern. Usually, local allies were available; often colonial intervention was actually solicited as defensive protection against other aggressors (Botswana, Lesotho), or as tactical support against local enemies. In making their calculations, African groups tended to project forward the patterns of relationships with European enclaves they had known in the past, when the coastal outposts were relatively equal players in an ongoing diplomatic game rather than aspirants to comprehensive hegemony; few had any inkling as to the character of the new colonial state whose birth they may have chosen to assist.

By way of illustrating the illusions of the epoch, one may note the 1885 impressions of an emissary of the ruler of Timbuktu, then wooed by the French as a possible ally in the final assault on the Tukulor state at Segu. The Timbuktu ambassador, en route home from a visit to Paris, confided to a Senegalese agent of the administration:

> When I was in Paris, I told the Minister that we want to engage in commerce with the French, but we wish to remain masters of our own country. I saw that the Minister had the intention of withdrawing all the troops and outposts from Senegal, because they cost too much money. . . . If the French do wish to come take over our land, we will gather all our goods, and give them to the King of Morocco, who is our ruler. He will share everything, and give his country to the Prussians so that they may defend us. The Prussians are the strongest of all the whites.

As the clinching point, he added that railway construction in Senegal had ceased, final proof that withdrawal was near.[25]

A hesitant disposition to African expansion within the metropolitan state also opened policy space for a generation of buccaneering empire builders to force initiatives the metropolitan state then covered, however reluctantly. These individual agents of conquest found that the fluid circumstances of the partition era supplied an extraordinary opportunity simultaneously to enact their intense nationalism and engrave their names on the tablets of history. Karl Peters played such a role in German East Africa. From 1876 to the closing of the colonial frontier, Afrique Occidentale Française (AOF) was etched onto the maps by a coterie of French military officers, often acting in disregard of formal instructions from Paris. Colonel Louis Alexandre Brière de l'Isle, Lieutenant Colonel Gustave Borgnis-Desbordes, Louis Archinard, Captain Joseph Simon Gallieni, and their associates plunged ever deeper into the upper Niger valley and ultimately Chad. The pattern was established well by Marshal Thomas-Robert Bugeaud in Algeria, who offered a peremptory response to Paris instructions forbidding a Kabylia advance in the early 1840s: "I have received your dispatch. It is too late. My troops . . . are already on the march. . . . If we are successful, the Government and France will enjoy the honor. In the contrary case, the full responsibility falls upon me. I demand it."[26] These sentiments are precisely mirrored in Gallieni's instructions as commandant in the upper Niger to his then subordinate, Archinard: "You won't pay any more attention to the missives of [Paris] . . . than you think necessary. The Commandant-Superieur . . . can alone decide what measures have to be taken. . . .

Everything I accomplished during these two campaigns was done in spite of the Ministry which was always afraid to commit itself."[27]

The apotheosis of the individual agent of empire, driven by intense nationalism and sense of personal mission, was Cecil Rhodes. The 1889 grant to Rhodes of a state charter as director of the British South Africa Company provided him with an institutional weapon for imperial aggrandizement up to the northern limits of the Zambezi watershed. Through this device, Rhodes enjoyed an arm's-length latitude to plant the flag ever deeper in the African interior, with the British state retaining a degree of deniability as to his tactics and his risks. The wellspring of the Rhodes obsession with British expansion is captured in an 1877 statement, as well as a secret will drawn up at the same time: "It often strikes a man to inquire what is the chief good in life. . . . To myself, . . . the wish came to make myself useful to my country. . . . I contend that we are the first race in the world, and that the more of the world we inhabit, the better it is for the human race." His will pledges his fortune to a secret society whose purpose was prescribed as:

The extension of British rule throughout the world . . . the colonization of British subjects of all lands where the means of livelihood are attainable by energy, labour and enterprise, and especially the occupation by British settlers of the entire Continent of Africa, the Holy Land, the Valley of the Euphrates, the islands of Cyprus and Candia, the whole of South America, the islands of the Pacific not heretofore possessed by Great Britain, the whole of the Malay Archipelago, the sea-board of China and Japan, the ultimate recovery of the United States of America as an integral part of the British Empire . . . the foundation of so great a Power as to hereafter render wars impossible and promote the best interests of mankind.[28]

Thus, with gathering force and momentum, the tides of alien conquest swirled over the continent. Africa by the early twentieth century—save only Ethiopia and Liberia—was reconfigured into colonial space. And these two formally independent states were in their present form products of the partition: Ethiopia as a subimperial polity whose Amharic core had acquired title over a substantial new periphery through adroit diplomacy and the stinging defeat administered to the invading Italian army at Adowa in 1896; Liberia as a precarious polity subsisting by American patronage and Franco-British sufferance, loosely managed by a small Americo-Liberian minority. The multiple vectors driving the scramble, once in operation, unleashed a dynamic that could stop only when the frontiers of occupation were closed. There were moments of hesitation, when doubts about the foreseeable costs set against the uncertain benefits afflicted the official mind in the metropolitan capitals. African aggrandizement, for the colonizing state, always required placement within the broader security calculus of global relationships. There were momentary setbacks, as when Italy was humiliated at Adowa or when imperial enthusiast Jules Ferry was briefly driven from office by the fallout from military fiasco in Tonkin in 1885. At times rivalry was tempered by negotiated ground rules, as at the 1884–1885 Berlin Congress or the Anglo-French Entente Cordiale of 1903–1904. At other conjunctures, the spillover tensions from the competitive momentum of partition came close to triggering broader conflict: Anglo-French tensions over Egypt in 1882–1983, the Fashoda incident in 1898, the Moroccan crisis of 1906.

Cumulatively, it was a tumultuous chain reaction that left the participating powers with vast tracts of newly acquired territories, subject populations negatively stereotyped but mostly little known, and the necessity of devising systems of rule to protect metropolitan treasuries from further outlays. In 1875 no state elite in Europe could have imagined such an outcome, and no Africans—other than those in Algeria and the Cape already under colonial rule—could have conceived of the new political order about to be fastened on them.

THE CONQUEST PHASE

The initial phase in the life cycle of the African colonial state subdivides into (1) a brief phase of actual conquest, a process occurring along a moving frontier, and (2) actual state construction, to institutionalize rule. Somewhat distinct state logics characterize these subdivisions of the first epoch. Conquest occurred, whether by negotiation or military action, grounded in an immediate reason of extending jurisdictional claim. Construction, the heart of the matter, required more systematic, integrated reflection on patterns of domination sustainable over time.

Within the special context supplied by the scramble, the first establishment of a domination claim had a dual aspect. Either by diplomacy or force, acknowledgment of colonial authority by the African community concerned had to be extracted. But this title by itself did not suffice. Recognition of the territorial claim by competing colonizers was indispensable as well. Particularly in the many zones of contending encroachment, the second requirement was often more onerous than the first.

The advantages in occupation by negotiated accord are obvious enough, in terms of economizing coercive resources. African rulers were frequently willing to sign treaties, for several reasons. Some, as noted earlier, had reasons of their own for seeking European allies against their adversaries. Others were attracted by the (usually trifling) gifts that might attend treaty signature and were misled as to the sweeping sovereign claims that the imperial authority would deduce from it. Those rulers with long proximity to coastal enclaves had some experience in European legal concepts. States like Morocco, Egypt, and Ethiopia were subsidiary participants in the Europe-centered international system of states, and they operated with a shrewd grasp of what was at issue, even if the first two did fall prey to the colonial system. Southern African rulers in Basutoland, Bechuanaland, and Swaziland had some access to legal advice from those professionally schooled in the European system. But the protection treaties urgently pressed on African rulers by imperial agents, exploratory missions, or chartered-company delegates were usually documents of obscure purpose and uncertain consequences.

The real meaning of the treaties also went through major metamorphosis, as the colonial state transformed from coastal trading enclave into hinterland occupying force. This abrupt modification in colonizer interpretation of the protection concept, from mere commercial trading preference and exclusivity of extra-African relations to actual sovereignty, is illustrated well in the travails of the canny King Jaja of Opobo, a Nigerian trading city-state of the Niger delta. When he signed a treaty with the Oil Rivers Protectorate in the early 1880s, he had the prudence to ask Consul Edward Hewett for a definition of protection. The consul responded: "With reference to the word 'protection' as used in the proposed Treaty . . . the Queen does not want to take your country or your markets, but at the same time is anxious no other natives should take them. She undertakes to extend her gracious favor and protection, which will leave your country still under your government. She has no wish to curb your rule, although she is anxious to see your country up."[29] Three years later, Jaja was astonished to receive a deposition order as ruler. When he inquired of Foreign Secretary Lord Rosebery as to the curious extension of the protection notion, he met the disdainful response that, as part of a larger administrative unit, he could not obstruct what the new rulers viewed as progress. Britain, wrote Lord Rosebery, wanted "promotion of the welfare of the natives of all those territories, taken as a whole, by insuring the peaceful development of trade, and by facilitating their intercourse with Europeans. It is not permitted that any Chief who may happen to occupy a territory on the coast should obstruct this policy in order to benefit himself."[30]

The British in particular began with a circumscribed notion of what protection treaties entailed. When the Oil Rivers Protectorate was approved in 1883, accompanying cabinet instructions stressed the limitations of the commitment, explicitly excluding colony institutions "with all the necessary expensive machinery of government." As John Flint points out, "The fact is that the protectorate system emerged not as a consciously thought-out policy, but as an expedient within the limitations which history had placed upon the free action of British politicians and officials. These limitations operated so widely that of all the vast areas acquired by Britain in Africa between 1880 and 1900, only one, British Bechuanaland, was given Crown colony status."[31]

The legal meaning attached to the notion swiftly expanded, however, as Jaja painfully discovered. An increasingly Austinian view of international law prevailed, which perceived international law as founded upon positive acts of will on the part of European states, and sovereignty as inherently indivisible. By 1895 the British law officers held that protection entailed unrestricted sovereignty: "The exercise of a protectorate in an uncivilized country imported the right to assume whatever jurisdiction over all persons may be needed for its effectual exercise."[32] The more rigorous and centralist public-law tradition in Europe precluded the necessity for such a debate.

However dubious in origin and malleable in content, the protection treaties played an important role in determining axes of penetration and lines of division. Astute maneuvering by Leopold at the Berlin Congress to achieve the international laying on of hands that would bring the gift of international juridical life to his African estate relied heavily upon the sheaf of treaties, on standard forms, bearing the "X" of Congo-basin rulers collected by his energetic agent Henry Morton Stanley. As Stanley stated the case,

> The Association [the camouflaged forerunner of the Congo Free State] were in possession of treaties made with over four hundred and fifty independent African chiefs, whose rights would be conceded by all to have been indisputable, since they held their lands by undisturbed occupation, by long ages of succession, by real divine right. Of their own free will, without coercion, but for substantial considerations, reserving only a few easy conditions, they had transferred their rights of sovereignty and of ownership to the Association. The time had arrived when a sufficient number of these had been made to connect the several miniature sovereignties into one concrete whole, to present itself before the world for general recogni-

tion of its right to govern, and hold these in the name of an independent state, lawfully constituted according to the spirit and tenor of international law.[33]

Not only "substantial considerations" but also the visible threat of force were important to the collection of treaties. As one French agent wrote in 1888 concerning his treaty-signing mission in eastern Senegal, "Among the Malinke or at least among those I visited, any other sentiment than respect for force is unknown, we are respected, we are considered as masters because we are strong and we have proved it. . . . Everywhere we are considered as masters, everywhere one accepts with alacrity to sign the treaty I present which places these villages and states under French protectorate.[34] The treaty diplomacy of French West African expansion mirrored its peculiarly military character, but the preoccupation with visible displays of strength was general to the conquest phase.

Major nuclei of resistance to colonial expansion were subdued by force. Pure military conquest had the advantage of leaving no semblance of rights in the hands of the dominated community. Bugeaud pioneered the *razzia* model of colonial expansion in Algeria, with ruthless mobile warfare conducted against Abd-el-Kader and others who combated the expansion of the French coastal enclaves acquired in 1830. His large armies confiscated animals and grain to ensure their mobility and crushed resistance by destroying the means of livelihood of unsubdued groups. In describing one of his campaigns in 1843, Bugeaud wrote: "Here I am . . . burning the tents and huts of these unsubdued tribesmen, driving off their flocks, emptying their granaries, and sending to Miliana all the barley and wheat that I can. . . . I shall leave them no peace until they submit."[35]

In many areas, therefore, subjugation came not through treaty but by punitive expeditions. Sometimes these were relatively mild, even symbolic battles, such as the *barroud d'honneur* through which much of the Moroccan *siba* (zone of dissidence) came to accept French overrule.[36] They frequently included burning of villages and pillaging whatever possessions might be found. Sacralized symbols of African power were a special target: the golden stool of the Ashanti state, the "long juju" of the Aro Chuku in eastern Nigeria. The objectification of Africans as "barbarian" meant that the brutalities associated with this mode of subjugation rested lightly on the imperial consciousness; the commander of the Aro campaigns in 1901 and 1902 characterized his methods as "not unduly severe," "as humane as could be expected under the circumstances."[37]

They needed to be repeated through annual punitive expeditions for the first decade of this century before conquest in eastern Nigeria was completed.

The strongly military cast of the nascent colonial state in the conquest phase led to a preference for armed defeat in the instance of large African states with strong armies. Even though such African leaders as Ahmadu of Segu and Samori based in Futa Djallon signed treaties with the French, domination was believed insecure until they were militarily defeated. Rabah and his marauding forces in Bornu and Chad and Kabarega of Bunyoro also fell in this category. Frederic Lugard was determined to ground British control over northern Nigeria on the military defeat of the Fulani emirates, and he found an occasion to provoke such a test of force. His celebrated address to the defeated rulers in Sokoto in 1903 captures well the advantages of conquest as a derivative principle of domination:

> The old treaties are dead, you have killed them. Now these are the words which I, the High Commissioner, have to say for the future. The Fulani of old times under Dan Fodio conquered this country. They took the right to rule over it, to levy taxes, to depose kings and to create kings. They in turn have by defeat lost their rule which has come into the hands of the British. All these things which I have said the Fulani by conquest took the right to do now pass to the British. Every Sultan and Emir and the principal officers of the State will be appointed by the High Commissioner throughout all this country. The High Commissioner will be guided by the usual laws of succession and the wishes of the people and chiefs, but will set them aside if he decides for good cause to do so. . . . You need have no fear regarding British rule, it is our wish to learn your customs and fashion, just as you must learn ours . . . you have always heard that British rule is just and fair, and people under our King are satisfied.[38]

By 1900 the basic grid of colonial partition and subjugation was in place, excepting Morocco and Libya. The axes of conquest followed established lines of communication—waterways and trade routes—and flowed around numerous communities initially protected by their isolation. Pastoral groups, rendered elusive by their mobility and decentralization, generally remained beyond colonial reach, particularly along the southern fringe of the Sahara. In the remaining years before the outbreak of World War I, colonial state attention focused on these remaining zones of autonomy and dissidence. With only a few exceptions, when the guns of

August signaled the onset of carnage in the European trenches, the silence of subjugation covered the African landscape.

CONSTRUCTING THE COLONIAL STATE:
BASIC PREMISES

The phase of partition and conquest in most regions occurred before a clearly articulated colonial state existed; the major exceptions were Algeria, Senegal, Sierra Leone, and the Cape. The great majority of the agents of state creation were of military background; their professional mentality permeated political action in this era. The logic of warfare dominated reason of state; immediate triumph eclipsed other considerations. In the metropolitan chancelleries, the Foreign and Defense ministries—which monopolized colonial partition policy during this brief moment of relentless expansion—applied a primarily security-driven calculus, in a more global context. On the ground, conquest became an end in itself for the partition generation of imperial agents. Unconstrained by the disciplines of a state reason balancing competing imperatives, pursuit of short-term domination was a consuming objective. Anticipating the Kwame Nkrumah injunction, "Seek ye first the political kingdom," they had little difficulty assuming that all other things would be added to the colonial domains they were creating.

New political kingdoms were indeed created—in the form of partitioned territory and subjugated populations. These political facts, usually so swiftly inscribed on the tablets of imperial history, summoned a wholly different order of statecraft: constructing Bula Matari. Conquest was perhaps a single act; its inarticulate major premise was the subsequent construction of machinery of permanent domination. Modalities of institutionalization of rule needed to follow at once. Whether accomplished by diplomatic guile or military force, the first assertion of European sovereignty was inherently precarious, and certain to dissolve unless the initial demonstration of superior power could congeal into enduring forms of dominance. To unravel the logic of this crucial phase in the life history of the African colonial state, I turn first to the operational code of axiomatic premises that guided its construction, before examining the application of the six imperatives of raison d'état.

The Procrustean bed of colonial state construction derived from European international legal notions of the time. The doctrine of sovereignty was the lynchpin. In the phrasing of the classic text on territorial acquisition, "The mission and purpose of international law has been the delimitation of the exercise of sovereign power on a territorial basis."[39] Warfare and conquest remained fully recognized modalities of engrossing new territory. Periodic confirmation of spatial rearrangements of sovereignty occurred through the occasional congresses of the European concert of nations, which then controlled international norm creation. The nineteenth-century system of states, through formal acts of recognition, conferred on imperial claims an apparent juridical sanctification beyond challenge by the dominated. The ubiquitous protectorate treaties, however ambiguous their meaning to the African rulers who affixed their signatures to them, became elevated, through external recognition in the European diplomatic realm, into the more potent doctrine of imperial sovereignty. These international norms soon began to erode, beginning with the 1907 Porter Convention proscribing the use of force to collect sovereign debts. The League of Nations Covenant, the 1928 Kellogg-Briand Pact, and especially the 1945 United Nations Charter progressively banned force or its threat as a basis for territorial change and incorporated the idea of self-determination, initially without abrogating the validity of older titles originating in conquest.[40]

"Effective occupation" became, in the intensely competitive politics of partition, an indispensable prerequisite to the consolidation of colonial sovereignty claims. This doctrine dates from late sixteenth-century French and English challenges to Spanish and Portuguese claims to sole title to the "Indies" grounded in loosely applied doctrines of "discovery," the 1493 papal bull, and the Treaty of Tordesillas. But it acquired far greater saliency through formalization by the Berlin Congress of 1884 and 1885, convened to codify rules of behavior in the vortex zones of colonial rivalry, the Niger and Congo basins. Although the congress did not, as is sometimes asserted, provide a comprehensive blueprint for partition, metaphorically it represents the diplomatic dimension of conquest, through its central purpose of keeping the tensions inherent in the scramble short of a European war.[41]

The affirmation at Berlin of the "effective occupation" doctrine made clear that sketching out vague spheres of influence would not suffice for confirmation of proprietary title. Recognition of sovereignty by the European system of states was a first step, but it needed to acquire prescriptive force by the creation of a visible infrastructure on the ground of garrisons that affirmed imperial presence and served as an embryonic framework for assertion of rule. Here the quintessentially competitive character of the partition dynamic came into play; empty spaces might be left within the zone of claimed sovereignty, but the zone's frontier marches required some form of physical presence. Competing predators were swift to advance their own claims to ungarrisoned territory, particularly far from the coast, where the first generation of diplomatically bargained boundaries were only vaguely defined.

Metropolitan treasuries, citadels of skepticism concerning the material benefits likely to accrue from colonial expansion in Africa, insisted on an iron law of fiscal self-sufficiency of the newly acquired colonial territories. In the British case, the older West African settlements had required small periodic parliamentary appropriations to rescue them from insolvency; for example, a 38,000 pound appropriation cleared Sierra Leone's debts in 1877.[42] Although past amounts were small, the projected expenses for the vast new territorial domains were ominous. The principle of colonial self-sufficiency dates from 1815, but as partition unfurled it acquired new urgency.[43] In the French case, the principle of colonial self-sufficiency became a fiscal keystone of overseas rule with the fiscal law of 1900, by which colonies were reconceptualized as distant collectivities with control of their own financial resources and responsibility for their own expenses.[44] The claim was made that, under prior French state responsibility for "expenses of sovereignty," 44 percent of colonial costs had been absorbed by the French treasury.[45] The status of the Congo Free state, as a royal agency alien from the Belgian state, automatically insulated the metropole from the Leopoldian domain, although some state loans were made during this period. The 1908 colonial charter defining juridical ties when Belgium assumed sovereignty made fiscal autonomy a foundational principle of the imperial relationship.[46] Only Italy was a systematic exception to this rule; Eritrea, Somalia, and Libya were costly ventures, requiring metropolitan financial commitments throughout the colonial period.[47]

The object of colonial rule was metropolitan advantage. In the phase of colonial state construction, justification for the imperial venture was required only in Europe. A liberal spokesman for empire in France, Jules Harmand, spoke for an epoch in 1912: "That the colonies are made for the metropolis, for the many and varied advantages that the metropolis may draw from them, is evident: if colonies, the foundation of which nearly always costs the metropolis so much money and sacrifices and which exposes them to such great risks, were not made to serve those metropoles, *they would have no raison d'être,* and one cannot see by what aberration civilized states would dispute them with so much rude jealousy."[48] Only Leopold II really believed that the colonial exploits of an earlier age (by Spain and Portugal in the Americas, Britain in India, the Netherlands in the East Indies) could be replicated in the form of direct fiscal extraction from Africa to fill metropolitan treasuries. But the array of strategic and commercial advantages itemized earlier in this chapter as motivations for conquest were expected to accrue; part of the task of the managers of the colonial state was to ensure that they did.

The conviction of African "savagery" permeated European thought at the moment of colonial state construction.[49] Racialist perceptions of the subjugated other intruded in innumerable ways in the everyday application of domination. Such a premise gave natural rise to the conclusion that the new colonial regime, no matter how harsh and extractive, was axiomatically beneficial to the African subject. Few colonial agents at this period entertained the slightest doubt on this score. Further, at this apogee of Social Darwinism, enacting the role of Bula Matari was a living morality play through which European superiority was validated. As Sanderson observes, "For a Social Darwinist, the most convincing possible demonstration of his own racial superiority is his ability to crush 'inferior races' by force."[50]

Finally, the germ of nationalism infiltrated the official mind. For the unwary potential African subject there lurked the dark fate of conquest by a rival colonial power of less beneficent disposition. An 1884 Foreign Office minute expresses views widely shared by British colonial agents: "The French are jealous and bad colonists, they oppress the natives, repel foreign capitalists and have to fall back upon Slavery, slightly disguised, for the labor required on their plantations. They are monopolists and protectionists and judge all other nations by their own standard."[51] Anglophobia and Germanophobia played an analogous role in early French colonial policy.[52]

A silent corollary to this ensemble of premises was the presumption of permanence. Often a short time might pass before an initial territorial seizure slipped under the cloak of imperial proprietary beliefs. Although Algiers was stormed in 1830, the final decision for permanent occupation and hinterland conquest came only in 1840. British military debarkation at Alexandria in 1882 initially had only immediate objectives; its very military success created a new crisis which, from a British perspective, required temporary occupation of the entire country. By 1889 the Egyptian financial crisis was resolved, and debt repayments secure, but the British official mind had become persuaded that new diplomatic imperatives made withdrawal unwise.[53] The territorial imperative intrinsic to the state came into play; space, once occupied, is almost never voluntarily relinquished.

Such were the assumptions embedded in the official mind as the construction of the African colonial state began. The six imperatives of reason of state will structure my consideration of this process. The first of these is hegemony, the consolidation of which was the prime preoccupation of the colonial state in formation. In turn, the nature of the colonial state response to the challenge of institutionalizing hegemony goes far to explaining its structural physiognomy and modes of operation.

BUILDING HEGEMONY

Hegemony was dearly won. Resistance intensified when African societies realized that the modest intrusions of informal empire were supplanted by a comprehensive apparatus of domination, placing a wholly new set of demands on their populations for taxes, forced delivery of goods, labor, and surrender of their land and livestock. A wave of major uprisings occurred. In Algeria, large rebellions took place in 1871, 1876, 1879, and from 1881 to 1884; in South Africa, Zulu wars in 1879 and 1906; in Tanganyika, the Maji-Maji revolt in 1905; in Rhodesia, the great Ndebele and Shona risings of 1896 and 1897; in Sierra Leone, the hut-tax war of 1898; in Angola and the Congo Free State, rebellions in many parts.[54] The widespread pattern of revolt conveyed important lessons. Once triggered, such uprisings could long delay efforts to build settled administration. Perhaps the most dramatic instance of extended combat was that of Sayyid Muhammad 'Abdille Hassan of British Somaliland, whose combined message of anticolonial resistance and religious solidarity sustained his struggle from 1900 to 1920, and whose final defeat came only through the first colonial use of aerial bombardment.[55] Further, rebellions were costly to repress and ran the risk—especially in Britain—of attracting unwelcome public attention to the devices employed to ensure domination.

Some variation in the nature of hegemony reflected contrasting state traditions and ideologies, environments of occupation, and teleology of rule. The British state stood apart from its Continental counterparts in terms of its less centralized historical personality, a less thorough impregnation with an earlier absolutist tradition, and a less prefectoral model of regional administration. Also, the diversity and dimensions of the British Empire supplied a variety of models of domination, from which concepts of rule might be extracted. There was in consequence less uniformity in the superstructure of domination in zones of British rule.

France stood at the other end of the spectrum, with the powerful Cartesian, Jacobin impulses that are a recurrent refrain in its imperial statecraft. The potent legacy of a fully formed absolutist tradition, modernized in the Bonapartist rationalization of the state, informed the inner spirit of republican institutions. Germany incorporated the older ethos of the Prussian state, a parallel model of highly articulated bureaucratic authority. Belgium as state was consciously modeled on a French pattern. Unified Italy was inhabited by an intense nationalism, which was to give birth to the exaltation of the state of the fascist period.

Modalities of state construction were influenced by variations in the African environment. The scale and nature of existing African polities determined what extent intermediary structures were available for possible co-optation or, alternatively, dissolution. The character of incorporation of African communities shaped an initial security map for the state. African states like Buganda, Mossi, or Barotseland that had chosen alliance needed some reward in the short run; those like the Sudanese Mahdists that were associated with resistance were long viewed as zones of danger. The natural economy determined where immediate resources could be found, and population densities measured labor supply. Islam, where present, was a potent ideological force, with important policy implications. Sedentary cultivating populations were far easier to bring within the net of domination than were pastoral and nomadic communities.

Fundamentally affecting the character of the colonial state was the role envisaged for European settlement, and the degree of occupation contemplated. In what became South Africa, Namibia, Zimbabwe, Kenya, Algeria, and Libya, at this stage settlement was the core logic of the state. In British and French Somaliland and Mauritania, only minimal and preemptive purposes informed state construction, and skeletal structures resulted. British Somaliland served no other end than to supply meat and related provisions for the Aden base; Djibouti was only a strategic port. Bechuanaland and Basutoland, and to a lesser degree Swaziland, were pawns in evolving South African space, and they were held separate by Britain in deference to their immediate forceful opposition to incorporation by the Union, but with the notion of their eventual transfer to South Africa. The Moor sultanates and confederacies of Mauritania were subjugated simply as a security zone.

The hegemony imperative, driven by the doctrine of effective occupation, immediately required a skeletal grid of regional administration. Its priorities were clear, its tasks minimal: the imposition of a basic order and the creation of a revenue flow. Its means were also slender, above all its ultimate coercive capacity as demonstrated in the conquest phase. The isolated outpost of the colonial state in these early years might have a couple of European agents, a few African interpreters, messengers, and ancillary staff, as well as a small military detachment. Its provisioning from the colonial center was sporadic and spartan; most of its sustenance had to be drawn from the surrounding countryside, whose precarious subordination had to be routinized.

The early administrators were drawn largely from seconded military personnel; the professionalization of colonial services did not really take hold until after World War I. The initial personnel pool was even multinational in some instances: Slatin (Emin) Pasha, an Austrian who had served the Turko-Egyptian state, was a key architect of British "native policy" in the Sudan;[56] nearly half of the cadres in the Congo Free State were non-Belgian (mainly Scandinavian and Italian).[57] The slender communication lines to the more remote posts necessarily left local commandants with a large range of initiative to adapt the broad directive of hegemony to their own judgments of situational strategies. They could not afford, however, to be lax in asserting their authority and fulfilling their basic tasks. Their daily duties were captured well by a British administrator, Captain O. H. Stigand, reflecting on his Ugandan experience on the eve of World War I: "Ask any official what he is doing in his district, and he will reply that he is administering it. Ask different officials, 'what is administration?' and you will get divergent answers. The general idea will be that it is to hear cases and get revenue for the government."[58] The identical themes emerge in the words of a French official, with respect to AOF: "The European commandant is not posted in a region, is not paid to observe nature, to carry out ethnographic, botanical, geologic or linguistic studies. He has a mission of administration. This word translates into the obligation . . . to impose regulations, to limit individual liberties for the benefit of all, to collect taxes."[59] These sentiments were echoed by Governor Gabriel Angoulvant in his 1908 instructions to local French commandants:

> What must be put in place above all, is the undebatable principle of our authority. . . . For the natives, acceptance of this principle must be translated into a genuine welcome, an absolute respect for our representatives whoever they may be . . . integral payment of the tax on a uniform scale of 2.50 francs, a serious contribution to the construction of roads, acceptance of compensated portage, observation of our advice concerning the necessity of labor, recourse to our system of justice.[60]

The nature of this early administrative infrastructure varied considerably. In northern Africa, where states recognizable to European jurisprudence were in place and the protectorate notion had greater force, the existing structures were simply placed under the direction and supervision of European residents; such was the case in Egypt, Tunisia, and the

Moroccan *makhzen* (zone of settled administration). In Tunisia this system quickly supplied such a stable apparatus of low-cost and relatively frictionless domination that it was regarded as a model; a generation of Senegalese sons of chiefly families in training for intermediary roles as canton chiefs were sent to Tunis for extended periods of observation of an ideal colonial apparatus.[61] In Bechuanaland and Basutoland, British administration was long confined to a supervisory role over the existing states.

In colonial states where settlement predominated, the logic of hegemony was likewise distinctive. White settlers regarded themselves as entitled to the prerogatives of citizens in a civil society and could not be ruled by command. The colonial state itself, during this period, was in part intermediary between the settler community and the indigenous populations. Both because its resource base depended on the settler economy and because it was partly susceptible to political pressures exerted by settlers, directly or circuitously through their access to metropolitan institutions, the colonial state needed to accommodate some settler demands, particularly with regard to labor supply and land rights. Yet even in the construction phase it could not afford total subservience to settler interests, whose rapacious excesses would threaten the security and ultimate resource base of the state.

Thus, the colonial state developed distinctive modes of rule to apply to indigenous subjects. Although these operated within an overall umbrella of extraction, their aim was partly protective. This pattern was exemplified in the *bureaux arabes,* first created by Marshal Bugeaud in 1841 as a means of consolidating rule over zones where his muscular repression had decimated resistance. For the subjugated, a paternal military control was proposed, with the army interposed between Algerian communities and the already strident settlers, who were swift to accuse these agencies of blocking land alienation and the "civil rights" of settlers in zones of military administration.[62] Their mission was summarized in Napolean III's instructions of 1865: "It is essential that they be constantly in contact with the tribes, but without meddling; that they visit the chiefs and listen to their demands and complaints; that they explain patiently to them the objectives of measures which affect them, which are often intentionally misrepresented. Their mission consists of transmitting the intentions, advice, and opinions of the authorities to the population, and of keeping their superiors abreast of what transpires in Arab territory."[63] By the 1870s the dimensions of the settler influx had pushed the bureaux arabes far from the coast, into the Saharan fringes;

this model, however, was later also applied to southern Tunisia and the Moroccan siba.

HEGEMONY PRIVATIZED:
CHARTERED COMPANIES

Confronted elsewhere with vast domains over which to establish rule, and the cost-avoidance axiom, the colonizing states exhumed the ancient formula of delegation to the private sector in a number of regions (AEF, the Congo Free State, the Rhodesias, East Africa, Somalia, the German territories). A relic from a past age, when the European state itself had far more limited capacities, and when overseas expansion was more exclusively mercantile in telos, this formula had done yeoman service in India and the Dutch East Indies in the creation of a basic framework of colonial domination. Elsewhere, however—in West Africa and the West Indies—it had been notoriously unsuccessful.

The basic compact with the chartered companies was a grant of virtually unrestricted delegated sovereignty, in return for their capitalizing and organizing the initial framework of hegemony. In recompense for sovereign services, the concessionary companies were awarded trade monopolies within their domains, and they could use the proceeds both to finance their exercise of domination and remunerate their shareholders. It was presumed that the concessionary regime was transitional; ultimately, the colonial state, once settled and stabilized, would be able to supplant the private exercise of its authority, as eventually occurred in India and the East Indies.

In the British instance, there were three major undertakings of this nature: the Royal Niger Company (chartered in 1886), the British East Africa Company (1888), and the British South Africa Company (1889). The first, under the direction of Sir George Goldie, did establish a number of treaty relationships in its zone of operation, but it fell short of clearly establishing the effective occupation that would thwart French and German encroachment; the company aimed to administer only foreigners and merely to manage trade relations with Africans. Its attempt to engross all trade led to constant frictions, contravening as it did the provisions of the Berlin Congress purportedly assuring free trade in the Niger and Congo basins. The company, modestly capitalized, did pay substantial dividends during its period of operation; when it was bought out in 1899 by the British state, it laid claim to 865,000 pounds compensation for "administrative losses," treaty-making costs, and military stores.[64]

The British East Africa Company in Kenya had an even shorter life. Its capital was a mere 250,000 pounds; in 1892, its income was only 25,000 pounds, set against outlays of 80,000. In 1894 its directors managed to peddle their sovereign rights back to the British government for the amount of their original capital stake.[65]

The British South Africa Company was a uniquely hardy specimen: of all the chartered companies, it alone retained its delegated sovereign powers (over the Rhodesias) throughout the state construction period. A creation of the unquenchable imperial energies of Rhodes, its attraction for the British state was its capacity to preempt German and Portuguese expansion in a vast tract of central Africa, and to organize assured occupation through European settlement. The BSAC initially expected to replicate the Rand gold strikes in Matabeleland. But Rhodesian gold diggings proved much more limited than anticipated, and the BSAC and the settlers it sponsored had to content themselves with expropriating the land and cattle of the Ndebele and Shona groups, provoking the costly rebellions of 1896 and 1897. In its political assignment, the BSAC was an undoubted success; British dominion over the Rhodesias was accomplished by the company. By vesting the settler community, at negligible cost, with title to the land and cattle it seized, and by assuring a flow of coerced labor, it equipped the settlers with a rigged market in which to prosper. But it was unable to pay dividends to its own shareholders until it divested itself of sovereign responsibilities in 1923 and 1924; thereafter, the absurdly advantageous terms of this settlement guaranteed an abundant flow of passive rents on mineral exploitation in the Rhodesias throughout the colonial period.[66]

The most notorious of the concessionary companies were those operating in the Congo Free State and the AEF territories of Congo and Ubangi-Chari. In the Leopoldian case, the two largest of the concessionaries, Anversoise and the Anglo-Belgian India Rubber Company (ABIR), were awarded vast tracts in the central Congo basin, with a license to collect wild rubber by whatever means might occur to them in return for assuming responsibility for control over the area. In fact, they brought little capital—a mere 8,000 pounds in the ABIR case—and instituted a reign of terror sufficient to provoke an embarrassing public-protest campaign in Britain and the United States at a time when the threshold of toleration for colonial brutality was quite high.[67] Leopold himself was the largest concessionary, engrossing one-eighth of the territory as a private domain, from which he derived an 1896 profit of 71 million francs, or roughly twice the total colonial budget for 1906. But eventual abandonment of the concessionary system was forced by tapping methods that progressively destroyed the wild rubber vines within reach, a sharp fall in the price of wild rubber when a plantation competitor entered the market toward the end of the first decade of the twentieth century, and the vehemence of the international protest campaigns, which a weak state like Belgium could not easily shrug off.

In the case of AEF, the life history of the concessionary companies was very similar, except that they were more numerous. Between 1898 and 1900 some forty-one charter companies in AEF received concessions, covering 70 percent of the territory of Congo and Ubangi-Chari. The smallest received 1,200 square kilometers, the largest (Compagnie des Sultanats du Haut-Oubangui) received a hundred and forty thousand square kilometers. Their total capital, for the exercise of delegated sovereignty in seven hundred thousand square kilometers, was 60 million francs (or 360 million 1967 francs).[68] Central African historian Yarisse Zoctizoum exaggerates only slightly in observing that "the principal capital contribution was force, the violence exercised by the state apparatus and the agents of these companies."[69] By 1906 the calamitous impact of the concessionary regime was apparent, and the colonial state moved to phase it out.

In most places, however, a basic grid of territorial administration was set in place, with two or three echelons of European administration radiating from the capital. The district officer, although usually a civil official by 1914, was invariably clad in uniform and expected to be saluted by all Africans. Although the germs of specialized health, public works, and judicial structures appeared, the basic structure was one of command rather than service.

THE COERCIVE ARM OF HEGEMONY

The colonial state required at once to underwrite its hegemony with a local security force; the Bugeaud strategy of enforcing domination with a hundred thousand French troops was impossible to contemplate. The Indian Army and the West Indian regiments supplied the British with a model of locally recruited troops under European officers. In East Africa colonial occupation briefly benefited from the imperial services of the Indian Army, but African replicas were quickly needed. From the Indian experience came the "martial races" doctrine, which held that certain ethnic stocks were summoned by culture and history to military vocations. Thus, the military units created in the early days utilized an ethnic recruiting strategy: Tiv in Nigeria, Acholi in Uganda, Kamba in Kenya.[70] These forces were augmented by sizable armed police forces; as early as

1895, the Sierra Leone frontier police numbered nineteen thousand.[71] In the Sudan, the British loaded military costs onto the Cairo budget by utilizing the Egyptian Army.

In the French case, the Armée d'Afrique, based in Algeria, remained an integral part of the French Army; however, separate Tunisian and Moroccan armies were quickly developed. In AOF and AEF the military requirements of hegemony were basically met by the tirailleurs sénégalais, units dating from 1823. By 1910 only one battalion of French troops remained below the Sahara, based at Dakar. The garrisoning and conquest of AOF and AEF were accomplished by the tirailleurs (rifles), whose ranks were primarily filled by Wolof, Tukulor, Bambara, Mossi, and some Sara from Chad. One of their commanders, Lieutenant Colonel Charles Mangin, touted their virtues as not only the hammer of sub-Saharan empire but also the strategic reserve for France: "We cannot be astonished to observe the warlike qualities of the blacks completed by professional discipline which make them usable in modern armies; the West African races are not only warlike, but essentially military. They not only love danger, the life of adventure, but they are essentially amenable to discipline. . . . The attachment of the Senegalese to France is absolute."[72]

The Congo Free State also swiftly equipped itself with an armed instrument of hegemony. The Force Publique was created in 1888, and by 1897 it had fourteen thousand African troops; its European officer and noncommissioned cadres numbered 360 in 1905. During its early years this force was in almost constant military operation; it experienced serious mutinies in 1895, 1897, and 1900, which led to a careful strategy of ethnic blending down to the smallest unit level.[73]

The Portuguese, during the construction phase, lacked both coercive and administrative resources to go beyond the minimal occupation required to prevent rival colonial encroachment. Portuguese military forces were limited to sporadic punitive expeditions; in Angola, Clarence-Smith estimates that by 1910 no more than a tenth of the territory was under real Portuguese control. Its military was a mélange of slave soldiers, some local militia, and the contingents still commanded by African rulers.[74]

Italy, after the catastrophe of the 1896 attack on Ethiopia with its largely Italian force, moved to build a force based on indigenous auxiliaries. Although Eritreans were readily recruited, and were used in Libya and Somalia as well as Eritrea, in Somalia local conscription proved difficult. In 1914 the Colonial Troops Corps had four thousand men, but only 10 percent were Somali, with the largest number coming from the Arabian Peninsula.[75]

Only in South Africa had European settlement become so comprehensive in shaping state and society that hegemony could be exercised without intermediation. The Congo Free State in 1908 had only 756 European civilian officers and 482 military cadres to assure domination over nine hundred thousand square miles.[76] Nigeria had fewer than two hundred European administrators.[77] Moyen Congo in AEF had only one hundred European administrators.[77] Moyen Congo in AEF had only one hundred in 1905, of whom fifty-four were in Brazzaville.[78] In 1914 the colonial administration in the Sudan had only 110 British officers and officials.[79] For rule to have substance, African collaborators were indispensable.

INTERMEDIARIES OF HEGEMONY

The obvious place to seek such allies was in the existing African political structures. Those holding authority, or having some locally recognized claim to it, could rely on a reservoir of legitimacy and the familiarity of prescriptive usage. Long before "indirect rule" was elaborated into a theoretical doctrine of efficient domination by Lord Lugard in 1919, accommodation with local power structures was almost everywhere a practical fact. Often there were competing claimants to authority, on whose rivalries the colonial state could play, and among whom it might select a contender willing to accept the diminished but still real power that colonial alliance could secure. Exceptions to this general rule occurred only where African ruling elites persisted so long in resistance that the colonial state dared not make them its agents (which seldom happened), where societies were so decentralized that no authority figure suitable for intermediation could be discovered (fairly frequent in the forest zones), or where European settlement marginalized African societies. Thus, below the bottom echelon of European regional administration an array of African chiefs were recognized, and vested with the authority of the colonial state, in addition to whatever title they enjoyed on their own. Furthermore, the colonial state insisted that those chiefs it recognized were the sole authority holders within the reconfigured political space subject to its design.

The political cultures and state ideologies of the colonizing polities were not identical. They produced somewhat different underlying perspectives concerning the value of African institutions, even if in the early phases all were equally compelled by the stringent circumstances of constructing hegemony to seek, where available, the collaboration of indigenous rulers. A paternalistic, aristocratic view of natural hierarchies in society permitted incumbent rulers once deferent to British direction to fit easily within the colonial official mind, although no intense dissonance was felt when, as in the Ashanti case, the conquered African state was dismantled. The French state was more disposed toward clear, unified chains of command extending from the governor down to the village in a single hierarchy. As Joost von Vollenhoven, then governor-general of AOF put the matter in a 1917 administrative circular, "there are not two authorities in a *cercle,* French and indigenous authority; there is only one. Alone, the [French] *cercle* commandant commands; alone he is responsible. The indigenous chief is only an instrument, an auxiliary."[80] At the same time, administrators recognized the pragmatic virtues of precolonial structuration of domination in molding societies for subjugation. The "anarchy" of the decentralized societies of AEF was frequently bemoaned. As one Moyen Congo administrator wrote in 1908,

> A tropical country such as this, with its very primitive black populations, who were never in the past educated and domesticated by the strong hand of powerful conquerors, as had been the case in West Africa, can never be brought by simple persuasion or even by the sheer virtue of our moral principles into the current of Western civilization. . . . In this respect, it would be puerile not to frankly recognize, whatever repugnance we may have for their barbarous procedures, that the energetic methods of African potentates have admirably prepared the terrain for our administration and our influence . . . societies certainly still barbarian, but strongly hierarchical, disciplined, fashioned for obedience and work.[81]

The extractive pressures placed on African societies in this phase of constructing Bula Matari were so extensive in taxes, porters, and other forms of corvée labor, and the administrative infrastructure was so skeletal, that the colonial state was inevitably led to incorporate existing structures (where available) within its hierarchy, or to designate those believed to have some customary claim to leadership, even where no special respect attached to these institutions—as in the Congo Free State or the Portuguese territories. In some instances a comprehensive alliance was achieved with a dominant faction within an existing state; in Buganda an intimate working relationship developed between an emergent Protestant chiefly faction and the British. In return for resolute British backing for their own reconstruction within the Buganda kingdom, this group supplied not only a ruling caste of intermediaries for

Buganda but also a reservoir of "Ganda agents" designated as colonial chiefs in many parts of Uganda, to create an administrative infrastructure on the Buganda model.[82] The Germans organized much of inland Tanganyika with the help of coastal Swahili agents, who served as imperial delegates. In Senegal, the *ceddo,* Wolof royal slaves who as a military caste achieved dominance in the unsettled politics of the nineteenth century, supplied many canton chiefs for the French administration.[83]

Intermediaries were supplied in the cultural sphere as well. The Christian missions might not have regarded their evangelical endeavor as an auxiliary agency of colonial hegemony, but there can be little doubt that it served that function. The embryonic Christian communities that took form around the mission stations were outposts of European influence beyond the religious sphere. As Dan Crawford, an early Plymouth Brethren missionary in the Katanga region of the Congo Free State, wrote, "Many a little Protestant Pope in the lonely bush is forced by his self-imposed isolation to be prophet, priest and king rolled into one—really a very big duck he, in his own private pond. . . . Quite seriously he is forced to be a bit of a policeman, muddled up in matters not even remotely in his sphere."[84] Armed with the Book and its mysterious powers, the cultural project of the missions indeed went far beyond that of the state, limited at this stage to domination and extraction. As Beidelman observes, "Missionaries invariably aimed at overall changes in the beliefs and actions of native peoples, at colonization of heart and mind as well as body. Pursuing this sustained policy of change, missionaries demonstrated a more radical and morally intense commitment to rule than political administrators or business men."[85]

In some cases—colonial Malawi, for example—in the early years the mission infrastructure was more powerful than that of the state. In western Nigeria, the Gold Coast, and Sierra Leone the African clergy that had emerged in the nineteenth century played an influential role in the extension of a religious culture whose silent partner was imperial domination.[86] Where conversion of the ruling class was possible, as in Buganda, rapid evangelization of much of the population could swiftly follow.[87] Often, however, missions were forced to begin with whatever social categories might be accessible; these were frequently dislocated persons, orphans, or former slaves, for whom the mission became a shelter, and over time the education it provided became a weapon for status reversal and social ascension.

In the latter instance, the mission might be a source of turbulence, challenging existing hierarchies. The theology proposed by Christian missionaries desacralized African kingship, frequently assaulting rituals and symbols of power as idolatrous. Most early missionaries shared the administrators' low view of African culture; an 1891 Church Missionary Society dispatch in East Africa expressed a representative view: "Undoubtedly the races of Africa with whom we have come into contact have been so miserably low, intellectually and morally, in the scale of humanity, apparently so dull and unimpressionable, that to persons who take no account of the generating power of the Holy Spirit, it must seem incredible that any of them should become intelligent Christians."[88] At the same time, the new African Christian culture they proposed was not to be modeled on the West, above all not on urban Europe's sinkholes of sin. The schools they were quick to establish had as didactic objectives, in the first instance, the creation of self-reliant Christian communities insulated from rather than incorporated into the new society that colonial space began to call forth.[89] Although bourgeois civil society is bound together by the reciprocities of exchange and necessities of cooperation, this "ethical moment" could not produce a sufficiently robust shared moral universe for a self-regulating system to operate. Only the state could discipline and rise above the egoism intrinsic to civil society.[90]

Islam represented the most comprehensive ideological challenge to hegemony available to Africa at the moment of subjugation. In the hands of determined adversaries of colonial rule, it offered a transcendental justification for resistance and a religious imperative for politico-military organization on a scale beyond ethnos and polity as these then existed.[91] The epic sagas of Abd-el-Kader, Al Hadj Umar, the Sudanese Mahdi Muhammad Ahmed, or the Somali "dervish" Muhammad 'Abdille Hassan were well known, and the sepoy mutiny in India in 1857, with its Muslim overtones, was a very recent memory for the British. Given the huge gap between its Bula Matari pretensions and its still frail infrastructure of control, Islam was a mortal danger if not managed with care.

Missionaries had a visceral animosity toward Islam, and they regarded combating its spread as a sacred vocation. Many longed to carry the struggle for African souls onto Islamic terrain. Administrators, however, were prepared to surrender cultural terrain and concede salvation to Islam, provided that political control of the secular realm could be assured. Here the colonial state soon discovered that Islam offered not only perils but also opportunities.

The British, after the searing experience of Khartoum in 1885, gave particular care to religious strategy in building their Sudanese colonial state. The essence of their doctrine of hegemony was a demonological exegesis of the Mahdiyya epoch. Religious charlatans, in this view, had exploited popular animosity to Turko-Egyptian rule and had packaged an appeal to rebellion in the religious motif of heterodox Islam. The British design was to supplant the Mahdiyya in exploiting the anti-Egyptian animus they took to be general in Sudan, while using orthodox Egyptian Islam as an instrument to combat and marginalize Sufi Islam from which the Mahdiyya sprang. Lord Kitchener set the tone in 1899 with his initial religious instructions:

> Be careful to see that religious feelings are not in any way interfered with, and that the Mohammedan religion is respected. At the same time, Fikis teaching different Tariks [Sufi orders] . . . should not be allowed to resume their former trade. In old days, these Fikis, who lived on the superstitious ignorance of the people, were one of the curses of the Sudan, and were responsible in a great measure for the rebellion. . . . Mosques in the principal towns will be rebuilt; but private mosques, takias, zawiyas, Sheikhs' tombs & c., cannot be allowed to be re-established, as they generally formed centres of unorthodox fanaticism.[92]

Scarce public revenues (in significant part drawn from the Egyptian budget) were indeed devoted to mosque construction. Decorations were showered on loyal Muslim leaders, especially (in the first years) those associated with Khatmiyya.[93] The British, by 1914, were able to present themselves as veritable defenders of the faith. In a ringing appeal for Sudanese support against the perfidious Turks as World War I broke out, Governor Wingate told the assembled ulama: "Not content with the overthrow of Sultan Abdul Hamid . . . unrestrained by the loss, through their mismanagement and maladministration, of the European and other former provinces of their Empire, these men [the Ottoman rulers]—this syndicate of Jews, financiers, and low-born intriguers—like broken gamblers . . . have gone to war with the one Power who has ever been a true and sympathetic friend to the Moslems and to Islam."[94] The British administration also strongly opposed pressures to allow Christian missions to operate in northern Sudan, and it was initially even reticent about their deployment in the south. In northern Nigeria, Islam swiftly became a bulwark of colonial hegemony through a combination of rigorous exclusion of Christian missions from Muslim areas and the Lugardian feat of bringing the "commanders of the faithful," the emirs of the Hausa-Fulani states, into his system of rule after their military defeat.

The French encounter with Islam produced contradictory and fluctuating tactics. The first instinctual reaction, in Algeria, was resolute hostility; Bugeaud believed that the Arab population should eventually be assimilated, and Cardinal Charles Lavigerie initially felt that a Christian Algeria was possible (although settlers strongly opposed any policy that might lead to equal treatment for Algerians). Subsequently, in West Africa, there was a period of Islamophile policies; when Louis Faidherbe initiated interior conquest he firmly believed, on the basis of his Algerian experience, in the possibility of a collaborative relationship with Muslim elites. Paul Marty, the first serious student of West African Islam, wrote critically of what he regarded as the naive excesses of Faidherbe:

> We made abundant use of Moor auxiliaries, and especially of their Tukulor and Wolof pupils and disciples; we carried out a thoroughly Islamophile policy. Even yesterday did we not make use in Casamance of the services of Muslim Malinke to administer and to soften up the anarchical and fetichist Diolas. By these methods: by the organization of a more or less Muslim legal system, an Arab and Moor justice; by constructing mosques, by the effect of the theory that, to bring fetichist natives to French civilization, one must pass through the stage of Islamic evolution. Frenchmen of the preceding generation have heavily contributed to the spread in Senegal of the Religion of the Prophet.[95]

As the French resumed their conquest of the Soudan (contemporary Mali) in earnest in the late 1870s, a more hostile attitude toward Islam reappeared. Leaders of the jihad states were among their most tenacious adversaries. The French became aware that, in much of the upper Senegal and Niger regions, only the ruling and mercantile classes were Muslim; the rural hinterland was not. There was a brief spell of relative receptivity to Catholic mission action targeted at these populations, before events in France toward the turn of the century reinforced the anticlerical currents that tended to form part of the "republican" ideology which suffused the administrative cadres.[96]

During this moment of anti-Islamic apprehensions, the French perceived the emergence in Senegal of the new Mouride order, a splinter from Qadiriyya led by Amhadu Bamba, as a subversive threat to the colonial order. In a spectacular gesture, Bamba was deported to Gabon in 1895. After his return in 1902, the swift assemblage of new disciples led to a second relegation, to Mauritania, in 1903. By the time he returned in 1907, French Islamic strategy was shifting toward co-optation. The implicit compact was freedom of action for the Sufi orders that dominated West African Islam in the religious sphere, in return for acceptance of the colonial order. Some leading Muslim clerics, such as Al Hadj Malick Sy, head of Senegalese Tijaniyya, came to view the colonial order as positively beneficial, since it marginalized African political rulers hostile to Maraboutic influence. In his celebrated letter to all Tijanis on 8 September 1912, Sy exhorted his followers to civil obedience:

> Adhere fully to the French government. God—may He be blessed and exalted!—has granted victory, grace and favor particularly to the French. He has chosen them to protect our persons and our goods. That is why we must live in perfect harmony with them. Let them hear nothing concerning us what would not have them rejoice.
>
> Before their arrival here, in effect, we lived on a footing of captivity, of murders and of pillages. . . . Had they not come we would still be in such a condition. . . . Do not consider yourselves unfortunate in fulfilling the obligations they have established. For on sound reflection, in fact, it is clear that this is a contribution which they ask of you, and not a burden they impose upon you.[97]

There were mutual benefits to this compact. In Senegal, Mali, and Niger in particular, probably only a minority of the population was Muslim at the moment of colonial penetration; by the end of the colonial era, the overwhelming majority was. For the colonial state, an injunction such as that of Malick Sy was worth many battalions of tirailleurs sénégalais.

The settled view by the eve of World War I held that much of Islam could be minimally compatible with, and maximally even actively supportive of, colonial hegemony. In Algeria, Islam was at least neutralized as a hostile force. In Tunisia and Morocco, the preservation of the precolonial states as the apparatus for French rule had as corollary a protected status for Islam. For West Africa, the French concluded that Islam was syncretic and largely malleable to colonial purposes, provided only it were kept isolated from Middle Eastern Islamic currents held to be "fanatic" or "xenophobic," terms that appear frequently in the discourse of the colonial state to refer to the protonationalist implications of Islam. Perceived as the most dangerous carrier of a Middle Eastern version of Islam at this period was Sanusiyya, spreading along the trade routes of the Sahara from its Cyreneica base. In Niger and Chad, active steps were taken to stem its advance.[98]

Where Islam was of recent vintage and lacked the religious infrastructure and theological articulation of high Islam, the colonial state was more disposed to isolate it and block its spread; Uganda, Nyasaland, and the Belgian Congo are cases in point. Especially in the Congo Islam was viewed as a dangerous source of subversion, associated with the Zanzibari mercantile states whose defeat had been so costly in the 1892–1894 "Arab wars."[99]

LAW AS AN INSTRUMENT OF HEGEMONY

From the set of assumptions concerning stateness implanted from the European model in the minds of the agents of state construction, the notion of law as a codification of hegemony sprang naturally. In these early stages, the creation of a legal framework for the institutionalization of domination was a several-pronged offensive. At the highest level, it consisted of the basic public law, promulgated by the metropole, defining the juridical relationship between the colonizing power and the colonial state and prescribing the basic institutional framework within which the state agents operated. In the Belgian instance, this occurred through the 1908 Colonial Charter, elaborated at the moment when the Belgian state took over from King Leopold II as sovereign ruler of the gigantic African domain he had amassed.[100] In the British case, the basic model was the crown colony, developed essentially out of Western Hemisphere experience, whose essence was the delegation of sovereign power to the colonial executive.[101] Even when the protectorate label was retained, as in Uganda, the mode of operation was identical.

In the French instance, the powerful Jacobin, centralizing currents in French state ideology that postulated a *république une et indivisible,* with the empire forming an integral part of a greater France, collided with the practical requirements of the colonial states for a public law of hegemony unencumbered by the constitutional constraints applicable in metropolitan France or even the old colonies. Thus, a Colonial Ministry was created only in 1894;[102] as late as 1910, imperial spokesman Jules Harmand still needed to remind his compatriots that a clear distinction was indispensable between overseas domains peopled by settlers (coastal Algeria) and those "populated by natives subjugated by force." For the latter, an imperial framework should give the colonial administration "the greatest possible degree of administrative, economic and financial independence compatible with political dependence."[103] The basic juridical framework for what Suret-Canale termed "pure colonial despotism" was created by the 14 July 1865 *Sénatus-consulte,* which stipulated that new colonies "will be regulated by decree of the Emperor, until a statute for them will be defined by a *Sénatus-consulte.*" In fact, none was ever adopted, and the Third Republic maintained this framework.[104] Accordingly, metropolitan law did not apply overseas unless explicitly extended by presidential decree. Colonial law issued from the president, and in wide areas was in practice exercised by ordinances promulgated by the governors-general.

Within this overarching framework of colonial public law, one may identify three legal sectors. A criminal and civil code drawn largely from metropolitan law governed relationships among Europeans and between Europeans and Africans. The code was clearly an arm of the overall relationship of dominance between European and African, as the European in most instances held all the trump cards through superior access to and familiarity with the legal framework. This assured the physical security of the Europeans clustered around the institutions of colonial hegemony and provided the guarantees of property and contract covering their economic activity.

A second sphere was wholly African and was classified by the colonial state as "customary law." So long as a given conflict concerned only African subjects, the colonial state was content to permit its regulation according to existing societal norms, although the proviso was usually added that these could not be "repugnant to civilized standards," as determined by the colonial state. An unstated but equally important premise was that customary jurisprudence not be subversive of colonial authority. Indigenous precepts of conflict regulation—or *shari'a* in Islamic zones—became instruments of colonial state hegemony through the state's assertion of a supervisory power over African jurisdictions, and the authority vested in its local agents to interpret and apply customary law. In the early years of building Bula Matari, this was a potent weapon. District officers found little difficulty in attracting as many disputes as they wished to resolve; those who believed themselves unlikely to prevail through existing African juridical institutions, however constituted, viewed the district officer as an alternative opportunity for litigative action. Within the limits set by their own capacity to cope with a flood of cases, and in their desire to uphold the authority of the African chiefs they had invested, the territorial agents of the colonial state had an interest in using their insertion into the fabric of local dispute resolution as one more wedge for rendering hegemony operational.

Nonetheless, the early converts of the mission stations were a small but critical social group whose interests were tied to the colonial state, and who were often willing collaborators in its construction. Particularly for those of low traditional status, absorption into the new order provided an opening for social ascension and status reversal not otherwise available. Whether directly as interpreters, messengers, clerks, and occasionally even "chiefs," or indirectly as catechists and auxiliary mission personnel, this emergent social category largely identified its own future with the colonial order during the construction phase. Its backing and intermediation played no small part in making the construction of hegemony possible.

In the process of appropriating customary jurisprudence, the agents of the colonial state transformed it in subtle ways into another weapon of domination. The participation of the colonial state in authoritative interpretation of African legal concepts, argues Martin Chanock in a seminal study, "changed the nature and use of custom. It could no longer be primarily a political resource in a continued re-negotiation of status and access to resources. . . . Custom became a resource of the instruments of government, rather than a resource of the people."[105]

Between these two dimensions of colonial law as a state-building weapon was a crucial third dimension of simply arbitrary authority vested in the lowest echelons of European-staffed territorial administration. The local commandant in this period, as Fuglestad puts the matter, was "local chief administrative officer (in the sense that he could interpret local customary law as he wished), judge, police chief, military commander, prison superintendant, tax-collector, chief medical officer. . . ."[106] Emblematic of the vast reservoir of arbitrary authority in the hands of the local European administrator was the French *indigénat* code.

This code originated in Algeria as a comprehensive inventory of acts by Muslim subjects whom the local administrative officer was empowered summarily to punish. In 1893 an analogous decree extended the system to French West African colonies, and subsequently elsewhere. In its various permutations, the list of proscribed behavior was sometimes of astonishing length—more than fifty items, in one version. These included such offenses as "refusal to furnish information of public interest" and "refusal or ill will in the execution of labor or support required by written or verbal requisition in cases concerning order, security or public authority." But the key, *passe-partout* provision authorized summary punishment (brief imprisonment or fine) for "any act, statement, speech, or chant uttered in public, disrespectful towards a European agent or representative of the state, or of a nature to undermine respect owing to French authority or its European representatives, or to injure the exercise of this authority or to provoke disorder or indiscipline."[107] In practice, during the construction phase, all local territorial agents of colonial states exercised essentially unrestricted arbitrary authority over their African subjects, circumscribed only by their practical capacity to enforce it.

At the same time, the groundwork for a more sophisticated framework of domination was being laid. In the French case, there was an apostolic succession of crucial imperial proconsuls, from Bugeaud, to Faidherbe, to Gallieni, to Lyautey; each began his career under the tutelage and influence of his predecessor in a chain of colonial conceptualization of hegemony.[108] Cumulatively, a vast distance separates the brutal *razzia* style of Bugeaud in Algeria and the sophisticated colonial diplomacy of Lyautey in Morocco, with Faidherbe in Senegal and Gallieni in Madagascar falling in between. Maurice Delafosse and Paul Marty in AOF ushered in a new school of colonial sociology, located within the logic of hegemony but grounded in a far more subtle grasp of the inner workings of the subjugated societies.[109] In the Belgian Congo, missionaries and administrators contributed major ethnographic works; the colonial state instructed its agents systematically to assemble basic information concerning the societies under its rule.[110] In the British instance, proconsuls like Lord Lugard and Sir Harry Johnston were shrewd observers of the societies they ruled, and their perspectives were influential in the construction of hegemonic doctrines.[111] Some Africans closely associated with the colonial state construction, such as Samuel Johnson, the Nigerian Anglican cleric, or Sir Apolo Kagwa, the great Protestant *katikiro* (prime minister) of Buganda, were also important contributors.[112]

SECURITY

Hegemony was in these years of construction by far the most critical imperative in state reason, along with the requirement for generating resources to finance it; the imperatives of security, autonomy, and legitimacy require briefer notice at this stage. The internal dimension of security was considered in our discussion of the military arm of the hegemonical apparatus. There was, in addition, an external dimension. Although the basic grid of partition was in place by 1900, it was far from stable. Italy and Germany—latecomers to the partition—were still seeking to enlarge their share as World War I approached. The occupation of Morocco and Libya in 1911 and 1912 had ripple effects elsewhere. Italian southward expansion into the Sahara, for example, triggered a French countermove to occupy the Tibesti region, then attached to Niger. As the Niger authorities were required to supply the military expedition and garrison through local forced requisitions of camels and grain, the precarious equilibrium of newly won hegemony in the Niger valley was placed at risk.[113] The substantial Italian population in Tunisia gave rise to French nervousness about Italian claims. The sizable territorial satisfaction Germany demanded as the ransom for acquiescence in French occupation of Morocco not only unsettled AEF but also led Belgium to fear that Germany coveted its colonial realm. Until the outbreak of World War I, however, this external security concern operated mainly at the level of European diplomacy. It did not greatly affect the force structure of the colonial state, which remained firmly focused on its potential internal challengers.

AUTONOMY AND ITS LIMITS

Autonomy, like security, has both an internal and an external face. As I suggested in chapter 2, a state is engaged in ongoing struggle with civil society to preserve the capacity for autonomous exercise of state reason; civil society seeks to make the state a passive register of its preferences. In the colonial state of the construction phase, civil society—as this notion was defined—was limited to European settler communities, where these existed, and elsewhere to the small nonofficial communities of traders, missionaries, and corporate agents, as well as the administrative cadres themselves. In Freetown and the four old communes of Senegal, the Creoles and *originaires* had a degree of empowerment won in an earlier phase of colonial evolution. But generally speaking the construction of hegemony had produced comprehensive subjugation of African society. The ever-present threat of revolt did impose some indirect limits on the internal autonomy of the colonial state. Whereas in Egypt, Tunisia, and Morocco the existing state infrastructure was retained, the clientelistic ties with local populations that then subsisted produced a distinctive type of colonial polity–subject society relationship, which imposed some limits on state autonomy.[114] In Mauritius, the established planter community, of French origin, was assertive and vocal, gingerly treated by the British administration.[115] But these were the exceptions, not the rule.

The missions and mercantile agents had some access to the colonial state but were in no position to dictate its policy. State agents might vary in their individual sympathies with the objectives of the evangelical and commercial sectors; this was particularly marked in the French case with regard to the missions, which evoked bitter partisan struggles in France between confessional and anticlerical laic orientations. State agents had to recognize that the representatives of European trading houses (though not the purely local operatives) might have influence in metropolitan parliaments or ministries. But they all perceived that the interests of the colonial state and those of merchants or missionaries were not identical. In my judgment, the degree of state autonomy with respect to the nonofficial European sector was substantial.

Especially in West Africa, as Anne Phillips argues, the demands of the most aggressive agents of capital ran up against the security requirements of the colonial state. Clearing land rights for large plantation concessions and guaranteeing a labor supply would have threatened a still tenuous hegemony; colonial state agents were not disposed by mentality or interest to accommodate such requests. So long as the peasant economy produced enough revenue to support the colonial state, there was insufficient incentive to risk public order by catering to the interests of capital, which ultimately had little leverage over colonial officialdom.[116]

Settlers, where numerous, were a different matter. They carried the perquisites and expectations of citizenship with them and believed that the basic purpose of the colonial state was to assure conditions for their prosperity. To an important degree, colonial state agents shared this perception; Sir Charles Eliot, newly appointed commissioner for Kenya, remarked on his arrival in 1901 that, like New Zealand, his territory was "a white man's country, in which native questions present but little interest."[117] The extravagance of settler demands for land and labor, however, inevitably raised conflicts with the state interest in order and security. But they had already won strong influence in the Kenya Legislative Council, were clamoring for self-rule and annulment of the British South Africa Company charter in Southern Rhodesia, and received a dominion status tantamount to independence in 1910 in South Africa. In this last instance, the colonial state established its hegemony over the Afrikaner republics of the Transvaal and the Orange Free State in the Boer War of 1899 to 1902, Africa's greatest colonial war (nearly half a million British troops, a cost of 222 million pounds, 224,000 Afrikaners and Africans herded into concentration camps, with at least forty-one thousand fatalities. It then transferred its powers to the settled white population (English and Afrikaner) on a basis constitutionally excluding the majority of the population. In this act of abdication, which took more than eight decades to undo, the colonial state and British politicians were intoxicated by their master stroke of reconciling the two components of the white community. "The few lonely voices raised against the dangers of a constitution which excluded the vast majority of the population from the political community," writes Shula Marks, "were ignored in the atmosphere of mutual congratulation."[118]

In Algeria, settlers and those assimilated to them (the Jewish, Maltese, and other Mediterranean populations) were a factor as early as the late 1830s. The basic framework for their representation was created in 1900 in an assembly designated the Délégations Financières. Although this body included twenty-one Algerian delegates, it was dominated by the settler community, who held forty-eight seats. Its formal charge was review of the budget, but in practice its voice extended beyond this.[119] With the birth of the Third Republic, they had (initially) six seats in the National Assembly as well, where through their alliances with right-wing political formations they could be certain that their voice was heard. Until 1870 the colonial state was dominated by the Armée d'Afrique, with which the settler community was locked in unremitting hostility and combat.

A particular spin to the settler political role in Algeria (and, to a lesser extent, Tunisia) was the non-French derivation of the majority, which produced a struggle within the struggle. Settlers sought dominance over the colonial state institutions, and French *pieds noirs* strove to assert a privileged status within the community classified as European (which came to include the Jews, long resident in Algeria, who were accorded collective naturalization by the Crémieux decree of 1870). "Assimilation," in Algeria, essentially referred in practice to the absorption of all non-Muslims into a Franco-Algerian settler identity, largely achieved by the interwar period. From 1889 on, all children born of European parents were automatically French citizens.[120]

Settlers, where they were dominant, therefore imposed major limits to the internal autonomy of the colonial state. In two special cases, Freetown and the four old communes of Senegal, the Bula Matari form of colonial state ensuing from the partition faced disconcerting limits on its autonomy by local African communities who had acquired political rights and a degree of representative government in the earlier era of informal empire. The town councils had important prerogatives in the taxation and budget fields; the Creole and originaire communities had acquired a keen awareness of their political rights, becoming civil societies in the full sense of the term. Their status in the new legal field created by the colonial polity could not easily be overriden in the more arbitrary hegemony characteristic of post-1875 state construction. As dominion spread inland the colonizer developed sharp legal distinctions between new territories, to which those political rights exercised in the old zones did not apply, and the old colonies.

Metropolitan personnel displaced the Africans once numerous in the local executive ranks, especially in Sierra Leone.[121] In Senegal, originaires succeeded in blocking moves in the early years of the century to remove their citizenship. Their status gave them some immunity from the arbitrary powers of French administrators even outside the communes; some were a constant irritant to the administration by serving as public scribes for aggrieved colonial subjects and assiduous cataloguers of administrative abuses. Their special standing included a parliamentary seat (permanent during the Third Republic), held on occasion by mulattoes from 1848 on, then won for the first time by an African, Blaise

Diagne, in 1914.[122] Although the Sierra Leone and Senegal colonial states made determined efforts to free themselves from the irritating constraints imposed on their internal autonomy by these politicized and partially empowered communities, Creoles and originaires could never be fully excluded from the political arena.

Externally, the autonomy imperative played itself out in the defining of the colonial state's relationship with the metropolitan state, the repository of sovereignty. Once conquest was assured, the colonial state acquired a distinctive personality, even where, as in France, Portugal, or to some extent Italy, the colonial domains were perceived as a direct extension of the home state. In the British case, two centuries of colonial public law clearly established the overseas territories as separate jurisdictional fields; only Ireland was an ambiguous case. For Belgium too the notion of constitutional separation was absolute.

For France, the occupation of Algiers precipitated an 1833 decree sharpening the distinction between the old slave-plantation colonies—Martinique, Guadaloupe, Guyana, and Reunion, with a more assimilated relationship—and Algeria and Senegal. The assimilationist themes deeply embedded in French political culture and state ideology emerged periodically—during the revolution, in 1848, during the early years of the Third and Fourth Republics—but these never had a compelling attraction for the agents of colonial state construction, confronted with the task of dominating the alien other. Even those, such as Marshall Bugeaud in Algeria, who made occasional assimilative statements, regarded this project as so far in the future that it had no practical application. For the settlers, the assimilation slogan at this juncture essentially meant full citizenship rights for themselves, the elimination of the colonial state as a military persona through full departmentalization of the settled territories, and unrestricted rights over Algerian land and indigenous populations, who were destined for some combination of absorption, disappearance, or *refoulement* to the desert fringes.[123]

As a superstructure of rule took form in the colonial territories, by natural processes it acquired a large degree of autonomy from the imperial center. In the British case in particular, this occurred through conscious disposition to trust the judgment of "the man on the spot." Development of telegraphic cables coincided with the implantation of colonial states, so metropolitan capitals were not curtained off by a screen of time. But their information was limited, and dominated by the reporting of the colonial state agents themselves. Once the spurt of conquest had spent itself, diminishing the risk-laden possibilities of conflict with imperial rivals, the interest of metropolitan state and civil society in colonial issues subsided.

Colonial state agents had no doubt that their assessments of state-building requirements were superior to those of the metropolitan ministries that supervised them. For example, the average tenure in office of French colonial ministers during this period was only a year; the governors-general and territorial governors served much longer terms. In practice, the governors had leeway to disregard whatever instructions from Paris they found unwelcome and to screen carefully the information reported, practices copied at the level of the bush administrators.[124] A distinctive official mind took form within the colonial state apparatus, with its own operational code, standing assumptions about subject society, and established routines. Views diverged over particular issues, but most united around the principle of autonomy for the colonial state, an instinctual aversion to "meddling" by the imperial capital.

The surest path to enhanced autonomy was avoidance of situations requiring metropolitan intervention. These were most likely to occur in the security and revenue fields. Once hegemony was established, the colonial state ran the risk of inviting intensified metropolitan scrutiny and oversight if its action provoked an uprising of sufficient visibility to attract metropolitan attention, especially if there were any prospect that it could not be repressed without resources from the imperial capital. As the principle of financial self-sufficiency became set as a cornerstone of the colonial system, budgetary deficits were also an invitation to intervention. Not only did the supervising ministry become involved, but in Britain, France, and Belgium, where parliamentary control of budgets was important, the actions of the colonial state became subject to a more public scrutiny.

Beyond these conjunctural constraints on its external autonomy, the colonial state was of course circumscribed by its fundamental legal status as appendage of an imperial system. Above all, sovereignty lay with the colonizing center. The top layer of colonial state officials were appointed by the colonial ministries and were subject to removal. Occasional visiting missions from the metropole played some censorial role. And apart from the private motivations that at times influenced colonial agents, most regarded themselves as servants of an imperial project, participants in a mission whose ultimate aim was the enhancement of the national state, as they interpreted its interests.

LEGITIMATING THE COLONIAL STATE

The impact of the legitimation imperative on colonial state reason, in its construction phase, was modest, and primarily directed toward a metropolitan audience. Hegemony was in places initially won by guile and diplomacy, but force was everywhere in the background. The powers of self-deception of imperial agents were not sufficient to persuade them that subjugation came because of any African conviction that the colonizer was intrinsically superior. And the wisdom of colonial expansion was debated in Europe, where it could have been stopped in its tracks. The battle for legitimation took place in the conquest stage, and it required persuasion of ministries, parliaments, and publics that African colonial expansion was advantageous.

The debate really began in the 1830s in France, over the issue of retention of the Algerian footholds. Some strategic opinion held that too great a diversion of military resources from the European front was required, an argument that reappeared in the first phase of the partition. Dominant economist opinion was deeply skeptical about the feasibility of the agrarian cornucopia of tropical and temperate produce, the old Roman granary reborn that annexationists promised; Algerian populations could not be compelled to produce these crops, and slave importation was no longer permissible.[125] Not until the designation of Bugeaud as governor with a full conquest mandate in 1840 was this debate resolved; Algeria had acquired prescriptive legitimation as colony through the irreversibility of his savage and costly actions, but salutary inferences were drawn as to tolerable expense levels.

The pact of legitimation basically secured by 1900 within the colonizing states was grounded in the array of arguments for conquest summarized earlier in this chapter. The calculus of political and economic advantage set against costs and risks was more finely computed at the level of state reason than within civil society. During the period in the 1880s and 1890s when the debate was still animated, opposition to colonial conquest was never strong enough to arrest its gathering momentum on the ground. It subsided partly because African empire was a fait accompli. Also, active agitation by imperial enthusiasts, within and without the state apparatus, had greatly strengthened the annexationist camp; of such groups, the *parti colonial* in France was a prototype. The risks and costs of colonial expansion were now sunk. But the ransom for the pact of legitimation in the colonizing state was the bedrock principle of no charges to the metropolitan budget for managing the colonial states. On this understanding, former adversaries could rest assured that, even if their skepticism concerning prospective benefits were proven correct, the disappointment would be cost-free.

The issue of slavery was a lynchpin of legitimation as well. Although state treasuries and private purses alike had drawn rich dividends from slavery in preceding centuries, its moral repugnance was now firmly rooted in the public mind. Forms of domestic slavery were widespread in Africa, and following the end of the Atlantic slave trade they probably assumed greater importance in some parts of West Africa.[126] Slave-trading systems centered in Zanzibar and Khartoum rapidly expanded. These phenomena permitted clothing colonial conquest in the legitimating garb of an abolitionist crusade. Leopold II was perhaps the most adroit in using this stratagem, summoning an international conference to Brussels in 1889 and 1890 to beckon "Christian Europe to undertake a great modern crusade against the Arab slave-trade in Africa."[127] The very success of the antislavery gambit as a mechanism of legitimation impaled the colonial state on the horns of an excruciating dilemma, conflicting as it did with the accumulation and revenue imperatives—a point to which I shall return shortly.

With respect to subject society in Africa, the colonial state rested mainly on its overwhelming conviction that those under its yoke would in the fullness of time come to recognize and appreciate the benefits of its rule. Tangible immediate legitimation in African eyes was not to be expected in the disarray that would accompany the shock of conquest. But colonial agents did believe that the imposition of an enforced peace and the vivifying impact of expanded trade would of themselves bring greater prosperity in a near future. Legitimation, for Bula Matari in the early years, was accomplished in the field by self-assertion and self-celebration. For the moment, this was more than sufficient. By the end of the construction phase, African societies had for the most part reluctantly acquiesced in colonial rule. When World War I loomed, declarations of loyalty attended their public expressions of support; the seeming acknowledgment by most colonial subjects of the colonizer's right to rule greatly eased the cost of hegemony. At this point, Bula Matari could be said to enjoy a tacit legitimacy among the bulk of the subjugated.

THE REVENUE IMPERATIVE

Meeting the revenue imperative, however, posed excruciating difficulties for the colonial state, with only few exceptions. South Africa already had an economy easily capable of supporting its state apparatus. Although in Egypt fiscal crisis and a debt of 100 million Egyptian pounds set in motion the forces leading to British occupation in 1882, the territory had well-established taxation machinery, long-existing habits of high extraction from the peasantry, and diverse proceeds from port fees, the Suez Canal, and state monopolies, which permitted a rapid restoration of its balances without any far-reaching reorganization of society or the economy.[128] Tunisia also had an adequate fiscal base, which with modest administrative reforms could be made to support both the extant Tunisian and the new French bureaucratic layers; indeed, taxation levels were four times those in France. The French found, in the words of one official, "all the elements of a complete, solid and durable administration" with which to strengthen its collection.[129]

But these circumstances were the exception. So too were the handful of situations where one colonial state could be compelled to help cover the deficits of another. The most noteworthy was the Sudan, where the serviceable fiction of the condominium permitted Britain not only to rely on Egyptian army units for security services but also to force Egypt to cover its budget deficit and capital outlays, up to 1912. This considerably eased the task management of the hegemony imperative, permitting application of a colonial fiscal doctrine from India that "low taxation" of newly incorporated subjects (relative to what they were previously paying) made domination more tolerable. The Sudan's revenue in 1900 was a mere 126,569 Egyptian pounds; by 1923 it had reached 3,766,133 Egyptian pounds, and the levy on the Egyptian budget was no longer necessary (or for that matter possible, as Egypt was nominally independent).[130] The Cape budget was nicked for small sums to augment the minuscule revenues of Basutoland in the years before creation of the Union in 1910. The grouping of the West and Equatorial African territories under French rule was partly motivated by the desire to fund a portion of basic administrative costs from the then more prosperous coastal colonies. But for the most part each territory was on its own.

The self-sufficiency rule thus came into rigorous play, most completely with the British and the Belgians, for whom the juridical separation of the overseas territories was most complete. The 1900 French law stipulating self-financing for the colonies did not apply to Algeria, and in practice it could not at the time be enforced for AEF. Military costs in theory fell on the metropolitan treasury, although repression of local uprisings was frequently the financial as well as political responsibility of territorial administrations.

The small coastal establishments had earlier subsisted on taxation of trade; in 1875 Sierra Leone's customs and other revenues were not much more than 50,000 pounds.[131] But no extensive infrastructure of domination was then required. Nile valley peasantry had endured heavy taxation from time immemorial, as had other settled populations on the Mediterranean rim. Sahel states erected on an Islamic model possessed a fiscal jurisprudence. More widely, larger African states drew their resources from levies on long-distance trade and tribute, in addition to conjunctural booty and predation.[132] In most places, however, there was no established revenue base to support the construction of Bula Matari.

The clusters of European merchants or—where present—settlers were not a viable fiscal source. The trading communities on the West African coast were long accustomed to battling the custodians of colonial footholds against any direct taxation; the chronicles of the nineteenth-century councils in Senegal and Sierra Leone bear witness to the losing struggle to generate revenue from this source. Traders connected to mercantile houses based in Europe had the means to carry their combat back to home territory. In Egypt, the swelling expatriate commercial community benefited from the comprehensive array of judicial and fiscal privileges embodied in the capitulation treaties, which the British could not repeal. Settlers were recipients of state-enforced subsidization, by way of land and stock confiscations and coerced labor supply, rather than suppliers of the treasury.

In a word, all fiscal trails led to the African subject. In one way or another the newly wrested hegemony had to be transformed into a self-sustaining resource flow for the colonial state. With a rural economy whose exchange relationships were limited and usually not monetized, as they lacked a capital stock, fiscal capture of subjects was much more difficult than military defeat. The heart of the revenue dilemma boiled down to converting the labor—the sole extractable resource—of state subjects into the ways and means of meeting state subsistence needs.

This alchemy proceeded in several ways. The most obvious was the imposition of a head tax, which occurred almost everywhere as soon as hegemony was established. The main exceptions were the Gold Coast and southern Nigeria, where anticipated African hostility was especially strong, where the cautionary experience of the Sierra Leone hut-tax war of 1898 was a deterrent, and where precocious development of palm products and cocoa as taxable exports provided an alternative fiscal base. As the following tables demonstrate, in most colonial territories the bulk of the revenue came from this tax during the construction phase.

Although payment in kind was initially permitted, within a few years colonial states required the tax to be met in cash. The capitation levy was much more than a cash-flow source for the colonial administration; it was a multipronged instrument for forcing African labor into channels that would ultimately produce state revenue. The village economy was coerced into restructuring its deployment of labor into export-crop production, whose output was taxable as export levies. And young males were

Table 4-1. Ivory Coast Budgets, 1903–1908 (Francs)

Year	Budget	Customs[a]	AOF	Head Tax	Licenses
1903	3,125,250	1,917,193		546,106	106,585
1904	3,943,442	2,484,691		776,993	283,290
1905	2,994,946		1,380,000	910,778	280,183
1906	3,277,184		1,480,000	1,183,204	323,322
1907	3,636,393		1,320,000	1,438,511	441,229
1908	4,321,374		1,250,000	1,713,497	459,229

Source: Timothy C. Weiskel, *French Colonial Rule and the Baule Peoples: Resistance and Collaboration, 1880–1911* (Oxford: Clarendon Press, 1980), 173, from official figures.
a. From 1905, customs revenues, previously collected at the territory level, were transferred to AOF.

often compelled to seek wage employment in European enterprises to acquit their fiscal obligations.

The capitation tax was thus the mortar with which, block by block, the colonial state was built. Through it subjects became units of production in an economy slowly penetrated by capitalist forms—in the revealing census categorization of the Belgian Congo, *hommes adultes valides*. Although one may doubt claims that colonial state agents considered themselves builders of "capitalism,"[133] as architects of empire they were convinced that the natural economy they encountered had to be restructured into a prolongation of the imperial system; in this sense reason of colonial state and the functional requisites of capitalism converged. In the Althusserian discourse of Rey, the colonial administration "had in effect to accomplish a social and economic revolution (replacing the lineage mode of production by a capitalist mode of production) by a *political* action in the name of an *ideology* which tells them that the latter system . . . is better than the former: all empirical perception is thus assimilated with difficulty because the administrator, unlike the capitalist or the lineage head, . . . cannot accept empirical knowledge which contradicts this ideology."[134] Governor Angoulvant of the Ivory Coast expressed the settled view on the crucial role of the head tax as a weapon of both economic reordering and revenue:

It is an established fact that the tax plays, in all the colonies, at once a productive and morally developmental role. The native, who, before our rule had no needs which could not find immediate satisfaction, almost without effort, in the resources at hand which nature

Table 4-2.   Congo Free State Revenue, 1906 (Belgian Francs)

Category	Amount
Domain produce (ivory and rubber), taxes in kind	16,100,000
Customs	6,350,000
Transport and other services	6,400,000
Stock income	5,000,000
Direct and personal taxes (on Europeans)	600,000
Miscellaneous	1,425,000
Total	35,875,000

Source: L. H. Gann and Peter Duignan, *The Rulers of Belgian Africa, 1884–1914* (Princeton: Princeton University Press, 1979), 92.

offered him, *must* be brought to produce ... there is no doubt ... that the obligation for the native to pay a higher capitation tax would be extremely efficient, the tax being, I repeat, in the present state of native mentality, the best stimulant to indigenous energy.[135]

The necessity to collect a tax from all households linked the hegemony and revenue imperatives through the intermediary system. Only an apparatus reaching down to the village could assure a mechanism of extraction. The hierarchy of African chiefs could not be expected to carry out these onerous obligations without both the coercive support of the state and a share of the rewards. Police operations and punitive expeditions were widely required to establish this tax; Governor Frederic Cardew in effect spoke for his counterparts across the continent in pleading with the Colonial Office in 1897 for authorization to expand his Frontier Police in anticipation of the imposition of a hut tax: without it, "the Government will not be in the commanding positions which is so necessary in order to fully collect the revenue. ... I do not anticipate there will be any active opposition ... but unless there is a good show of force ... the natives may passively resist the authorities collecting the tax, and do all in their power to evade it."[136]

The chiefs were generally given a commission on the taxes collected, which doubtless often exceeded state demands. Governor-General William Ponty, in a 1913 memorandum calling for more direct French administrative involvement, no doubt had ample cause for his excoriation of the canton chiefs serving the colonial state: "My long familiarity with French West Africa and the populations who inhabit it have allowed me to verify absolutely that the native intermediaries between the taxpayers and the fisc, that is between those who pay and the administrators of the *cercles* ... are nothing but parasites living off the population,

Table 4-3. Algerian Department Revenue, 1899 (Francs)

Department	Arab Head Tax	Total Receipts
Algiers	1,815,225	3,726,123
Oran	1,315,884	3,349,764
Constantine	2,598,272	5,419,322
Total	5,729,381	12,495,209

Source: Algérie, Conseil Supérieur de Gouvernement, *Procès-Verbaux des Délibérations et Exposé de la Situation Générale de l'Algérie* (Algiers: Imprimeur du Gouvernement Général, 1901), 12–13.

without any profit to us. . . . So many intermediaries, so many thieves."[137] Material incentives by no means sufficed to ensure vigorous tax collection by the chiefs. Revocations, imprisonment, and public whippings of chiefs, especially local, were frequent in the early period for derelict performance in fulfilling tax and labor demands of the administration. The chiefs were ordered to collect taxes; the means used were up to them, so long as the revenue was delivered.[138]

By an imposing demonstration of extractive capacities, Bula Matari rapidly increased the revenue flow in the first decade of the century. By the time of World War I, with the head tax leading the way, most colonial territories had achieved a basic equilibrium between the requirements of hegemony and revenue. In the lower Casamance in Senegal—a region of sustained resistance whose occupation was achieved only at the close of the construction era—the administration calculated that about 46 percent of the cash income of the two hundred thousand Casamance villagers entered the state coffers.[139] The laconic observation of Fuglestad with respect to Niger on the eve of World War I is of much broader application: "The fact that the French were able to squeeze more than a million francs out of the impoverished and hunger-stricken peoples of Niger can only be described as a major performance."[140]

The head tax was far from the only means of metamorphosing African labor into state resource. However impressive fiscal extraction from the African natural economy might be, its absolute yield was modest, and far from sufficient to support even the skeletal apparatus of governance the colonial state put into place. The supplies of the colonial garrisons, many of which were distant from the river or embryonic rail systems, required haulage. Pack animals were available from the Mediterranean to the Sahel and in southern Africa; everywhere between, human portage was necessary. Even when porters were given nominal payment—far from a universal practice—they could only be acquired by conscription. The

Table 4-4.   Metropolitan Nonmilitary Subsidies to French Colonies,
1900–1906 (Francs)

Colony	1900	1903	1906
Martinique	833,685	499,000	390,000
Guadaloupe	1,010,670	700,000	590,000
Reunion	774,454	280,000	180,000
Guyana	400,000	135,000	0
Senegal	6,580	0	0
St. P./Miquelon	95,347	78,000	80,000
Mayotte	34,083	19,000	10,000
Tahiti	314,016	199,000	169,000
New Caledonia	710,985	499,000	469,000
Fr. India	175,235	138,000	75,000
Madagascar	2,070,832	not available	not available
Fr. Somaliland	300,000	200,000	180,000
Congo	500,000	700,000	665,000
Totals	7,225,890	3,447,000	2,808,000

Source: France, Chambre des Députés, *Documents Parlementaires,* Sess. ordinaire,
1906, 1490.

French Congo in 1912 required a hundred and forty thousand man-days
of porterage, a voracious cavalry that few adult males could escape.[141]
Until completion in 1898 of the rail link between the port of Matadi
around the lower Congo River rapids to Kinshasa (then Leopoldville) at
the head of the upper-river navigation system, some fifty thousand porters were required to carry on their heads all supplies required for the
vast Congo Free State interior, more than two hundred miles of rugged
terrain.[142] Lonsdale estimates that a hundred thousand porters were
used along the communications routes in Tanganyika around the turn of
the century.[143] Rubber exports in Guinea kept between forty thousand
and fifty thousand porters on the road ten hours per day with head loads
of twenty-eight kilograms for half a franc per day and a small ration.[144]

The capacity to produce porters was defined as the very essence of
sound administration; the governor of Senegal, then Angoulvant, commented in 1916 on the exemplary performance of the Sine-Saloum *cercle*
in meeting the porterage demands of a touring geologic mission:

> The sole *cercle* where Mr. Hubert encountered no obstacle, where the
> recruitment and feeding of his porters took place without requiring
> his personal intervention, where the village chiefs furnished the di-
> rections and guides which were necessary, was Sine-Saloum. Yet this
> *cercle* is inhabited by the same races as the neighboring jurisdic-

Table 4-5.   AOF Revenue, 1905–1912 (Francs)

Year	Ordinary Revenue	Customs
1905	15,421,825	13,595,595
1908	17,073,802	14,979,955
1911	26,986,759	23,940,241
1912	29,164,440	22,526,382

Source: Gouvernement Général de l'Afrique Occidentale Française, *Budget Général Exercice 1914,* 5–6.

tions. If the natives are in hand here whereas they were not in the other stops, this state of affairs can only be attributed to the fact that Sine-Saloum is administered in the real meaning of the word, whereas the other areas are not to a sufficient degree.

The deficiencies of administrative performance in the neighboring districts was revealed when local residents had the impudence to suggest that Hubert could use readily available donkeys for his baggage rather than human beasts of burden.[145]

Road building was another source of labor imposition, although this became much more important in the next period, when motor vehicles appeared. The construction and upkeep of the colonial outposts also used requisitioned labor. Particularly burdensome were the requirements of military expeditions, with their extensive supply trains.

Thus, in diverse fashion the African colonial state in this construction phase devised modalities of extraction that assured its survival needs. The most painless revenue source was customs levied on overseas trade, which usually passed through a single seaport. Overland interterritorial commerce, then as now, was far more difficult to tax, as the French discovered when they tried to impose a series of forlorn and functionless customs posts along the Niger-Nigeria border during this period.[146] But even collectible sea-trade customs were far from sufficient to cover colonial state occupation costs. Few territories yet had significant export crops, nor did their impoverished economies consume many imports, particularly now that the two most lucrative customs sources of an earlier age, guns and alcohol, had fallen from administrative favor.

The basic sustenance for Bula Matari, therefore, came from what amounted to a levy on African labor. In its visible form, this was the head tax, whose collection compelled the subjects to redeploy their labor in ways that would avoid the punitive ire of armed fiscal agents. But in these early years of colonial state construction, a large part of the extrac-

Table 4-6. Revenue Sources by Territory, AOF, 1911 (Francs)

Colony	AOF Subsidy	Head Tax	Total Revenue[a]
Senegal	717,429	4,442,000	8,071,080
Guinea	0	4,901,000	6,192,000
Ivory Coast	2,063,000	2,300,000	5,474,254
Dahomey	1,700,000	1,250,000	3,582,400
Haut-Sénégal-Niger	−500,000	7,167,805	8,325,000
Territoire Militaire du Niger	0	0	1,510,000
Mauritania	921,000	598,000	1,619,200

Sources: France, Chambre des Députés, Sess. ordinaire, 1911, *Rapport fait au nom de la Commission du Budget chargée d'examiner le projet de loi portant fixation du budget général de l'exercice 1912* (Budgets locaux des Colonies, 3ème partie, Afrique Occidentale Française), 67, 69; Gouvernement Général de l'Afrique Occidentale Française, *Budget Général Exercice 1914,* 7.

a. The head tax and total revenue figures are estimates made at the beginning of the year. The head-tax figure for the military territory of Niger is included under Haut-Sénégal-Niger.

tion consisted of invisibles not recorded in government budgets: often unpaid porterage service and corvée labor for clearing roads, building and provisioning the colonial outposts, and supplying military units in transit. The revenues available to the colonial state tended to concentrate in its center; as with many earlier forms of state, the regional apparatus through which rule was extended to the periphery was in large measure expected to live off the land. Yet the tasks that the colonial state in its territorial occupation was summoned to perform went well beyond those of older state forms. The European district officers, and the African chiefs below them, were held accountable for imposing an increasingly comprehensive hegemony, universal tax collection, and initiation of rudimentary communications and other infrastructure. Whatever the personal dispositions of the state agents, the gap between their means and the ends defined for them could be filled only through a tenacious, often ruthless, always improvised assertion of extractive authority. For the subject, the alternatives of flight or rebellion progressively narrowed during this period; the default option was submission to the manifold demands of labor service.

In the French case, the creation of the two sprawling territorial federations of AOF and AEF had important repercussions in the fiscal realm. Customs receipts were vested in the federation, a fact of particular consequence in AOF. The necessity for individual territories to meet their internal administrative costs via the head tax (although there was a rebate from the federation, especially to the poorer hinterland territories) in-

Table 4-7.   Revenue Sources, British Colonies (Pounds)

Colony	Year	Head Tax	Customs
Uganda	1904–05	36,701	8,026
Somaliland	1904–05	0	28,522
Swaziland	1905–06	34,780	5,676
Nyasaland	1915–16	76,679	21,571
Bechuanaland	1903–04	10,566	13,353
Sierra Leone	1905	44,691[a]	143,538
Gold Coast	1910	0	458,722

Sources: Annual Colonial Reports.

a. The Sierra Leone head-tax figure includes trifling amounts for licenses and hawker fees.

creased the pressure for its energetic collection. The drain on the coastal territories with taxable agricultural exports (peanuts in Senegal, rubber in Guinea, palm products in Dahomey) was substantial; Manning argues that more than half the gross national product was siphoned out of Dahomey between 1905 and 1914, when the territory's net payment to the AOF was 23 million francs.[147] Coastal products also had some impact on territorial configurations; when Mauritania was created in 1904 by the tenuous subjugation of the turbulent Moor clans, the sedentary (and thus taxable) Wolof, Tukulor, and Soninke populations on the north bank of the Senegal River were detached from Senegal to provide a fiscal base for this territory. Although Moor desert warriors could be compelled to accept a truce with the colonial state, collection of a capitation tax was impossible.

ACCUMULATION

The final imperative, accumulation, only began to assume importance during the construction phase. Its intimate link with state revenue was of course recognized; the overwhelming predominance of customs and head taxes in sustaining the state made this obvious enough. Customs returns measured trade induced (or forced) into European channels; head taxes could be increased if African agriculture would produce cash crops.

The notion of state-fostered "development," which was to assume prominence in the following phase of the colonial state life cycle, was not yet in evidence. By inertial force, older mercantile notions that regarded enlarging trade as the consuming economic goal continued to hold sway, especially in West Africa. Trade, however, was beneficial only if captured by colonial channels; there was an active effort to supplant African long-distance trade, particularly the trans-Saharan routes.[148]

An axiomatic premise in colonial state reflection on accumulation was the beneficial role of European settlers in regions where climatic conditions favored their installation. Whether by ranching, as in German South West Africa, or large farms, as in the Maghreb, Kenya, and the Rhodesias, European agriculture was commercial, and thus supported an economy that would yield a nurturing flow of revenue through customs and other conduits. On the basis of such reasoning, the official mind found justification for spoliation of African lands and livestock and conscription of plantation labor, even if the support supplied to the settler sector fell short of its insatiable appetite for subsidization.

Promotion of export crops was a way of enhancing revenue, although in only a few places did this occur on any scale during the construction period. Two major successes, however, established a pattern for the future: peanuts in Senegal and cotton in Uganda. Both took place in special circumstances, where the peasant cultivator was directed into these crops by the potent authority exercised through indigenous social hierarchies who shared with the state a hefty proportion of the returns. In the Senegal case, discovery by the Maraboutic class that the humble groundnut was a holy instrument of generating wealth created a moving peanut frontier settled by villages of disciples under religious leadership. For the French, the happy pattern by which peanut exports rose from twenty-five thousand tons in 1885 to 140,000 in 1900 without any grid of state agricultural agents to enforce its cultivation created durable illusions about the ease with which export crops could be imposed.[149] In Uganda, the exceptional authority enjoyed by the *bakungu* chiefs in Buganda, and the landed status vested in them by the 1900 agreement, fostered a cotton-promotion campaign of evangelical force. The value of cotton exports rose from 1,000 pounds in 1905 to 165,000 pounds six years later.[150]

The most important capital expenditure in the colonial sphere was on rail lines. The birth of the African colonial state coincided with a moment in railway history when supply-side reason ran rampant. The imagination of the official mind was fevered with visions inspired by the dramatic impact of such epic lines as the Union Pacific (1872), the Canadian National (1885), and the Trans-Siberian (1891–1893). These examples of wild lands tamed into productive estates engendered a plethora of railway schemes, based on an assumption that running iron tracks across any stretch of territory would fructify impoverished lands and make deserts bloom. The mere whistle of the locomotive would beckon the traffic necessary for amortization of the capital costs. The legends surrounding such colossal railway schemes as Rhodes's Cape-to-Cairo or the Trans-Saharan stoked colonial imaginations in the early years of state construction. Funds for planning the Trans-Saharan were actually appropriated by the French parliament in 1879 but were promptly diverted by military commanders in the field to finance new conquests in the western Sudan.[151]

Within the colonial sphere, the success of the British rail system in India provided a seemingly applicable model. Although the colonial state paid a high ransom for railway construction—free land for the contractors who built and managed the railways, plus state guarantees of 4.5 to 5 percent on their operation—two decades after the first construction in 1852 there was a five-thousand-mile net that functioned in the black.[152]

Some early African railways served areas with a sufficiently commercialized economy to cover their costs without great difficulty: South Africa, Algeria, Egypt. Others were constructed at low cost over flat terrain with few obstacles: Port Sudan–Khartoum, St. Louis–Dakar. The former, built from 1896 to 1899, used the Egyptian Army for its construction and had few capital costs. The latter, whose tracks were laid between 1879 and 1882, benefited from an immediate extension of peanut cultivation along its route to ensure its viability. Mineral exports from Broken Hill and Katanga gave basic revenue to the Rhodesian railway net, which reached Elisabethville (now Lubumbashi) in 1911.

But many rail projects encountered excruciating natural obstacles to their construction, required a risky level of labor conscription, and had doubtful commercial prospects. The Matadi-Leopoldville rail line illustrated well these dilemmas. The security and hegemony imperatives of the Congo Free State made its construction an absolute necessity; in Stanley's lapidary phrase, without it the Congo "is not worth a penny." Available labor in the region was completely mined for porterage; most of the laborers had to be imported from other African territories (and even, briefly, from China and the West Indies). Although the line was only 409 kilometers long, it took eight years and major loans from the Belgian state to build.[153]

Private capital did not share the visions of sugarplums dancing in the official mind at the mere thought of new railways. In some instances the state was compelled to construct the lines itself (as in the Sudan). Elsewhere, private capital was solicited; railway companies were open to persuasion as public contractors for construction and as sellers of management services. But they were adamant in their refusal to risk their capital; guaranteed returns and other inducements were the price of their technical services. For example, in the case of the Compagnie des Chemins de Fer du Congo Supérieur aux Grands Lacs (CFL), the Empain financial group in its dealings with Leopold and the Belgian administration parlayed a modest capital stake of 370 million Belgian francs into a grant of four million hectares of transferable land and mineral rights along the eastern frontier, and a 4 percent guaranteed return on its capital. Empain spun off its highly remunerative land and mineral ventures and took the losses on the rail line, to which, by 1939, the colonial state had paid some 160 million francs in interest guarantees.[154]

The consequence of the railway mirage was a heavy debt burden for the colonial state in its construction years, as it struggled to create a revenue base for itself. For example, 40 percent of the 1912 AOF budget expenditures were devoted to debt repayment, primarily incurred in railway construction.[155]

Egypt probably had a higher degree of public capital investment than any other colonial territory during the state-construction period. The state commitment to accumulation was in this instance not a colonial innovation but a resumption of policies dating from early in the century, initiated especially by Khedives Muhammed Ali and Ismail and energetically pursued until the debt crisis suspended these efforts in the 1870s. The debt impasse overcome by 1889, this foundation of public infrastructure provided a basis for major development of the hydraulic system and an attendant rapid rise in cotton exports (from 12 million Egyptian pounds in 1885 to 36 million in 1910).[156]

But in most of Africa public investment during this period was small, and private capital influx even smaller. Capital was reticent even where, as in the Congo Free State, major mineral deposits were identified early (copper in Katanga, diamonds in Kasai, gold in the far northeast). The most powerful Belgian financial group, the Société Générale de Belgique (SGB), despite the large holdings by the royal family itself, remained deaf to Leopoldian appeals until 1906. By this time Leopold himself was reaping an abundant personal harvest from the Congo Free State, some of which was committed to sumptuary adornment of the Belgian capital.[157] Despite the attractiveness of the Congo evidence, the SGB—like the Empain group with the CFL—drove a hard bargain in return for its first capital commitments. Only South Africa really attracted (mostly British) capital at this juncture; French financiers were supremely skeptical of African opportunities. The most visible French private economic interests in Africa were the Marseilles and Bordeaux trading houses, but although their mercantile presence was ubiquitous, their capital exposure was small and short-term.

Availability of African labor was crucial to the accumulation imperative. Virtually all operations, vegetal and mineral, were labor intensive. Among other issues posed by the labor dilemma was the realization by colonial administrations, particularly in West Africa, that the most readily conscriptable might be persons of servile status. Here the colonial state was entangled in embarrassing contradictions with its discourse of legitimation, which portrayed its occupation as a relentless fight against slavery. In the early stages of construction, a "see no evil" policy was widely followed. The architect of British native policy in the Sudan, Slatin Pasha, warned his subordinates at the beginning of colonial rule that "if in an official document I find again that he calls Sudanese servants 'slaves'—a finger from his right hand will be cut off."[158]

In parts of Senegal, upper Guinea, the French Soudan, and Niger, as well as northern Nigeria, the proportion of slaves in the population was very large—a third or more. The early administrators were well aware that their corvée requisitions would not be met without accepting the provision of conscripts who were in reality slaves. As Roberts observes, "Most local administrators were convinced that the end of slavery would mean economic and political chaos. Ending slavery would change the state's role in reproducing the means and relations of production."[159] In 1895 the prospective governor of Guinea, Penel, declared: "No man of good sense having experience of the land will counsel immediate abolition of slavery. That would provoke a general uprising, in which slaves would participate and which would ruin the colony."[160] Future AOF Governor-General Ponty, then head of Haut-Sénégal-Niger, called for caution in a 1901 circular:

> You are quite aware that we cannot recognize the condition in which people called captives, slaves or non-free are found. If we are in some cases obliged to support this organization so dear to the blacks, we must be consistent with the traditions of republican France, and little by little take measures destined to take this secular sore disappear.
>
> Above all, we must not forget that to act ex-abrupto would suddenly provoke large political disorder. We must thus proceed with prudence but with firmness, without losing sight of the goal we must follow here.[161]

By 1905 the French administration had backed away from its de facto tolerance of domestic slavery, partly finding its hand forced, as happened earlier to the British in the Fulani emirates, by large-scale desertions by captives and others of servile standing. Zanzibar and coastal Kenya were other areas where existing slave-based plantation agriculture was approached with caution by the British. The officials believed, as Frederick Cooper suggests, that "development required that labor be steady, that it be under the direction of a property owner and the supervision of the state, and that laborers be made to learn and internalize new values and attitudes."[162] Thus, a strategy was required that would change the legal status of the cultivating class without endangering the production system on which state revenue flow was based.

Here and there a colonial officer with unusual developmental energies and ambition sought to break out of the narrow constraints of sustaining hegemony. The efforts of Sir Walter Egerton to promote an ambitious (in its day) program of public capital investment in southern Nigeria is a case in point. The relatively buoyant southern Nigerian revenues, even without a head tax, gave him some latitude; budget levels were well above those for the entire AOF in this period, and revenues increased from 535,902 pounds in 1900 to 2,668,198 in 1913. But he was held on a tight leash by the Colonial Office, which regarded a budget deficit as prime evidence of gubernatorial incompetence. Fiscal dogma held that the less spent, the better spent. Steady, no-growth budgets were the password, as customs-derived revenue was inherently volatile. Or, as a Colonial Office official commented on an Egerton budget submission, "The comfortable principle that the more you spend the more you will have cannot be applied blindly. It is all to the good that Sir W. Egerton should have such an abounding faith in the future of Southern Nigeria. . . . The responsibility is on the S. of S. [secretary of state] to judge such proposals calmly and dispassionately, and with a long look ahead. If any mistake is to be made in the Colonial Office, it should be that of excessive caution, rather than the opposite."[163]

THE COLONIAL ORDER CONSTRUCTED

As the 1914 war clouds darkened in Europe, the colonial state in Africa was digging itself in for the *longue durée*. The final colonial occupations— Morocco and Libya—were far from completed, but save for a shrinking number of remote areas the basic superstructure of hegemony was in place. The allocation of colonial space among the imperial occupants had been resolved; the territorial grid of alien domination was firmly in place, although it would be somewhat reworked as a consequence of the elimination of the Germans in World War I. More fundamentally, the operational code through which the colonial state resolved the conflicting and complementary demands of the six imperatives of its reproduction across time had crystallized. Given the ground rules fixed by the metropolitan proprietors of colonial sovereignty, and the limits set by the character of the subjugated economies and societies, its logic was implacable. Self-financing hegemony and security demanded effective resource generation from the primary factor of production, African labor. The individual European district officers and the African chiefs who were the primary agents in the construction of Bula Matari labored within a tightly bounded set of constraints in the daily performance of their functions. Whatever their personal dispositions, they were imprisoned by the imperatives of reproducing the system they served.

Thus, Bula Matari, crusher of rocks, managed in a short time to assert a powerful hold on subject society and to smash its resistance. Yet the colonial state was also acutely conscious of its weakness. Its resource base remained painfully limited, and its hold was fragile. Its battle for legitimation on the European front was won, but colonial agents were well aware that its command over its subjects relied ultimately on force. Accordingly, Bula Matari lost no opportunity to represent itself as an invincible leviathan, as the sole alternative to the nasty, brutish, and short existence of the Hobbesian state of nature that its discourse portrayed as the precolonial African condition. But no social contract other than conquest bound its subjects to its rule. Therefore, however strong its despotic ascendancy appeared, hegemony remained precarious.

One may perceive, as have some able analysts, a servitude of the colonial state to broader processes of capitalist penetration, with the superstructure of European rule as "a system of political domination which takes the form of a separate and *apparently autonomous* complex of institutions and practices which establish and maintain in juridical and political forms the social relations that ensure the reproduction and accumulation of capital." In its most sophisticated form, this argument concedes that "the interests of the state authorities diverge from the interest of capital over the need of the state to sustain the conditions of its own legitimacy. At the same time, the state remains tied to capital by its dependence on the process of accumulation for the fiscal conditions of its own reproduction."[164] Certainly colonial state agents assumed that the European form of economic organization, like all other aspects of the European social, cultural, and political realm, were axiomatically superior. But in the short run—the quintessential time frame for the official mind—a purely political form of extraction was the indispensable instrument for reproduction of the colonial state. For both the architects and the masons constructing Bula Matari, in my view, the logic governing their behavior was essentially political.

The builders of the colonial state generally assumed that their handiwork was permanent—or at a minimum extended so far beyond any time horizon practical statesmen might usefully contemplate as to render debate about its ultimate ends utterly fruitless. But there were distant omens; particularly in the British case, as B. R. Tomlinson observes, decolonization—which began with the 1840 Durham Report in Canada (or perhaps the American Revolution)—proceeded simultaneously with colonization. Thus, applying the older model of transferring power to white communities, Britain granted South Africa dominion status in 1910. More portentous for the rest of Africa, the congealing of a civil society in India forced constitutional reforms on the colonial state, beginning a process of empowerment of subject society that could only lead to the eventual transfer of sovereignty.[165] Were one to use 1875 as the benchmark for the beginning of the colonial era, the colonial epoch in Africa was nearly half over when World War I transformed some of the fundamental parameters of the international system.

Chapter Five

THE COLONIAL STATE INSTITUTIONALIZED

The Negroes are becoming ungovernable in all the European protectorates, said the governor. University graduates, worker agitators, Black
Americans incite them to disobedience and hatred. . . . The most ardent in
combatting us are the university graduates, who owe us everything. For
them, higher education means "Africa for the Africans."

—Paul Salkin, L'Afrique Centrale dans cent ans

Egyptians are not a nation—they are a fortuitous agglomeration of a
number of miscellaneous and hybrid elements. . . . To suppose that the
characters and intellects of even a small number of Egyptians can in a
few years be trained to such an extent as to admit of their undertaking
the sole direction of one of the most complicated political and administrative machines the world has ever known, and of guiding such a machine
along the path of even fairly good government, is a sheer absurdity.

—Consul General Lord Cromer

Assuming . . . that this collection of self-contained and mutually independent Native States, separated from one another, as many of them are, by
great distances, by differences of history and traditions, and by ethnolog-
ical, racial, tribal, political, social and religious barriers, were indeed
capable of being welded into a single homogeneous nation—a deadly blow
would thereby be struck at the very root of *national self-government in
Nigeria, which secures to each separate people the right to maintain its
identity, its individuality, its own chosen form of government,* and the
peculiar political and social institutions which have been evolved for
it by the wisdom and the accumulated experience of generations of its
forebears.

—Governor Sir Hugh Clifford

DISTANT OMENS

The compressed but momentous epoch of the colonial state in Africa at
the start of the interwar period was at the end of the beginning. Its hegemony was consolidated and its rule thoroughly institutionalized during
this phase. Paradoxically, the end of the beginning was also the beginning of the end, although the gathering forces, within and without Africa,
that were to force European withdrawal were only dimly perceived, and
they were largely discounted by the colonial state agents.

These distant omens found their way into the colonial consciousness here and there through such pessimistic fantasies as the 1926 essay *L'Afrique Centrale dans cent ans,* by a distinguished Belgian colonial magistrate, Paul Salkin.[1] Retired French administrators from the Maghreb penned novels about indigenous insurrections to come.[2] Colonial security departments opened files on "Bolshevism" and "Garveyism" as new forms of ideological challenge to the colonial state appeared on the external horizon. These still inchoate apprehensions found official voice from French Colonial Minister Albert Sarraut in 1923: "The profound shudders that are running, in swelling, unseemly waves through the immense flood of the colored races, marking the new awakening of aspirations . . . may again bring together the old fanaticisms, the nationalisms, or the mysticisms against the enlightenment that has come from the West."[3]

There were, indeed, more immediate portents. The interwar period began with the 1919 Cairo riots—a virtual urban insurrection—that shattered the British complacency so eloquently expressed by Egypt's former British consul general, Lord Cromer, in the epigraph above. The short-lived protectorate, given full juridical colonial incorporation into the British Empire in 1914, was hastily abandoned in favor of nominal transfer of power in 1922, with Egyptian sovereignty substantially circumscribed by treaty cessions assuring imperial security (especially the military occupation of the Suez Canal zone). The earlier South African transfer of power—also subject to imperial security limitations—proved a false precedent, in permitting the instruments of sovereignty to fall into the hands of a white immigrant minority. But in the same way that the initial 1882 occupation of Egypt had served as the trigger event—for some analysts, the prime detonator[4]—of African partition, the recovery of sovereignty by an African leadership was to provide a beacon of nationalism and a Mecca for those combating colonial occupation.

But this lay in the future. Egyptian independence, at the time, was an isolated, even aberrant event. For nearly everybody, the colonial order seemed in the ascendant. The notion of yielding power to those who were beginning to articulate nationalist voice seemed preposterous—the Cromer and Clifford quotes illustrate the disparaging contempt reserved for the visionaries who perceived a world beyond colonialism. Indeed, the system was still expanding: the Ottoman Levant was the object of an unseemly scramble whose cynical diplomacy layed the groundwork for the intractable postcolonial civil strife in Lebanon and the former Palestine mandate. In Africa the conquest of Morocco and Libya was still incomplete and required massive military operations in the 1920s. And Italy initiated the final episode in colonial occupation with its invasion of

Ethiopia in 1935, an aggression requiring half a million troops. Berque, writing of the interwar Maghreb, captures the essence of the period: "Not only, at the time we are concerned with, was decolonization not under way or even in prospect, but colonization dominated everything. Only a few bold spirits at that time defied it, only a few pioneers realized its fragility."[5]

I treat the interwar period as a single analytical moment in the life cycle of the African colonial state because the overarching parameters that conditioned the imperatives of system behavior are broadly similar. However, the period breaks down into two relatively distinct phases: the era of expansion and relative prosperity in the 1920s, and the prolonged world depression of the 1930s. The sharp economic contraction hit hard in the colonial world, by this time sufficiently incorporated into the global economy to feel the repercussions of its overall trends. The institutional elaboration of the colonial state—acquiring some momentum in the 1920s—stopped in its tracks, and the top echelons of its apparatus required some compression. But its strength was more than sufficient to impose most of the costs of the depression on the subject population, by increased fiscal pressure and enforced maintenance of export-crop production in the face of steep reductions in purchase price.

THE IMPACT OF WORLD WAR I

Except for Portugal and Spain, the colonial occupants were all caught in the maelstrom of World War I. "World War" etymologically derived from the projection into Africa (and Asia) of a conflagration originating in Europe. The four German colonies became theaters of conflict; although Togo and South West Africa were quickly overrun, Cameroon and Tanganyika were the scenes of prolonged campaigns, requiring the mobilization of large numbers of African soldiers and porters and inflicting substantial casualties from combat and disease.

For Britain and France the carnage in the trenches in Europe generated demands for exploiting the imperial reserves of manpower. In the British case, the vast human reservoir of India filled this need; nearly one million Indian troops were dispatched overseas, many to France.[6] African troops and carriers were utilized primarily in the Cameroon and Tanganyika campaigns. In West Africa some twenty-five thousand mainly Ghanaian and Nigerian soldiers and an indeterminate but larger number of porters took part in the Cameroon campaign; casualty rates for porters were nearly 50 percent.[7] For the German East Africa campaign, which lasted throughout the war, huge numbers of Africans were conscripted, with high casualty rates. Some 175,000 porters were recruited in Nyasaland, and between fifty thousand and one hundred thousand in Northern Rhodesia. Nearly eight hundred thousand East Africans served in the war, from which more than one hundred thousand did not return.[8] For the French, the African manpower pool appeared crucial to survival; a total of 177,000 Algerians, fifty-four thousand Tunisians, thirty-seven thousand Moroccans, 181,500 Africans from AOF, and ten thousand from AEF were pressed into service, with varying degrees of coercion.[9] Of the African total, some 24,762 perished.[10] Belgian Congo units and porters also participated in the East African campaign.

Recruitment of such large numbers tested the hegemonical talents of the colonial state, especially the French. The still potent coercive capacities of existing social structures were amply demonstrated; Suret-Canale estimates that three-quarters of the AOF contingents were of slave ancestry.[11] In AOF, after recruitment pressures had played an important part in triggering serious uprisings in northern Dahomey, Niger, and what soon became Upper Volta, recruitment was suspended in 1917. Later that year the French manpower crisis was sufficiently severe to prompt resumption of recruiting, with the aid of Senegalese deputy Blaise Diagne, sent back to AOF with the rank of governor-general. Diagne—who in the preceding year had extracted confirmation of citizenship for the inhabitants of the four communes as the price of his collaboration—was effective in his campaign, but even the local French administrators warned of its risks. Governor-General Joost van Vollenhoven resigned his post (partly affronted by the colonial rank accorded Diagne), and the governor of Niger cabled that additional conscription was impossible. The succeeding governor-general, Gabriel Angoulvant, archly responded: "It is in full knowledge of the difficulties that you describe that the Government of the Republic has demanded that the West African colonies furnish a new and important military effort. . . . Whatever the importance of the difficulties encountered, you must meet them head on. . . . When the higher interest of the country is involved, that which appears impossible to achieve becomes possible."[12]

What accomplishing the impossible actually meant, in this context, is described in the report of an Upper Volta local officer:

To bring together the young men to present to the recruitment commission (five needed for each actual recruit) was not always easy. It was necessary to surround the village at dawn to obtain, during the day, the submission and assembly of the men hidden in the nearby bush. A first summons consisted of burning a few huts, after evacuating their inhabitants, with the threat of continuing the process with the rest of the village. The youths thus taken or surrendering were chained one behind the other, a rope around their neck, herded by horsemen and directed towards the recruitment commission, after being lodged in the prison.[13]

The imperatives of war led the metropolitan states to demand not only manpower but also an effort in the economic sphere to sustain deliveries of vegetable oils and other exports, and in the Algerian case to supply workers (about seventy-seven thousand in 1918).[14] The war thinned the superstructure of the colonial state by summoning to service many European agents and by sharply reducing the pool of available rural labor. In Algeria one-third of the males between the ages of twenty and forty were recruited either into the military ranks or the industrial work force in France.[15] Although the colonial economies were less equipped to supply the war machines than they later were during World War II, the pressures exerted on the subject population by a weakened colonial state were substantial.

The war years were thus a coda for the epoch of construction of the colonial state. Even though the colonial state was compelled by the security requirements of the ruling power momentarily to shrink its superstructure of domination, its hold on the population was not seriously shaken despite the apprehensions of some. The harshness of its wartime pressures, especially military recruiting, certainly played a part in triggering revolts here and there (in AOF and the Chilembwe uprising in Nyasaland in 1915), but there was no widespread or organized effort to seize the opportunity to throw off the newly imposed colonial yoke. In part, this attested to the effectiveness of the intermediary structures of rule that had been created, which in the short term proved generally capable of performing the quotidian routines of sustaining hegemony at the local level, even if the European overlayer was stripped of some of its personnel.

The colonial state had also succeeded in imposing a certain negative legitimation, a prescriptive familiarity. In the discourse of the colonizer, the colonies remained "loyal" to the imperial cause. In the Islamic arc from the Sudan to the Maghreb there were real fears at the outset of the war that an appeal of the Caliphate to Muslim solidarity might find some audience. However, only in Libya, seized from the Ottoman state on the eve of the war, was there any nostalgia for Turkish rule. Elsewhere, the assiduously spun "black legend" concerning the venal and oppressive character of the Ottoman polity proved resilient, and the strategic alliances with elements of the Muslim leadership left no mobilizational space for jihad movements. Despite the intense barrage of war propaganda, the dominant mood was no doubt distance and detachment from the "white man's war." Yet the conflict seemed to present no option other than incorporation into someone else's imperial domain.

Colonial state agents, well situated to measure the costs of the war effort to newly institutionalized rule, tended to resist the more extreme demands of the metropole for an ever-greater contribution; the most spectacular example was van Vollenhoven's resignation as governor-general of AOF. At the same time, they were susceptible to the *union sacrée* psychosis induced by the war. Thus, for a time the exigencies of total war in the European theater diminished the relative autonomy of the colonial state, reducing the colonies to imperial appendages in a titanic global combat.

This interlude created a sense that the postwar epoch was a new moment in colonial life. Across the African continent there was a moment of conscious review of the formal legal arrangements structuring the colonial state. Where settler communities spoke with loud lungs, demands were heard for transfer of authority from the colonial administration to white-run "representative" bodies. In British territories generally, the composition of legislative councils was reviewed, with small concessions to an African voice. Significant reformulations of the ideological justifications of the colonial state were also in the air; the fidelity of colonized populations merited some recognition, ran the argument.

These reconsiderations occurred in the context of important developments in world political balances and the international jurisprudence of colonial rule. Three major new players appeared on the global scene: the Soviet Union, the United States, and Japan. The Soviet Union, while providing a territorial base and doctrinal support for the idea of anticolonial revolution, was soon engulfed in civil war and subsequently in building "socialism in one country"; the United States quickly retreated to interwar isolationism; and Japan busied itself with building its own colonial empire in Asia. Yet all three, in different ways, contributed toward the emergence of a world order no longer prescriptively committed to upholding European imperium in Africa.

Vladimir Lenin and Woodrow Wilson separately injected the doctrine of self-determination into the discourse of international law and politics, a norm ultimately absorbed into the law of nations and providing a decisive ideological weapon for anticolonial movements. The doctrine was partly incorporated into the Covenant of the League of Nations, even though self-determination in the Soviet case was swallowed up in the convoluted sophistries of Leninist "nationality" doctrine in the new Bolshevik polity, and Wilson later confessed to sleepless nights at the parade of nationalities beckoned from the deeps by his vision of popular sovereignty as the basis for a postwar order.[16]

In the early stages of the war the British, French, Belgian, and South African armies moving into German territories expected that the older international law of conquest would apply, permitting simple annexation to be blessed by postwar treaty among the victors. However, new rules were applied. The colonizing powers held only contingent sovereignty under the mandate system, and they acquired the novel obligation to rule in trusteeship for the subject "peoples not yet able to stand by themselves under the strenuous conditions of the modern world." Those sharing the African spoils of war were persuaded to accept these arrangements because they believed at the time that the status defined in the league's covenant was a distinction without a difference. South African Versailles delegate General Louis Botha affirmed his acceptance of the mandate arrangement on the assumption that "the League of Nations would consist mostly of the same people who were present there that day, who understood the position, and who would not make it impossible for any mandatory to govern the country."[17] Sir Donald Cameron, soon to assume the governorship of the Tanganyika mandate, later confided that "the terms of the Mandate in the case of Tanganyika did not trouble or preoccupy my mind in any way; the principles embodied in that document were in complete accord with those with which I had become so accustomed in the administration of Nigeria—the ordinary and recognized principles of British Colonial Administration."[18] Although Cameron expressed the settled view in colonial milieux at the time, trusteeship in the near term and ultimate self-determination in a very distant future were norms that slowly corroded some of the prewar certitudes about the perpetuity of the colonial state.

HEGEMONY ROUTINIZED

The interwar years saw a rationalization and routinization of the exercise of hegemony. The basic structures of rule were in place, but principles of colonial science were elaborated to perfect their operation. A series of colonial congresses took place, where jurists, anthropologists, missionaries, and colonial agents debated the application of Weberian state-building reason to the management of the colonial estates; virtually no Africans participated in these assemblies.[19] The discipline of colonial anthropology emerged, and a more professional corpus of ethnographic literature slowly became available, augmenting the early descriptions by missionaries and administrators.

The specialized institutes created in France and Belgium before the war to train colonial administrators now became the primary source of the top cadres. With improving medical and other physical conditions, colonial service became an attractive career; the French Ecole Coloniale began to compete with the other Grandes Ecoles for a middle-class clientele.[20] Sir Ralph Furse, who during this period single-handedly selected the cadets for colonial service, recruited from the elite ranks of the Oxford and Cambridge colleges by using a scout system of tutors to identify the type of candidate drive by "the challenge to adventure, the urge to prove himself in the face of hardship and risk to health, of loneliness and not infrequently danger, the chance of dedicating himself to the service of his fellow men, and of responsibility at an early age on a scale which life at home could scarcely ever offer; the pride of belonging to a great service devoted to a mighty and beneficent task; the novelty of life in unfamiliar scenes and strange conditions."[21] In 1927 Oxbridge supplied seventy-nine of eighty-three new administrative appointments; in 1937, 123 of 157.[22]

The numbers of the commanding echelons of the colonial state were spare throughout this period. In AOF, for example, there were 341 French administrators in 1912, and 385 in 1937.[23] "The essence of the steel frame lay not in its size but in its strength," Anthony Kirk-Greene remarks. The supreme self-confidence of the state's territorial officers was yet unshaken by nagging doubts about its mission or the security of its dominance. The district officer performed his prefectoral role "rooted in an unquestioned assumption of his authority. . . . This authority needed nothing more than his person; of other support, he seemingly had or needed none. Of course, in the background, at various stages of remove, lay the whole might of the colonial state; yet this was a force which, after c. 1910, was rarely invoked."[24] Hubert Deschamps, like Kirk-Greene a former colonial officer, offers a similar description of the unchallenged ascendancy of the "kings of the bush":

> To imagine a police state, founded on force, would be to be totally deceived. In my last district, which contained 100,000 inhabitants, dispersed in the bush, forty policemen, recruited in the same area, largely sufficed to ensure order and the observance of regulations. I always went about, from ten to fifteen days per month, without escort and unarmed, and everywhere I was well received, without servility and with dignity. . . . It is through all these "kings of the

bush" . . . that the incoherent whole of the French possessions had been upheld and had been able to give the impression of a solid bloc, despite the absence of doctrine from Paris, despite its unkept promises and its horror of the future."[26]

IDEOLOGIES OF DOMINATION

The status of the chiefly intermediaries found sharper definition in these years, as administrative ideologies were cast in philosophical form. The great debate about the hegemonical merits of "indirect" versus "direct" rule emerged, initiated by the publication in 1919 of the Lugard *Administrative Memoranda*. In its most extended form, as practiced in northern Nigeria, indirect rule prescribed a caring nurture of existing institutions and their development as agencies of local government. Governor Clifford of Nigeria reflects this doctrine in a 1922 minute: "In all that he does or leaves undone in his control or management of the administration of a Native State by its own local Government, the Political Officer must be careful, whenever possible, to lend his support to the authority of the Emir and his officers. *They, and not he, as I have said, constitute the de facto Government over which their operations extend.* . . . The Political Officer should be the Whisper behind the Throne, but never for an instant the Throne itself."[26]

From its Nigerian genesis, the ideology of indirect rule spread through much of British-ruled Africa. It was applied with particular zeal in Tanganyika and Northern Rhodesia, and had significant influence in all but the settler territories of Southern Rhodesia and Kenya. Its concept of hegemony is well conveyed in the 1927 Tanganyika White Paper defending its adoption:

> Being convinced that it is neither just nor possible to deny permanently to the natives any part in the government of the country, the Government of this Territory has adopted the policy of native administration which aims . . . at making it possible for this to evolve in accordance with their traditions and their most deeply rooted instincts, as an organized and disciplined community within the State. . . . It enlists on the side of law, order and good government all responsible elements in native society, and it aims at preserving that society intact and in protecting it from disintegration into an undisciplined rabble of leaderless and ignorant individuals.[27]

As an instrument of rule, the mechanism of sanctified "native authorities" required the exercise of guided hegemony. "Development" had be-

gun to enter the doctrinal pantheon of the colonial state, and the reproduction of hegemony alone was not a sufficient goal. Thus, even in its
extreme form, indirect rule required more than a whisper behind the
throne; custom, even if worshiped as the cornerstone of bureaucratic
predictability, had to serve other purposes.[28] Prospective successors were
subjected to schooling; little by little, the British version of the colonial
state sought intermediaries who combined the useful authority derived
from some customary title to office with the literate skills and exposure to
basic administrative training that would make them serviceable auxiliaries of the would-be Weberian state.[29]

In the scholastic debates over the science of hegemony, France appeared to represent the polar opposite to Lugardian doctrines. Beyond
doubt the prefectoral, hierarchical, centralizing, and Cartesian impulses
that permeated the French state tradition instilled a different ethos in
the relationship between the European echelons of administration and
the African canton and local chiefs. The dominant view of the senior administration was expressed by Inspector of Colonies Maret in 1930: "[The
canton chief] is not the successor of the former petty native chiefs. . . .
Even when the person is the same, there is nothing in common between
the former state of things and the new order. . . . The canton chief, even if
the descendant of the king with whom we once dealt, holds no power in
his own right. Named by us, following a choice in principle discretionary,
he is only our auxiliary."[30] In practice, after the routinization of hegemony, Bonapartist prefectoral command was modified by the art of politics. Even at the doctrinal level, it was challenged by some: Félix Eboué,
of Afro-Guyanan origin, who held various AEF posts, and especially Marshal Lyautey, the first Resident of colonial Morocco. A disciple of Gallieni
in Madagascar, Lyautey regretted that French agents "had direct administration in the skin," and he ordered his "native affairs" officers to "become penetrated by the very spirit of the Protectorate in carefully ab-
staining from directly administering, in limiting their intervention to a
broad, enlightened and discreet although very active intervention with
the caids to whom must be left all the initiative and the responsibility."[31]

In the Tunisian case, although French colonial doctrine did not employ
the same discourse and the administrative occupation was relatively
dense (14,500 French functionaries by 1939, as against only 3,500 Tunisians), its operations were mediated through a ramifying network of
Tunisian patrons and brokers, and more generally an emergent bourgeoisie.[32] In AOF and AEF a few canton chiefs were nothing more than
former tirailleur noncoms, but in most instances they were recruited
from ruling families. The image of the pure command hierarchy con-

veyed by the doctrine of direct administration needs to be set against the practical contingencies of rule at the local outposts of the colonial state. "It led to the emergence of a particular breed of bush-administrators— mainly bachelors, who felt more at ease in the African countryside than in France, who more than often spoke the local tongue (thanks to their African mistresses), who knew everyone, and in particular everything that went on. At ease in the tortuous labyrinths of 'traditional' African politics, they were not only aware of local intrigues and cabals, but were often instrumental in launching them."[33]

Algeria was a case apart in the physiognomy of colonial hegemony and its intermediation. By the 1920s the administrative cadres of the colonial state were in good measure recruited among the settler population. Through the local councils in the *communes de plein exercice* and *communes mixtes,* which structured local government during the interwar years in all but the military zones of the desert fringe and some remote mountain areas, obstreperous settlers found the institutional means to bend state reason to their own security and needs. To boot, the nine settler deputies in Parliament tended to dominate legislative interest (except during the Popular Front period between 1936 and 1938). Thus, the extraordinary weight of the European community—the full empowerment of a civil society from which Algerians were all but excluded— relegated the intermediaries as well as the subjects to an exceptionally peripheral status.[34]

The Belgian administrative ideologies, as the colonial state consciously sought instruction from its neighbors of long-standing experience in the art of domination, blended notions inspired by British and French doctrines. The dark shadow of the Leopoldian regime and the scandals its improvised exploitation generated still lingered at war's end, giving added impetus to the quest for rationalization of rule. Its basic administrative ideology is set out in the official manual guiding its agents:

We must make use of indigenous leaders. These know the indigenous milieux and their customs; their authority in the eyes of the populations has a character of legitimacy which commands respect and their compensation weighs less heavily on the treasury. For these reasons, our organization maintains the populations under the authority of traditional chiefs and within the framework of ancestral customs. . . . By this form of indirect administration, the colonial Government is enabled to attain more easily and more surely its goal: promoting progress in all fields. . . . Governing through the intermediary of chiefs, we have an interest in reinforcing their authority, in repressing separatist tendencies and a spirit of insubmission amongst their subjects.[35]

The ideology of indirect rule was most thoroughly applied in the mandate territories of Ruanda-Urundi. In the Congo, it confronted the political fragmentation of the equatorial forest area and the ravages of the Leopoldian era, as well as the interventionist dispositions of the territorial service. There were significant regional variations in bureaucratic style. Within the Congo, Orientale province developed an administrative culture placing more emphasis on cultivation of chiefs, while in Katanga a residue of suspicion toward chieftancy as a residual focus of resistance obtained, partly fed by the small but noisy settler group and some influential Catholic mission milieux, especially the irascible Benedictine prelate Jean-Félix de Hemptinne, archbishop of Elisabethville.[36]

During the interwar period the juridical framework of intermediation was cast, absorbing the intensely legalistic culture of the Belgian state. Particularly important were the 1926 decrees governing indigenous tribunals and, above all, the long-nurtured 1933 decree on *circonscriptions indigènes*.[37] The Cartesian impulses inherent to the Belgian state, so closely modeled on France at its birth in 1830, was mirrored in the disposition to seek basic units of native administration of comparable dimensions. Thus, to remedy the fragmentation and small scale of many African communities, especially in the western half of the Congo, "sectors" were created, amalgamating several smaller natural jurisdictions; by 1938, the 6,095 recognized chieftaincies of 1917 had been reduced to 340 sectors and 1,212 chieftaincies.[38]

In the Portuguese territories a slow, halting process of rationalization of a singularly weak and underdeveloped metropolitan state spilled over into the colonial domains, which throughout the construction phase of the colonial state, despite its seeming antiquity, remained a series of patrimonial satrapies improvisationally run by an amalgam of settlers, renegades, and officials. A colonial institute was created in 1907, and a slow alignment of its African rule on the models supplied by what were regarded as the pace-setting European states began, accelerated by the creation of the Estado Novo in Portugal by Antonio Salazar in 1928. By the end of the era of consolidation, in the words of one analyst, "For the first time in Portuguese colonial history, the writ of Lisbon began actually to be obeyed in the colonies. The settler and the official were made increasingly aware that they might in reality be called to account for their conduct. Mozambique and Angola ceased to be a rag-bag of separate customs zones, railway corridors and company concessions and began to evolve as integrated states."[39] However, the Portuguese system never developed the elaborate and systematized network of intermediary "native authorities" set up by the other colonizers. Intermediation occurred through a more diverse net of Afro-Portuguese traders, settlers, and some chiefs.

The dictates of hegemony for the Italian colonial state, especially in Libya, became permeated by the fascist doctrines that served as ideological charter in Italy with the advent of the Mussolini regime in 1922. Its exorbitant exaltation of the state reverberated in the colonies—overpoweringly in the "fourth shore" of Libya, strongly in Eritrea and Somalia. In this philosophic text, the state was "infinitely superior" to civil society. For Mussolini the fascist state was "the single, unitary state, the sole repository of all the history, of the entire future, of all the force of the Italian nation . . . a moral idea which incarnates itself and expresses itself in a system of hierarchies. . . . I intend to re-establish with all the means at my disposal a single national discipline binding upon sect, faction, and party."[40] Thus doctrinally armed, Italy resolutely embarked on a reconquista in Libya which consumed a decade, and which was so relentlessly and ruthlessly conducted that by some accounts the population was reduced by half and the livestock by much more (sheep, goats, and camels fell in number from 713,000, 546,000, and 83,000, respectively, in 1910, to 98,000, 25,000, and 2,600 in 1933). The structures of rule and intermediation bequeathed by the Ottoman state in Libya were pulverized, and the Libyan political community was forced back into kinship structures, a "political identity of last resort."[41] Reason of state pivoted around Italian settlement; the subjugated populace was ancillary to this end.

In Eritrea and Somalia a basic framework of rule had been created in the prewar period, which was less overwhelmed by the overlay of fascist-regime doctrine. Although settlement was an important determinant of state action, rural colonization remained limited, and its main characteristic was a thorough grid of Italian territorial administration covering the countryside. A British official who took it over during World War II regarded it as exemplified by "high paper efficiency, meticulously thorough, minutely organized."[42]

Spanish domination was weakly structured and belatedly imposed, and requires no further attention. Until 1934 the Spanish Sahara was no more than a precarious coastal garrison; its military occupation of the hinterland in the mid-1930s was primarily preemptive.[43] The Spanish presence in Fernando Po was mainly sustained through individual and corporate planters, who displaced an earlier generation of black Creole elites from Sierre Leone and elsewhere. In Rio Muni exercise of hegemony only slightly extended beyond the range of timber concessions.

HEGEMONY AS ARBITRARY AUTHORITY

Although hegemony was infrequently challenged during this period, it continued to rest on a wide latitude for arbitrary repression at its rural periphery. Its more distasteful impositions—especially tax collection and labor conscription—often required what in French administrative idiom were described as *moyennes energiques*. The institutionalization of rule at the upper echelons of the colonial state witnessed a progressive infusion of juridical texts and legalistic discourse. Public law, however, held sway mainly at the top; it was a shroud enclosing the operations of the colonial state, which as one moved down the state hierarchy veiled the quintessentially arbitrary character of its rule over the subject population. In the supple reservoirs of tradition as interpreted by the African adjuncts of the colonial state the customary tribunals could readily discover rules enjoining any form of disobedience to a ruler.

The European administrators themselves had ample legal weapons for summary punishment of subjects challenging their hegemony. In the Belgian case, for example, a decree of 24 July 1918 stipulated that a territorial administrative and plenary power to impose seven days' imprisonment and/or a 200-franc fine for "any disrespectful act or word committed or uttered towards a European agent of public authority in his presence."[44] Any territorial agent had plenary power to arrest and incarcerate any African who "was guilty of threatening state security, provoking disobedience of the laws, or in other ways compromising public tranquility or the stability of institutions."[45] By administrative action, subject to governor-general promulgation, any troublesome individual could be relegated to remote internment. In the case of collective disobedience, the administrator could occupy the recalcitrant community with a detachment of troops, "with the obligation, for the inhabitants to provide the occupying personnel, if need be without remuneration, lodging, food and service."[46] If more vigorous military action were required to ensure that administrative orders were executed, the administrative manual warned: "There is no more perilous conduct than to allow the natives to believe that they have nothing to fear from the effects of an armed action; beyond the fact that such a belief would annihilate the very prestige of our force, it would inevitably validate the superstitions of the natives, who readily believe in immunization by magical ritual against the European arms."[47] With this arsenal of authority, any administrator lacking the resourcefulness to apply instant punishment to those troubling the colonial order deserved to lose his chevrons.

The indigénat code, as a singularly visible instrument of arbitrary colonial authority, came under some attack in France, both in the middle 1920s and at the time of the Popular Front. The colonial state responded by enlarging the pool of exempted categories—chiefs, veterans, the educated, women—but insisted on retaining the code, both in Algeria and in sub-Saharan Africa (it remained in effect until the close of World War II). In 1924 and again in 1936, the AOF territorial governors were queried as to possible reform or elimination of the indigénat; the responses were unanimous in demanding its retention. The Guinea dispatch offered typical arguments in its insistence on keeping this repressive arm, "owing to the necessity in which we find ourselves to maintain the prestige of our authority and to assure the security of individuals (settlers and natives). In effect, in a recently formed colony, where the natives are of different races and religions, among them a rather large number still refractory to European civilization . . . it is indispensable that political actions which might trouble public order be swiftly repressed, or rather prevented . . . a system of preventative defense, a procedure of intimidation."[48] Formal judicial process, the dispatch added, was much too slow and complex. In 1937 the Ivory Coast governor had recourse to the same arguments: "Those who command in these countries still little evolved, must be able to punish themselves, and rapidly . . . the primitive Black often does not recognize the right to command except to he who may punish."[49] Throughout the interwar period, use of the indigénat remained substantial, as table 5-1 demonstrates.

Table 5-1.   *Indigénat* Convictions, AOF, 1933–1935

Territory	1933	1934	1935
Senegal	1,568	1,890	2,423
Mauritania	1,704	998	1,108
Soudan	5,130	4,773	3,023
Guinea	3,084	3,362	3,398
Ivory Coast	1,881	1,652	2,036
Dahomey	8,988	7,548	3,588
Niger	1,332	1,696	1,823
AOF Total	23,687	21,919	17,399

Source: ANS, 17 G 97 (17), Réforme de l'indigénat. Documentation fourni par Labouret en prévision d'une campagne contre l'indigénat.

MISSIONS AS PARTNERS IN HEGEMONY

The interwar years also saw the routinization of relationships between the Christian missions and the colonial state, and the substantial incorporation of mission into the superstructure of hegemony. Mission personnel were nationalized, with only minor exceptions: French and Canadian White Fathers, and Italian Verona Fathers in Uganda; British, American, and some Scandinavian Protestant missions in the Belgian Congo and Angola. Some residual mutual suspicions existed in these instances, but generally the missions came to view the colonial state as one of the familiar and reassuring certitudes of life, while the state realized that the missions could cheaply operate sectors of social policy—such as education and health—that began to be recognized as the responsibility of government to encourage, if not necessarily organize. More broadly, the cultural project of the colonial state—bringing "civilization" to subject society—could be largely delegated to the Christian missions, outside the Islamic zones.

The surge of anticlericalism that for a time seemed a necessary concomitant of "republican" engagement in France subsided, facilitated by the union sacrée of the war years. The new mood of mission engagement in consolidating the colonial state was expressed by leading Upper Volta prelate Father Thevenoud when accepting his 1920 appointment to the AOF Conseil d'Administration: "If I may one day bear witness to having contributed, however little, to the development of this country for which I dream of a so beautiful future, it would be for me the sweetest of consolations, for I would feel at the same time that I have made my small contribution to rebuilding the Mother Country. I believe in effect that laboring here, is to work for France."[50]

For the Belgians, who gave far more generous material backing to the Catholic (national) missions, the obligation of the administrators to support mission action was explicit: "The government agents are not working alone in the task of civilization. The religious missions participate to an least equal degree. Government agents, whatever their own opinions, have the strict obligation to aid the Christian missionaries."[51] The Congo missions had as many personnel as the state, and three times as many stations. Throughout the colonial domains, particularly when administrators began to have their families resident, the missionaries were in far more comprehensive encounter with the populations among whom they worked. They normally remained for extended periods—even a lifetime—in the same area, took infrequent home leaves, and (particularly in the French case) were far more likely to know local languages.

There were occasional episodes of conflict between the colonial state and the missions. Perhaps the most intense, in the 1930s, pitted the White Fathers against the Upper Volta administration over an array of issues. The administration and some Mossi chiefs accused the missions of encouraging young women to desert the husbands imposed on them or to flee their families to avoid arranged matches. For the missions, the basis of the Christian family was at issue. The conflict escalated when elements in the administration accused the missionaries of complicity in fomenting a flare-up that briefly appeared to presage a major rebellion in an area swept by insurrection in 1915 and 1916.[52]

The apparatus of colonial hegemony also embraced European enterprises—especially mines and plantations—with large work forces. Through the common practice of controlling estates that housed workers, enterprise monitoring and management of labor extended far beyond the market sale of workplace services. Where the subjugation of the work force was most complete, as in the Katanga copperbelt, Fetter can argue that a veritable totalitarian society existed. The copper corporation Union Minière du Haut-Katanga, in alliance with the state and the Benedictine mission, had achieved "full control over its human milieu," extending to "virtually all aspects of the life of its African workers."[53] In this "hegemonic bloc" of state, mission, and corporation, the distinctions were hard to draw for the subject at the high tide of colonial rule. To the Congolese, as Douglas observed, "they were as one," the orders of each carrying the irresistible weight of Bula Matari.[54]

In territories lacking large mining or plantation sectors, the colonial trading corporations played a similar role as auxiliaries in hegemony. They often enjoyed de facto monopoly mercantile privileges accorded by the colonial state in particular commercial niches. In turn, they functioned in practice as "tax collectors of the empire," in the words of one writer.[55] With its internal hegemony not subject to serious challenge, the security imperative of the colonial state had only modest valence during these years. Security forces were for the most part small and lightly armed; total Nigerian defense costs from 1937 to 1938 were only 366,366 pounds.[56] The Armée d'Afrique in Algeria, partly a reserve force for metropolitan defense, numbered nearly one hundred thousand (by the interwar period, one-third Algerian, one-third Foreign Legion, one-third French). The Spanish and French mobilized several hundred thousand troops in the 1924–1926 campaign to suppress the Riff republic that

Abdelkrim el Khatabi had created in 1921. Large Italian Army forces were deployed in Libya during the 1920s, then in the Horn as the Ethiopian conquest required half a million troops. But these were the exceptions; the rule was a small, constabulary force.

THREATS TO SECURITY

As World War II approached, Italian and German ambitions began to stir colonial security fears. In Tunisia the Italian community by the late 1930s (one hundred thousand) was nearly as large as the French (120,000), and occasional discourse from the fascist state exalting itself as heir to the Roman Empire sent tremors through the colonial bureaucracy. In Germany imperial pretensions as well as *Lebensraum* and German in-gathering claims gained force apace with rearmament. Among the many injustices of Versailles was stripping Germany of its colonies. The British and French, desperate to avoid military confrontation, scanned the African landscape for territorial gifts (other than their own) that might propitiate Hitler; they toyed with offers of the Belgian Congo or Angola.[57]

Such exhuming of the scabrous diplomacy of the partition era sowed insecurity among the smaller and weaker colonial powers, Belgium and Portugal. There was little that they could do in response, save to tighten their grip on their colonies. In the Portuguese instance, the running theme of insecurity, extending back to the partition era, was an important factor propelling completion of the occupation and administrative organization of Angola and Mozambique, despite the slender power resources and instability of the Portuguese state, especially in the 1920s.

The colonial state detected some hostile, even dangerous ideological currents in an international environment less dominated by the imperial ethos than before 1914. Communism, nationalism, and Garveyism attracted the notice of the colonial state and entered its security calculus. The creation of the Soviet Union and the founding of the Communist International (Comintern) brought fears of the potential appeal of socialist revolutionary doctrines. To a handful of Africans in France, the novel doctrines of international communism did appeal; the important Maghreb nationalist movement Etoile Nord-Africain, a lineal ancestor to the Front de Libération Nationale, emerged in 1926, initially close to and supported by the French Communist Party.[58] For the most part, Soviet and Communist influence in emergent African nationalism was very small, but it sufficed to trigger a security response by the colonial state. Measures were taken to prohibit or curb entry of printed materials labeled "Communist propaganda," and to seal off the colonies from persons suspected of Communist connections.

Egypt was an epicenter of Arab nationalism, judged particularly dangerous in the Sudan and Maghreb. The British continued to promote assiduously anti-Egyptian sentiment in the Sudan, expounding on the misdeeds of the Turko-Egyptian regime. The French limited as best they could the numbers of pilgrims to the holy places and scholars bound for al-Azhar University or other Middle Eastern centers of Islamic study.

Garveyism, and the radical pan-African ideas associated with the movement, had some influence in coastal West Africa, from the Congo to Senegal.[59] The official mind readily fused it with communism and Middle Eastern Arab and Islamic nationalism into a hydra-headed subversive menace. In the French case, a decree of 27 March 1928 placed new powers in the hands of the colonial administration to seize periodicals and other printed matter "susceptible to threaten respect for French authority." The governor-general noted with satisfaction that the new legislation "will permit, in imposing useful sanctions, the restraint of subversive propaganda, particularly harmful in the field of colonization, whose volume has until now been increasing in rather alarming fashion."[60]

THE AUTONOMY OF THE COLONIAL STATE

The colonial state stood at its apogee in its quest for autonomy. The progressive institutionalization of its apparatus, for most territories, and the professionalization of its cadres liberated the colonial state from detailed management by its metropole. Internally, the completeness of its domination freed the state from responsiveness to its subjects to a remarkable degree; only strong settler communities, and corporate interests where its revenue and accumulation requirements were contingent on their good will, could significantly constrain its choices.

Colonial ministries had final statutory power, acting on behalf of the holder of sovereignty.[61] But it exercised this power with a light hand, so long as no deficit occurred, no unsavory military operations were required, and no other scandal attracting public attention appeared. The default option during the interwar period was passive observation, an inertial disposition to permit the "man on the spot" to "get on with the job." In the words of a former senior French colonial officer with long service in Chad, on the eve of World War II the governor-general was all powerful; if he had some personal standing, he "could generally ignore the bureaux of the Ministry of Colonies."[62]

The colonial state of course operated within a broad policy framework set by the overrulers. By the 1920s, however, a basic set of policy parameters were in place, and there were few really major new departures. Perhaps the most consequential proposed changes—schemes for closer union in East and Central Africa, the Blum-Violette reforms in Algeria— never went into effect. The Colonial Ministries did name the territorial governors, perhaps their most visible prerogative at the time. Some were individuals of unusual talent and energy, who put a personal mark on their territory—like Sir Gordon Guggisberg of the Gold Coast and Pierre Ryckmans of the Belgian Congo. But they were almost always drawn from a pool of imperial proconsuls who made their careers in colonial service. To an important extent, they were interchangeable parts in the colonial apparatus, skilled practitioners in the reason of colonial state, whose life histories embodied this special form of polity, the purest modern form of autonomous bureaucratic autocracy.[63] State and administration were coterminous.

Changes in political tendency in the metropole had some impact. Governments of left complexion—the short-lived Ramsey MacDonald government of 1929 to 1931 in Britain, the "cartel of the left" in the mid-1920s and the Popular Front between 1936 and 1938 in France— yielded brief flurries of reform, but no fundamental alterations. The three less important colonial powers, Italy, Portugal, and Spain, all experienced changes of regime during this period, which in the first two cases did result in significantly reduced autonomy for the colonial state; the consolidation of fascism in Spain occurred too late in the period to make a difference. For Italy and Portugal, the overseas dominions were elevated into exhibitions of national aggrandizement, exalted as memorials of grandeur. To some degree, colonial governance became tributary to the rhetorical extravagances washing across the overseas territories.

For the parliamentary regimes, colonial issues received only sporadic attention. Particularly in the British case, there was a small but vocal set of MPs who made active use of question time to compel public defense of some policies. Of the 325 parliamentary questions raised in the House of Commons between 1925 and 1929 concerning East Africa, 258 were put by only six members.[64] These might be a cause for embarrassment, and colonial administrations had to be sensitive to the risk of exposure in question time. But they were not a serious constraint on policy choice. In France, the nine deputies representing Europeans in Algeria had a virtual stranglehold on parliamentary debates on North Africa. Senegalese deputy Blaise Diagne was a voice for colonial reform, especially at the beginning of the 1920s. As time went on, his relations with the colonial establishment in Dakar grew increasingly cordial.

In Belgium, Parliament devoted even less time to colonial affairs, except briefly in the 1930s when a bailout was needed. Although it voted on the colonial budget, the administration in the Congo was free to shift expenditures from one category to another; frequently, the budget was not submitted until six months after the fiscal year began. The Colonial Ministry itself, a fiefdom of the Catholic party, was a well-insulated world of its own. The "empire of silence" was already well protected by the penumbra of self-satisfaction that had grown around it.

The League of Nations Mandates Commission did not seriously compromise the autonomy of the territories under its jurisdiction. All it required was conscientious application of the settled principles of responsible colonial administration, and open access for sales agents and missionaries from all parts. As Lord Hailey observed with respect to native administration in Tanganyika, but with general application, "the influence exercised . . . by the League of Nations was unimportant." The Mandates Commission was dominated by such respected elder colonial statesmen as Lord Lugard, who characterized the "sacred trust" described in Article 22 of the League's covenant as "only a more precise definition of the ideals of the British Colonial system."[65]

On the internal front, the primary limitation on the autonomy of the colonial state was the strength of the settler community. As citizens in the land of subjects, they inevitably viewed themselves as a constituted and exclusive civil society, whose interests the state was obligated to serve. Where the formal structure of the preexisting state was retained as the instrument of colonial domination, the administration was able to limit the settlers' role. Thus, in Morocco, Tunisia, and Swaziland, although the immigrant community might constitute as much as 10 percent of the population and acquired extensive land holdings, the colonial state generally held the upper hand, if sometimes with difficulty. Settlers in such circumstances could not so easily claim standing as the core legitimate element of civil society. At the other extreme lay Algeria and Southern Rhodesia, where in different ways the settler community had gained almost total ascendancy.

In Algeria this was accomplished by settler exploitation of the assimilation doctrine simultaneously to bring about a juridical incorporation of Algeria with France (the departmentalization of the settler-populated zones) and to retain as a shield the apparatus of a separate Algerian administration under settler domination. Within the colonial state, occasional impulses to reassert its autonomy in order to create the conditions for its long-term reproduction inevitably withered in the face of settler intransigence, as in the case of the reform efforts of Maurice Violette, governor-general from 1926 to 1928. Nor could Paris impose political changes directed toward winning the loyalty of then-important currents of Algerian opinion seeking equality and a form of assimilation (the Jeunes Algériens). The determined effort of the Popular Front government to force passage of the Blum-Violette law, whose central provisions would have accorded citizenship status to a series of special categories of Algerians who had served the colonial state, totaling about twenty-four thousand, foundered on the resolute opposition of the settler lobby.[66]

In Southern Rhodesia surrender of the colonial state to the settlers took the form of granting full self-government on the basis of franchise provisions that excluded all but a tiny handful of Africans. At this juncture, colonial sovereignty was still exercised by the British South Africa Company, now convinced that it could never make government a profitable enterprise for its shareholders. The issue became posed as a choice between incorporation into the Union of South Africa or "responsible" government, meaning a settler regime. A referendum among white voters revealed a 8,774 to 5,989 preference for a separate settler government, established in 1923, with the colonizing power retaining a nominal legislative veto right (never exercised in these years) and residual sovereignty (asserted only when "independence" was unilaterally declared in 1965).

Elsewhere, landed settler interests achieved significant influence and large representation on colonial councils but never a decisive voice in instances where colonial state reason placed officialdom at odds with the settlers. The struggle between settler and state was particularly intense in Kenya, where official statements proclaiming the colony as "white man's country" since the era of construction were contradicted but not entirely superseded by postwar doctrines of the "paramountcy of native interests." Resolution of these teleological anomalies, in the last instance, remained in the hands of the colonial state, which in these years asserted and—imperfectly—upheld its autonomy.

The High Commission territories of Bechuanaland, Bastuoland, and Swaziland were a case unto themselves in the autonomy issue. With British overrule supervised from the High Commission in South Africa, and the bulk of the colonial personnel recruited in South Africa, these territories stood somewhat apart from the main stream of British imperial ideology. Indeed, an investigatory report in 1931 by Sir A. Pim found that in Basutoland the colonial state pursued a policy of noninterference rather than indirect rule; indeed, his report concluded that the colonial state hardly existed at all.[67] The logic of colonial rule here was grounded in the ultimately contradictory axioms that the territories would eventually find beneficial incorporation into South Africa, though this could only take place with their consent. The immediate inference, for the colonial state, was that rule was a minimalist holding operation pending the evolution of South Africa in a direction that would facilitate transfer of the territories.

PURSUING LEGITIMATION

At this flood tide of empire, the colonial state was not sorely tested in meeting its imperative of legitimation. Both in Europe and Africa the bedrock validation was simply its unchallenged existence. For the colonizing powers the debates that had raged at the time of conquest about the wisdom of African annexations were long stilled. The innate proprietary impulses of a state, commanding preservation of its territorial heritage, held sway. In Africa, although anticolonial nationalism was already a tangible force in parts of the northern rim, and its precursors were beginning to be visible in a number of other regions, subject populations (other than Egyptians) could see no way of dislodging it. No one could foretell the possibility of successful armed struggle or imagine that the colonial state would voluntarily relinquish power.

There were, however, some new vectors in the postwar configuration of forces in Europe and Africa that induced the development of more elaborated doctrines of justification. As I noted earlier, the interwar world system was no longer entirely dominated by the imperial states and the ethos associated with their ascendancy. Novel themes began to emerge in the international jurisprudence of colonial rule, in particular the unsettling notion that imperial sovereignty comported obligations toward the subject population, as yet unenforceable. The demon of self-determination had escaped confinement. For Britain, the ransom of the war effort was concession of self-rule to the oldest colony, Ireland, and the 1917 pledge of "the progressive realisation of responsible government in India as an integral part of the British Empire."[68]

The terrible carnage of the war unhinged the social consensus and brought a surge of lower-class militancy, translated into the strengthening of socialist parties and the emergence of Communist representation. In the short term the apparent equation of capitalism and imperialism, for the socialist parties, was obscured by the hiding hand of nationalism. As Raoul Girardet put the matter in the French case, socialist reticence to engage in a fundamental critique of empire in Africa demonstrated that "the colonial idea tended henceforward to form part of the very powerful system of restrictions and taboos which dominate everything touching upon the expression of national sentiment . . . any basic challenge, direct or indirect . . . ran the risk of seeming suspect in the face of the exigencies and imperatives of elementary patriotism."[69] In a compendium of its colonial policy positions from 1885 to 1960, published in the wake of the decolonization debacle by the Belgian Socialist Party, only twenty-nine of 381 pages covered the period before 1956.[70] Nonetheless, new social and ideological forces on the left foreshadowed future sources of challenge to the legitimacy of the colonial vocation. Thus, within the metropolitan state and to a small extent externally, doctrines investing the colonial mission with beneficent purpose helped disarm potential critics—most of whom, at this time, wanted only to be convinced.

Within Africa the emergence of a class of Africans armed with Western education created an audience for the discourse of legitimation beyond the customary ruling classes or Islamic notables whose co-optation had been the preeminent concern in the construction phase. The educated Africans—often lexically characterized in terms betokening their proximity to European culture (*évolué, assimilado*)—were viewed in patronizing terms, as in a 1920 address by Governor Sir Hugh Clifford to the Nigerian Council:

> There has during the last few months been a great deal of loose and gaseous talk . . . which has for the most part emanated from a self-selected and a self-appointed congregation of educated African gentlemen who collectively style themselves the "West African National Conference." . . . It can only be described as farcical to suppose that . . . continental Nigeria can be represented by a handful of gentlemen drawn from a half-dozen Coast tribes—men born and bred in British administered towns situated on the sea-shore, who in the safety of British protection have peacefully pursued their studies under British teachers.[71]

The colonial state still embraced the comforting thought that it protected the subject population from, in Lugard's phrase, "the will . . . of a small minority of educated and Europeanized natives who have nothing in common with them, and whose interests are often opposed to theirs."[72] Nonetheless, the inevitable growth of this category of the African population, and its necessary role in the auxiliary ranks of the colonial state, meant that texts of legitimation required some reformulation to accommodate its interests and concerns.[73]

DISCOURSES OF LEGITIMACY

Several new themes thus appeared as salient components of the discourse of legitimation in the interwar period. They were not entirely novel; their innovation lay not in their originality but in the stress they received. The most important of these themes were good government, development, and trusteeship.

Good government, in this context, meant "sound administration." Rational, prudent management of the colonial estates by a professional cadre of administrators applying increasingly scientific methods to their development and impartial adjudication of conflicts: this was the refrain of the self-composed encomium to colonial rule. As a Platonic guardian class, colonial officialdom represented itself as the disinterested servant of the subject population, basking as philosopher-king in the full sunlight of wisdom, ruling firmly but justly over those still enclosed in the cave of ignorance, who could see only distorted shadows of their true interests flickering on the darkened walls.[74]

The sturdy confidence of the official class in the legitimacy of its own role was rooted in this notion of guardianship, which doubtless in subtle ways enhanced its credibility. As E. A. Brett notes, "It is important to understand that the colonial system was seen by its agents as essentially a moral force; as an agency whose primary purpose was to bring Africans to civilization."[75] Each colonizer tended to perceive its own version of good government as perched on the summit of virtuous guardianship. For Lugard, only under the British Empire "does the African enjoy such a measure of freedom and impartial justice, or a more sympathetic treatment."[76] Comparable notions may be found in the colonial myths of the other colonizers: immortal and generous France, offering its civilization and republican heritage to Africa; prudent Belgium as the custodian of prosperity; the rulers of tropical Portugal, who "like no other people, made their enterprise of exploration and conquest a transcendent campaign, a sharing of spiritual values";[77] Italy as the new Rome, sharing its imperial grandeur.

The idea of good government and visions of its potential impact perhaps reached their highest development in the Belgian system, which took the form of a comprehensive paternalism. In the hands of an expert administration the subject was malleable clay, to be reworked into a willing cog in an efficient productive machine. In the words of Louis Franck, colonial minister from 1918 to 1924, "We wish to form . . . not a black Belgian, but a better Congolese, that is, a robust, vigorously healthy, and hard-working Negro, proud of a task conscientiously accomplished, respectful of the collectivity to which he belongs."[78] For both metropolitan and African audiences, good government found frequent expression in familial metaphors; in this idiom, the harsher realities of daily hegemony—police operations and military occupations—became softened into the formative discipline of the stern but loving parent.

In the imagery of interwar discourse the colonial realm was portrayed as a vast estate awaiting fructification. A series of major works by influential colonial statesmen elaborated on this theme. For Albert Sarraut, French colonial minister from 1920 to 1924, *mise en valeur* was not only an opportunity for the colonial state but also a duty to the world at large. No single state had a right to allow its fertile soils to lie fallow indefinitely, in this view; not just France but the whole industrial world needed colonial raw materials. "The France that colonizes does not work for herself alone, her advantage is inseparable from that of the world."[79] Lugard, in his 1922 work *Dual Mandate in British Tropical Africa,* made a parallel argument: enlightened rule and the development it made possible fulfilled the mandates from both the subject populations and the world as a whole. Franck, as colonial minister and as publicist, was a tireless apostle of mise en valeur; he even managed to extract an annual 15-million Belgian franc parliamentary contribution to colonial development, which came to an end as soon as he left the ministry.[80]

Sarraut also fought hard to wrench from the French treasury some public development capital for the African territories. Although Algeria received significant French state loans and subsidies between the wars (4 billion francs in loans during the 1930s), this was tribute to the settler lobby rather than funding for mise en valeur discourse.[81] The subtext remained fiscal self-sufficiency; development was merely declaratory vision.

The same observation applies to the British territories. The 1929 Colonial Development and Welfare Act was a symbolic statement of historical importance, asserting the developmental purposes of the colonial state with a resource base enhanced by imperial contributions. The substance fell far short of the symbols; the anemic funding level of one million pounds annually provided only a whiff of development capital.

Trusteeship as vindication of hegemony catapulted into the language of domination with the Versailles peace treaty debates. In jostling for the repartitioned German territories, colonizers found it expedient to clothe their claims in the advantages that would be conferred on populations to be placed under their sovereignty. Thus, the exercise of colonial rule in the League mandates—and by implicit extension other colonies—became a "sacred trust of civilization." The landmark statement articulating the trusteeship doctrine as colonial state policy was the 1923 Devonshire White Paper, precipitated by the obstreperous claims of immigrant communities to entrenchment of their domination through "responsible" government:

> Primarily Kenya is an African territory, and His Majesty's Government think it necessary definitely to record their considered opinion that the interests of the African Natives must be paramount, and that if and when those interests and the interests of the immigrant races should conflict, the former should prevail. . . . In the administration of Kenya His Majesty's Government regard themselves as exercising a trust in behalf of the African population, and they are unable to delegate or share this trust, the object of which may be defined as the protection and advancement of the Native races.[82]

In appointing itself trustee, against the claims of the nine thousand whites and twenty-five thousand Indians then settled in Kenya, the colonial state simultaneously filed its brief for legitimation, hegemony, and autonomy. The paramountcy theme, also of immediate application in Tanganyika and Northern Rhodesia, played a critical role in defining future patterns of political evolution.

Empire entered state discourse in Europe as a part of the European nationalist charter. Empire was perceived as underpinning a state's claims to its importance on the international scene. Without its Central African colonies, Belgium would be a small buffer state, with provincial perspectives: *"petit pays, petit esprit,"* ran the saying. For Britain and France, after the numbing costs of the Great War, empire was more critical than ever to the "great power" standing that for nearly four centuries they had come to regard as a natural right. For both, the imperial reserves of military manpower and economic resources were seen as critical to survival; some two hundred and fifty thousand overseas subjects, mostly African, died under the French flag.

The mystique of empire in the paroxysm of nationalism found its most intoxicating expression as one foundation of the Estado Novo. For Salazar, the central place of the colonies in the renaissance of the Portuguese state was "a perfect expression of our national consciousness, and a close affirmation of the colonizing temperament of the Portuguese, [designed] for the aggrandizement of Portugal . . . and to make clear to the rest of Europe our position as a great colonial power."[83] Another Portuguese writer defined the imperial charter of the Portuguese state in lyrical terms as "the notion of vast territories over which . . . our flag

167

flies. . . . It is the knowledge that our sovereignty as a small European state spreads prodigously over three continents and is summed up in the magnificent certainty that we are the third colonial power in the world . . . the ancestral memory of an astonishing gallery of discoverers and builders, who, moved by a sacred impulse, carried to the ends of the world our ships, our dominion—and our faith."[84]

Mussolini echoed these sentiments, with a trace of sexual innuendo, in declaring that Italy had "a right to empire as a fertile nation which has the pride and will to propagate its race over the face of the earth, a virile people in the strict sense of the word." The expression of virility through conquest was extraordinarily expensive to the Italian state; state budget deficits rose from 2,119 million lira in 1934 and 1935 to the ruinous level of 60,389 million in 1939 and 1940 (before Italian entry into the war).[85]

Such poetic statements notwithstanding, the colonial state in its quest for metropolitan legitimation began to encounter difficulties on the profitability front. There were exceptions, such as the Belgian Congo, but overall the promises of untapped wealth at the hour of conquest were not fulfilled. A literature appeared drawing up "balance sheets" of imperialism. Grover Clark, in a 1936 study, concluded that the colonial system—especially its African component—had failed in all its claims to deliver benefits to the imperial powers.[86] Constant Southworth, focusing on the French Empire, reached identical conclusions in 1931.[87] Jacques Marseille, a French Marxist economic historian, offers persuasive evidence that by the 1930s capital had determined that few profitable outlets for colonial investment existed and lost interest in the imperial venture.[88] All the more important for the colonial state was its rejoinder to metropolitan skeptics that its administrative costs were imposed on its subject population.

A message of welfare started to appear in the text of legitimation addressed to the colonized audience as well. Schools began to symbolize uplift, and there slowly percolated into the popular consciousness the linkage between schooling and life chances. Primary schools sprinkled the landscape, although secondary schools were few and far between and there was no university except Fourah Bay between Algiers and Johannesburg. The moral charter of the colonial state required recognition of government responsibility for education—not only for its functional contribution in producing subaltern personnel but also as the vessel for conveying "civilization." Budgetary penury and the requirement of financial self-sufficiency, however, kept its expansion limited. In 1925 Nigerian educational expenditures were just 116,301 pounds, or 1.8 percent of state outlays.[89] In most places only the capacity of the missions to provide education at rock-bottom prices made its growth possible.

Health as a significant policy sphere for the colonial state emerged not simply as a welfare service valued by the subject population but also in response to a growing fear that population was stagnant or even declining in a number of areas. The harsh impositions in the years of construction and the ravages of epidemics that accompanied colonial penetration had decimated communities, and often the animal herds on which their livelihoods depended. Jan Vansina estimates that Central Africa lost at least one-third and perhaps one-half of its population during the first phase of colonial state rule.[90] Libyan population losses during the Italian reconquista campaign were comparable. In Algeria the murderous campaigns of Bugeaud and his successors and the ravages of refoulement sent the Algerian population into a prolonged decline that ended only in the 1890s.[91] Governor-General Angoulvant wrote in 1917 that sleeping sickness in French sub-Saharan Africa "had followed a path parallel to our colonization. . . . We have been the principal agents of propagation. . . . These facts create a special obligation toward the affected population."[92] According to a contemporary observer, France had come to the realization after World War I that "West Africa was a country without Negroes," yet that labor "would to no small degree determine the extent and direction of development.[93] No Africans, no taxes, no porters, no tirailleurs, no road builders: a rudimentary public-health system was an evident necessity, as well as a legitimating amenity.

Finally, the appearance of elements within the subject population demanding some definition of the pathway to the future compelled the beginnings of a colonial state response. This aspect of the legitimation dilemma in the consolidation phase appeared only in the French and British colonial realms. In the former, with the French state firmly committed to the perpetuity of its sovereignty, enlarged political voice and African promotion could only come through changed personal status. Thus, the primary issue was the combating of disabilities tied to subject status: the indigénat, labor obligations, differential civil-service pay, denial of political rights. Although citizenship through naturalization was possible, there were exacting requirements, including completion of military service; more important, for Muslims (except in the four Senegalese old communes), naturalization necessitated abandonment of Islamic civil status in favor of the French civil code. Africans enjoying citizenship were not numerous—about seven thousand Algerians, the originaires of the four Senegalese communes (five thousand people voted in the epic 1914 election that sent Diagne as the first African deputy to Parliament, including several hundred whites), a few thousand elsewhere. But in this period nearly all sub-Saharan elites, and a significant fraction of the elites in Algeria, structured their claims through the vehicle of the citizenship question and allied political rights. Among the évolué class, the French system had a greater capacity than any other of eliciting loyalty.

In the British case, political advance could occur only at the territorial level. One might say that three models of political evolution were available: the Egyptian, the South African, and the Indian. The first involved constrained sovereignty hemmed in by treaty restrictions, particularly in the security field. The South African path led to transfer of power to the "civilized," or white, population. The emergent Indian paradigm of decolonization prescribed progressive devolution to representative institutions, with the colonial state withdrawing upward to the center and inward to the security and financial core of the government apparatus. Neither the model to be applied nor the timing of its application was at all clear. Neatly summarizing the opaque vision of the future was a 1922 statement by Winston Churchill regarding Kenya, in the midst of heated controversy over both immediate and ultimate political rights and roles for its European, Indian, and African communities. His statements had some southern African echoes, suggesting invocation of the Rhodes dictum of "equal rights for all civilized men." Africans and Indians might thus qualify, but only if deemed to conform to European standards, in the definition of which the European community had "a right to be fully consulted." Churchill continued: "We do not contemplate any settlement or system which will prevent . . . Kenya . . . becoming a characteristically and distinctively British colony looking forward in the full fruition of time to complete responsible self-government."[94] The full fruition of time, in the official mind, was still measured in centuries.

Equally unresolved were the basic institutional units around which evolution would occur and the issue as to which categories of Africans would be the ultimate heirs to the colonial state. The Lugardian view, dominant through most of this period, foresaw native administrations serving as the operative centers of political evolution. From these would emerge some loosely defined "federation of native states." In this view, the central administration—the colonial state per se—would remain a purely European echelon of tutelary governance, in which African elites had no place.[95] Combinations of the African territories into larger units were contemplated—East Africa, Central Africa, even a West African grouping. Some thought was given to transferring the southern Sudan to

Uganda. In the French case, Upper Volta was divided between the Ivory Coast and the Soudan in 1932, apparently to facilitate labor recruitment for Ivory Coast plantations and the newly created Office du Niger.[96] Chad lost its status as a separate territory from 1934 to 1938. Thus, not only was decolonization not on offer even as a remote objective for any colonial occupant save Britain, but the territorial frame for ultimate political evolution also remained indeterminate. For the subject, discourse of legitimation was confined to promising some advance for those accepting European cultural norms within the colonial frame.

REVENUE: THE COLONIAL STATE AS FRUGAL GOURMET

The basic patterns of revenue generation for the colonial state established during the era of construction remained in place during the consolidation phase. The principle of financial self-sufficiency was now firmly rooted, with only nominal amounts of public mise en valeur capital from the metropole and occasional deficiency appropriations for the most impoverished territories. The exceptions, noted earlier, were settler Algeria and the Italian colonies, where substantial sums were committed, not to indigenous uplift but to creating the conditions for Italian settlement. For the imperial center, the doctrine was colonial state self-sufficiency; for the colonial administration, this dictum translated into compelling the African subjects to finance their domination. To accomplish this feat was the essence of the revenue imperative, and it continued to be the pivot around which much of routine territorial administration turned.

Almost everywhere, the head tax continued to be a substantial (usually the dominant) source of state income. Bula Matari had by the 1920s routinized its collection. The exception was the Gold Coast, where it was never found expedient to create such a tax, although it was debated at times during the interwar period. Some transhumant Saharan populations escaped its bite, where the cost and security risks of its collection would outweigh its returns. Most African communities had come to accept the head tax as an inescapable component of colonial servitude, even if they perceived almost no returns for it. In Ubangi-Chari in 1910, for example, 63 percent of the revenue derived (mostly) from the head tax went to paying the salaries of the agents of domination, with only 1 percent each to education and health;[97] these proportions changed little in the interwar years.

As African incorporation into the cash economy grew, the head-tax rates were steadily increased. In the Abomey region of Dahomey, for

Table 5-2. Percentage of Territorial Revenue from Head Tax, AOF

Territory	1925	1930	1936
Senegal	22.3	13.1	24.3
Soudan	53.4	49.3	51.9
Guinea	69.5	61.2	54.0

Source: Jean Suret-Canale, *Afrique Noire: L'ère coloniale, 1900–1945* (Paris: Editions Sociales, 1964), 436.

example, they rose from 8 francs in 1920 to 33 in 1938, while in impoverished northern Dahomey they went up from 3 to 11; during the 1930s, the capitation tax constituted 90 percent of territorial receipts.[98] In Uganda newly arrived Governor Robert Coryndon as his first measure in 1918 raised the African poll tax by 50 percent, while imposing a nominal one-pound tax on Europeans.[99] Sustaining head-tax collections when the depression brought sharp drops in crop prices and wage opportunities was a severe test of the state's hegemonical capacities; that it largely succeeded reaffirmed its entitlement to the image of Bula Matari.

The fiscal burden born by the subject population was by no means limited to the head tax. In most territories the bulk of export taxation hit African crops; in this case the incidence of the tax was exclusively on the producer, as the marketing intermediaries were able to transfer its impact back to the farm gate in the price paid. In one of the rare studies that endeavors to estimate relative tax incidence, Vali Jamal calculates that in Uganda in 1938 rural Africans paid an effective tax on income of 28 percent, whereas the vastly more prosperous non-Africans paid 6.7 percent. When the differential impact of import and export taxes are factored into the equation, the disproportion becomes more dramatic. In 1927, for example, common salt (consumed by Africans) paid a 42 percent levy, while table salt (bought by immigrants) was charged 20 percent. Gray cloth paid 35 percent duty, wools and silks 20 percent; candles were dutiable at 24 percent, light bulbs at 3 percent. The colonial treasurer report for 1936 stated: "In Uganda the bulk of the taxation is paid by large numbers in rural areas and the amount paid by each individual represents a very large proportion of his money income. In many cases, the proportion approaches 100%. In Uganda taxation is the principal incentive to labour and production."[100] These calculations were verified by an anthropological monograph that measured total cash flows and fiscal incidence in a relatively isolated part of Uganda, the Baamba region of Toro; the colonial state managed in one way or another to engross two-thirds of total peasant revenues. The fraction that came from cus-

Table 5-3.   Belgian Congo Revenues, 1929

Category	Amount (Millions of Francs)
Customs	196.6
European taxes	110.0
African taxes	84.6
Ivory	14.6
Administrative receipts[a]	57.6
Portfolio[b]	114.2
Total	577.6

Source: Louis Franck, *Le Congo Belge* (Brussels: La Renaissance du Livre, 1930), 1:194–95.

a. An important part of administrative receipts were court fines.

b. Portfolio revenues came from dividends in colonial corporations in which the state held shares.

toms levies was not visible to the Amba, although the impact of the export tax was recognized by those closer to the center.[101]

The crushing weight of taxation on Africans partly measured the capacity of Europeans effectively to resist responsibility for the revenue imperative. The Swaziland figures in table 5-6 are eloquent in this respect, if one recollects that the first task of the colonial state when it assumed power in 1906 was to sort out the anarchy in land rights resulting in venal and disorderly concessions to Europeans made by Swazi chiefs. The settlement had allocated 967,558 hectares to Europeans, 687,635 to the Swazi nation, and 63,549 to the crown. The European beneficiaries of this eleemosynary arbitration of fraud-riddled land claims displayed no fiscal gratitude. In Algeria interwar estimates calculated that Algerians paid 27 percent of the total tax burden, with rural households paying 15 to 20 percent of their income to the state; almost no French residents paid this much. This tax rate can be set against the fact that expenditures overwhelmingly favored the European community; in 1930 Algerians made up only 8.6 percent of the secondary school enrollment, for example. At least 90 percent of state salaries went to Europeans; more than seven million hectares of land had been confiscated from Algerians and been given at nominal cost to settlers.[102]

Impossible to quantify but of enormous importance during the interwar period was the use of forced labor, often unremunerated, for the construction of the communications infrastructure, above all the road network, which assumed growing importance as motor vehicles became the primary means of transport. In 1928 AOF Governor-General Jules Carde attempted to measure the importance of this labor tax, in an ad-

Table 5-4.   Main Budget Receipts, AEF, 1928 (Thousands of Francs)

Category	Gabon	Congo	Ubangi	Chad
Head tax	2,925	7,000	7,675	7,500
Licenses	1,275	442	660	70
Forest	7,025	35	3	0
PTT	466	1,455	294	89
Registry	125	822	90	0
Domain	300	1,505	2,385	88

Source: Georges Bruel, *L'Afrique Equatoriale Africaine* (Paris: Lerose, 1930), 463.

dress to the AOF Council: "In addition to a monetary expenditure of about 56 million francs, there was a commitment of *prestation* [obligatory labor] days which corresponded to an expenditure of 258 million francs. In this fashion, we were able to construct and maintain in French West Africa in six years some 32,000 kilometers of roads for an average cash outlay of 10,000 francs per kilometer."[103]

In all colonial systems during this period, public infrastructure developed was largely financed by what amounted to a labor tax. In the British case, what was termed "political labor" was impressed for construction of the Port Harcourt and Baro-Kano rail lines in Nigeria and the Uasin Gishu branch in Kenya. In Uganda the Native Authority ordinance of 1919 authorized sixty days per year of forced labor on building the arteries that serviced the cotton system, which in turn provided in various ways the bulk of state revenue at this time. Compulsory public-works labor was also widely employed in Kenya and Nyasaland.[104]

Forced labor as a fiscal resource was most heavily utilized by France; only the rhetorical skills of the immensely presentable Blaise Diagne pleading the French case at the 1930 International Labor Organization (ILO) conference on forced labor saved France from an embarrassing rebuke. In AOF the Popular Front governor-general, Marcel de Coppet, a critic of the prestation policy, conducted an inquiry into the practice,

Table 5-5.   Main Expenditures, AEF, 1928 (Thousands of Francs)

Category	Gabon	Congo	Ubangi	Chad
Central admin.	272	138	324	369
Local admin.	4,432	4,547	5,285	3,447
Health	1,430	2,443	950	787
Education	356	524	409	164

Source: Georges Bruel, *L'Afrique Equatoriale Française* (Paris: Lerose, 1930), 463.

Table 5-6. Main Revenue Sources, Selected British Territories (Thousands of Pounds)

Category	Sierra Leone 1938	Swaziland 1935–36	Kenya 1938	Uganda 1935
Customs	402	20	835	437
African taxes	238	41	532	650[b]
Immigrant direct taxes	not available	6	153	29
Licenses	38	10	57	21
Other	210	74[a]	969	56
Total	886	151	2,546	1,193

Source: Annual Colonial Reports.
   a. Includes 48,000 pound imperial grant-in-aid.
   b. Includes 100,000 pound cotton tax, whose incidence was entirely on African growers.

which put its finger on the revenue dilemma as the driving force in the policy. The *commandant de cercle* was ordered to construct and maintain a basic road network, as well as local airfields and rest houses for touring administrators. On the one hand, it was made clear that his efficiency report would depend on his success; on the other, he was provided with little or no funding—perhaps 10,000 francs, barely enough to purchase shovels. Thus, de Coppet concluded, "the lack of means had to be filled by the exercise of constraint on the natives."[105]

Officially, in the French case, prestations were limited to about ten days per year, organized outside the agricultural season and limited to work within five kilometers of the village unless rations were provided; after 1930, when French practices came under unwelcome ILO scrutiny, persons could make a cash payment in lieu of labor service. In practice, these limits were widely exceeded by administrators, indigénat in hand. As de Coppet noted in a 25 January 1937 dispatch, "We lie in France, in Europe, before the entire world, at Geneva to the International Labor Organization when, regulations and circulars in hand we speak of labor in the colonies on public works projects. We dishonor our colonial administration and we demoralize the functionaries in asking them to apply on paper only regulations which are in practice inapplicable."[106]

Sundry juridical devices were employed to meet the urgent infrastructure requirements of the cash-strapped colonial state. Beyond prestations, another widely employed mechanism was the military conscription obligation. Manpower not needed for actual military service was assigned to a *deuxième contingent,* which was in effect a forced-labor battalion assigned to road construction.[107] Massive coerced recruitment of labor was required for the two gigantic state infrastructure projects of this period, the Office du Niger and the Congo-Océan rail line linking Brazzaville and Pointe Noire in AEF. The terrible mortality rate on the Congo-Océan project was etched into the popular consciousness in the saying that every railway tie symbolized the corpse of a worker. The Sara regions of southern Chad bore the brunt of this conscription; characterized in official reports as a *belle race,* strong, docile, and passive, the Sara were tapped for some 20,900 men for railway building, of whom ten thousand paid not just a labor but a life tax.[108]

ACCUMULATING: DEVELOPING THE COLONIAL ESTATES

Tightly bonded to the revenue imperative was the accumulation imperative. With mise en valeur now an integral part of colonial state discourse, development was an active item on the agenda. But how could this be accomplished, based simply on commercial linkages with the natural economy of rural Africa, whose limits by the close of the construction era were well recognized? To foster accumulation, there were three basic strategies that appeared available: to attract metropolitan capital, to induce European individual or corporate commercial farming, and to reorient African agriculture toward export-crop production. All three of these avenues of accumulation dated back to the first phase of the colonial state, but they took on new importance and stress after the Great War.

Although some major projects were undertaken directly by the state— the Gezira cotton scheme in the Sudan, the Office du Niger in the Soudan—the liberal economic doctrines then dominant held that state action should be limited to developing the infrastructure. The simple capacity of the colonial state in the 1920s to manage an economic endeavor was limited; the Belgian Congo did try to operate the Kilo-Moto gold mines in the far northeast but found itself unable to assemble the technical skills required for the task. It was forced to negotiate an extraordinarily generous management contract, turning over control to a private group for a negligible $2 million capital stake.[109]

The three avenues were in turn tightly bound to the revenue requirements of the state. All three necessitated important public overhead investment: in the short run, the road, port, and railroad facilities, without which profitability on any of these fronts was impossible, and in the longer term, education and health investments in human capital. The head tax—in spite of the vigor of its collection and the increase in its level—had an absolute ceiling, in terms of its ability to finance a long-term expansion of the colonial state and meet the requirements of public infrastructure. Even when revenue was enhanced by the disguised taxation of forced labor, colonial state agents were acutely aware of the urgent need for an enlarged resource base.

Private capital, however, was on the whole reticent and skeptical. High-value minerals might be attractive: copper in Northern Rhodesia and the Belgian Congo, diamonds in Angola and the Belgian Congo, gold in the Gold Coast. But most territories had no such lures, and for the boardroom in London and Paris, the African landscape, aside from South Africa, was barren. The colonial state, on its end, was reluctant to solicit capital sources outside the ruling power; foreign capital sent tremors of apprehension about possible threats to colonial security. Thus, metropolitan capital held the whip hand in the conditions imposed for its colonial involvement. These came down to favorable tax regimes, generous land concessions, and guarantees of inexpensive labor supply.

The fiscal concessions meant that in the interwar period colonial revenues did not benefit greatly from such investment as did occur. In the Belgian Congo, as table 5-3 indicates, the state did derive significant returns for the passive shares it claimed in return for land and other concessions. For the most part, the head tax and customs receipts funded the state. Peemans demonstrates that during this period corporate profits were untaxed and distributed dividends at a maximum rate of 12 percent; personal income taxes for Europeans in the private (or public) sector ranged from 0 to 9 percent.[110] Large land concessions had the disadvantage of provoking domestic challenges to colonial security. In Nigeria persistent Lever group requests for land concessions for oil-palm plantations were rejected by the colonial administration in the 1920s, fearful of the contention that granting them would arouse. The Belgian Congo, of more hegemonical disposition, was willing to pay the ransom to secure the Lever investment; by 1930, title to some 350,000 hectares in five zones had been accorded, though only thirty thousand had been developed. Lever also received monopoly buying rights to palm products collected from wild trees in the surrounding regions.[111]

European agricultural settlement continued welcome in Kenya, southern Africa, the Belgian Congo, Tunisia, Morocco, and the Italian colonies. Elsewhere, the colonial state had concluded that accumulation was only viable through African peasant export agriculture. The day of the crass spoliations on a gigantic scale as in the initial phases of Algerian and Southern Rhodesian occupation were over, but where settlement was still favored the colonial administration had the task of extinguishing indigenous land rights in conceded areas, and often granting the property at low cost along with diverse start-up subsidies.

European enterprise of whatever form operated on a labor-intensive basis. In many areas it was unwilling to offer working conditions or compensation sufficient to attract a voluntary flow. Doubtless many enterprises could not have functioned without what amounted to a state subsidy imposed on the subject population for its labor costs. To this one may add the still powerful factor of the resilient social self-sufficiency of many rural communities; for many, purely economic incentives would not have sufficed to induce acceptance of wage labor for European enterprises.

The magnitude of the labor recruitment challenge is illustrated by figures from the Belgian Congo. In 1915 there were only 37,368 wage earners; in 1920 this figure rose to 125,120; in 1925 to 274,538; then in a single year leapt to 421,953.[112] The diamond, gold, and copper mines each required labor forces of twenty thousand, which until the late 1920s worked on short-term contracts and experienced high mortality rates, thus needing constant replenishment.

From such needs emerged the administrative ideology that for the African subject work was not only an ennobling virtue but also an absolute obligation. A 1922 circular from Governor-General Maurice Lippens in the Belgian Congo placed local administrators under strict orders to take whatever measures were required to ensure a labor flow to mine and plantation: "It is a mistake to believe . . . that once taxes are paid and other legal obligations met, the native may remain inactive. Under no circumstances may magistrates or officials express this opinion. In every case, I should consider this to be a lack of discipline violating the recommendations of the government and our most positive obligations toward our black subjects."[113] Implementation of such instructions turned local administrators into man catchers and by the late 1920s led to a severe labor crisis. To protect this crucial pillar of accumulation, the colonial state and major corporations turned to a policy of stabilizing their labor force and encouraging family establishment in the worker compounds.

Analogous doctrines are found in other colonial state doctrines. In the Portuguese case, former Estado Novo Colonial Minister Vieira Machado wrote: "It is necessary to inspire in the black the idea of work of abandoning his laziness and his depravity if we want to exercise a colonizing action to protect him. . . . If we want to civilize the native we must make him adopt as an elementary moral precept the notion that he has no right to live without working."[114] This concept remained enshrined in what was advertised as a reform of the labor code in 1926, which continued the practice of requiring Africans to accept assignment to labor service unless they could prove that they were marketing a crop surplus, trading, or employed by the administration. Under this arrangement the administration delivered to plantations and other employers a flow of contract labor, a system that persisted until 1962.[115]

The head tax itself, throughout colonial Africa, was valued not only as a revenue source but also as a compulsion to work. The settled view of the time, for state and private sector, is conveyed in a communication from two Belgian Congo company officials: "[The tax system] is not only to reimburse the government in some measure for the cost of occupying all the territories, and of providing protection for the native population. Taxes also have a higher purpose, which is to accustom the Negroes to work."[116]

A final cornerstone to accumulation-driven policies was directing African agriculture into export-crop production, which simultaneously assured income for head-tax payment and a second strike at the resource flow through export taxes. Thus, the colonial state developed agricultural services to promote and if need be enforce cultivation of crops with an external market, the most widely favored being vegetable-oil sources (peanuts and palm products) and cotton. These commodities had the additional attraction, for the colonizing state, of supplying important industries in the home market.

Although peanut cultivation generally spread without state intervention more muscular than encouragement, cotton was a different matter and necessitated extensive coercion in such scattered sites as Mozambique, the Belgian Congo, Soudan, and Uganda. This mechanism was found in its most perfected form in the Belgian Congo, where the state devised a legal weapon in the ordinance of 20 February 1917 obliging all peasants to devote at least sixty days annually to crops prescribed by the administration; this was most vigorously used for cotton, which from tiny beginnings rose to seven hundred thousand planters by the late 1930s. Local administrators drew up an "agricultural program" for their territory, consisting of minimum surface areas for cash and some food crops. Failure to exhibit such cultivated acreage on the visit of the agronomist was prima facie evidence of contravention of the obligatory cultivation ordinance and exposed the offender to fines, beatings, or prison. Local administrators, as Zairian scholar Mulambu Muvulya laconically observes, were informed by circular that the 1917 ordinance equipped them with "the means necessary to induce cultivators to expand their crops." These means, he adds, "were nothing other than military or police occupation."[117] The dominant view of the newly created state agricultural service was expressed by one of its local agents in 1918: "The sole way to improve native agriculture is to force the blacks to place their crops following the principles indicated by competent agents. At this time, only the territorial administration, backed by armed force, can achieve this goal, and even this only temporarily."[118]

Although the impact of state response to its accumulation imperative was not evident in added revenue flows, there was a steady growth in basic infrastructure, which positioned the colonial economies to profit from the long commodity boom that followed World War II. Multipronged pressures on African societies to force labor into cash employment or cash-crop production also had their effect. Peasant societies may in some areas and in some respects have remained "uncaptured," as Hyden has argued.[119] But young men in growing numbers were actively seeking, not merely conscripted for, wage employment. And rural households had been incorporated into a regime where, one way or another, enough cash had to be generated to propitiate the wrath of the tax collector. Their products were drained by a transport system which, if not reaching everywhere, did come within reach of a large portion of the population.

THE COLONIAL STATE AT FLOOD TIDE

In its hour of consolidation, entrenched for what was still believed to be the longue durée, the African colonial state had fully developed its singular features, as a pure model of alien bureaucratic autocracy. Wayne, writing of Tanganyika, offers a cogent characterization: "The colonial state has been theorized as either the class agent of the metropolitan bourgeoisie, on the one hand, or as a relatively autonomous body which mediated among class forces in the colony, on the other . . . the colonial state was neither. It was, rather, a political bureaucracy, a form of rule in which bureaucrats are politicians and in which political actors outside the bureaucracy are suppressed or given a minimal role."[120] He adds that such a political formula is inherently unstable.

Indeed it was. On the eve of World War II the African colonial state, having weathered the tempest of the Great Depression, seemed securely rooted. Neither within nor without could anyone perceive the forces that were gathering to bring about its downfall only two decades later.

There were, it is true, some signs in the wind, which only a handful of the clairvoyant read accurately. The serious rioting in the Northern Rhodesian copperbelt in 1935 and 1940; the great cocoa holdup in the Gold Coast in 1937: small but portentous precursors of the militant popular action to come. The symptoms were more numerous of impending changes in the colonial world outside Africa: the West Indian disorders between 1935 and 1937, leading to the very pessimistic conclusions concerning the colonial status quo of the Moyne Commission; the long, bruising struggle in Britain and India over the 1935 Government of India Act; serious nationalist unrest in Indochina and the Levant mandates. If pressed, all might agree that, at some remote time, the colonial state in its existing form might be superseded by something else. Only Britain had even a vague project as to what this might be; for the others, whatever world lay beyond the colonial state was axiomatically within the permanent zone of sovereignty of the colonizing power.

Thus, the world drifted toward war, and the colonial state in Africa to a shattering of the operational code that had hitherto governed its exercise of rule. Memories of the carnage and terrible human costs of World War I were too recent for colonial state agents to contemplate the coming conflict with the chauvinistic enthusiasms widely present at the start of the previous conflagration. Neither did they dream that Bula Matari, in the final phase, as a consequence of the momentous changes wrought by the war, would be served by technicians of decolonization rather than commanders of domination.

—— *Chapter Six* ——

TOWARD
AFRICAN INDEPENDENCE

We all know in our heart that most Colonies, especially in Africa, will probably not be fit for complete independence for centuries.

—Colonial Office memorandum, 1942

The aims of the civilizing effort accomplished by France in her colonies rules out any idea of autonomy, any possibility of evolution outside the French bloc of empire; the eventual or even the ultimate institution of self-government must be avoided.

—Brazzaville Conference, 1944

A large number of Congolese interlocutors asked immediate independence. . . . [On the basis of their explanations,] the *Groupe de Travail* concluded that its interlocutors meant by immediate independence the immediate liberation of the individual.

—Belgian Government Working Group, 1958

THE CHANGING INTERNATIONAL ENVIRONMENT

Bula Matari, convalescent but apparently on the road to recovery after the debilitating impact of the Great Depression, was mortally wounded— at least as an alien construct—by World War II. The robust aura of invincibility and comfortable certitudes of the era of consolidation were progressively undermined by a newly hostile international environment and the burgeoning forces of African nationalism. The official mind was increasingly forced to contemplate that brooding nemesis: a future that could not simply be a reconstructed reproduction of the past. A progressively foreshortening time horizon enclosed the colonial state with narrowing options to avert or defer what then appeared as the apocalypse: African independence. The final phase of the life cycle of the African colonial state—the decolonization era—saw remarkable and accelerating transformations in colonial reason of state.

The swiftness of the changes, however, was not foreseeable by colonial officialdom as the Axis armies faltered and fell back. Nor did the assembly of nationalists gathered for the 1945 Manchester Pan-African Conference anticipate that a decade later they would find independence within reach. Of the colonial occupants, only Britain even contemplated a distant eventuality of transfer of sovereignty. In 1938, in a major policy statement, Colonial Secretary Malcolm MacDonald had declared:

> I think it is the gradual spread of freedom amongst all His Majesty's subjects in whatever part of the earth they live . . . a slow . . . evolutionary process. . . . There may even, sometimes, be inevitable setbacks. But over generations the evolutionary process goes on. . . . Even amongst the most backward races of Africa our main effort is to teach these peoples to stand always a little more securely on their own feet. . . . The trend is towards the ultimate establishment of the great commonwealth of free peoples and nations. . . . But it will be generations, perhaps even centuries, before that aim is accomplished in some cases.[1]

The grant of responsible government to Ceylon in 1931, the inevitable commitment to dominion status in the 1935 Government of India Act, and the official recognition that the West Indian rioting of 1935 to 1937 portended similar unrest elsewhere, necessitating political concessions, established a framework of policy postulates permitting leisurely movement toward self-government, although within a calendar measured in generations or centuries. In the French case, however, the colonial officialdom assembled at Brazzaville in 1944 resolutely excluded evolution outside the ambiguous frontiers of an enlarged France; as Overseas Minister René Pleven told the conference, "In the great French empire there are neither people to liberate nor racial discrimination to abolish. There are peoples who feel French, who wish, and to whom France wishes to give, an ever greater part in the life and in the democratic institutions of the French community."[2]

For the other colonizers, the notion of abandonment of imperial sovereignty was even more remote. Belgium's most distinguished imperial proconsul, Pierre Ryckmans, declared in his final address as governor-general in 1946 that "les jours du colonialisme sont révolus," but what he had in mind as the replacement for "colonialism" was a renovated colonial state less subservient to mendacious private corporate and settler interests and more rigorously obedient to its obligations of paternal tutelage to the subject population.[3] The postulate of perpetuity was unshaken for Portugal and Spain. Only Italy was stripped of colonial title as an immediate consequence of the war, and even in this instance Rome managed to recover Somalia for a final decade of trusteeship.

In this last act of the imperial drama Africa's destiny became more interwoven. In new ways Africa came to be seen whole, and the interconnectedness of its regions and peoples impinged on political events. In turn, the dynamic of events themselves upon a web of circumstance enclosing Africa: the Algerian war of liberation forced the pace of evolution in francophone sub-Saharan territories; de Gaulle's promise of independence in Brazzaville echoed loudly in Kinshasa; the Portuguese coup in 1974 decisively altered the balance of forces in the Rhodesian struggle. The relative insulation of prewar imperial compartmentalization eroded in the face of interterritorial solidarities of common combat, as well as the "imagined community" of pan-African discourse. The nominal independence of Egypt in 1922 could remain an encapsulated occurrence; Libyan sovereignty in 1952—however feeble and barren of resources the initial regime—was perceived as an immediate threat to French colonial security in the Maghreb, and it was opposed with all the dilatory diplomatic skills Paris could muster.[4]

The effects of World War II on Africa were far more consequential than those of the first war, a fact symbolized by the greater scale of military operations on the continent. In contrast to World War I, where the modest expeditions to wrest Germany's colonial possessions involved only European-officered African armies, the North African campaigns from Somalia to Morocco from 1940 to 1943 engaged large German, Italian, British, and American military detachments. Sea, air, and supply bases scattered throughout the continent infiltrated normally exclusive colonial spaces. In the first war only France used African troops outside the continent on a large scale. In World War II the British too made extensive use of African contingents, especially in Asia and the Middle East; the West African Frontier Force was expanded from eight thousand to 146,000, and the East African contingents from five thousand to 280,000, creating in the process the volatile vector of disgruntled ex-servicemen at war's end.[5] Smaller Belgian Congo contingents also served in Burma and the Middle East.

The mystique of colonial invincibility was damaged by the early successes of the Axis armies, above all in the humiliating defeat and fall of France in 1940. The Bula Matari image of irresistible force was always fundamental to colonial security, even in the consolidation phase when challenges to its hegemony were infrequent. This was shaken, though not shattered, by the spectacle of German occupation of Belgium and much (eventually all) of France. To boot, the sectarian divisions that honeycombed the French colonial administration with clans of Freemasons and Catholics, left and right, republicans and admirers of authority, crystallized into bitter cleavages between Vichy loyalists and Gaullists. Not until 1942 were Vichyites, practicing a singularly implacable colonial rigor, ousted from control of AOF and Madagascar. In the Belgian case, German occupation conferred almost uninhibited autonomy on the colonial administration, little subject to the dictates of the London government-in-exile. After a brief flirtation with "neutrality," the colonial administration committed its resources to the war effort.[6]

The insatiable manpower demands of the war stripped colonial administrations of their European cadres, while imposing new rigors of economic production pressure. The Japanese sweep through southeast Asia interdicted supply sources of an array of tropical commodities; war planners inevitably turned to Africa as an alternative producer. In this chain of war mobilization the ultimate object was the African peasantry, solicited to redouble its efforts. The war effort was especially implacable in Belgian and French territories; in the former, obligatory cultivation was extended from sixty to 120 days, and collection of wild rubber—abandoned since the Leopoldian "red rubber" days—resumed. In 1943 a leading Catholic prelate issued a public warning to the government-in-exile: "In one place, the food situation is becoming aggravated to the point of threatening famine; in another, the villages are disintegrating; elsewhere, there is depopulation."[7] The territorial administration, thus cast in a man-catching and plantation-overseeing role, was—in the words of an influential liberal jurist—"the great sacrifice of the war: decimated in its cadres, prostituted in its mission."[8]

The war effort prompted a remarkable extension of state management of the economy, with lasting effects. A felt necessity to control the flow of major export commodities led in a number of territories to the creation of the parastatal marketing monopolies that became so prominent a feature of subsequent rural policy. The exigencies of conflict also spawned comprehensive price and wage controls, manpower allocation, and rationing of goods. The war brought a surge of revenue and made possible extension of income taxation; state financial intakes generally rose from 50 to 100 percent. This racheting action in the scope of state economic direction and control, though improvised and temporary in initial conception, became joined in the postwar world with novel state doctrines of planning and development to foster a far more elaborated state apparatus.

Finally, the war marked not only a hiatus in colonial routines but also a rupture in expectations. No one believed the war could end with a simple restoration of the status quo ante. The colonial subject had made important contributions to the imperial cause, whether voluntarily or by imposition. The fruits of victory had to include rewards of improved political status and greater economic well-being. "Progress"—as yet undefined—

was the ransom for colonial wartime participation. The British envisaged new colonial constitutions with added African legislative representation, especially in West Africa, mechanisms for incorporating educated
Africans into central administrations and local governments, and expanded educational opportunities. The French contemplated opening the
doors of citizenship, enfranchisement, and African parliamentary representation, and they began to employ the notion of "federalism" as an
institutional device for holding the colonies within the framework of an
enlarged republic, while keeping them partly separate from it. The Belgians cast about for modalities of enhanced indigenous welfare and rationalized development. All recognized that metropolitan public capital
would have to be found and that the perennity of colonial rule now depended on some degree of subject consent.

As metropolitan officials and colonial state agents pondered these
dilemmas, they found their options constrained in jarring ways by an
international environment increasingly hostile to the imperial system.
Colonial conquest and occupation, a half-century earlier accepted as a
providential act conferring the blessings of civilization on benighted
lands, was now under attack as a blight on the international order, and
even a threat to peace. In the construction phase the colonizing powers managed the international system. In the period of consolidation
they remained the dominant players, with the United States and Soviet
Union on the sidelines. In the epoch of decolonization they encountered a
bipolar world order dominated by powers who for different reasons had
no stake in the colonial system and desired its abolition.

Neither great power in the postwar system really placed its entire
weight behind African nationalist demands for independence. In the Soviet case, although state discourse resonated with anti-imperial affirmations, European affairs came first, and priority was accorded to the tactical interests of the metropolitan Communist parties. Further, until the
passing of Stalin, African political leaders faced classification as "bourgeois nationalists," susceptible to imperialist blandishments and unreli-
able as allies. In the American case, the strong antipathies to colonial
rule held by President Franklin D. Roosevelt and some members of the
foreign policy establishment did translate into proposals for placing all
colonies under international trusteeship in the early war years. Roosevelt's encouragement of Sultan Mohammed V of Morocco played some
part in raising nationalist hopes. The Roosevelt antipathy to colonial rule
was evident in a press conference statement after a February 1944 stop-
over in the Gambia: "It's the most horrible thing I've seen in my life. . . .
The natives are five thousand years back of us. Disease is rampant, abso-

lutely. . . . For every dollar the British, who have been there for two hundred years, have put into Gambia, they have taken out ten. It's plain exploitation of the people."[9]

But strategic security reason, within the premises of a novel global perspective, began to permeate the American official mind as the war wound down. The navy eyed annexation of the Japanese-ruled Pacific islands as military outposts even before the war ended. Once the cold war came to dominate policy thought, propitiation of European allies became a consequential consideration. The animus toward the colonial system did not wholly disappear, but it did recede into the background and was informed by a different rationale: the need to preempt possible Communist leadership in nationalist movements by phased, prudent evolution toward independence.[10]

The crucial point, however, is that the power configuration of global politics no longer served as a nurturant womb for the colonial system. Although neither Soviet nor American diplomacy was as forceful in seeking the swift liquidation of the African colonial state as its public rhetoric might have implied, the colonizers now had to include possible great-power pressures in their policy calculus, at least as a future contingency. As the pulses of political change quickened in the 1950s and the inevitability of independence became daily more apparent, the leaders of the two ideological camps intensified efforts to curry favor with prospective postcolonial successors, which in turn induced colonizers to court as well as thwart their nationalist adversaries.

Although its impact was only gradually felt, another critical change was the emergence after the war of what began as an Asian neutralist grouping, then broadened into an Afro-Asian, and eventually a third world front of states for whom anti-imperial orientation was a unifying doctrine. For this set of states, for whom anti-colonial struggle was the core element in the ideological charter of nationhood, freedom for subjugated peoples was the transcendent issue of the times and the primal focus of their diplomacy. In the conventional algorithms of power politics their valence was modest, but they grew increasingly resourceful in using ramifying international forums for transforming the moral imperative of national liberation into an international norm, as well as exploiting the opportunities opened by the cold war obsessions of the great powers. As the numbers of independent states in Africa grew, they could also serve as sanctuary, communications bases, and even military supply conduits for nationalist movements in territories still under colonial rule. The idea of anticolonial nationalism was abroad during the phase of consolidation, but its bearers were isolated and within easy reach of the colonial apparatus of repression and intimidation. African nationalism in the postwar years was sustained by the conviction of inevitable triumph, its struggle swept victoriously forward by the irresistible tides of world historical process.

The emergence of the United Nations system became another potent weapon against the colonial system. Even in its charter drafted at the 1945 San Francisco Conference, a decade before the Bandung Conference symbolized the emergence of an Afro-Asian bloc in world affairs, there were major changes leading to an internationalization of the colonial question. The U.N. Charter included references to "equal rights and self-determination of peoples" in Articles 1 and 55, although profound ambiguities surrounded these notions. More troubling to the colonizing powers, Article 73 obligated them "to develop the capacity [of colonial subjects] to administer themselves, to take account of the political aspirations of the populations, and to aid them in the progressive development of their free political institutions." Worse yet, the composition of the Trusteeship Council was entirely different from that of the League of Nations Mandates Commission, dominated by elder colonial statesmen. By 1951 its triennial visiting missions were adversarial inquisitions, and their reports insistent on accelerating progress toward self-rule. Although only Togo, Cameroon, Rwanda, Burundi, Namibia, and Somalia were trust territories, the recognized interconnections of political advance exerted powerful pressures on neighboring colonial administrations. The perils to colonial interests were well understood, especially by the Belgians and French, even leading to Belgian parliamentary reticence about ratification of the charter.[11]

As the roster of Asian and African members swelled during the 1950s, U.N. affirmation of the rights of the colonized became more explicit, culminating in the solemn declaration by the General Assembly in 1960 on the "Granting of Independence to Colonial Countries and Peoples," adopted by overwhelming majority after several years of preparatory labors. This resolution established as an unchallengeable norm of international law that "all peoples have the right to self-determination; by virtue of that right they freely determine their own political status." The juridical foundations of this doctrine were solidified by the 1966 International Covenant on Civil and Political Rights and the companion International Covenant on Economic, Social and Cultural Rights, incorporating similar affirmations.

The rising decibel level of assaults on colonial rule in the U.N. organs and other international bodies could not in itself dismantle the system. Yet the impact was profound, isolating the colonial powers and placing them on the defensive. This was particularly important once nationalist combat moved into armed insurrection; France took a fearsome pummeling at the United Nations during the years of the Algerian war. Although de Gaulle might refer to the United Nations contemptuously as an infernal gadget in the hands of demagogic adversaries, the energies of French diplomacy were for a period entirely consumed in defending Algérie Française theses that persuaded almost no one.

In this process the anticolonial dossier gradually congealed into a new international jurisprudence. Alongside the classical Westphalian system of international law, which tolerated territorial acquisition by conquest and offered normative order for colonial occupation, there emerged a UN charter code, which stipulated decolonization as a fundamental legal right. More recently, this has been extended into an "international law of development" by third world jurists. "Effectivity" has always constrained the reach of international law, but the mere existence of novel norms in juridical garb became a factor—among others—that acquired weight in policy thought. Indeed, for colonizing states, where public law permeated the official mind and constitutionalist reasoning was unconscious habit, indictment as international culprit produced private dissonance even for the diplomatic representatives schooled in the casuistries of the defense attorney for state interests.[12]

A profoundly altered international environment thus confronted the African colonial state. The other half of what functioned as a gigantic historical pincer movement was the rise of African anticolonial nationalism, which I shall consider in more detail in the next chapter. Suffice it to note that what could be dismissed in the era of consolidation as mere "loose and gaseous talk" took on the aura of a seemingly invincible force. Colonial officialdom and the metropolitan state gradually became persuaded that the growth of nationalism was an inexorable process, which might be temporarily contained or momentarily diverted but which could not be permanently defeated. Its leaders could no longer be regarded as a "self-appointed congregation of African gentlemen" but had to be acknowledged as popular heroes who officials recognized "had the mass behind them."[13] Characteristic was the lamentation of a senior Belgian international jurist who served on a number of delegations to New York to plead the Belgian case: "Anti-colonialist nationalism has thus become one of the main revolutionary forces of our times. Its virulence has grown in the course of recent years to the point of subjecting the colonial powers, both within and without their non-self-governing territories, to a pressure which—failing recourse to totalitarian methods—tends to become irresistible."[14]

189

The perception of irresistibility found potent reinforcement in the nationalist discovery of guerrilla warfare as a possible option. Violent resistance to colonial rule was of course not new; even the colonial state at flood tide encountered occasional uprisings, most notably the Rif war in the 1920s. But earlier revolts were episodic, usually regional, always isolated, never able to persist over time. But in postwar Africa the epic Algerian struggle demonstrated the possibility of independence by armed combat. The pedagogy of the Vietnamese and Indonesian liberation wars played a part, as did the doctrines of protracted guerrilla struggle germinating in the Chinese Revolution. But for Africa it was above all Algeria that haunted the colonial imagination; half a million troops, sophisticated weaponry, and well-crafted counterinsurgency methods could contain but not root out and destroy the nationalist armies. The very dialectic of warfare progressively aligned colonized society behind the insurrection; the existence of a credible military option provided leverage for simultaneous nationalist diplomatic action. Guerrillas need not win militarily; stalemate eventually becomes victory, as metropolitan army morale is corroded by prolonged commitment to the brutalities inherent in repressive campaigns and ultimately the legitimacy of the regime itself is compromised. The Fourth Republic in France and the Estado Novo in Portugal both perished in colonial battlefields. Armed uprising did not always and inevitably succeed; insurrections in Cameroon and Kenya (and Malaya in Asia) were repressed. But even in defeat insurgents triumphed in decisively altering the premises of colonial policy, even if different political forces might prove the beneficiaries of their action.[15]

Anticolonial nationalism began to acquire an audience within metropolitan public opinion, initially at the left end of the spectrum; over time, the political costs of a military response to African challenge rose. Following on the heels of the eight-year colonial war in Indochina, the revolution in Algeria destroyed the Fourth Republic and deeply polarized French society. The three major Belgian political parties in 1956 for the first time adopted major statements on colonial policy in their congresses, anticipating in different ways an acceleration of change. Repressive excesses during the Kenya emergency and in Nyasaland attracted barrages of hostile parliamentary questions.

Especially in the French case, capital progressively defected from the coalition of forces resisting decolonization. In the Belgian case, where colonial investment was immensely profitable in the first postwar decade, by the late 1950s the mood grew more pessimistic, not just because of emerging political uncertainties. The colonial budget, long enjoying not only rising revenues but also buoyant surpluses, fell into deficit in 1957, which by 1960 appeared structural. In the final three preindependence years, a billion-dollar debt—very large at the time—was accumulated.[16]

Bula Matari, in the final phase, was embattled. Beset by adversaries externally and internally, colonial state reason operated in a radically altered context. Even the most fundamental, instinctual goal of any state—its own reproduction over time—became impossible. Thus, in a setting of rapidly narrowing options, the colonial state reached a point where it could at best aspire only to its dignified demise in conditions that projected onto its successor a theory and doctrine of state derived from the metropole, and witnessed the maximal incorporation rather than repudiation of its residues.

VANISHING HEGEMONY

The hegemonical drive evolved rapidly during the decolonization phase. At the outset, domination was still securely maintained. In the final act, hegemony was surrendered, vanishing with the final midnight lowering of the imperial flag. Between these two moments the colonial state, where skillfully managed, could still retain the capacity to orchestrate the process of transferring power.

Dexterous management was of course not inevitable. In some cases the doctrines of state through which hegemony was justified were too rigid to accommodate the adaptations required to meet new circumstances. This was most notably the case for Portugal, mesmerized by its Estado Novo dogmas concerning the Luso-African domains as central to Portuguese standing in the world and even its identity as a nation. When nationalist insurrection broke out in Angola in 1961 and then spread to Guinea-Bissau and Mozambique by 1964, Portugal responded with a military commitment eventually reaching nearly two hundred thousand troops and diverted half its budget to the colonial war effort.[17] In those colonial states whose apparatus had fallen largely into European settler hands—Algeria and Rhodesia—deeply instilled presumptions of entitlement to monopolization of civil society and bending the state to its service blocked any accommodation with a mobilizing subject society. In the Belgian Congo the very penumbra of hegemonical effectiveness enshrouding the official mind froze policy in a time warp. Gratifying contemplation of the perfection of its apparatus of domination anesthetized policy reform; success is the opium of the state, and its intoxicating euphoria suppresses the normal critical processes of the official mind.

Britain and France did begin adapting the framework of hegemony at war's end, in divergent ways. Britain possessed a usable model in the concept of a dominion still tied affectually through the Commonwealth to the metropole, as adapted to non-European subjects in Ceylon and India. Until the interwar years the boundaries of dominion sovereignty were unclear, and some objected to the admission of Australia, New Zealand, Canada, and South Africa to the League of Nations on the grounds that they were merely added votes for Britain.[18] But the Asian pattern clarified the pathway and identified the mechanisms of transforming hegemony.

A vague British commitment to self-government dated from 1938, made more explicit by Colonial Secretary Oliver Stanley's July 1943 House of Commons statement pledging "to guide colonial peoples along the road to self-government within the framework of the British Empire."[19] This engagement, reaffirmed by Labour Colonial Secretary Sir Arthur Creech-Jones, was the keystone. A relatively coherent model of programmed evolution accompanied the self-government pledge: gradual enlargement and democratization of the Legislative Council, through increase in unofficial African representation, then a shift from appointment to election as the mode of selection, with progressive extension of the franchise. Subsequently, African members are introduced into the Executive Council, whose members eventually become responsible before an elected African Legislative Council majority: responsible government. Finally, an embryonic prime minister emerges from the legislative majority, whose actions remain subject to gubernatorial veto. This schema, from representative to responsible to self-government remained in place throughout the decolonization period, but with rapidly foreshortening time horizons in the movement from one stage to another.[20]

The essence of the strategy was to capture emergent political forces and temper their militance with responsibility. Rural Africa was still acquiescent, perhaps even loyal, ran official thought. The chiefs were by and large satisfied with the opportunities provided them in the native administrations. An institutional niche was required for the growing numbers of educated Africans, whose disaffection in the postwar world threatened the stability of the entire system. These were to be provided at three strategic locations in the colonial state: the political sphere, the central administration, and local governments. The broad and in many respects prescient design of Lord Hailey, commissioned by the Colonial Office in 1940 to devise a strategic plan for postwar colonial development and completed in 1942, set the tone in its call "to identify potential political and administrative elites who could gradually be trained to assume the enlarged responsibilities of the colonial state."[21] In such roles African incumbents unwittingly became accountable in the first instance to colonial authority and were given incentives to please the governor rather than mobilize the discontents of the hustings.

The commitment to self-government, rendered credible by the Indian model and soon by the Ghanaian example, and the ample openings provided to the aspirant generation of educated Africans kept African protest within civil bounds and moored nationalist organization to constitutional process in most instances. The principal exceptions occurred where the devolution model appeared not to be applied: Kenya until 1960, Rhodesia, the Central African Federation. Not all African nationalist politicos could be ensnared in this cooperative, if not co-optive, machinery: such tormenters of the colonial state as I. T. A. Wallace-Johnson in Sierra Leone or Ignatius Musazi in Uganda were beyond reach. But most were receptive to the new openings offered, and the others could be isolated.

In the French instance, the hegemonical impulse long operated under the aegis of the principles enunciated at the Brazzaville Conference: emancipation of subject society within the framework of a renovated colonial state permanently joined to France but remaining distinct from the metropole.[22] The profound contradictions in French colonial ideology, which in earlier phases required no resolution, now rose to the surface. The republic had to be indivisible but could not in the full sense be one. If colonized societies could no longer be relegated to mere subject status, neither could they be fully empowered without placing sovereignty at risk, especially in Tunisia, Morocco, Algeria, and—to a lesser extent— Madagascar, where former advocates of full application of the assimilation doctrine (such as Ferhat Abbas) now wished autonomous national identity and development. The long-standing debate between "assimilation" and "association," a merely hypothetical quandry resolved in favor of simple domination in earlier eras, assumed new saliency. The formal status as protectorates of Morocco and Tunisia, built on modified forms of their historical states, and the status as trust territories of Togo and Cameroon, entangled in international legal obligations, offered formidable obstacles to their permanent incorporation into an enlarged France. At the apogee of the colonial state these had been distinctions without differences in the everyday practice of hegemony. But they now became crucial.

To resolve the many contradictions, the French introduced the amorphous notion of "federalism" as master principle. Hegemony, it was acknowledged, now required the consent of the colonized; Overseas Minister Marius Moutet told the National Assembly in January 1946, "The colonial fact, in its brutal form . . . maintenance of a sovereignty which reposed only upon force is today impossible. *This historical period of colonization is over.* A nation—ours in particular—will only maintain its influence over the overseas territories with the free consent of the populations who inhabit them."[23] To secure these ends, formal citizenship and attendant civil liberties were conferred on the subjects, but—aside from the three settler-dominated departments of Algeria—African territories were juridically separate from France, as associated states (Morocco and Tunisia) or overseas territories (the sub-Saharan colonies), with the trust territories in a singularly ambiguous limbo. Separate electoral colleges (except in AOF) were defined for voters who had French civil status (settlers and French residents, and small numbers of Africans previously naturalized as citizens)[24] and those who retained indigenous personal status. Significant representation was accorded in Parliament for the overseas territories, although the fatal logic of the pure assimilation doctrine, which would have yielded a substantial overseas majority, was averted by limiting the number of overseas deputies. More abundant representation was provided in what proved a functionless assembly, the French Union (which included the associated states), while elected assemblies were created at the territorial and administrative federation levels (AOF and AEF).

This complex and contradictory structure provided important opportunities to involve emergent African elites in metropolitan institutions, a fact of particular importance in sub-Saharan Africa, where dominant political forces were willing to accept some form of autonomous status within the framework of French sovereignty until the very eve of political independence. Such pivotal leaders as Léopold Senghor, Félix Houphouët-Boigny, and Modibo Keita were deeply immersed in metropolitan as well as territorial politics, with all of the satisfactions that ministerial office and the deferential honors attendant on distinguished political service could provide. A wider segment of the évolué class benefited from the provisions of the 1946 Lamine Guèye law, which guaranteed to African functionaries of high rank perquisites and remuneration identical with those of their French counterparts, including the diverse special compensations for the hardships of colonial service. This expensive but seductive policy was accompanied by a new effort to encourage recruitment of African administrative candidates; a 1955 AEF administrative circular required that "any position that can be filled correctly by an African must be entrusted to him rather than to a European. . . . Between two equally qualified candidates, the African must always receive preference."[25] As M'Bokolo persuasively argues, a lasting consequence of this policy was that it swiftly made "bourgeois the second generation of the modernist elite at a time when the first generation was embracing moderate political views."[26]

The hegemonical impulse of overseas France had a mailed fist as well as a silver chalice. Revolutionary insurrections in the Setif region of Algeria in 1945 and in Madagascar in 1947 were met with ruthless force: between six thousand and eight thousand deaths in Algeria, more than eleven thousand in Madagascar, where the uprising was more extensive and military repression lasted longer.[27] The inability to identify and retain credible indigenous allies, the legal obstacle of circumscribed sovereignty over the Maghreb protectorates, and the impossibility of simultaneous pursuit of three North African colonial wars in the shadow of Dienbienphu soon ruled out armed repression of a growing violent challenge to the colonial state in Morocco and Tunisia once the Algerian Revolution began in November 1954. But the war to sustain French domination of Algeria was carried out with tenacity and determination, and it was abandoned only when the political and economic bankruptcy of metroplitan France was at risk.

Yet however riddled with contradictions and derogations from the Cartesian modes of jurisprudence, the French strategy of offering junior partnership in the colonial state to the postwar African elite was remarkably successful in the sub-Saharan zones, an effectiveness demonstrated by the extraordinary and unique intimacy of postcolonial ties with most of the successor states. The final effort to refurbish the federal concept to preserve an umbrella of French sovereignty over the African territories came in the French Community design of the Fifth Republic Constitution, primarily drafted by Houphouët-Boigny. Although the formulas proposed could not contain Algerian nationalism, the subsequent independence of the sub-Saharan African territories came less from the sustained nationalist will of the party militant than through a complex dialectic of events, propelled by contending political ambitions of leading figures and parties and by almost accidental misunderstandings, such as the personal animosity between Sékou Touré and President de Gaulle that triggered the 1958 Guinean vote of *non* in the constitutional referendum.[28] The ultimate irony was that the final official dissolution of the French Community and its replacement with an informal though pervasive network of postcolonial ties was the work of its principal architect, Houphouët-Boigny, who only four years earlier had dramatically asserted: "To the mystique of independence we oppose the reality of fraternity."

In the Belgian case, although the trust-territory status exposed the colonial state to decolonizing pressure in Ruanda-Urundi—the 1951 and 1954 visiting missions were sharply critical of glacial political evolution—hegemony in the Belgian Congo seemed secure almost until it was shattered. Indeed, the rapid economic expansion of the postwar years financed a broad-front expansion of state action in the social and economic realms that appeared to make domination more elaborate. To a striking extent hegemony as postulate was internalized by the growing évolué class until 1956; only on the eve of independence did Congolese nationalism become radical. The vast distance traveled between the intransigent demands for immediate independence in 1959 and the deferential assimilation of colonial state ideology a decade earlier is shown in a 1949 paean by Antoine Omari, who in 1960 was a militant lieutenant of Patrice Lumumba's:

> [Before the Belgians,] idolatry and superstition governed all. Ignorance was hereditary. Hygiene was unknown. Epidemics were rife. Cannibalism was of daily occurrence. . . . While the existence of some good customs must be recognized, it is appropriate to acknowledge that there was no rational law; this gave rise to innumerable conflicts and interminable internecine wars. . . . In short, we were a backward people, overwhelmed by all the evils of nature and remote from world civilization. . . . Belgium, to Thee all our gratitude, in Thee our unshakable confidence. We owe all to Thee, thy tenth province through colonization.[29]

For the first postwar decade the Belgian colonial state concentrated its policy efforts on defining a special status for the évolué class, with some corresponding privileges: exemption from the battery of discriminatory measures that permeated colonial practice. However, in contrast to British and French adaptation of the colonial state, no access to authority or share in hegemony was offered.[30] Not until 1959 was the term *independence* officially uttered, or provision made for African access to the executive ranks of the administrative service.

The seeming solidity of Belgian colonial hegemony, which as late as 1958 made thirty-year timetables for political autonomy audacious, was in unseen ways growing more brittle in the late 1950s. Its fragility was suddenly demonstrated by the trauma of the eruption of urban discontent into days of rioting in Kinshasa in January 1959. In the months that followed, the colonial administration found itself confronted with widespread civil disobedience in the Kongo zones between Kinshasa and the sea, with early symptoms of a parallel evolution in Maniema and Kwilu districts. Shorn of the certitudes of secure domination, in a twinkling Belgium and its colonial state found few available choices. The reliability of the once feared Force Publique, engaged over time in repression of nationalist outbreaks across the country, no longer seemed sure. Reinforcement by Belgian Army units was politically unpopular and constitutionally difficult, as conscripts could not be sent involuntarily. Over all hung the dark cloud of the endless Algerian war in neighboring France, with its multifold costs. Thus shattered, hegemony could not be reconstructed at any reasonable price; this premise of the official mind led to the astonishing January 1960 acceptance by Belgium of the maximal demand of Congolese nationalists—immediate independence. What became known as *le pari congolais* was, in essence, the calculation that an amicable transition after formal independence would result from transfer of sovereignty and constitution to a wholly African political sector—parties, assemblies, ministers—while keeping the administration and security forces under almost exclusive Belgian personnel at executive and command levels. This formula lasted exactly five days, swept away by the mutiny of the African other ranks in the army.[31]

In the Portuguese (and to some extent the Spanish) case, the tenacious insistence on unreformed hegemony persisted until no possibility of negotiated and phased transition was possible. The corporatist autocracy in Portugal could not contemplate a co-optative strategy through representative institutions. The colonial state was perfectly willing to integrate in its ranks those Africans assimilated to Lusitanian culture and perspectives, especially those of partially Portuguese ancestry; the many Verdeans in its service, especially in Guinea-Bissau, are a case in point. Above all, the Estado Novo doctrine of the indissoluble global Lusitanian community was an insuperable barrier to politically inspired management of interactions with emergent nationalist forces. Once the April 1974 military coup swept away the *ancien régime,* the successor regime was far too weak (as its colonial army was no longer willing to fight) for any option other than negotiated withdrawal to exist.

In the Spanish instance, the African colonies were of very peripheral interest. In 1945 what is now the Western Sahara still had a minimal administrative and military infrastructure. Until the final colonial days, only fishing was exploited, an economic activity that required little onshore infrastructure. In 1966 Spanish Vice President Admiral Carrero Blanco could assert on an official visit, "We will never extract the slightest material benefit here; and, on the other hand, we have given you as much as we have been able."[32] Phosphate production did not begin until 1969. In Rio Muni, Spanish administration was minimal, sufficient only to assure secure conditions for small lumbering enterprises. Fernando Po—to be joined in decolonization to the mainland enclave as Equatorial Guinea—there was a socioeconomic partition of the domain that long deferred decolonization pressures: the Spanish operated a skeletal colonial administration, and their private planters operated profitable cocoa plantations with imported contract Nigerian labor, while the indigenous Bubi occupied diverse mercantile intermediary positions.[33]

The international community suddenly impinged on Spain when it joined the United Nations in 1955. Asked by the secretary-general the following year to submit information on its non-self-governing territories, as required by Article 73, Spain after some hesitation declared the African territories incorporated as provinces in 1958. A decade later, with a growing desire for respectability in Europe as it wiggled out of the now tattered skin of its Falangist past, Spain bowed to the international clamor for decolonization. A truncated moment of political transition and party organization placed power in Equitorial Guinea in the hands of Francisco Macias Nguema, who soon degenerated into a sanguinary and paranoic tyrant. In Western Sahara the Spanish state lost control of a transition it was reconciled to accepting; with Franco on his deathbed and acute fears of domestic uncertainties ahead, Spain abdicated to Moroccan annexationist pressures and simply withdrew in February 1976.

In sum, the dictates of hegemony for the colonial state were constantly shifting during the postwar period. As time went on, the stress shifted from assertion of undivided domination to retaining control over the process of change, and eventually to optimizing postcolonial advantage. Because only Britain began the decolonization era with a conscious recognition of its end goals, the greater consistency of policies pursued comes as no surprise, and it gave the colonial state real latitude in the brokering of emergent political forces. The decolonization doctrines of the British colonial state also provided a framework for collaborative sharing of hegemony with African political forces and leaders whom it had once opposed: Kwame Nkrumah, Jomo Kenyatta, Hastings Banda, among others. Still, the metamorphosis of hegemony was so belated and so brief that the institutional superstructure of power transfer did not long survive in its intended form.

France contemplated an Africanization of hegemony under French sovereignty until near the end of this period. The institutions and political configurations to which this strategy gave rise proved more resilient than might have been anticipated. Italy, in its final decade in Somalia, was internationally bound to a ten-year calendar for decolonization, and thus its terminal hegemony had a vocation of power transfer from the outset, executed with reasonable fidelity. In the other cases, hegemonical habits remained essentially unaltered until overtaken by circumstances in which state reason was swallowed up in immediate crisis contingencies.

There were crucial changes in the cast of intermediaries in the exercise of hegemony. In the earlier phases chiefs and sometimes religious notables were the key figures. As the colonial state slowly absorbed the perspective of decolonization into its premises, the realization took root that the chiefs—however faithful they had been as executants of the colonial will—could not provide the leadership for a territorial state. The issue first acquired saliency in the British realm, where chieftaincy, for tenants of indirect-rule ideology, had acquired the most dignity, even reverence. In cases like Nigeria and Uganda, where indigenous kingdoms played a particularly vital role in the colonial superstructure, earlier political thought envisaged some undefined federation of native states as the end point in imperial evolution. The influential Hailey wartime report had called for some de-emphasis of indirect rule as quasi-religious dogma, and it suggested reformation of native authorities into regional councils. Even Margery Perham at this point believed that chiefs could be used to "head off the intelligentsia from the state system."[34] But by war's end Colonial Office opinion swung to the view that a new departure in local government was necessary, based on elected councils and offering access to a young generation with some schooling who fitted uncomfortably into customary institutions. Creech-Jones in his critical 25 February 1947 dispatch on local government sounded the death knell for indirect rule as state doctrine and declared his belief that "the key to success is the development of an efficient and democratic system of local government." Andrew Cohen, then his chief lieutenant, added at the same time that "taking a longer view, however, a time may come when . . . chiefs will no longer be in a position to make an effective contribution to the development of local government. It is suggested that the evolution of native administration be conceived in the light of this possibility."[35]

The new policy was applied with energy, particularly by a new generation of district officers not tied by habit and inclination to their chiefly allies and auxiliaries. The notion of local affairs as a vocational school for intending politicians had natural appeal to colonial administrators. Chiefs were not without resources under the new rules of the game; the more effective ones could enter the political party lists themselves, with such movements as the Northern People's Congress (NPC) in Nigeria or Kabaka Yekka (KY) in Uganda. Indeed, the exceptional standing of the Buganda king led even elected District Councils in Uganda to demand emulation of the Buganda model and the creation of ceremonial rulers to dignify their own districts, a fact noted with some dismay in a 1953 British report: "All the [District Councils] made it plain that they are bent upon reaching the status of a native state. Their object is to achieve a constitution as like that of Buganda as possible. In short they aim at Home Rule. . . . Moreover, it seems to them that this is the logical development of past administrative policy."[36]

Chiefs had never enjoyed such standing in the French system, although some had acquired important influence; the insistence of the *moro naba* of Ouagadougou and other Mossi rulers was an important factor in the 1947 reconstitution of Upper Volta territory. Ironically, one of their most tireless supporters, Governor-General Eboué of the wartime AEF, won new standing for them at the moment that attention was shifting to co-opting the elites emerging from the school system. A new role for chiefs, as administrative adjuncts, emerged with the institution of elections, beginning with the 1945 Constituent Assembly. For an administrative apparatus long accustomed to a command role and disposed to cynicism about the value of the electoral process, the temptation to use the chiefly conduit for balloting instructions was naturally strong. This form of intervention, most flagrant in Algeria, tended to diminish over time and was far from universal. It did leave in its wake an animus toward chieftaincy on the part of a number of nationalist politicians; for example, abolition of chieftaincy was one of the first actions taken in independent Guinea.

Finally, the exercise of hegemony tempered its harsh and brutal edge. Colonial administrations lost some of their arbitrary weapons. The indigénat in French territories was abolished in 1945. In the Belgian Congo whipping as punishment ended in 1952. If, in Machiavellian metaphor, the district officer had always combined the qualities of lion and fox in the exercise of command, in the new environment of terminal colonialism the lion's mane shriveled, and the fox's tail grew longer. The emergence of representative institutions and the appearance of the professional politician brought unaccustomed hazards for the artisans of colonial hegemony: novel arenas where abuses could be pilloried and colonial agents called to account. In short, a civil society was taking form, with which state agents had to relate through a political process rather than a command hierarchy.

ALTERED SECURITY PREOCCUPATIONS

Colonial security posed entirely new challenges. The state gradually lost the capacity to isolate subject populations from external influences, and the broad currents of ideological debate agitating the world at large percolated into the colonies, although at different rates. The Maghreb was especially affected; significant numbers of young North Africans pursued either religious or political education in the intensely politicized Middle East, with its heady broth of radical secular and Islamic doctrines. The very large contingent of Maghreb, especially Algerian, workers in France were exposed to radical nationalist and socialist perspectives. The growing numbers of African students in Britain and France naturally gravitated to the left, where a sympathetic hearing for anticolonial views was available. By the early 1950s the West African Students Union in Britain and the Fédération des Etudiants de l'Afrique Noire en France were dominated by members of Marxist-Leninist persuasion.

Although far less successful at excluding revolutionary ideas and their advocates than in the era of consolidation, the colonial state was not wholly unarmed. Colonial intelligence services were developed, and outsiders were carefully screened and monitored, especially those who were not citizens of the metropole, for whom visas could be judiciously limited. The Belgian Congo was perhaps the most rigorous in this regard; until the late 1950s its subjects remained hermetically sealed from external influences. Only when they were put on display in large numbers at the 1958 Brussels World Exposition did substantial contingents of Congolese visit Europe.

The most feared external threat was the Soviet bloc and "international Communism." In fact, as I noted earlier, Soviet and other Communist state assistance to African nationalist movements was small, assuming some significance only in the armed nationalist revolutions marking the end point of anticolonial struggle, particularly in Angola. Some funds, travel opportunities, and other organizational facilities were available to nationalists, selectively allocated to those close to Soviet positions. The network of Soviet-operated international front organizations in the trade union, youth, student, and other sectors (the World Federation of Trade Unions, World Federation of Democratic Youth, International Union of Students) directed most of their energies toward the anticolonial campaign.

The psychosis of the cold war that so thoroughly permeated both official and public minds in Western states doubtless magnified the perception of peril. If doctrinal dreams were read as literal intent, then the Soviet camp—and the Chinese, when they became a separate and yet more radical threat in the 1960s—sought not only the destruction of the colonial state but also its replacement by antiimperial successors actively hostile to metropolitan and other Western interests. Such perceptions explain the close monitoring of leading nationalists, official suspicions of leaders like Nkrumah (arising from some of his London associations and the tenor of a 1945 tract he wrote), or the widespread belief in Belgium when nationalism exploded in 1959 that a master plan of "Communist penetration" was afoot.[37] One may also grasp the importance attached in France to severing the Rassemblement Démocratique Africain from its tactical alliance with the French Communist Party in 1950, and the collaborative rather than confrontational posture adopted by the colonial administration with its leadership once the RDA had regrouped.

The military coup in Egypt in 1952 by the Young Officers, and especially its radicalization after 1954 when Gamal Abdel Nasser assumed power, opened a second external front against colonial security. With the communications revolution making the airwaves an increasingly potent weapon, Radio Cairo became a beacon of radical nationalism, and Cairo a crossroads of itinerant African nationalist organizers. The catastrophic 1956 Anglo-French-Israeli attack on Egypt following its nationalization of the Suez Canal was motivated as much by the two colonial partners' fears and frustrations over Egyptian patronage of African nationalism as by the Suez Canal issue itself. The real objective of the attack was to eliminate the Nasser regime. Soon thereafter, with the independence of Ghana and Guinea, centers of nationalist sanctuary began to proliferate rapidly. Colonial state security reflexes brought actions with lasting consequences: the 1970 Portuguese operation in Conakry, targeted at decapitating both the Guinea-Bissau nationalist revolutionaries who used Guinea as rear-echelon headquarters and the Guinean regime itself; the creation of a Mozambiquan rebel movement by Rhodesian security services in 1976 (*Resistência Nacional Moçambicana,* or RENAMO) to punish the independent Mozambiquan government for its active backing of Zimbabwean insurgent forces; the arming by the Portuguese of Zairian exiles from Shaba province as leverage against Zaire for its sheltering of the Frente Nacional de Libertação de Angola (FNLA), later to achieve notoriety as the Front pour la Libération National du Congo (FLNC), or the "Katanga gendarmes" who invaded their homeland in 1977 and 1978.

Colonial security calculus in the terminal period also had to reckon with the possibility of nationalists acquiring external arms supplies and secure sanctuary for their guerrilla forces in neighboring independent states. This development, which paralleled in importance the shift in the balance of forces in the second half of the nineteenth century that made colonial conquest possible in the first place, became evident only with the Algerian war. In the initial anticolonial uprisings after World War II—in Algeria in 1945 and Madagascar in 1947, and the more scattered episodes of violence in Ghana in 1948, the Ivory Coast in 1949, and Tunisia and Morocco in the early 1950s—participants had only rudimentary armaments, or even none at all. But the Algerian army of liberation acquired a level of armament and sophistication in its guerrilla activity to keep nationalist combat alive despite formidable French politico-military counterinsurgency mobilization.[38] Even though the best-armed Algerian units remained in their Tunisian and Moroccan sanctuaries, the elaborate frontier fences could not wholly interdict resupply of the internal units. Availability of arms, both from state sources (Egypt, the Soviet bloc, sometimes others) and the murky nether reaches of the international arms market, opened the possibility of protracted guerrilla warfare. New doctrines of revolutionary warfare defined means of survival in the face of apparently superior colonial state armies.

These developments brought the possibility of security challenges that the small and lightly armed colonial constabularies were inadequate to meet. Even the Land Freedom Army ("Mau Mau") in Kenya, although lacking external supply, forced dispatch of regular British troops. The necessity of metropolitan contingents involved political as well as economic costs for the colonizing state, which over time altered the parameters of state reason.

Significantly, the existing colonial factors were not considerably expanded; the metropolitan army served as security reserve. In those instances—the majority of cases—where the politics of decolonization were not forced into violent channels, these security establishments sufficed; Nigeria became independent with an army of fewer than ten thousand troops. Despite the extensive measures taken, in recruiting strategy and troop indoctrination, to insulate colonial security forces from nationalist contagion, the reluctance to enlarge African troop levels doubtless reflected not only cost preoccupations but also uncertainties about the long-term reliability of such units if continuously engaged in active repressive service against national liberation movements, as opposed to the local revolts they were long accustomed to crushing.

As the inevitability of decolonization over a near term became more apparent year by year, security decisions were pushed upward to the metropolitan capitals. In the process, they became suffused with the more global reason of the imperial states. The Sudan is a case in point;

the abiding fear in London of an enlarged and militant Egypt astride what was still regarded as the Suez "lifeline" to British positions in Asia played a pivotal role in London's decolonization strategies. Overriding priority was given to organizing a power transfer process assuring an independent Sudan separate from Egypt. This required orchestration of terminal colonial politics to favor northern Sudanese political groupings that were reliably anti-Egyptian. The ransom for this strategy was a decolonization formula that marginalized the southern Sudan. In defining the arrangements for the landmark 1946 conference on constitutional development, Governor Robertson overruled the warnings of British administrators serving in the south regarding apprehensions in their region about a unified, northern-dominated framework. He argued that any other policy "would be received with great disappointment in the Northern Sudan and would incline many of those who are now supporters of the Sudan Government to go into opposition and drift across to the Egyptian side."[39] Especially with the advent of the Nasser regime, deemed irremediably hostile to British security interests, added weight attached to bringing about a Sudan antipathetic to Egyptian aspirations for "unity of the Nile valley." The success of this strategy came at the cost of setting the stage for a civil war that has sputtered on, with a remission from 1973 to 1983, since independence.

LOSS OF AUTONOMY

The Sudanese case illustrates a broader pattern in the terminal colonial period: the loss of autonomy by the colonial state itself. In the era of consolidation the exercise of sovereignty by the colonizing state was only sporadic; the colonial bureaucracy within Africa largely managed statecraft. But as the locus of sovereignty itself came into question, power drifted upward to the metropolitan capitals, which asserted control over the final phases of political evolution and negotiated the terms of power transfer.

This occurred first in the British case, precipitated by the wartime debate over the final objectives of colonial rule. Once the commitment to self-rule was clarified and made explicit in 1943, the Colonial Office assumed much greater authority and initiative in defining its blueprint. Two key 1947 dispatches drafted in London established overall policy directives, enunciating democratic local government and hastened development as immediate requirements. The second of these, in May 1947, declared that "within a generation . . . the principal African territories will have attained . . . full responsibility for local affairs."[40] This implied a radical foreshortening of the time horizons previously assumed, a pattern reinforced by the conclusions drawn by the Colonial Office in the wake of the 1948 Accra disturbances, making it more urgent that an understanding be reached with nationalist forces.[41]

Changes were made in colonial governorships, to ensure that those directing territorial affairs were sympathetic to the new policy directions. Indeed, there was substantial resistance to the Colonial Office directives from those still attached to indirect-rule dogmas and skeptical about democratic change. Sir Philip Mitchell, then governor of Kenya, forcefully argued that the proposed changes should apply in the first instance only to West Africa, that a wholly different timetable and framework was required for East Africa. The Colonial Office, however, remained firm, responding that "there was no prospect of the policy being changed except in the direction of still faster policy."[42]

Assertion of metropolitan direction occurred not only through the executive arm of the state but also through parliamentary pressures. The number of parliamentary questions concerning colonial policy multiplied. Both the Conservative and Labour parties created research sections on colonial affairs. The Fabian Society produced a stream of decolonization studies,[43] and other policy institutes and academic centers added their voice.

As political evolution progressed through the responsible government stage and duly anointed African leaders rose from the institutional matrix of the terminal constitutional process, final bargaining on the terms and timetable of power transfer matched the metropolitan state and the presumptive successors to the colonial state. By this time the colonial administration itself had receded into a merely advisory role, its autonomy with respect to both the metropole and civil society nearing vanishing point. The final act was a formal conference determining the modalities of independence, organized at Lancaster House or some other suitably dignified location, attended by the British government and the nationalist elites mandated by electoral process.

In the French case, except in AEF, the deflation of colonial state autonomy began in World War II with the serious tarnishing of its standing through "collaborationist" Vichy associations. In the Maghreb the colonial administration faced an obstreporous settler community, whose voice was well represented in the parliamentary combines of the Fourth Republic. In Algeria, as I argued in the preceding chapter, the colonial state apparatus had been largely captured by the settlers. In Tunisia and Morocco the retention of the precolonial shell of the state partially insulated the colonial administration from settler claims, but it also provided institutional bastions for nationalist forces. When Sultan Mohammed V of Morocco was deposed under settler pressure in 1953 for his refusal to sign decrees that would have accorded a share of Moroccan sovereignty to French citizens, no viable replacement could be found, and the state apparatus could not enforce its hold.[44] Paris intervened and accepted independence settlements, in the higher interest of concentrating repressive energies on the Algerian nationalist challenge.

In Algeria, Paris recognized at war's end the necessity of reforms granting some share in colonial state affairs to the Algerian populace. Although by this time a significant segment of the nationalist movement would accept nothing short of independence, and even the moderate wing wanted full autonomy under Algerian leadership, the French state endeavored to entice the moderates into cooperation with a 1947 statute, whose essence was the creation of an Algerian assembly half of whose members were Algerian. The settler-dominated colonial state was in charge of its application and systematically voided the statute of its substance; elections to the Algerian seats on the assembly, and to Parliament in Paris, were cynically rigged, and the Liberal Socialist governor Yves Chataigneau sent to apply the reforms was driven out by settler interests within a year. In Charles-André Julien's words, "Electoral fraud became an institution of state."[45]

When the war of liberation began in November 1954, the colonial state was progressively eclipsed by the army, which quickly became convinced that its mission of permanently securing French sovereignty could only be accomplished by a total strategy of psychological warfare joined to military repression. As in the days of Marshal Bugeaud, the army came to view the settlers' intransigent defense of their exclusive privilege as an impediment to the higher aim of French domination. In the final stages, the French state all but lost control of its military instrument in Algeria, and eventual extrication of France from what became a ruinous conflict required not only surviving the 1961 coup effort by the army in Algeria but also a tortuous campaign to regain full control over its armed forces. In the process, the colonial state disappeared as a factor, and power transfer took place amid the paroxysm of destruction by extremist settler elements in the Organisation de l'Armée Secrète (oas).[46]

In sub-Saharan Africa the colonial state's loss of autonomy, upward to Paris and downward to autonomous territorial governments, accelerated from 1954. France, under growing pressure from the U.N. Trusteeship Council, granted autonomy statutes to Togo and Cameroon in 1954, making it difficult to withhold political advance from neighboring territories.

Deteriorating French positions in North Africa also made Paris's initiatives for AOF, AEF, and Madagascar appear imperative. Colonial services began drafting a new statute in 1954, which ultimately became the *Loi-Cadre* of 1956. This provided for elected territorial assemblies with a quasi-prime minister, distinguishing between "sovereign functions" remaining under French control and "territorial services" under the jurisdiction of the assembly. The decisive step of fixing autonomy at the level of the territories, rather than the administrative federations, swiftly marginalized the colonial superstructure at Dakar and Brazzaville, which by buffeting the territorial administrations against monitoring by Paris had been a critical agency of colonial administrative autonomy.[47]

The loss of autonomy for the Belgian colonial state was as sudden as the decolonization process overall. In the mid-1950s metropolitan political issues began to spill into the colony in new ways, especially the bitter disputes over school control and Flemish language rights. In 1956 the three major political parties all adopted colonial positions, an important break with past practice. Auguste Buisseret, the aggressively anticlerical Liberal colonial minister from 1954 to 1958, in constant conflict with the Kinshasa administration, set about creating his own network of allies and favorites within the colonial administration. The Groupe de Travail constituted in July 1958 to define a blueprint for political evolution had only two of eight members representing the colonial administration (and no Africans). When in the wake of the January 1959 Kinshasa riots King Baudouin promised independence, the colonial administration was not consulted at all. In the tumultuous final year of colonial rule, the governor-general became all but irrelevant, as power transfer terms were finally negotiated between the Belgian parliamentary parties (not even the government) and the major Congolese nationalist parties. Bula Matari, so long apparently omnipotent, was, as Stengers observes, "short-circuited in the decision-making process. It passively observed the institution of a policy it disliked or even roundly disapproved of."[48] The final disgrace was dispatch of a minister from Brussels to supervise directly the final moments of power transfer.[49]

Inherent to the decolonization process, then, was a progressive loss by the colonial state of its capacity for initiative, of its ability to respond to the autonomy imperative. This process was most gradual where an African civil society came into being through constitutional processes and shared power within the colonial state itself. It was most total when a civil society was fashioned in guerrilla warfare, outside the grasp of the colonial state. In such settings, when insurgents and the metropolitan state finally came to terms on power transfer, colonial officials—in Algiers, Bissau, or Luanda—were reduced to a dispirited removal of the regalia of domination, and unceremonious departure.

LEGITIMATION: WELFARE COLONIALISM AND HONORABLE EXIT

The requirements of the legitimation imperative for the terminal colonial state were likewise transformed. Continuation of imperial rule now required active defense in the international arena, where in the consolidation phase plausible claims to responsible trusteeship and camouflage of such distasteful policies as forced labor had more than sufficed. But moral and even juridical norms ascendant in the international system tolerated no less than the phased demise of the colonial state. Metropolitan civil society, previously indulgent and disposed to avert its eyes from the daily devices of enforcing domination, now grew more critical of manifest brutality or egregious inequities. At the same time, nostalgic attachment to days of empire and flags aloft in all time zones persisted; when forced into decolonization, the colonizers required a mythology portraying the change as a fulfillment rather than abandonment. Finally, the colonial state—really for the first time—faced a sustained and serious challenge of legitimating its rule to the subject population.

For a time the colonial powers mounted a concerted campaign in the international sphere. Such distinguished elder colonial statesmen as Sir Alan Burns and Pierre Ryckmans were dispatched to the United Nations to plead the imperial brief. Arguments of the *tu quoque* variety were embellished; the deplorable treatment of indigenous populations in the Americas and the quasi-colonial reality behind Leninist-Stalinist nationality theory in Soviet Central Asia were exhibits in the dossier.[50] Only Britain's declared policy of self-government in the Commonwealth was marketable; international impatience with Britain was far less than it was with the other major colonial occupants.

The Commonwealth was also a pivotal idea within Britain—permitting the simultaneous argument that nothing was surrendered (for the metropolitan audience) and that everything was granted (for the African subjects). In the 1950s the British idea of Commonwealth had a resonance entirely different from that it enjoys today. Its implicit model was the Britain-centered consort of white dominions of prewar times, which in British (and even other) eyes operated as a closely consulting, coordinating international entity that greatly enhanced British standing as a world power. The accession of neutralist India ruptured the inarticulate premise of a politically cohesive conglomeration of states, but the image persisted of a close-knit association of states bound by affective ties: a family of polities, in the metaphor of the day. The chasm may be vast between these expectations and the fractious reality of the Commonwealth gatherings of the 1980s, with their intense pressures on Britain's South African policy; in the 1950s, however, misty-eyed toasts to the Commonwealth as a dynamic third force in world politics in the twenty-first century were standard fare at patriotic banquets.

For France, there was an urgent need for a legitimating doctrine of ultimate purpose that would provide respectable clothing for the fundamental goal of preserving French sovereignty. The French Union was the first version; this ramshackle structure never gained credibility. "False calculations on the symbolic power of colonial empires," writes Ageron, "stubborn rigidity in the defense of outdated principles, mindless juridism prevented the French Union from becoming other than a still-born venture."[51] The French Community idea included in the Fifth Republic constitutions was far more plausible, while still clinging to the idea of ultimate French sovereignty. The exceptional intimacy and clientage ties most African territories retained with France, when they did move beyond the Community formula of reserved functions of defense, finance, and law resting with the French state, eliminated any trauma in power transfer for the metropole.

To the modest extent that Belgium contemplated a future beyond Bula Matari, a similar presumption of permanent institutional ties existed. Some thought loosely of a "tenth province," but the more common vision was a two-tiered association: between Europeans and Africans in the Congo, and between this Eurafrican autonomous community and Belgium as senior partner. The Belgo-Congolese community as legitimating telos vanished once the African voice entered the debate on the future.

Except in the case of the two colonial occupants that were corporatist autocracies, Portugal and Spain, democracy assumed growing importance in the terminal colonial scripts of legitimation. The conviction that democracy was a defining attribute of the moral realm was deeply seated in metropolitan political culture. To speak of political evolution for a colony axiomatically included representative institutions, an enlarging franchise, free political competition, and civil liberties, none of which existed in the pure colonial state.

Less obvious as a corollary to the idea of democracy as intrinsic to decolonization was the overpowering tendency to discover the empirical content of the notion in metropolitan institutions. After the epochal February 1947 Colonial Office memorandum enunciating democratic local government as British policy, senior administrators were summoned to the first in a series of summer institutes at Cambridge to discover what in fact this commitment implied; English local government was the inevitable model, as Westminster was for the central institutions. Both colonial administrators and metropolitan opinion demanded that departure, if it had to come, should be honorable. Inevitably, honor was measured by the closeness of the apparent approximation of metropolitan institutions.

Such an outcome was inexorable because, as an element of decolonization, democracy was equally desired by the nationalist elites. This was partly an instrumental preference; the representative arenas, electoral politics, and civil liberties provided forums for the independence cause and legal protection for political mobilization. But metropolitan political institutions also enjoyed high prestige; however swiftly these institutions were—in many instances—dismantled after independence, few proposals were heard during the independence struggle of alternative structural forms, save in cases of prolonged armed combat. The juridical exegesis of the Congolese provisional constitution by socialist public-law specialist François Perin is of wider application:

> The big argument which tipped the scales in favor of the European tradition is the confidence which the functioning of the Belgian regime inspires in the Congolese. The political regime of Belgium has shown itself to be endowed with a rather surprising prestige, even amongst certain Congolese leaders least suspect of indulgence toward the colonizing nation. It is curious to note how often the newly independent nations have yielded to the temptation of trying to adopt the institutions of the erstwhile imperial power. This experiment often proved disappointing, as the historical, economic and sociological conditions were profoundly different from those of the former rulers.[52]

Honorable departure also implied a due concern for the "viability" of the successor state. The British long presumed that some minimum-size threshold existed for full independence, and they were therefore drawn to seek territorial regroupings. Just before World War II, brief consideration was given to some integration of the West African territories, but their dispersion and other logistical obstacles made this impractical. But the East African and Central African federation schemes were pursued much further, the former aborting at the stage of several common services, and the latter eventuating in the ill-fated Federation of Rhodesia and Nyasaland. African fears—well validated in the actual operation of the latter scheme—that such territorial integration would serve as a vehicle for enlarging the reach of white-settler domination made such frameworks impossible to sustain.

Honorable departure, for the metropolitan state, also led to a proprietary solicitude for the European immigrant communities, and—as free riders on this protective disposition—Asians. This factor particularly marked decolonization politics in East and Central Africa, where until 1960 Britain remained committed to a doctrine of "racial partnership." The import of this doctrine was that equality would apply only to communal units. The small European and Asian minorities, touched by the empowering wand of partnership theory, would each win entitlement to a representational share equal to that of the huge African majority. Self-impaled on the institutional formulas to which this doctrine gave rise, and the inevitable deepening African revolt against their absurd disproportions, Britain faced its worst decolonization moments when retreating from this flawed framework in Kenya, Tanganyika, and Nyasaland in 1959 and 1960.[53]

Two central themes in terminal colonial legitimating discourse, directed above all to the subject population but also to the metropolitan and external arenas, were development and welfare. The colonial state, ran the argument, through its prudent and rational management, assured a growing prosperity. At the same time, its patient efforts had finally created a basic infrastructure that could guarantee rapid improvement in the social welfare of its subjects. Premature transfer of power to populist and irresponsible politicians threatened the stability and continuity of this process.

There was some plausibility to these claims; the performance of the colonial state in its last years in managing development and extending welfare far exceeded that of its earlier phases. The 1950s in particular were beyond dispute a decade of broadly shared increase in well-being, probably the sole such extended period of the colonial age. Indeed, this moment of expanding prosperity, deeply instilled in the experiences and expectations of a generation, became a liability for the postcolonial states from the 1970s on, when economies turned sour and the older citizenry developed negative yardsticks to measure performance, this exceptional moment of expansion as base.

Development, as state charter, was not new to the postwar years; the first Colonial Development and Welfare Act dated from 1930, and a successor statute, of more serious purpose, was adopted in 1940. But development took on a radically different meaning after World War II, as it became a master concept in world affairs and an influential subfield within the "dismal science." In the mainstream versions of development economics a consensus emerged by the 1950s that was, as Tony Killick notes, "highly interventionist. It established powerful theoretical and practical arguments against reliance upon the market mechanism and advocated a strategy of development which placed the state in the center of the stage."[54] In such words the colonial state heard itself summoned to be the apolitical custodian of planned rationality. Across the colonial spectrum "plans" were adopted, cataloguing public investment aspirations as texts of prospective developmental accomplishment.

Over its life cycle, the colonial state had gradually accumulated an institutional capacity that positioned it to seize the developmental initiative when propitious circumstances—booming commodity prices, metropolitan public capital, swelling domestic revenues—offered the opportunity. A professionalization of its administrative cadres had occurred in the consolidation era. To this still skeletal structure was added, from the early postwar years, a rapid enlargement of its technical and specialized services: "technicians of decolonization," Hargreaves labels them. This remarkable influx, he adds, "produced a 'second colonial occupation' in the form of a large-scale infusion of technical experts, whose activities not only increased the 'intensity' of colonial government, but seemed to imply its continuance in some form until the new policies had an opportunity to mature."[55]

As the colonial economies expanded, a substantial welfare infrastructure was constructed, by now almost universally desired and mirroring the development of the welfare state in the metropolies. The most visible icons of the colonial welfare state were the school and the clinic, but there were other aspects: safe drinking water, access roads, public housing. To cite but one example, from an absolutely rudimentary African school system before World War II, the Belgian Congo had by 1959 created a huge primary network serving 70 percent of school-age children. Although in the 1920s a medical service for Africans hardly existed, by the late 1950s the Belgians could justifiably claim that their colonial health services was "without doubt the best in the whole tropical world."[56]

The discourse of legitimation was of limited force; it certainly could not stem the tides of nationalism. But the effects were more than negligible, and they help explain the long delay in the appearance of overt nationalism in the Belgian Congo, as well as the willingness of AOF and AEF political elites to cooperate so long and so closely within the institutional framework that French sovereignty provided. The different course taken by nationalist forces in Algeria and the Portuguese colonies may be explained not only by the complete negation of African political advance and empowerment but also by the monopolization of most benefits of postwar economic advance by the European communities. In 1954, for example, Algerians—90 percent of the population—made up a mere 18 percent of secondary school pupils; only 12.5 percent of school-age children were enrolled. Europeans accounted for 92.8 percent of executive and professional cadres, 82.6 percent of technical positions, and 83.4 percent of office workers.[57]

REVENUE: THE GOLDEN YEARS

The revenue imperative during the final phase ceased to constrain the colonial state in the same ways as previously. Pent-up wartime demand, followed immediately by the effects of the Korean War, meant a prolonged period of record price levels for major African commodities, both base metals like copper and agricultural exports like cotton, coffee, cocoa, and peanuts. Through export taxation and "price stabilization" schemes, whereby state marketing boards built surpluses by withholding from producers a significant part of their windfall earnings, the state shared generously in the commodity bonanza. The emergence of a small industrial sector, and other economic advances, permitted some diversification of the fiscal base.

This translated into a spectacular expansion in revenue flows. In the Belgian Congo expenditure levels increased elevenfold between 1939 and 1950 and tripled in the final colonial decade. In the last ten years of British rule in the Gold Coast, state expenditures multiplied by ten; in the preceding thirty-five years, they had only doubled.[58] Nigerian revenue, which had been just 7 million pounds in 1937, rose to 17 million in 1947 and to 71 million in 1957.[59] These orders of magnitude are encountered in most African territories during this period, as is illustrated in tables 6-1 and 6-2.

The old shibboleth of colonial self-sufficiency was finally abandoned, and metropolitan states—for the first time on any scale, except for military costs and emergency bailouts—began contributing substantial amounts of public capital. In the British case, prior to World War II total African colonial grants-in-aid were only 27 million pounds, of which 10.8 million went to the Sudan (after Egyptian independence made it impossible to force Egypt to finance British rule) and 5.7 million to Nigeria (mostly to finance Lugard's years of military action in Northern Nigeria); other colonies received no more than 3 million pounds each. By way of contrast, the 1945 Colonial Development and Welfare Act provided for 120 million pounds.[60] The first phase of French colonial public invest-

Table 6-1. Expenditures, Selected British Territories, 1940–1956 (Pounds, Current Value)

Year	Kenya	Nigeria	Uganda
1940–41	not available	6,220,691	2,060,199[a]
1943–44	6,782,466	8,431,777	not available
1946–47	8,795,237	11,263,265	3,574,194
1947–48	9,023,624	16,032,038	4,473,773
1949–50	10,761,676	25,215,393	8,000,380
1952–53	18,858,631	44,103,000	15,299,871
1955–56	38,313,735	55,386,554	25,517,826

Source: Annual Colonial Reports.
  a. Figures for 1938.

ment, through the Fonds d'Investissement pour le Développement Economique et Social (FIDES), covering 1946–1952, was 285 million pounds.[61] By contemporary standards, these are small figures; by comparison with prior colonial experience, they were immense.

The incidence of taxation remained heavy on rural Africans. Head taxes continued to be collected almost everywhere; they were a significant bite in peasant incomes, even if their total return was a rapidly shrinking portion of total state revenue. Export taxes fell entirely on rural producers. The state marketing monopolies and other intermediaries in these highly regulated markets were invariably permitted to deduct their operating costs; their profit margins, with the peasant price being a residual, were further reduced by the practice of withholding as marketing-board surpluses a portion of the returns in years of especially high prices. During the 1950s the effective rate of taxation of such crops as coffee, cotton, and cocoa was frequently 50 percent or more of the world market price. Mention should also be made of fees collected for some state services, above all for primary and secondary schools.

Concealed taxation in the form of forced labor did rapidly diminish, although in different guises it still persisted in Portuguese, Belgian, and some parts of French Africa. One may note that urban areas, of growing importance, were in practice less heavily taxed than rural ones. The rates of income tax were low; successful merchants could largely evade taxation. And urban dwellers were not subject to export taxes.

Overall, the terms of exchange with the state altered. Before the war colonial subjects endured heavy fiscal extraction whose sole purpose was financing the superstructure of alien oppression. In the terminal phase an array of valued services became available.

In the process, there began a dynamic of expansion of the state ap-

Table 6-2. Expenditures, Selected AOF Territories, 1940–1955 (Millions of CFA Francs)

Year	Senegal	Mauritania	Guinea	Ivory Coast
1940	162.9	21.2	73.0	147.9
1943	119.1	24.2	97.3	174.6
1946	611.2	102.0	241.0	532.0
1949	3,206.0	239.0	1,246.0	1,873.0
1952	5,640.0	1,275.0	2,934.0	3,885.0
1955	6,236.0	1,063.0	3,357.0	6,356.0

Source: *Annuaire Statistique* (Paris: Imprimerie Nationale, 1949–55).

paratus, supported by the revenue revolution, that was carried forward and accelerated in the first two decades of independence. The developmentalist, welfare state of the terminal period was an apparatus very different from the minimalist vehicle of alien hegemony of the earlier phases. Its successor soon came to operate in a far less favorable revenue environment.

ACCUMULATION AND DEVELOPMENTALISM

Driven by the developmentalist doctrines dictated by terminal colonial logic, the accumulation imperative played a much more central role than in earlier phases. To meet the colonial states legitimating pledges of an expanding welfare sector, economic growth was indispensable. As nationalist forces gained voice in the institutional arrangements of transition, the weight of their insistent demands for a forced pace of developmental advance entered the equation. The development plan became the icon of the accumulation imperative, articulating a discourse of intention and aspiration.

As growth moved to a more central position in policy calculus, some curious contradictions deeply embedded in the colonial state surfaced. From the metropolitan state and society sprang the presumption of a capitalist order; despite the significant nationalization and public-sector expansion that occurred in various colonizing states in the immediate postwar era, in Britain, France, and to a lesser extent Belgium the fundamentals of a market economy remained in place. Yet the now profoundly rooted hegemonical habits of the colonial state had produced in Africa a more hybrid capitalist order, where the postulates of a market economy became interwoven with the political reflexes of action by command.

The cross-pollination of the premise of capitalism and the practice of state control produced a singular form of market statism. This bore no resemblance to the command economies of the state-socialist model; indeed, the intimate association in the public eye of colonial capitalism and alien domination largely explains the widespread adherence, at least rhetorical, by the postcolonial state to socialism as a legitimating creed. But market statism was manifest in a number of ways. Prices of key commodities were frequently established by the state, as were wage rates for unskilled labor. Marketing structures for export crops, which had become the revenue lifeblood of the state, were tightly regulated, and—often—were state monopolies. The extensive wartime controls justified by emergency conditions were only partly dismantled. Although forcible conscription of labor diminished, except in the Portuguese territories, management of labor flows remained, through such practices as internal passport systems, urban influx controls, and informal designation of some regions as reserves of labor (northwestern Uganda, northern Ghana, lakeshore Tanganyika, Upper Volta).

Within the developmental frame, light industrialization aimed at African markets was now encouraged; earlier, production of items like textiles had been deliberately hampered to protect metropolitan industries. Also, the *chasse gardée* exclusivism regarding nonmetropolitan private capital and imperial preferential trade policy protectionism lessened, as private investment was actively sought. Even the most suspicious guardians of metropolitan economic monopoly, the Portuguese, had loosened their restrictions by the 1960s.

There was, however, no major influx of private capital in much of terminal colonial Africa. There were some exceptions: Morocco, the Belgian Congo, the Rhodesias. In the latter instances, much of the private capital was in fact reinvestment of the extraordinarily high profits from mineral and plantation export commodities. Public capital predominated in the momentum of accumulation that did occur, through colonial development funds, state loans, and public guarantees of commercial borrowing. Its central role was also apparent in such giant public development projects as the Office du Niger, Gezira, and the Tanganyika groundnut scheme.

The long commodity boom sparked a search for mineral and hydrocarbon deposits in Africa. A number of major undertakings were initiated from the 1950s but, given the long lead time required for production, they really came on line only after independence (Nigerian oil, Gabonese oil, manganese, and uranium, Mauritanian iron ore). They invariably needed extensive commitment of public capital to provide the necessary supporting economic infrastructure. Emblematic of the ironies of the colonial era was the failure of the Italians, in their costly campaigns of conquest, domination, and settlement in Libya, to discover that their occupation was camped on a sea of oil. And yet, especially in the interwar period, Italy was acutely aware of its lack of domestic hydrocarbon resources; this strategic handicap became increasingly important as the fascist regime grew more bellicose. The costly Ethiopian aggression was justified in part by the illusion that rich oil resources were awaiting discovery.

Until the final years, colonial state reason continued to be governed by an inner desire for its maximal prolongation. Even when eventual power transfer was accepted as a policy objective, the state's ruling agents were disposed to believe that the transition would be more secure the longer it could be delayed. This instinctual logic of self-preservation often—though not always—collided with an incipient postcolonial state reason, promoted by the nationalist movements.

The essence of terminal colonial politics was the implanting of fragile graftings of a constitutional polity onto the robust trunk of colonial autocracy. Tunisia was a rare instance in which a resilient array of linkages between the state and society emerged, incorporating continuities with a precolonial state; it was a colonial polity that, although bent to the logic of French domination, retained linkages of incorporative clientelism with a civil society never wholly destroyed, which could then be rewoven by nationalist mobilization behind the Neo-Destour Party.[62] Botswana may be another case where the very minimalist character of the colonial state did not press down on subject society with so comprehensive an apparatus of domination, thus permitting the emergence of a civil polity incorporating elements of a precolonial African heritage with the constitutional accoutrements of the terminal colonial state.[63] But in most countries the experimental life of a truly civil polity prior to transfer of sovereignty was too brief to override the more enduring heritage of the colonial state, its bureaucratic autocracy animated by its vocation of domination. Permeating the state tradition bequeathed by the colonial era was the ethos of Bula Matari.

—— Chapter Seven ——

THE AMBIGUOUS
CHALLENGE OF
CIVIL SOCIETY

Whenever, therefore, any number of men so unite into one society as to quit every one his executive power of the law of Nature, and to resign it to the public, there and there only is a political or civil society. And this is done wherever any number of men, in the state of Nature, enter into society to make one people one body politic under one supreme government.

—John Locke

In the East the State was everything, and civil society was primordial and gelatinous; in the West there was a correct relationship between the State and civil society.

—Antonio Gramsci

For Africa, truly to escape the West involves an exact appreciation of the price we have to pay to detach ourselves from it. . . . It implies that we are aware of the extent to which the West, insidiously perhaps, has been moving closer to us. It implies that we know what is still eastern in that which permits us to think against the West, and that we assess to what extent our recourse against the West may still be a ruse.

—V. Y. Mudimbe

IN SEARCH OF CIVIL SOCIETY

Bula Matari and civil society evoke utterly antithetical images. In the preceding chapters I have argued that until the final hours of the colonial state its system of rule was rooted in an exclusionary hegemony. The rise of a civil society inevitably marked the decline of Bula Matari as both cause and effect. Yet embedded within the complex process of the crystallization of African civil society were ambiguities and contradictions that were to haunt the postcolonial state. Ghostly residues of Bula Matari were concealed within an apparently triumphant civil society.

No comprehensive review of the rise of African nationalism, normally considered the embodiment of civil society, is proposed, nor does this chapter seek to synthesize all aspects of African reaction to the colonial state. My more modest objective is to illuminate aspects of the crystallization of civil societies that seem particularly pivotal for an understanding of the contemporary African polity. By way of prologue, let me begin with some reflections on the notion of civil society itself.

Although civil society as trope, a collective signifier for a politically defined human aggregate, has antique lineage, only during the 1980s did it acquire widespread currency in comparative African analysis and, indeed, more generally in everyday discourse. At the apogee of African liberation in the 1950s and 1960s, no one—actor or analyst—employed the term, whose return to current usage reflects a paradigmatic metamorphosis in how relationships between the state and society are perceived.

This striking temporal dimension invites parenthetical notice; beyond any doubt conjunctural factors explain its lexical resurrection. Within Africa the transparent and widespread decline of the state as an agency of development led to a search for new instruments of progress. Powerfully reinforcing this trend was the stunning implosion of the most comprehensive form of the modern state, the Soviet-type system ("really existing socialism"). An increasingly assertive East European and Soviet intelligentsia characterized the space grudgingly abandoned by retreating state socialism as civil society, through which the last redoubts of a discredited "totalitarianism" could be breached.[1] The global pressures for democratization that swept across Africa and other regions in the late 1980s gave added force to these trends. As counterpoint, a more diffuse animus against a state deemed to be overextended and overweening permeated the Western world, symbolized in its most belligerent form by Reaganism and Thatcherism.

The return of civil society into the language of politics was not matched by a consensus as to its meaning. An academic conference in Jerusalem in 1992 devoted to "civil society in Africa" revealed a remarkable diversity of understandings.[2] These in turn reflect the intellectual history of the idea, whose schematic recapitulation could suggest why it may be helpful to impose on the past an analytical metaphor alien to the epoch that is our subject. I would stress three particularly important antecedents: Lockean, Hegelian, and Gramscian.[3]

COMPETING MEANINGS OF CIVIL SOCIETY

For Locke and other philosophers stressing the concept of social contract, civil society was an essential construct to juxtapose with the state. As a basis for the legitimacy of sovereign authority, and suggestive of limits to it, the idea of a collective human entity capable of rendering its consent was an artifact indispensable to the structure of the theory. What defined the civil nature of society was its political vocation; one may note in the prefatory quotation that Locke used the words *civil* and *political* interchangeably.[4] Civil society and state are at once clearly distinct and intimately—contractually—joined.

Hegel enveloped civil society in a new penumbra of meanings when he designated it as a "moment" in the unfolding of the world historical spirit. In this reading, civil society became dialectically joined to the state in a very different fashion. In a lucid gloss on Hegelian thought, Z. A. Pelczynski writes:

> Men are primarily concerned with the satisfaction of their private, individual needs, which they do by working, producing and exchanging the product of their labour in the market. This creates bonds of a new kind. While individuals behave selfishly and instrumentally towards each other they cannot help satisfying other men's needs, furthering their interests and entering into various social relations with them. Men are "socialized" into playing socially useful roles for which they are not merely rewarded with money but also with respect and recognition.[5]

Avineri adds that civil society is "a necessary moment in man's progress towards his consciousness of freedom" but "is subordinated to the higher universality of the state."[6] Although bourgeois civil society is bound together by the reciprocities of exchange and necessities of cooperation, this "ethical moment" could not produce a sufficiently robust shared moral universe for a self-regulating system to operate. Only the state could discipline and rise above the egoism intrinsic to civil society.[7] Thus, as an antecedent but transcended moment in Hegelian idealist dialectics, civil society is imaged in a manner quite different from the contracting partner proposed by Locke.

The Gramscian *lecture* casts a long shadow over contemporary African usages. Here civil society is defined above all by its structuration. It is the ensemble of "institutions, ideologies, practices, and agents . . . that comprise the dominant culture of values."[8] Intimately joined to civil society is his notion of hegemony, whereby the ruling bourgeois class achieves the acquiescence of the classes it dominates by its capacity to diffuse an ideology legitimating the social order through the organizational and ideological structures of civil society. The revolutionary project to which Gramsci dedicated his life could succeed only by challenging and contesting, trench by trench, the hegemonical ideology in the many battlefields that define civil society. But a fate worse than submission to the hegemonical bourgeois order was possible: a society not yet "civil" by its structuration but rather "primitive and gelatinous"—and thus wholly helpless before a powerful state, as in Czarist Russia.

Various of these themes are interwoven in the contemporary search for civil society in Africa. Bayart, in the first extended essay on this theme, stresses the relational dimension and the heterogeneity of both state and civil society as juxtaposed entities.[9] He joins Robert Fossaert in defining civil society as "not so much a structured set of institutions, but the 'social space,' large or constrained, as it is shaped by historical forces."[10] Both in colonial and in postcolonial times civil society finds itself in confrontation with a state driven "to seek to control and to shape civil society . . . to enlist the dominated social groups within the existing space of domination and to teach them to be subject to the state."[11]

Others have stressed more specifically associational life. Michael Bratton, drawing on Alfred Stepan, defines civil society as an "arena where manifold social movements . . . and civic organizations from all classes . . . attempt to constitute themselves in an ensemble of arrangements so that they can express themselves and advance their interests."[12] The essence of the relationship with the state is interactive rather than necessarily confrontational; however, it must include a zone of autonomy. Joel Barkan et al., who also underline organizational action as a defining feature, borrow an implicitly Hegelian imagery in locating civil society in "the space that exists between the state and the household."[13] The suggested existence of a zone of private action, which is neither state nor civil society, implies a potentially large sphere governed by other mores and hierarchies. Naomi Chazan prefers to locate civil society above all in organizational life, excluding from her purview wholly parochial associations with only local concerns, communal agencies (ethnic associations), or fundamentalist groups with an exclusive vision of the true path; this sharply narrows the field.[14]

Patrick Chabal, in emphasizing structural dissensus, identifies civil society in Africa as "a vast ensemble of constantly changing groups and individuals whose only common ground is their being outside the state and who have . . . acquired some consciousness of their externality and opposition to the state."[15] In this view, two important dimensions are stressed. Civil society is defined by otherness and exclusion; its essence lies in its externality to the state. Further, that essence acquires meaning by consciousness. Transcending "primitive and gelatinous" latency requires awareness, a recognition of a collectivity perhaps defined by exclusion, or even multiple communities evoking a sense of attachment or belonging.

What, then, may be distilled from the foregoing review of civil society as discourse? Meaning varies sufficiently, particularly in the stress given to particular aspects, to alert one to the elasticity of the notion. In my usage, which is closest to the Lockean conception, the essence of civil society lies in its relationship to the state. In the particular case of the colonial state (and for that matter, historically, most other states), the emergence or creation of the state is antecedent to civil society. The political space bounded by a state creates a sphere of public action and exchange within which a civil society may germinate. The greater the extent to which civil society shares this public space and actively interacts with the state in determining its modalities and rules, the more completely formed it becomes. Consciousness is a constitutive dimension; so is membership, not just in the collectivity but in the potentially vast array of organizations, institutions, and communal forms that provide its structuration. The relationship between the state and civil society combines cooperation and conflict in ever-changing measure. The state protects and provides while it dominates and extracts; civil society responds with exit, voice, or loyalty.[16]

THE COLONIAL STATE:
CIVIL SOCIETY DENIED

From the foregoing it follows that there were precolonial civil societies reflecting the rich diversity of historical political architecture in Africa. The existence of states—of varying dimensions, degrees of centralization, ideological underpinnings, and economic bases—implies their interactive relationship with societies. Vansina, in his brilliant portrayal of the equatorial polity, shows how what he terms a political tradition was rooted in "a changing, inherited, collective body of cognitive and physical representations shared by their members," which defined a political world of communities and big men, sometimes kings, in shifting symbiosis but stable guiding principles.[17] The political tradition often had contractarian practices; Abraham, describing the Akan heritage, notes that "according to Akan political theory, the whole power of a ruler was derived from the people and held in trust for them. This was safeguarded in the provision for the removal of rulers, and the grounds for removal."[18] One need not claim that fully empowered civil societies were everywhere present to observe that in many precolonial states relationships with populations were not grounded in the exclusionary hegemony the colonial state was to introduce.

For most of the continent, what did exist by way of a shared political tradition commonly understood by rulers and ruled was swept away by the nature of the colonial partition. In only a handful of instances did the pre-existing state units coincide with and to some degree persist within the territorial frame of the colonial order: Morocco, Tunisia, Egypt, Zanzibar, Swaziland, Lesotho, Botswana. A much larger number retained some identity as subordinated units of native administration but were now enclosed within a novel territorial entity and stripped of even the merest shadow of their former sovereignty. In those cases where the former state retained a significant portion of its precolonial identity, the trajectory of civil society differed markedly from that in cases where it was extinguished from the outset. In contemporary Swaziland, for example, the notion of civil society as "Swazi nation" resonates more powerfully than most other African national identities.[19]

Chapters 4 and 5 detail the comprehensive nature of the hegemonical project of the colonial state in its construction and institutionalization stages. Nothing was more alien to the telos of the colonial state than a civil society. Sovereignty required forcible subjugation; there were few illusions that it could rest on any principle but overwhelming military power.[20]

Not only was a radically reconfigured Africa imposed in a territorial sense; extant, perhaps partially "civil" societies also experienced a deconstruction in the cognitive realm. An "invented" Africa took form, the product of an external imagination, reconceived as the subordinated other. In the elegant semiotic exploration of V. Y. Mudimbe, the colonial state through its dominance of both physical space and discourse "transformed non-European areas into fundamentally European constructs."[21]

Running through these constructs were two core notions that made subjugation imperative: savagery and childhood. The barbarian other extends back into Hellenistic thought and doubtless beyond; with the rise of European imperial expansion from the fifteenth century, it became tied to notions of race. The authoritative compilation of Enlightenment wisdom, the French *Encyclopédie,* summarized the prevailing in its 1780 supplement: "The government is nearly everywhere bizarre, despotic, and totally dependent on the passions and whims of the sovereign. These peoples have, so to speak, only ideas from one day to the next, their laws have no principles . . . no consistency other than that of a lazy and blind habit. They are blamed for ferociousness, cruelty, perfidy, cowardice, laziness. This accusation is but too true."[22] The emergence of Social Darwinism in the late nineteenth century provided a pseudoscientific gloss. Mission views of "paganism" as a defining attribute of the savage offered an alternative avenue to the same conclusion of barbarity.

The thesis of the incapacity of the African other rested on a second pillar of arrested development, the premise of perpetual childhood. This robust mythology persisted through much of the life cycle of the colonial state. As late as 1946 a published memorandum of the Belgian mining giant, Union Minière du Haut-Katanga, summarized its operating philosophy with respect to its African work force:

> The colonizer must never lose sight of the fact that the Negroes have the souls of children, souls which mold themselves to the methods of the educator; they watch, listen, feel, and imitate. The European must, in all circumstances, show himself a chief without weakness, good-willed without familiarity, active in method and especially just in the punishment of misbehavior, as in the reward of good deed. . . . [The European camp head] must interest himself constantly in the life of the natives, in their well-being; must guide them, examine their complaints; punish them when necessary with the tact, the calm and the firmness which are required.[23]

With the African subject thus firmly constructed in the official consciousness of the colonial ruler as a savage child, systematic exclusion was the essence of statecraft. In those intermediary roles where African participation was necessary—above all, the apparatus of native administration—firm tutelage was indispensable. Even in areas where doctrines of scientific colonial management appeared to vest the greatest degree of responsibility in the African rulers recognized as anointed intermediaries—the British territories where indirect-rule ideology was most thoroughly applied—the inner spirit of administration was pervasively autocratic, and chiefs were viewed foremost as "stewards of British rule."[24] The government anthropologist R. S. Rattray, working in Ashanti (the Gold Coast), remarked in 1930 on the irony of indirect rule as creating in reality a translation into local African society of the authoritarian principle so deeply imprinted on Bula Matari: "We are thus confronted with the curious paradox of the most ardent devotees of the principles of rule in Africa, by Africans, on African lines, having evolved a form of Native State, or government, really quite foreign to anything which the African left to himself could have conceived. It is, moreover, government from which a most important and ever-growing section of the African people seem at present largely to be excluded and debarred from being given a chance to play the part."[25]

The premise of African backwardness, and its corollary of imperative disempowerment of the subject, opened the door to the settlers' pretense that they constituted an embryonic civil society deformed by its restriction to the "civilized." The consequences, particularly in Algeria, South

Africa, and Rhodesia, where a racialized civil society captured the colonial state, have been examined in preceding chapters. What requires notice here is that elsewhere the colonial state long had the capacity to impose its cultural definitions on the formative processes of an indigenous civil society. To have voice in a public realm the subject needed to repudiate otherness, to master the discourse of the colonial state, to learn—perhaps conform to—its behavioral code. *Evolué* as a social label perfectly captures this dynamic; this status classification—largely accepted until late in the colonial game—connotes distancing from ancestral background, a schooled movement from the eternal childhood of the indigenous to proximity to the dominant cultural domain. The colonial state had achieved an overpowering hold over the nature of discourse; challenges to it could be effective only if rendered in its own language. In this important sense the sudden and swift colonial occupation of Africa marked a profound historical rupture. Resistance to conquest was widespread and in many cases prolonged. Indeed, as A. Adu Boahen and his collaborators argue in the UNESCO *General History of Africa,* resistance can be used as the orienting analytical theme in the overall interpretation of African history in the first two stages of the colonial state.[26] Yet equally striking is the absence of any direct link between the initial forces of resistance and the civil societies that eventually drove Bula Matari to cover. An utterly different language of politics and governing metaphors of society were to construct the new realities.

THE INTERNALIZATION OF
COLONIAL STATE DISCOURSE

The brilliant career of Blaise Diagne—who, we remember, won election in 1914 as the first French deputy of purely African ancestry, confirming citizenship for the Senegalese originaires—illustrates well the internalization of colonial state discourse. Of humble birth, he was raised in the household of a well-known mulatto family on Goree. He entered the French customs service in 1892 and served in various colonial postings (Dahomey, Gabon, Reunion, Madagascar, Guyana). Active in the Masonic order, he operated comfortably in French milieux, marrying a French woman in 1909. Although in his administrative career and the early years of his parliamentary service he was in frequent conflict with the colonial administration, his discourse was that of assimilation. He gave eloquent defense of the French colonial state at the 1919 Pan-African Conference, comparing it favorably to the repulsive racism dominant in the United States, and lent his prestige to the doubtful brief of denial of colonial forced labor as head of the French delegation to the 1930 Geneva International Labor Organization conference drafting a covenant on free labor. In his declaration of belief shortly before his death in 1934, Diagne spoke as a tribune of the colonial state: "France, in my person, surprises the world by staying true to the principles of the Revolution of 1789. The unity of our country is above differences of skin color, so much that it stupefies with admiration or horror foreign peoples . . . a lesson of high moral probity which only France is capable of giving."[27]

The magnitude of the cultural rupture imposed by colonial subjugation was characterized well by another important leader whose life and persona reflected its imprint, Ferhat Abbas of Algeria. For Algerians, Abbas observed in 1931, conquest was "a veritable revolution, overthrowing a whole ancient world of beliefs and ideas and an immemorial way of life. It confronts a whole people with sudden change. An entire nation, without any preparation, finds itself forced to adapt or perish. This situation is bound to lead to a moral and physical disequilibrium, the barrenness of which is not far from total disintegration."[28] Although Abbas ultimately rallied to the Algerian Revolution and for a time served as nominal head of the exile Provisional Government of the Algerian Republic, the singular power of colonial state discourse long held him in its grip. In the late 1930s he wrote:

> If I had encountered the Algerian nation, I would be a nationalist and, as such, would have nothing to be ashamed of. Men who have died for a patriotic ideal are honored and respected every day. My life is worth no more than theirs. And yet I will not die for the Algerian fatherland, for this fatherland does not exist. I have not encountered it. I have questioned history. I have questioned the living and the dead. I have visited the cemeteries. No one has spoken to me of such a thing. . . . You cannot build upon the wind. We have eliminated all fogginess and vain imaginings to link our future once and for all to that of French endeavor in this country.[29]

Inevitably, at the apogee of colonial state power its language shaped that of protest, especially the discourse that directly engaged the colonial state. Thus, endorsing assimilation was an assault on the hypocrisy of a situation where in the name of universalizing values the benefits of colonial domination were reserved exclusively to the French. Still, the discourse of the colonial state was above all invoked in conversations with European power. Diagne on the hustings often spoke a different language, avoiding reference to a colonial concept viewed with suspicion by rank-and-file subjects.[30]

In the early colonial period there began to emerge an embryonic social class defined by its capacity to enter the new roles defined by colonial encounter. Some members of this class were the product of precolonial mercantile interactions: the Afro-Portuguese traders who pushed the slave frontier inward in Angola,[31] the Creole community in Freetown, the "Brazilians" in Dahomey and Nigeria, the Senegalese originaires. Others were the product of the missionary endeavor that gathered momentum in the nineteenth century; the planting of Christianity required Africans capable of carrying the evangelical message, first as catechists, then as pastors or priests. Education and health—however rudimentary the networks—offered openings for African professionals; in anglophone West Africa the legal profession was accessible to Africans at an early date. The colonial administration itself needed subaltern personnel literate in the colonial language, as did the colonial corporations and trading companies. In these interstices of the colonial order a new elite took form. Its unique skill was its grasp of the discourse of the colonial state. Indeed, David Robinson perceives in this new social category the realization of a colonial state project; driven by its need for a fragmentary legitimacy in the eyes of its subjects, the colonial state "had to create the embryo of a 'civil society,' and to find the intellectuals, the persons of standing and relative autonomy, to achieve its formula of 'domination-hegemony.' "[32]

The nature of the vision imposed by the colonial state in its salad days necessarily shaped the response. Before World War II the language of domination had no recognized end point. Thus, for example, in the Belgian case, the évolué class framed its revendications in terms of a status securely differentiating itself from the mass of the population, as a Europeanized social category. In the Belgian Congo the first major political statement came from the Cercle des Evolués in Kananga (Luluabourg), who in 1944 asked for "if not a special statute, at least a special protection of the government, shielding them from the application of certain treatments and measures which could be applied to a retarded and ignorant mass."[33]

In 1944 it was impossible for the emergent Congolese elite to imagine a future outside the framework of a reformed colonial polity that opened status opportunities to them. Even in 1956 Patrice Lumumba, already visible thanks to his febrile charisma that later made him the martyred hero of Zairian nationalism, still remained enclosed within the imposed metaphors of the colonial order and the circumscribed future that Bula Matari offered. In a manuscript published posthumously but drafted just after the 1955 royal tour of the colony by King Baudouin (who accorded him two audiences), Lumumba wrote:

Our sole attitude must be ... to build together, in a spirit of harmony, of humanity, of justice, the solid bases of the Belgo-Congolese community ... we recall to you with pleasure the declaration made by our beloved King, His Majesty Baudouin, that "BELGIUM AND THE CONGO FORM A SINGLE NATION." The thought of the King is clear: Belgians and Congolese are all citizens, just like Walloons and Flemish. We must jealously defend our common undertaking ... a solid union between Belgians and Congolese which will be cemented by mutual esteem.[34]

The colonial state was long ambivalent toward this elite class. Their skills were valuable, and they often played useful auxiliary roles in the colonial state apparatus. But their mastery of the cultural forms and modes of expression of the colonial state permitted them to articulate claims to indigenous rights. The statements quoted above, speaking of equal treatment within the frame of acknowledged colonial domination, contrast clearly with a representative declaration of initial resistance by the paramount ruler of the Mossi state in contemporary Burkina Faso: "I know that the whites wish to kill me in order to take my country, and yet you claim that they will help me to organize my country. But I find my country good just as it is. I have no need of them. I know what is necessary for me and what I want: I have my own merchants: also, consider yourself fortunate that I do not order your head to be cut off. Go away now, and above all, never come back."[35] The heroic defiance of the *moro naba* could not halt the tides of imperial conquest; the discourse of rights by Diagne or Lumumba was a major solvent of colonial empire.

Colonial officialdom long sought to dismiss these claims of elite rights as "unrepresentative" of the disempowered subject, seen as a savage child, which was its cherished invention. Over time, this voice was marginalized through stigmatization and was bound to fail. By subtle metamorphosis the discourse of rights became the language of liberation.

RECONFIGURATIONS OF SOCIETY, CLASS, AND ETHNICITY

In the shadow of the colonial state new lines of social division that were to define civil society took form. Two primary lines of cleavage beckon our attention here: class and ethnicity. In both these realms of consciousness the colonial order fundamentally restructured societal categories.[36]

In class terms, the significance of coalescing patterns of stratification become apparent only in retrospect. At the upper end of the spectrum, the primary categories widely employed in late colonial times were "modern" and "traditional" elites: the products of Western education, and the chiefly auxiliaries of the colonial state who often enjoyed ancestral connections with precolonial ruling classes. P. C. Lloyd, in an influential text, expressed a still dominant view in 1967 when arguing that class conflict was only an "incipient" aspect of civil society.[37] Its emergence was occulted by the overpowering saliency of the chasm between the European estate and nearly all Africans: a comprehensive political, social and economic fault line that Georges Balandier aptly characterized as the *situation coloniale*.[38] Around this was constructed a core postulate of anticolonial nationalism: the natural unity of all Africans in the struggle for independence. Julius Nyerere of Tanzania spoke for a nationalist generation in saying, "I doubt if the equivalent for the word 'class' exists in any indigenous African language; for language describes the ideas of those who speak it, and the idea of 'class' or 'caste' was non-existent in African society."[39] Only class societies required multiple parties; the classless nature of African society was a prime justification for a single-party system.

In its economic management and social policies, the colonial state had gradually suppressed one type of differentiation—unfree, or slave, status—and introduced two others: worker and peasant. I have argued in chapters 4 and 5 that midwiving the birth of a wage labor force and transforming villagers into peasant producers were indispensable to the survival of the colonial state; in no other way could its revenue and accumulation imperatives be met. In the first two stages the work force was largely migratory in many areas, which slowed the emergence of class ideologies.[40] Linkages with rural areas remained strong; often only the male sought urban work, while families remained in the rural area. Also, two types of large employers—mines and plantations—frequently housed their laborers and subjected their social being to such comprehensive tutelage that a veritable "totalitarian" environment was created; Fetter and van Onselen offer Zairian copperbelt and Rhodesian examples.[41]

A distinctive worker consciousness and revendicative disposition did emerge, most notably in the transportation industry (the railways and docks) and among subaltern state employees (in good part clerical or other white-collar staff, more of a petty bourgeoisie than a proletariat). But railway workers in particular played a legendary role in confronting colonial power in Senegal, Guinea, the Sudan, and Congo-Brazzaville, immortalized in Ousmane Sembene's lyric novel portraying nationalism, *God's Bits of Wood*.[42]

If we understand the term *peasant* in the African context to mean "agriculturalists who control the land they work either as tenants or smallholders, are organized largely in households that meet most of their subsistence needs, and are ruled by other classes, who extract a surplus either directly or through control of state power,"[43] then we may conclude that this category comes into full existence with the birth of the colonial state. In some areas, especially in the Nile valley, well-organized precolonial states had extracted peasant surpluses for millennia. But more typically African precolonial states required relatively little revenue. Their sustenance came from control of long-distance trade (Ashanti), sporadic predation on neighboring groups (Buganda), use of unfree labor for production (Abomey, Zanzibar); most did not enjoy the extractive machinery to impose regular forms of taxation on their free subjects. As chapter 4 argues, for this reason the imposition of widespread fiscal obligations on newly subjugated rural populations involved the colonial state in bitter struggles, evoked widespread rebellions, and led to the extraordinary brutality and devastation that marked the early colonial years.

As the tax collectors and labor recruiters fanned out over the countryside, the peasantry necessarily became aware of its incorporation into a broader domain. By force or by choice, a part of the household labor resources needed to be diverted into salable crops. Taxes had to be paid; the diverse labor demands imposed by an increasingly intrusive state apparatus (for portage, road construction, and not infrequently tilling the fields of the chiefs serving the colonial masters) were as difficult to evade as they were distasteful. Over time, the possibility of upward mobility that schools might offer the next generation, at least the boys, made school fees a crucial investment.[44] Although some have maintained that the peasant communities retained a large degree of autonomy and in the last analysis did not need the colonial state (or its successor),[45] the peasants were certainly aware of the state's existence and its claims to domination.

To an important extent, peasantries closely approximated the Chabal definition of a civil society defined by its opposition. Multiple mechanisms of evasion and resistance sprang up, whose multiform dimensions are captured well by Allen Isaacman.[46] In some times and places there was open rebellion, but it was usually too risky and costly. What James Scott has termed "hidden transcripts" of subversion and subtle contestation were ubiquitous.[47] "Peasant intellectuals" crafted alternative discourses, often beyond the ken of the colonial state.[48]

Thus, social hierarchies were profoundly reworked by the political economy of the colonial state. The politically critical class was the elite whose work uniform was the white collar. This group did not view itself as a privileged category; rather, its members perceived themselves as anointed by history for leadership, as capable of translating the inchoate aspirations of the peasant countryside and a proletarianizing army of wage earners. Amilcar Cabral of Guinea-Bissau was a rare voice in labeling this rising class as a "petty bourgeoisie" summoned to commit "class suicide."[49] A more representative voice of the time was Nigerian nationalist leader Obafemi Awolowo, who noted that the politically conscious formed a small minority, but one with a sacred destiny. "It must be realized now and for all time that this articulate minority are destined to rule the country. It is their heritage."[50]

Colonial state doctrine and policy had an unequal impact on males and females, enlarging whatever gender inequality pre-existed. This outcome mirrored the masculine image of Bula Matari; colonial commandants were never women. Perhaps men experienced the whip more often than women and saw their labor power most directly channeled to the purposes of the colonial state. Still, such modest opportunities for social ascension or accumulation as the colonial order permitted were almost wholly reserved to males.

The functional requirements of the colonial state were invariably met by men: plantation or mine workers, construction teams, subaltern personnel for state or company. The missions in their first phase wanted above all catechists to spread good news, and they therefore directed their first rudimentary educational efforts at boys. The export crops assiduously promoted by a revenue-hungry state were cultivated and sold by men, who controlled the proceeds (or what was left after taxes and other state deductions had been levied). When a white-collar elite and, later, professional classes began to emerge, only a tiny handful of women appeared in their ranks.

As urbanization became an important social process, these imbalances intensified. Girls did begin to find school places in the terminal stage of the colonial era, but the gender disequilibria at the higher echelons of the educational system (secondary school and especially university) were immense. Women in towns thus had few options: petty trade, which they often dominated, sundry informal-sector pursuits, prostitution. In the rural sectors the colonial economy resulted in a new sexual division of labor: cash crops for men, food crops for women. To boot, in many regions men were absent from town or other employment centers for long periods of time, placing on their wives the full burden of assuring the subsistence of the family. Yet agricultural services of the colonial state worked exclusively with male cultivators.

The colonial codifications of customary law tended as well to follow a subliminal patriarchal text drawn from Western legal thinking. In succession, family relations, and property rights men were doubly advantaged: by those aspects of life governed by imported Western law, and by the remodeling of indigenous jurisprudence. One measure of the pervasiveness of the gender impact of the African colonial state is the relative frequence of female ascension to chief-executive office in postcolonial Asian societies—in India, Pakistan, Bangladesh, Sri Lanka, the Philippines by electoral mandate, but aborted by military intervention in Burma (Myanmar)—compared to the absence until the 1990s of any woman head of state in the far larger number of states in independent Africa.[51]

Although the class categories linked to the colonial order were not marked by a strong consciousness, the new ethnic map produced by the imperial era was another matter. The precolonial political order was not rooted in notions of nationality, nor were its borders coincident with the ethnic patterns that had crystallized by the end of the colonial epoch. The larger states generally incorporated a number of ethnolinguistic zones; the more diminutive polities were much smaller than the zones of cultural affinity that form the contemporary array of ethnic categories. There was a discourse of identity that antedates the colonial state, of course. The crucial point is that the vocabularies of classification were complex and fluid, giving recognition to ancestral descent, political grouping, ritual practice, and language. Distinctions considered socially important to establish could differ depending on whether the "other" was a subordinated group or a hostile adversary, a trading partner or an armed competitor. Identity issues were not commonly translated into political ideologies, nor would rulers have dreamed of commissioning anthropologists to prepare ethnic maps of their domains.

In the construction of its hegemony, the colonial state soon acquired a compulsion to classify. Particularly for the British and Belgians, administrative organization was rooted in a "tribal" image of Africa. The task of the ruler was to identify, rationalize, and streamline ethnic cartography. As Patrick Harries remarks, "Europeans implicitly believed their concept of ethnicity to be the natural order and not merely one convention amongst others used to make sense of the world. Caught within this mental structure, Europeans applied to Africans their own system of ethnic classification and accepted without question that Africans should use the same distinctions and concepts."[52]

Thus, ethnic boundaries were territorialized, and often novel taxonomies acquired the weighty sanction of official texts and printed maps.

Small entities, deemed unnaturally or unhealthily fragmented, were amalgamated under a common label. Large states were dismantled to form units of convenient scale, in the name of freeing "tribes" held in thrall to tyrannical rulers.

As Apthorpe observed of anglophone Africa (but with broader applicability), "what happened was the colonial regime administratively created tribes as we think of them today."[53] But administrators were not alone in their labors; missionaries had an equally far-reaching impact, although they were driven by a different logic to create an ethnic map. Particularly for the Protestant missions, the early translation of the scriptures was an urgent task, which in turn necessitated preparation of written forms for languages chosen as vehicles of evangelization. Much was at stake in these choices; in relation to the precarious resource base of early missions, the investment in a language chosen for transmitting Christianity was huge. Thus, a rudimentary sense of cost-effectiveness propelled the missions toward a preference for languages that seemed to cover significant areas and populations. In addition, once the written version with its paraphernalia of dictionaries and grammars existed, the missions automatically acquired a commitment to standardize and unify closely related speech codes as a single language. "The more bewildering the linguistic situation appeared, the more urgent became the need to create order, either by imposing 'vehicular' languages that already existed, or by promoting certain local languages to vehicular status," writes Fabian in a seminal account of language policy as an instrument of colonial power.[54] School and chapel were singularly powerful tools for this purpose.

The science of colonial anthropology, in its early years, was largely the province of administrators and missionaries, many of whom devoted years of dedicated effort to the ethnographic venture. The first generation of published monographs, generally bearing tribal designations, owes its existence to their labors. Often containing a wealth of descriptive information, these tomes were also, in a potent way, ethnic charters; their maps proposed a territorial definition (often vastly inflated, as their authors were proprietary advocates of the groups whose discovery was their copyright), as well as an official history. Through the schools, the young generations absorbed this distillation of an ethnic idea and frequently made it their own.

Colonial anthropology supplied a library of ethnicity, its shelves lined with tribal monographs. The traits of a community closely examined through the classical participant-observation methodology were projected onto a much larger ethnically labeled collectivity, portrayed as a once and future reality through the premise of the ethnographic present.

The colonial state was a remote *ceteris paribus;* the collective representations of dehistoricized, pristine ethnic units were, in the words of a historian of the discipline, "the shadowy dance of archetypes from the dreamtime of anthropology."[55]

In an ultimate sense, all identities are doubtless socially constructed. In the African case, the extraordinary impact of the colonial state and allied agencies of external domination has meant that the salient metaphors of civil society are of more recent vintage than is the case in most other regions. Also, the exceptional capacity of the colonial order to impose its own images of society means that contemporary geographies of identity have a larger alien imprint than is usual. But the novel communal partitioning of society was not simply implanted from above and beyond. An intricate dialectic unfolded, as Africans found the politics of identity to be one weapon in the long unequal battle to constrain and limit the oppressive intrusion of the colonial state and, in the state's latter stages, to build larger spaces of autonomous action.

Local administration, in its various forms, produced native authorities whose own standing was tied to the cultural categories through which domination was mediated. Uganda offers a particularly clear example of this dimension. Although Buganda and Bunyoro were large precolonial states whose political identity readily translated into ethnic ideology, most of the districts that served as the basis for British rule fell clearly in the category of "imagined communities."[56] Acholi, Madi, Bugisu, Kiga, Teso: all were novel ethnic entities whose district elites acquired a proprietary interest in the nurture and promotion of these identities.[57]

The uneven access to social advance that characterized the colonial era everywhere likewise gave incentives to exploit an ethnicized world, particularly to those categories who benefited from relatively positive stereotyping as being "open to civilization" or apt pupils of "modernization." Igbo, Kasai Luba, Chagga, and Ganda found advantages to using these images—indeed, internalizing them—to seize the slowly expanding opportunities in the interstices of the colonial order. Those laboring under negative stereotyping—like the "wild and lazy" Lamba of the Zambian copperbelt—were driven to accept a constructed collectivity to reverse the status attached to it.[58]

The social environment of urban life—which took on increasing significance in the decolonization era as cities began to grow rapidly—virtually imposed assimilation of the transcripts of identity now extant. Ethnicity as an active sociopolitical force was first noticed in the 1950s, above all as an urban phenomenon, in seminal monographs by Paul Mercier, Immanuel Wallerstein, and several scholars associated with the Rhodes-Livingstone Institute in Zambia.[59] Solidarities defined by ethnicity could serve as a veritable lifeline in surmounting the survival challenges of urban existence—employment, housing, schooling, assistance in life crises (sickness, death).

Solidarity became more efficacious when organized and led. Particularly in the last stage of colonial rule, ethnic associations proliferated, giving organizational expression to new identities. Political entrepreneurs and cultural brokers found leadership niches in this associational web, and they became articulate spokesmen for ethnicity, however recently constructed. Missionaries of identity then emerged to carry the message back to the rural hinterland, a dynamic vividly captured by Abernethy:

> What was the best course of action open to the urban migrant who was acutely concerned lest his ethnic group fall behind others in the struggle for wealth, power and status? Certainly the rural masses had to be informed of the problem. If the masses were not aware of their ethnicity, then they would have to learn who they really were through the efforts of "ethnic missionaries" returning to the homeland. These "missionaries" would also have to outline a strategy by which the ethnic group, once fully conscious of its unity and its potential, could compete with its rivals. . . . The gospel of ethnicity and the gospel of education were thus mutually reinforcing. Educational schemes sponsored by the tribal unions fostered ethnic consciousness in the rural areas; a heightened sense of ethnicity, in turn, facilitated the spread of education.[60]

The swift reconfiguration of identity patterns in the colonial era was further shaped by a parallel process of primordialization. The metaphorical oath of identity among the Kikuyu with which Harold Isaacs opens his ode to the primordial face of ethnicity—"I shall never leave the House of Muumbi"—captures the inwardness of communal consciousness once it has been internalized.[61] Ethnicity as discourse of consciousness inevitably absorbs the potent metaphors of kinship, attracts like a magnetic field emotion-laden symbols of selfhood. It takes on womb-life qualities of nurture and security; in turn, threats perceived in ethnic terms become more deeply troubled and emotionally charged.

One need not assume a Machiavellian master plan of deliberate division for economical hegemony; the colonial impact on identity dynamics was haphazard as well as intense. Perhaps suggestive of the limits of purposive ethnicity is the essential failure of French "Berber" policy in Morocco. In imagining a possible congealing of the many clans speaking related Tamazit dialects as a collectivity separated from the dominant Arab-Islamic cultural zone of core Morocco, Lyautey and his heirs contemplated a Berber ethnicity whose primary negative other was the Arab. "Arabic," wrote Lyautey, "is a factor of Islamization because this language is learned in the Koran; our interest commands us to promote the evolution of the Berbers outside the framework of Islam."[62] From this fostered antagonism would naturally spring a deepening affinity with France and even a predisposition to assimilation. But Berber policy proved so transparent a maneuver of division that it provided a potent unifying grievance for emergent nationalism. The underlying premise of a natural animosity toward the dominant Arab culture of those projected as Berbers was false; Bidwell notes that "they did not reject the idea of assimilation, but it was assimilation to the Arabs and not to the French that they sought."[63]

In sum, in asymmetric dialectic with the colonial state, subject societies acquired an array of ethnic fault lines far more pronounced than those in the precolonial world. Some of these lines had their origins far in the past; many others were constructions of the colonial era. Even established ethnic categories were altered in important ways. The instrumental incentives for mobilizing and using cultural solidarity, above all in the decolonization era, deepened its political impact and reinforced a process of primordialization already in course.

CIVIL SOCIETY EMERGENT: NATIONALISM

The organizational activity of an emergent civil society, first visible in the interwar years, crisscrossed the social field at the hour of decolonization. A proliferating web of associational life knit society together in ways that supplied the structuration indispensable for the coming nationalist challenge. Indeed, Thomas Hodgkin's masterful monograph *Nationalism in Colonial Africa,* long the scriptural touchstone for studies in African nationalism, devotes much of its space to cataloguing diverse forms of associational activity.[64]

In its earlier phases the colonial state maintained strict scrutiny of African associations, viewing them with suspicion as possible centers of subversion. There was usually legislation that required administrative screening of organizations before they could obtain legal existence, thus empowering colonial officers to ban unregistered organizations.

Group activity under the paternal supervision of the mission churches or corporate sponsorship was more acceptable. Ethnic associations were more likely to enjoy informal tolerance as harmless outlets for collective energies.

In the altered political environment of the postwar years, associational activity acquired formidable momentum. Indeed, if one defines civil society by its organizational life, the decolonization era was its golden age. Metropolitan civil society for the first time took a proprietary interest in promoting overseas auxiliary bodies; unions, religious movements, and political parties sponsored colonial affiliates and also provided training personnel and opportunities for overseas travel. The colonial state and its metropolitan parent hoped to superintend these efforts, to ensure that colonial unions and other organizations were instilled with a civic ethos of "responsible" collaboration with colonial authorities in the political reforms now promised.

These tutelary efforts were at best partially successful. In colonial Zaire associational life was contained within the frame of évolué circles, unions affiliated to the major metropolitan centrals, ethnic associations, and social movements sponsored by the mission churches or large corporations until the late 1950s. But containment was not usually so effective; the postwar years were punctuated with militant actions by unions, youth movements, student organizations, or ex-servicemen's associations.

The urban centers were the vortex of organizational life, but associational structuration spread into the countryside as well. Aside from political parties, the most noteworthy organizations were the marketing cooperatives, which in some instances became major focal points of rural identity, voice, and discontent; this was particularly true in Uganda, Tanganyika, and Ghana.[65] Although departments of cooperative development had supervisory powers and the audit weapon, the more assertive and effectively led cooperative unions slipped through the net of colonial tutelage, their influence augmented by the substantial assets and large cash flows they acquired.

For a brief moment in history—which passed totally unperceived at the time—a swiftly congealing civil society basked in the sun of relative autonomy. The weakening will and authority of the terminal colonial state opened hitherto closely guarded social space. With swelling voice, civil society demanded liberation, the dismanteling of the oppressive colonial state. Nationalist protest was its medium, articulated with growing force by the political parties to which civil society gave birth. No one at that moment of millennial expectations anticipated that these movements would by metamorphosis become the state instruments for a resubordination of civil society.

The idea of anticolonial nationalism offered a message of salvation and redemption. Although its lineages can be traced to the nineteenth century, except in Egypt, the Sudan, Tunisia, and South Africa, before World War II the dream of liberation was too remote and the obstacles to its articulation too severe for ideologies of protest to command a strong following. The various factors examined in chapter 6 that compelled the colonial state to temper and finally abandon its mission of domination facilitated the rise of nationalist organizations. As time went on, initiative increasingly passed to nationalist forces, whose growing strength drove Bula Matari to cover far more swiftly than initial timetables had anticipated.

Nationalism was foremost a discourse of protest, better recognized in a call to action than in the texts of classic works. In flood tide, as the bringer of liberation, it came to appear as a beneficent and irresistible historical force: in the words of one of its most thoughtful students, nationalism "intrudes itself not only with an aura of inevitability but also as the bearer of positive goods."[66] In its earliest voice, nationalism in a pan-Africanist guise beckoned to a global solidarity of Africans around the world. The scornful demeaning of the African heritage that permeated the colonial mind was challenged by historian-philosopher Cheikh Anta Diop, who argued that a black Egypt was the prime center of early civilization,[67] and by poet-politicians Léopold Senghor and Aimé Césaire, who asserted a uniquely African ontology (*négritude*) whose naturalist, nonmaterial values contrasted favorably with the hedonistic materialism of the West.[68] The sheer force and trauma of colonial oppression elicited a singularly powerful exegesis in the polemics of Frantz Fanon, a Martiniquan psychiatrist in the service of the Algerian Revolution.[69] Finally, nationalism held the promise of a revolutionary transformation of society, although by ways and means that were left unspecified.

Political parties were the organizational weapon of nationalism.[70] Ideologically, they articulated the message of nationalism and stitched it to the many-colored fabric of grievance woven by the colonial state. Structurally, they drew together the rich array of organizations in support of the liberation project; in a number of instances (like the "congress" type of party identified by Hodgkin), they were simply federations of such organizations. But they were much more, carrying their message beyond the collection of intermediary organizations to the far ends of the country.

The moment is vividly caught by Basil Davidson, a lifelong apostle of African liberation and companion of many nationalist campaigns:

> One's memories of those years are of jubilant young men . . . setting out on endless journeys delayed and harassed by endless troubles and upsets, lack of petrol, spare parts, cash, and even food. . . . By whatever transport they could find, on foot or horseback, in truck or "mammy wagon," their arrival was often "accompanied by brass bands, flute bands, cowhorn bands and dancers" in places never visited before. Meeting the "masses" in "schoolrooms, compounds, cinemas and churches, they touched the lives of hundreds of isolated communities in a way never known before."[71]

I recollect attending political rallies by the Neo-Destour Party in Tunisia at the time of independence in 1956, at which President Habib Bourguiba spoke. The air was electric, the crowd's adulation overpowering. Equally memorable was the almost universal esteem of the university student population, repeatedly expressed in speeches and resolutions at a congress of the Union Générale des Etudiants Tunisiens I attended, in an atmosphere free of the fear and intimidation that years later might influence public debate.

The energies of political party mobilization originated in part from the inner impulses of liberation. Circumstances created their own imperatives; the rules of the terminal colonial game made the search for a mass audience indispensable. Once the inevitability of power transfer was acknowledged by the colonial state, the nationalist leaders were asked to demonstrate electorally their mandate to claim the right to succession. In most cases there were multiple contenders, often with regionally defined clienteles. Not infrequently, competing parties differed in their ideological images—less in explicit divergences of doctrine than in tone and style. Some movements employed a more radical, aggressively confrontational language; others transparently enjoyed the state's favor, speaking of the coming independence in terms of a harmonious postcolonial entente (for example, the Union Camerounaise of Ahmadu Ahidjo in Cameroon, and the ill-fated Parti National du Progrès in Zaire). The nationalist movement thus had to become an electoral machine.

In the instances where the colonial state was dominated by an intransigent white-settler elite tenaciously defending minority racial privilege (Algeria, Rhodesia, Namibia), or in the Portuguese case where a beleaguered autocracy had tied its Estado Novo legitimating ideology to the permanence of empire, independence through the electoral and negotiated route was not available. The sole pathway for nationalism was the long, costly one of armed insurrection. As chapter 6 argues, these cases were supremely important in revealing the bedrock historical fact that sheer force, once the architect of empire, no longer sufficed to preserve it.

The civil society constructed out of liberated zones, guerrilla armies, and militarily enforced solidarity was different from the kind that emerged from voluntary associations and electoral campaigning.[72] At the time of independence many believed that the character of the mobilization that warfare involved, and the intimacy of the links forged between guerrillas and populace (civil society as an aquarium for the freedom-fighting fish, in the Maoist metaphor), offered a different and more hopeful future for the countries concerned. By the time of the 1981 coup overthrowing Luis Cabral in Guinea-Bissau a consensus had taken hold that, whatever the differences in itinerary of civil society, the similarity in the operating modes of the postcolonial states created broadly similar contemporary circumstances.

In its first stirrings anticolonial nationalism was essentially a discourse of protest. Its contours were to a degree defined by its hostile other: the colonial occupant in question. But the specific nation to which nationalism referred remained opaque. It was obvious enough in instances of historical states like Egypt, Morocco, or Tunisia but entirely obscure in the vast sub-Saharan zones under French rule. When the colonial state weakened, a territorialization of nationalism set in, embracing imperial partition. The British, persuaded of the higher viability of larger sovereign units, tended to promote regional units, such as the federations in Central and East Africa; they preserved Nigeria and the Sudan as single entities (opposing, as I noted earlier, a Sudanese reunion with Egypt). But these multiterritorial groupings were fatally compromised by their linkage to the preservation of exorbitant privileges for immigrant European and Asian communities, although elements of an East African Community survived until 1976. The individual territories into which British colonial sovereignty was divided served as successors.

Fragmentation was the more powerful force in the dialectic of decolonization, most dramatically triumphant in the sundering of the colonial federations of AOF and AEF. Political life—and consciousness of a civil society—took form mainly at the territorial level; the "federal" institutions at Dakar and Brazzaville were quintessentially colonial bureaucratic instances. Multiterritorial political movements did play a major role, most notably the Rassemblement Démocratique Africain (RDA); the opportunity in the French case for parliamentary participation at first provided important incentives in this direction, and during the period up to the mid-1950s, when this forum for action seemed most visible and efficacious, multiterritorial parties were the rule. But the large opening for local African participation offered by the political reforms for sub-Saharan imperial organization (formalized as the 1956 Loi-Cadre) altered the balance, placing African leaders in charge of newly autonomous territories and introducing a different calculus of relative advantage. The wealthier territories (the Ivory Coast and Gabon) calculated that they would be drained of resources to support the impoverished inland units (Niger and Chad). Dahomey long harbored resentments over Dakar's tutelage and nursed historical memories of net revenue losses to support the colonial federation.[73] France invested little energy in saving these federations and was widely suspected of a secret preference for smaller, more pliable postcolonial partners. Although the leading nationalist figures—Léopold Senghor, Sékou Touré, Félix Houphouët-Boigny—had at one point or another favored political spaces larger than those provided by the individual territories, the conflicting visions they held, and the pull of the divergent interests of the individual territories, introduced a fatal dialectic of fragmentation.[74]

NATIONALISM AND THE COLONIAL STATE: AMBIGUOUS TRIUMPH

What stands out above all was the capacity of the individual colonial territory to imprint its personality on its nationalist adversary. However alien the geographical grid of imperial partition, the logic of struggle compelled nationalist movements to embrace it. The most politically aware and articulate groups, in whose name nationalism spoke, had thoroughly absorbed this territorial identity, through their greater proximity to and interaction with the colonial state. In subliminal ways, the associational infrastructure of civil society territorialized identity; the peak organizations invariably bore the label of the country and deployed their activity within its boundaries. Formerly acknowledged as determining the boundaries of anticolonial engagement, the units of colonial partition became sanctified, even sacralized—a process symbolized in the 1963 charter of the Organization of African Unity (OAU), which declared colonial boundaries definitive and immutable.

The triumph of nationalism seemed, in its *annus mirabilis* of 1960, well-nigh complete. Although the term *neocolonial* quickly entered polemical vocabulary, to denote the continued economic dependence of the new states or their political subservience to the former metropoles, only gradually did it become apparent that independence had a more costly ransom. The silent revenge of the colonial state was surreptitiously to embed in its postindependence successor the corrosive personality of Bula Matari.

African independence remains a historic accomplishment of epochal dimensions. The robust growth of a civil society during the final colonial years serves as a beacon in the historical memory, more luminous than ever in the 1990s with the search for a democratized relationship between state and society. In the dispiriting years of African stagnation during the 1980s, one would occasionally hear from ordinary Africans expressions of nostalgia for the colonial era. Such jarring statements mirrored a profound disenchantment with the present condition; were they really an invitation to Bula Matari to return? Such affirmations applied to the recent years of crisis a yardstick fashioned in the gilded years of the 1950s—the one decade of the colonial era when real per-capita incomes at all levels of society were indisputably rising, when the colonial state for the first time was making major public investments in expanding the social infrastructure serving the mass of the populace, when an entire young generation had great expectations. One might perhaps also detect a trace of a recollected civil society. In this selective remembrance, the harsh oppression and relentless extraction of the colonial state for most of its life cycle disappear; none can wish the return of those years.

But the political history of the past three decades raises new questions. In using the discourse of the colonial state to confront and challenge it, the independence generation of leaders unwittingly absorbed elements of its inner logic. In Davidson's eloquent words, "Acceptance of the post-colonial nation-state meant acceptance of the legacy of the colonial partition, and of the moral and political practices of colonial rule in its institutional dimensions. . . . Along with the nation-state as necessary aim and achievement, the legacy of the partition was transferred practically intact, partly because it seemed impossible to reject any significant part of that legacy, and partly, as one is bound to think in retrospect, because there was as yet no sufficient understanding of what the legacy implied."[75] The fatal attraction for the nation-state vision of the polity, superimposed on the colonial territory, reinstated a superstructure of domination severed from civil society. "National integration" became an imperative that justified the single party and military forms of rule in the name of a national unity menaced by the activated and transformed ethnicity bequeathed by the colonial state. At the same time, the discourse of development, which only the central institutions of the state could rationally plan and competently execute, implied "bringing the state back in"—as undisputed master.

In fully committing itself to the nation-state model of modernity, nationalism unwittingly repudiated its ancestral heritage. "Africa's past achievements," writes Davidson, "could be useful as food for anti-colonial argument—essentially, by this time, anti-racist argument—but could offer no useable design for political action."[76] Accordingly, the moral realm associated with the state, as Peter Ekeh has argued, lacked any normative ties with civil society. The state domain, thus, was a site of amoral behavior by all hands.[77] Independent Africa, adds Vansina in a powerful argument, can "finally flourish" only when this "baneful dichotomy" between Western influences and the majority tradition, epitomized in the gulf dividing state and civil society, is at last overcome.[78]

Chapter Eight

THE IMPERIAL LEGACY
AND
STATE TRADITIONS

> You all went, but left so much behind that you couldn't carry with you
> wherever you were going, and these days those of you who come back can
> more often than not hardly bother to think about it.
>
> —*Lady Chatterjee in Paul Scott,* The Jewel in the Crown,
> *from* The Raj Quartet)

COMPARING COLONIAL STATES

The time has come to return to the broader genus of colonial states, so as
to argue the particularity of the African species. In chapter 3 the colonial
state was introduced as a subdivision of the still more incorporative category of "state." At that point I explored the rise of the imperial phenomenon from the fifteenth century onward and the major forms taken by
early colonial regimes that served as precursors for Bula Matari. My
objective was to catalogue the library of lessons in colonial statecraft
built up in the early centuries of imperial expansion, which supplied the
initial corpus of policy knowledge informing the incipient architecture of
domination in Africa. Chapters 4 to 6 sketch a portrait of the African
colonial state; with this image before us, a further stroll through the
gallery of global imperialism will illuminate the contrasts between the
African colonial state and its counterparts in other regions.

   The core thesis of this work is that one consequential factor in the crisis
faced by most African states by the late 1970s—and intensifying since—
was the singularly difficult legacy bequeathed by the institutions of rule
devised to establish and maintain alien hegemony. The credibility of this
proposition rests on showing differences between African and other colonial constructs. Thus, we need to turn to the broader universe of colonial
systems and their legacies in the modern world, identifying their points
of contrast with the African colonial state.

Our task is inevitably complicated by the sheer size of the universe we must explore—much of Asia, Oceania, the Americas—and the range of colonial actors—Russia, Japan, the Netherlands, and the United States, in addition to those active in Africa. Within the compressed frame of a single chapter, I cannot claim either encyclopedic documentation or definitive proof. But I do wish to establish at least the plausibility of my central hypothesis. I first throw the net of the six imperatives of state behavior over the broader realm of colonial state formations. I then consider some other differentiating factors shaping colonial states and enumerate overall characteristics of colonial state legacies beyond Africa. The chapter concludes with a listing of crucial dimensions particular to Bula Matari.

In the creation of imperial domains, all expanding states confronted the same half-dozen imperatives. The specific formulas developed for overcoming the dilemmas of rule varied widely in terms of historical circumstance, social setting, resource base, and prevailing modes of thought. The requirements of hegemony, security, autonomy, legitimation, revenue, and accumulation nonetheless appeared on all agendas of colonial statecraft.

HEGEMONY

The scope of hegemony varied from the loose suzerainty exercised by British residents in the Persian Gulf sheikdoms to the extraordinarily thorough policing of the Japanese colonial estates.[1] The imperial purposes served explain the British case; these satrapies were held solely for preemptive security reasons as part of a strategy linked to the defense of the Indian jewel in the crown. In the case of Japan, concepts of state deeply implanted in the culture and ethos of the Japanese polity appear to explain the densely structured apparatus of domination. The ways and means of hegemony also reflect the political sociology of the subjugated. Societies with complex and highly structured social hierarchies and richly elaborated theologies could only be managed by co-opted intermediaries, like the diverse array of rajas, princes, zamindars, and Brahmans who permitted a tiny cadre of British officials to rule India. In the instance of the Russian Empire, co-optation extended in some non-Russian territories to what Laitin calls "most-favored lord" status: that is, a recognized rank whose title gave access to high society at the imperial center as well as protected lordship in the peripheral region.[2] Scattered and decentralized populations could be driven back (as in much of the Americas, Australasia, and the Russian north) or be subjected to more direct domination. The denser the infrastructure of hegemony, the greater the imprint on successor states. Prolonged, comprehensive colonial hegemony largely obliterates the indigenous structures of rule and the political culture attending them.

At the moment of colonial conquest, imperial sovereignty over newly acquired territory was invariably presumed to be permanent. Even in the British case, where the distinction in public law between the overseas territories (except Ireland) and the imperial homeland was clearest, and the formula of self-government as an ultimate goal emerges at least by the time of the 1867 British North American Act, the concept of the British Empire as a united security community of autonomous dominions remained intact until the defection of the Irish Free State in 1937.[3] Thus, until World War II sounded the death knell of the colonial system, hegemony always required strategies aimed at permanence but able to adapt to changing circumstance.

SECURITY

The drive for security had both external and internal dimensions. In most times and places the external aspect dominated state behavior. The major threat to overseas estates came from fellow predators. As I argued earlier, preemptive expansion—pushing back the frontiers for strategic depth or to forestall an anticipated move by a rival—was a potent factor in imperial diplomacy: for example, the "great game" of nineteenth-century rivalry between Britain and Russia, stalking each other in the steppes and mountains of Central Asia. The British, French, and Dutch nibbled away at Spanish Caribbean holdings so as to acquire bases for intercepting the profits and plunder from contraband trade and even piracy.[4] In the age of the steamship the necessity for widely distributed coal stations to sustain a global naval strategy energized the scramble for island holdings in Oceania.[5]

Internal security was a surprisingly modest problem in the long period between initial conquest and wars of liberation. Large detachments of metropolitan soldiers were found in only a few places. A good part of Russia's huge army was deployed in non-Russian frontier zones. The Armée d'Afrique, garrisoned in Algeria, represented roughly one-third of the French Army, but other parts of the empire were mainly controlled by French-officered local auxiliaries. Until the Seven Years' War (1756–1763), Britain had no standing army in the American colonies. Between the sepoy mutiny (1857) and World War I, Britain kept an average of seventy thousand British troops in India, with an Indian Army twice as large. In relation to the Indian population, this force was not consider-able, nor was it frequently used in other than local skirmishes during those years. Its main role was as an imperial reserve, the mailed fist reinforcing British policy from China to Suez.[6] The Spanish domains as well were largely held by local contingents; in 1800 there were only 2,358 Spanish soldiers in Chile and 6,150 in New Spain (Mexico and Central America), with thirty thousand local auxiliaries in each case.[7] The slave-plantation Caribbean territories were secured by forces composed of free soldiers of color.[8]

AUTONOMY

The autonomy of the colonial state with respect to its conquered popula-tion was self-evident in instances where occupation was imposed by mili-tary action, as in Latin America. In the early phases of imperial ex-pansion, when absolutist ideas of state sovereignty were paramount, the newly acquired subjects overseas axiomatically had no more standing than those in the metropole. In North America occupation often occurred by treaty relationship with Indian communities, whose withdrawal be-yond the zone of colonial sovereignty was negotiated. Particularly ambig-uous were the cases of colonial states originating in chartered corpora-tions. In the East Indies and India they soon came to exercise authority of uncertain derivation over the territory they came to occupy (the Am-bonese islands, Batavia, the Madras strip); in 1765 the East India Com-pany was named by the Mogul emperor to serve as revenue collector for Bengal, Bihar, and Orissa. As crown-chartered satraps and tax farmers for an Indian empire, the company agents assumed an even more bizarre form of authority. Equally uncertain, especially on the ground, was the relationship between clusters of settlers and chartered bodies holding the delegated sovereignty of the crown in the North American colonies.

As a corporate entity distinct from the imperial center, the colonial state only gradually acquired a legal personality of its own. Such a notion was initially alien to the European states first engaged in expansion, Spain and Portugal. In its European domains the Spanish crown applied a feudal model of dynastic quasi-federation. Aragon, Naples, Sicily and the Netherlands were dependencies of the Hapsburg monarchy rather than integrated domains of the absolutist Castilian state.[9] But its new conquests—first the Canaries, then the Americas—were considered an overseas extension of the Castilian realm, following a model of incorpora-tion that had applied to the reconquista of Moorish Spain. In Brazil, after the initial period of quasi-feudal coastal captaincies bestowed by crown patronage on a dozen courtiers, from the mid-sixteenth century onward a royal bureaucracy was established that tended to grow stronger with time, culminating in the centralizing reforms of the architect of late absolutism, the Marquis de Pombal, in the third quarter of the eighteenth century. The essence of the Brazilian colonial state is captured by Schwartz: "Government and society in colonial Brazil were structured by two interlocking systems of organization. On one level, a metropolitan controlled and directed administration, characterized by bureaucratic norms and impersonal relations, tied individuals and groups to the political institutions of formal government. Parallel to this, there existed a network of interpersonal primary relations based on interest, kinship, and common goals, which while no less formal in one sense, nevertheless lacked official recognition."[10]

An ethos of distinct colonial personality was also absent in the Czarist domains, even though Russia's expansion, particularly the nineteenth-century surge into Turkestan, was indistinguishable from colonial conquests by other powers. But the Czarist state cloaked its relentless expansion in an incorporative imperial idea: the autocracy was ruler of "all the Russias" (Rossiiskaia Imperiia). The czar was not *russkii* but *vserossiiskii imperator.*[11] Thus, although Turkestan was ruled through indigenous intermediaries in a manner resembling colonial administration elsewhere, it was viewed as a simple administrative unit of the state.

The specificity of the colonial domains acquired by Japan (Taiwan, Korea, Karafuto [south Sakhalin], and the Nanyo [the equatorial Pacific islands]) was likewise ambiguous. The doctrine of "one nation, one emperor" was incompatible with full recognition of the newly conquered territories. Further, the cultural similarities of the subjects in Taiwan and Korea marked them as candidates for eventual assimilation; in Karafuto and the Nanyo, Japanese settlers were soon a majority of the population. With the exception of the Nanyo, where legal incorporation was constrained by the class C League of Nations mandate, the Japanese constitution was held partly applicable, with colonial governors enjoying in practice some ordinance-issuing autonomy. In 1942 the Ministry of Colonial Affairs was abolished, implying a more complete integration.[12] Ironically, by the 1930s the most enthusiastic empire-building by Japan was in Manchuria, which was formally just a puppet state under Japanese control, not an annexed territory. The public imagination was captured by the notion of "total empire," a joint project of a large contingent of Japanese settlers, the Kwangtung army, and the South Manchurian

Railway Company. Cultural images representing Manchuria as a miracle of Japanese developmental initiative, a veritable utopia mirroring a model for a future Japan, dominated the popular media.[13]

In the latter phases of the colonial era, however, insistence on the separate juridical personality of the overseas dependencies became the rule, with as corollary the autonomy required by the delegated agents of imperial sovereignty. French colonial theoretician Jules Harmand forcefully expressed this view in 1910, arguing that territories "peopled by natives subjected by force" necessitate an administration endowed with "the greatest degree of administrative, economic and financial independence compatible with their political dependence."[14]

LEGITIMACY

In the early phases of colonial empires the issue of legitimation scarcely arose. Only the crown and court needed persuading of the legitimacy of imperial domains, not a difficult test to meet. The plunder and mercantile advantages so visibly accruing to Spain and Portugal in the sixteenth century made overseas conquest in the age of absolutism seem profitable to ruling circles who had the sea power to embark upon it; before the activation of civil society, no other opinion counted. The phenomenal profits of the sugar trade in the eighteenth century, which rewarded royal treasuries, the planter aristocracy, and merchants engaged in colonial trade, injected new incentives to annex suitable areas. By the nineteenth century, however, expansion required justification to an audience beyond state elites, first reflected in the rise of an abolition movement in England. The final paroxysm of imperialism in the late nineteenth century was punctuated by active debate both within the state apparatus and the public at large. A now activated civil society was crosscut by intersecting currents of nationalism, racism, and jingoism supporting conquest, which were offset by deep skepticism (shared by a good part of the ruling class) about the likely balance sheet. From this came the explicit fiscal pact, applied more strictly to Africa, that stipulated the financial self-sufficiency of colonial territories.

Before the era of decolonization and anticolonial nationalism, legitimation relative to the subject population arose as an internal issue for the colonial state only with respect to settler populations, who believed they transported with them whatever "rights" attached to their standing as subjects of the realm. English settlers had the most extended concept of what such rights might comport, summarized well by Savelle:

Colonies were new "British" societies founded on the basis of ancient social compacts (the colonial charters) with the kings of England. The people were Englishmen, with all the rights of Englishmen; nevertheless, the societies were new bodies politic that were by natural right sovereign within their own boundaries. Thus the Anglo-American creole political philosophers introduced into the debate the concept of a divided sovereignty: the "Kings, Lords, and Commons" were sovereign in matters pertaining to international and intercolonial affairs, but this sovereignty did not extend to matters concerning only the internal affairs of any colony.[15]

Creole expectations of voice in Ibero-America did not rest on such robust foundations.[16] Spanish kings claimed authority directly from God, excluding accountability to the estates. Although loyalty was not at issue until the nineteenth century, creoles chafed under crown trading restrictions, as well as the royal monopolization of a number of profitable activities. Especially in the later period, creoles were largely excluded from some key offices in the Americas, another source of friction; of the 170 viceroys and 602 captains-general serving the crown in the new world, some 98 percent were Spanish-born, as were 85 percent of colonial bishops (although creoles were fairly numerous in Audiencia offices).[17] The crucial importance of legitimation in creole eyes is demonstrated well in the confused, prolonged wars of independence.[18] The trigger event was the Napoleanic occupation of Spain, which deposed the king in 1808. This forced the issue of whether New Spain and other Spanish territories in the Americas were Spanish colonies for Spaniards or federated royal realms coeval with Spain.[19]

A crisis of legitimation also immediately occurred in the few instances where nationalism was well rooted at the moment of colonial conquest. Korean nationalism challenged the Japanese occupation from the outset (even though its organizations were riddled with informers planted by the ubiquitous Japanese police). The head of the Japanese police in Korea warned in the early 1920s of the rise of nationalism, arguing that what he felt to be "soft treatment of the Koreans" was "risky because it will only provide further stimulus to the trend of increasing nationalist demands," a trend that would be "difficult to slow" and "maybe even impossible to stop."[20] American occupation likewise encountered aroused nationalism in the Philippines and Puerto Rico, where the American invasions to oust Spain turned into new colonial occupations, ferociously imposed in the case of the Philippines. In Puerto Rico, writes Carr, the United States "was confronted by a self-confident political elite that had

already grasped the local levers of power, not by a race of Latin illiter-
ates."[21] Nationalism also bedeviled the efforts of France and Britain to
impose effective rule on Arab areas formerly under Ottoman rule, which
they partitioned through the mandate system.

REVENUE

The revenue imperative drove colonial state construction along diverse
pathways. Russia was not preoccupied with imperial balance sheets, and
Japanese colonial expansion was largely dictated by strategic and cultural ideas of national strengthening; insistence on economic returns to
the state did not dominate policy thinking. In Taiwan and Korea the
Japanese nonetheless acquired sophisticated rural economies that could
supply a revenue flow covering a large part of their occupation costs.
Peattie points out that, informed by the land-tax reforms in Japan itself
that financed the rapid state construction following the Meiji Restoration, systematic organization of the agrarian zones provided most of the
resources required for the colonial project:

> One of the first concerns of the colonial regimes, beginning with
> that in Taiwan, was to establish a rationalized agricultural tax base
> which could provide a regular source of revenue. Just as the Meiji
> modernizers had recognized that this could only be achieved through
> the clarification of land ownership, so too did Japanese colonial gov-
> ernments undertake a series of land survey and registration pro-
> grams ... to classify land, identify and measure property ownership,
> simplify the sale and purchase of land, promote land utilization, and
> most of all provide accurate assessments for tax purposes.[22]

The most profitable part of Japan's expanding empire was its zone of
informal domination in Manchuria, exercised from 1908 until military
occupation in 1931 by the tentacular South Manchuria Railway Company, then the largest Japanese corporation, with profits of 20 to 30
percent during most of this period and a yearly revenue in the 1920s
equal to one-quarter of total Japanese state tax income.[23]

For the East India trading corporations, Dutch and English, trading
profits funded the costs of delegated sovereignty and often yielded comfortable returns for the shareholders. The Dutch East India Company,
during its seventeenth-century operations, assured shareholders an annual return of 18.7 percent a year.[24] Although it accumulated debts during the eighteenth century, many of its servants prospered through trading on their own account from the base it provided. When the company

was liquidated in 1798, the Netherlands acquired proprietary title to the sprawling Indonesian archipelago by clearing company debts of 140 million guilders. As systematic territorial administration was organized, first in Java and then in the outer islands, the Dutch colonial state could take over a fiscal system that designated 40 percent of the rice lands for tax payments to the rulers. The "cultures" system, which flourished from 1830 to 1870, required villages to allocate 20 percent of their land for commercial crops stipulated by the state, and each male subject to provide sixty-six days of labor service on state plantations.[25] The "liberal" policy that followed after 1870 shifted away from direct state management of agricultural production, but export crops continued to provide an ample flow of revenue. Throughout the nineteenth century the Indies were not only self-supporting but also contributed significantly to the metropole's revenues; only in 1900 were the two budgets separated. It is estimated that during the years of the cultures system the Indies contributed 189 million guilders to the Dutch revenues.[26] These impositions built on historically rooted patterns of a ruling elite; "peasants remained village residents whose contact with the colonial apparatus was cushioned and muted by a layer of native civil servants."[27]

In India, once the metamorphosis from mercantile body to colonial state had occurred, land revenue—the historical basis for Indian statebuilding—became key. "Land revenue administration," writes the chronicler of the elite Indian Civil Service, "has always been one of the primary duties of the civil service."[28] Given the scale of India and the size of its population, the British Raj could largely fund its thinly staffed apparatus of domination as well as meet its legitimation imperative by keeping the tax rate relatively modest. As Tomlinson observes, "The secret of successful Indian government was thought to be low taxation."[29] But British reliance on the Indian Army and the cost to the Indian budget of garrisoning the seventy thousand British regulars in India posed a major threat to revenue equilibrium. The Raj and London came into increasing conflict over British government efforts to force India to pay for growing imperial commitments: the 1867 Abyssinian expedition, East African colonial conquest, Egypt, Persia, Afghanistan. In 1920 London insisted on India supplying thirty-nine infantry battalions and four cavalry regiments for the costly military campaign to crush resistance in Iraq.[30] Indian colonial revenue requirements also precipitated the 1839–1840 Opium War with China, which remains one of the most sordid episodes in imperial history. In order to pay dividends to East India Company shareholders and to permit company agents to repatriate their capital to England, a mechanism for generating bullion was required. As India produced none and its exports to Britain were insufficient for this purpose, the solution was to compel China to purchase Indian opium with silver (and tea), and to abandon efforts to prohibit its consumption.[31] At the time, opium supplied one-seventh of colonial revenues to India.[32]

In Indochina one encounters a colonial structure whose revenue practices oppressed its subjects and defined a colonial situation that has some resemblance to its African form. French administration was relatively dense and costly—five thousand European colonial agents during the interwar period in Vietnam for a population of thirty million, as opposed to 4,800 British civil servants for 350 million Indians.[33] The substantial French population escaped most taxation, which bore heavily upon the peasantry, particularly in Tonkin and Annam, whose fiscal potential was greatly overrated by French imperial strategists. State monopolies for salt, alcohol, and opium were other major fiscal sources; even in Cambodia, more indirectly ruled than Vietnam, these impositions were heavy enough to trigger peasant delegations of forty thousand to the king to seek tax relief.[34] The high costs of a proliferating alien administration, unremunerative public investment in costly infrastructure (the unprofitable railway system), and the demands of settlers for coerced labor supply drove Indochina's administration to impose heavy taxation and—particularly before World War I—extensive corvée labor.[35]

In the Caribbean, colonial state establishments were quite small; the core structures of social coercion—the slave plantations—were private. The primary revenue considerations concerned the impositions on trade. In Britain the fiscal dividends reaped from sugar (along with tea and coffee, closely linked in consumption patterns) became a major revenue source when in the late eighteenth century it became an article of mass consumption. A historian of taxation in the United Kingdom said of the sugar excise in an 1884 work, "This tax, with those on tea and coffee, held . . . a position of peculiar importance: to be kept, in time of peace, at low rates at which, so evenly do these taxes lie over the whole surface of the nation, the pressure was not felt by anyone, they were powerful engines available when the nation should be called upon for a general effort in time of war. To abolish these taxes would be to remove the mainstays of our system of taxation."[36] Customs collected from the sugar trade had become a significant British revenue source by the later seventeenth century, along with those from tobacco. In addition, Jamaican sugar was an important source of bullion earnings: 200,000 pounds annually by 1700.[37] The state proceeds from the West Indies in the eighteenth century made the British willing during peace negotiations following the Seven Years' War to return Quebec to France in exchange for Martinique and Guadaloupe.

The Spanish colonial state was a more formidable engine of revenue, both in supporting the relatively sophisticated superstructure of domination and in generating an important flow to the metropolitan treasury. From 1503 to 1660 some 16,000,000 kilograms of silver and 185,000 kilograms of gold reached Spain from the New World, increasing the existing European stock by 300 percent and 20 percent, respectively.[38] The "royal fifth" accrued to the crown, accounting for 11 percent of state revenue in 1554 and 20 percent to 25 percent by the late sixteenth century.[39] The colonial state apparatus itself was financed by various mechanisms that fell heavily on the native population. A tribute tax was collected from all those within reach of the administration. By the mid-to-late colonial period an increasing number of state positions were sold by the metropolitan state. The local magistrates (*corregidores, alcaldes mayores*), the key link between local communities and the state, purchased their positions for a price far in excess of the position's derisory stipend, and they had to recoup their capital and make their livelihoods by diverse extortion. The colonial administration also collected the tithe due the Catholic church, although these proceeds probably found their way back into church maintenance and such social institutions as then existed. Substantial customs on land and sea routes were a good source of revenue, but enforcing them contributed heavily to the subverting of the empire because of the incentives for contraband trading with British, Dutch, French, and—later—American shippers. State monopolies on salt, paper, gunpowder, mercury, and tobacco were significant sources as well.

By a circular dynamic, these diverse fiscal sources both permitted a relatively large state structure and generated continuing pressures to sustain—even expand—it to carry out the functions implied by state revenue requirements. Particularly frustrating was its limited capacity to extract much from the wealthy, "a class," suggests Macleod, "which had to be pampered because it performed so many social control and other functions for the government."[40] The best that could be managed were "voluntary donations," in reality involuntary but negotiated payments, frequently underpaid. Needless to say, private wealth was in significant part generated by the coerced labor of Indians or African slaves.

The patrimonial colonial bureaucracy in Brazil, less elaborate than its Spanish counterpart, throughout its early, sugar-based period required only modest revenues, largely generated by tithes (which by a 1551 Vatican accord were collected by the crown). Portugal's revenues from sugar production and trade were by far the largest source of crown revenue from 1550 to 1650. The discovery of gold in 1694 and the rapid rise in mining output in the eighteenth century made the royal fifth and allied mining revenues the critical nourishment for the treasury. The insatiable demand for slaves in Brazil was another significant source of crown revenues; a per-capita tax was levied at the Sao Tome transshipment point. By the later eighteenth century the royal mint in Brazil was yielding six times as much as the tithes.[41]

ACCUMULATION

In the age of mercantilism, accumulation meant fostering metropolitan-dominated trade and accumulating bullion. In the early days of empire, trade entailed a small range of high-value commodities not easily available in Europe. At the beginning these were obtained by exchange: the spice trade or, later, peltries. With sugar and tobacco in the Americas, colonial states acquired an interest in production systems; initially luxury items, their markets steadily increased (in contrast to spices, with narrow and highly volatile markets). A class of plantation owners had to be attracted, by assured land grants and labor supplies; for sugar, a significant private investment in the processing factories was needed, raising the stakes. Only servile labor would meet the needs, which drew the colonial state into fostering the slave trade. The state also had to provide ultimate security guarantees to this highly coercive social hierarchy. In accumulation terms, colonial states had little direct interest in purely internal and local production, which did not give rise to trade or taxes.

Precious metals exerted a singularly powerful shaping force. The crown at home and royal officers overseas obeyed a compulsive instinct to secure as much as possible of this treasure for state ends. In the first years, gold and silver mainly came from confiscation of Indian possessions, but the sources were swiftly discovered, posing the challenge of organizing mining so as to secure a maximum share of royal returns. The established principle of the royal fifth of precious metals was naturally helpful, even if at times it had to be reduced to a tenth or even less as an inducement to develop new mines. States lacked the capacity to organize silver and gold mining directly as government monopolies, although there were some state mines. But the need to encourage prospecting, capital, and management capacity forced reliance on private operators. There was a running battle for state surveillance and monopolies of minting, assaying, and other choke-point controls to ensure that the state share was collected on everything that was produced; in the Americas the colonial state monopolized mercury, the indispensable metallurgical agent for refining gold and silver.[42]

As the colonial state became an appendage to a nascent industrial system in the nineteenth century, the accumulation imperative took on new dimensions. Textiles, the prototypical product of first-generation industry, required a cotton supply. American production, as the Civil War blockade demonstrated, was not necessarily reliable; the potential for peasant taxation joined with imperial industrial policy as motivating factors in cotton promotion. The strikingly remunerative nineteenth-century colonial state involvement in the "cultures policy" in Indonesia, promoting export-crop production (coffee and tobacco), was a compelling model for other colonial powers. Where colonial accumulation required a labor force not locally available through market mechanisms, and where coercive conscription would challenge legitimation and security, by the late nineteenth century colonial states had initiated indentured recruitment in zones where population and poverty pressures induced human flows: Indians for sugar plantations in Guyana, Trinidad, and Fiji, Chinese for Malayan tin mines, Indians for Malayan rubber plantations.

For the later phases of the colonial era, the logic of accumulation dictated large infrastructure investments, most visibly railroads—successful and profitable in India with a public investment of 95 million pounds,[43] a costly source of colonial debt in Indochina. In much of the Caribbean, the diminished profitability of sugar plantations and the abolition of slavery utterly deflated the colonial states, which became largely ignored backwaters: imperial slums, as Lloyd George called them. (Cuba, however, was an important exception.) Lacking for the last colonial century any impelling dynamic of accumulation, the West Indian colonies became minimal and self-reproducing structures of domination protecting a small white planter minority and an allied mulatto elite against the large Afro-Caribbean majority of tenants and peasant cultivators.

OTHER DIMENSIONS OF DIFFERENTIATION

Beyond the comparative reflections on colonial systems provided by the six state imperatives, other differentiating measures merit consideration. The state doctrines attaching to imperial polities shaped their colonial perspectives. These organic principles of state conduct reflected the particular traditions and trajectories of a given country, discourses of power, authority, and structuration that encoded a lived historical experience. Stateness, observed Nettl in welcoming the concept back to comparative analysis, is culturally designed, intellectually reasoned, and politically expressed in a particular pattern of institutionalization of power.[44]

Thus, the Spanish model of rule in Latin America drew inspiration from prior reflection on the strategic requirements for projecting royal control over newly acquired domains in southern Spain and the Canaries, and for controlling (or at least restraining) the unruly agents of conquest.[45] Portugal was a more maritime power; although influenced by Iberian ideas and practices (and under Spanish rule from 1580 to 1640), it was more inclined toward a pattern of expansion based on coastal outposts for a sea-borne empire. The Dutch mode of mercantile expansion by chartered associations of merchants followed logically from the uncertain nature of the metropolitan polity itself: the Netherlands was a precarious consortium of allied, merchant-dominated principalities at the time of the venture into the East Indies. Dutch historian H. L. Wesseling suggests that by the nineteenth century imperial policy in the East was shaped above all by a consciousness that the Netherlands was an imperial dwarf in a continent of colonial giants.[46]

Far more centralized state traditions shaped ideologies of colonial rule in the French case; the prefectoral, Bonapartist tradition infuses the apparatus of domination under the *tricouleur.* The debates over "assimilation" and "association" and the tendency of the French colonial presence to be bureaucratically dense reflect a certain intellectual history and state tradition. The thoroughness of German rule during its brief history likewise reflected the heritage of the Prussian state. The Japanese colonial empire, and those parts of the Russian Empire that approximated colonial realms, closely mirrored the normative models of stateness of the parent polities.

The United States brought to its expansionist thrust an incorporative premise that new territories would be populated with its citizens, and existing inhabitants shunted aside, overwhelmed by numbers, and stripped of much of their land rights. These state ideas could apply to the Hawaiian islands, annexed in 1898, but not to the territories swept into the national domain by the imperialist war with Spain (the Philippines and Puerto Rico). The Philippines in particular were indigestible; the incorporative implications of American state doctrine soon revealed policy consequences that mobilized potent interests and segments of opinion in support of conceptualizing the colony as temporary other. American public law led to integrated economic relations, much to the distaste of the sugar lobby. A looming threat of unrestricted Filipino immigration encountered the strong racist currents directed against Asian newcomers; a visiting Filipino delegation to Washington seeking statehood early in the century was told by cabinet secretary Elihu Root, "Gentlemen, I don't wish to suggest an invidious comparison, but statehood for Filipinos would add another serious race problem to the one we have already. The Negroes are a cancer in our body politic, a source of constant difficulty, and we wish to avoid developing another such problem."[47] Although there were "Indian agents," there was not a colonial administrative service per se, nor a theory of overseas rule. The relatively "stateless" early tradition of the American state found reflection in an unusually small colonial bureaucracy, far less developed than in any other southeast Asian colony in the interwar period.

Imperial states differed considerably in their organizational capacities. For sheer effectiveness of the administrative infrastructure of domination, Japan perhaps had no peer. Distilling what the Japanese considered the most advanced forms of rational and scientific colonial management—a synthesis of French and German state practice—the thoroughly organized twentieth-century Japanese state developed a highly bureaucratized imperial system. "With effective power concentrated at the center by highly efficient executive institutions, [the colonial territories] were managed by an elite corps of civil servants reasonably well trained, well paid, and honest."[48] The sheer mass of the Russian state, with its huge standing army and pervasive bureaucracy, endowed it with a potent capacity for dominating its periphery, reinforced by the contiguous patterns of its expansion.[49]

In its sixteenth-century version, the Spanish state—relative to state possibilities at the time—was a remarkably thorough apparatus. Its multiple structures of domination compensated for distant projection of royal authority by mutual surveillance: viceroyalties, audiencias, regular clergy, missions, and encomenderos provided hierarchies of control meeting at the crown apex. The periods of disarray and weakness at the imperial center—roughly, the seventeenth and nineteenth centuries—only partially undermined the colonial state in the first phase but fatally weakened the Spanish hold in the second. Portugal, in its days as imperial pacesetter in the sixteenth century, through its maritime abilities, merchant capital, and early centralization, enjoyed a brief moment of expansive splendor, in spite of its small size and limited population. In Brazil, particularly during the eighteenth century, a relatively elaborate patrimonial bureaucratic state was constructed. By the nineteenth century, however, Portugal lagged far behind its European imperial competitors in all major respects: administrative capability, capitalist resources, military strength.

Colonial states became of themselves an important source of imperial capacity. The Netherlands was a small and—by the nineteenth century—very vulnerable European state; however, by the mid-nineteenth century the colonial apparatus in the Dutch East Indies had its own momentum of expansion and occupation of its claimed territories, which depended very little on the capacities of the imperial center. Similarly, British India became a veritable regional hegemon as a colonial state, with its large and effective military force, its substantial state resource base, and its unusually competent administrative infrastructure.

The dominant structures of production influenced the physiognomy of the colonial state as well; in extreme cases, one might argue that they largely determined it, a situation illustrated in slave-plantation colonies, where colonial state operations revolved around the protection of the planter enterprises. In the case of the English West Indies, the strong voice of planter-dominated assemblies, before abolition made the representative principle too dangerous for the dominant class, reinforced the tendency of the colonial state to bend before an interest that was also its prime raison d'être.[50]

But in most instances one can perceive a more interactive process. As Martin Murray acknowledges in his influential monograph on capitalism in colonial Indochina, grounded in historical materialism, "What cannot be overemphasized is the fact that the contours of direct colonial rule depended as much upon political considerations of collaboration, efficient administration, and security, as upon opportunities for private profit."[51] The political considerations gave strong weight to the revenue imperative, which in turn was governed by the resource base and modalities of its exploitation. In colonial territories whose revenue-generating output came from agrarian activity based on free labor, a liberal market economy was the least-cost solution. If the nourishment for colonial state coffers came from a crop that could only be produced by coerced labor or imported indentured workers, then state priorities reflected these necessities. Export crops produced by peasant subjects—cotton, for example—inevitably involved the colonial state in organizing the marketing and processing infrastructure, fostering (if not compelling) planting, and supervising cultivation practices.

The political economy of large-scale mining conditioned state structures and practices. In most colonial circumstances, mining ventures were ardently desired by state officials, enchanted by visions of fertile flows of painlessly collected revenues. Mining capital, in return for the substantial risks and long periods of immobilizing capital inherent in their ventures, invariably negotiated its terms of entry with the state, demanding infrastructure support and guaranteed labor supply.

Where the colonial economy was complex and diverse—late colonial India, for example—the sheer multiplicity of production forms meant that no one type could shape the state. But colonial economies were not infrequently rooted in one major export commodity, whose production requirements necessarily set some of the major parameters for state operation. A politically calculated reason of state always filters the economic vectors through the screen of overall requirements for its reproduction. In other terms, the economy—the structure of production—constrains choice; the colonial state as political actor exercises choice.

The foregoing review of varieties of colonial experience brings us to the core of our analysis: the extent to which the African colonial state was unique. I tackle this central issue in two steps: first, by identifying the defining attributes of the major regional forms of the colonial state, building on chapter 3, with a particular eye here to their final shape and legacy; and second, by considering the precise ways in which the colonial state experience in Africa was particular in nature and consequences. My net is not large enough to capture every aspect, but I do hope to include a sufficient number of the most prominent to sustain the argument.

WHITE IMMIGRANT STATES

In the case of the large expanses of North America (the United States and Canada) and Australasia (Australia and New Zealand), from the outset the colonial state personality was defined by a white immigrant population.[52] As we saw in chapter 3, the thirteen colonies that became the United States had perhaps the most meager colonial state superstructure, and the most latitude for a precocious civil society, of any imperial construction. When belated efforts were made by the parent state in the eighteenth century to build a colonial state superstructure capable of managing the North American estates by a royal design, only where the white settlers needed security insurance from the crown could these measures succeed: in the West Indies, where by 1700 slave populations were a large majority and fears of servile insurrection began to spread. On the mainland, only in South Carolina was this the case.

The lessons of the loss of the American colonies were well learned; in Canada, Australia, and New Zealand, colonial state structures were fashioned that more closely reproduced, in an imperial setting, British constitutional designs: a representative principle but strong executive power, overlaid with effective surveillance of the imperial interest. Another, less visible dimension of the British tradition of colonial governance came to the fore: its military backbone. First fashioned in Ireland, where Tudor and Stuart kings discovered that Irish resources could sustain "royal forces that the king's revenue could not afford and that his English parliament would not permit,"[53] garrison government informed the inner spirit of British rule in the West Indies and in Canada, where most early governors-general were of military background, "military men," argues Webb, "intent on establishing security and imposing social order within their jurisdictions."[54]

The founding conceptions of Canada contrasted sharply with those of the settlements to the south. In his extended gloss on the Durham Report, Sir Charles Lucas observes, "Canadian colonization was the product of the State, and the State was the Crown. The [American] colonies, which were the neighbors and rivals of Canada, were largely the product of antagonism to the Crown." He adds, "Canada as a British possession, began with military rule, and it throve under military rule."[55] Nova Scotia, a separate entity until the creation of the Canadian confederation by the 1867 British North America Act, was propelled by its need for protection against French incursions and by its financial dependency into willing subordination, its high costs attracting the oratorical thunder of Edmund Burke, "Good God! what sums the nursing of that ill-thriven, hard-visaged, and ill-favored brat has cost. . . . Sir, this colony has stood us in a sum of not less than seven hundred thousand pounds. To this day it has made no repayment—it does not even support those offices of expense which are miscalled its government; the whole of that job still lies upon the patient, callous shoulders of the people of England."[56] The conquest of Quebec and incorporation of fifty-five thousand French subjects of uncertain loyalty reinforced the disposition toward carefully maintained executive colonial authority. The stream of loyalists, many dispossessed by punitive state assemblies, flowing into Nova Scotia and upper Canada helped build a society receptive to finding such governance legitimate. By the time "responsible government" was accorded in 1840 (followed by dominion status in 1867), a framework of attachment to the imperial consort was well established, even if periodically challenged by the francophone "founding people."

Australia and New Zealand were shaped by the model of imperial rule initially fashioned in Canada. The first Australian settlements were depositories for surplus English prison populations; the "fatal shore" of New South Wales and Tasmania was subject to harsh military rule in the early decades following the first arrivals in 1788.[57] Although South and Western Australia had different origins, the colonial political tradition of the continent, federated into a self-governing dominion in 1901, long bore the mark of its initial purposes. The penal genesis also meant a large Irish strain to the transported convict population, some of whose infractions were political, making their subsequent loyalty ambivalent. New Zealand, in contrast, was the most reliably English of the settler colonies. Although responsible government was granted in 1856, settler loyalty to the imperial connection was sustained not only by the English origins of the immigrants but also by the prolonged resistance of substantial Maori indigenous populations, and by the perceived threat of French expansion in nearby Tahiti and New Caledonia.

British imperial doctrine, by the later nineteenth century, was deeply marked by the dominion formula. The self-governing, self-financing, self-regulating white dominions nonetheless remained within a British Empire framework, which had an ethereal yet real collective existence as a security community until World War II. When added to the formidable contributions to empire security made by India until the 1930s, they offered a vision of a British-led ensemble, whose legitimation imperative in the subjugated periphery found continuous rebirth in ever-extending degrees of self-government "within the empire" (or, after World War II, the Commonwealth). The "illusion of permanence," concealing from the managers of empire the ultimate consequences of decolonizing reform outside the white dominions, was an indispensable self-deception.[58]

THE COLONIAL LEGACY IN LATIN AMERICA

The structure and dynamics of the colonial state in Latin America have been thoroughly described in chapter 3 and in the preceding pages, needing only a few summary observations here. Particularly in the major centers of Spanish rule—initially Hispaniola, subsequently New Spain and Peru—we find important parallels with Bula Matari. From the outset, the capacity to dominate and rule was intimately bound to a labor system based on coerced service. The colonial system was less territorial than demographic; it required control over population, and its frontiers were human rather than physical. Where Indian communities had the option of retreat deeper into lowland tropical forests or acquired the horseborne mobility and weapons to resist effectively, as in the vast grasslands on the southern and northern fringes of the Spanish colonial empire, Spanish authority remained sporadic and settlement minimal. Where dense indigenous populations were locked within elaborate social hierarchies and established structures of political domination, the exit option vanished; the conquistadores superimposed themselves at the summit of these hierarchies, and through the powerful cultural medium of spiritual conquest—the erection of churches with the building stones of de-spoiled temples—a divine discourse of hegemony complemented that of the sword.

The demographic holocaust produced by the conquest compelled the colonial state to augment its labor force with African slave imports. The mines and estates that were the basis for the colonial economy rested on largely unfree labor. Colonial state (and Spanish crown) revenues de-pended, in the several ways described earlier, on Indian tribute and labor service, and on commodities whose production rested on slave labor.

The sophistication of the colonial state structures and the policy direc-tions imposed by state revenue requirements are suggestive parallels. There were, however, important differences. The Latin American states were far less explicitly colonial than the African in conception; both for Spain and Portugal the New World domains were overseas prolongations of the realm. Free crown subjects in Iberia and the Americas were not clearly differentiated.

The heavily male composition of the first generations of Iberian mi-grants meant the swift emergence of an elaborate hierarchy of *castas,* or intermediate racial categories. Color implied rank, though much less sharply than in North America. *Limpieza de sangre* (genealogy free of Indian, African, or Jewish ancestry) was a prerequisite for ascent to the summit of social status, but respectability was within reach for the better-placed of the castas.

What particularly marked the Spanish and Portuguese colonial socie-ties was the hegemonical grip of a theory of society that viewed the ulti-mately color-driven principles of hierarchy as natural, yet understood the cultural master model of creole (native-born) Spanish or Portuguese as open and incorporative, even while it was class-ridden and sharply stratified. The colonial state bequeathed to its successor a dominant im-age of society as racially ranked but politically united. In the majority of the successor states, the creole population was a distinct minority, even a small one in Peru, Bolivia, Guatemala, or Paraguay. Yet the "imagined communities" that emerged from the debris of the Spanish empire assim-ilated the legitimating ideology of "nation." Racial polarization, though recognized, was far less rigid than that of a South Africa or a United States. Racial hierarchy was ultimately open to incorporative resolution, a racial fusion that would bring about the slow disappearance of "back-ward" races. Even where—as in Mexico or Paraguay—the public mythol-ogy of nationhood acknowledged the indigenous peoples, the vision artic-ulated a "cosmic race" of fused cultures, symbolized in the famed mural covering a wall of the National University of Mexico: a single yet dual face, Indian and Iberian. The idea of nationhood finds embodiment in the intertwined myths of Quetzalcoatl and Guadalupe: the Indian god of sea and wind whose return was impersonated by Cortes; the Virgin Mary miraculously appearing to an Indian maiden in 1531.[59]

The political legacy of the Spanish colonial state was much less serviceable, and its inadaptability brought a century of instability. The caudillo, like the African would-be life president, was the successor to the colonial state. However shrewdly conceived as apparatus of Iberian domination, the patrimonial bureaucracies of Latin America fared poorly as servants of the societies that shed Spanish rule.

CARIBBEAN SLAVE PLANTATIONS

The ultimate legacies of the slave-plantation colonies in the Caribbean were on the whole less negative than an eighteenth-century visitor might have imagined. The intensity of the exploitation of the slave population at the peak of the sugar system has few historical parallels; by the Curtin estimates, more than four million Africans reached the Antilles, ten times the number imported into the United States.[60] Yet today there are far fewer Afro-Caribbeans than people of African ancestry in America. The harshness of the slave era in North America requires no elaboration, and even postemancipation African Americans have not flourished in a favorable environment. The difference in numbers lies in the exceptionally high mortality rates in the British and French slave islands.

Yet postcolonial states in the Caribbean, particularly successor states to the British imperial regime, have fared markedly better than most African states, and indeed compare favorably, in political terms, with many Latin American polities, especially when their limited resource bases are considered. One may suggest that colonial state sequences may partly answer this riddle. During the slave period, the hierarchies of exploitation were mainly private, centered on the plantation unit. Hegemony was privatized; the colonial state was only an ultimate guarantor.

Emancipation transformed political as well as production relations. An immediate labor crisis ensued, anticipated by the under secretary of state for the colonies, Lord Howick, on the eve of emancipation:

> The great problem to be solved in drawing up any plan for the emancipation of the Slaves in our Colonies, is to devise some mode of inducing them when relieved from the fear of the Driver and his whip, to undergo the regular and continuous labour which is indispensable in carrying on the production of Sugar. . . . [Planter] inabil-

ity . . . to pay liberal wages seems beyond all question; but even if this were otherwise, the experience of other countries warrants the belief, that while land is so easily obtainable as it is at this moment, even liberal wages would fail to purchase the sort of labour which is required for the cultivation and manufacture of Sugar.[61]

Emancipation in 1834 (in British territories) and 1848 (in French) ended the sugar system as it had previously existed. White planters adapted with difficulty, although often—as in densely populated Barbados, with no available land—freed Africans had little option but to accept some form of disadvantageous labor on the plantations. In Jamaica, with a large mountainous interior, African peasant communities could take root in the areas outside plantation zones. But the colonial state was not heavily engaged in regulating the lives and allocating the labor of the emancipated; its modest revenue requirements could be met by customs imposts. Sugar boomed in Cuba, where slavery remained intact until 1880 and better production technologies were used. Beyond Cuba and Puerto Rico, sugar declined. It faced competition from beet sugar as well. It no longer played the role in imperial calculus it had a century earlier; the once-intense European rivalries for control of patches of the Caribbean evaporated, removing the security imperative from policy calculus.

The Caribbean colonies thus lost their allure. Planter aristocracies and an Afro-Caribbean elite of light color were socially dominant; colonial governors ran the islands, with a sometimes rancorous relationship with local assemblies that were a voice for privilege. These slowly became more representative; the first black member entered the Jamaican legislature in 1900. But until well into the twentieth century, power—limited in the scope of its exercise—remained in the hands of the colonial autocracy, still responding to a theory of governance expressed by a colonial official in Jamaica in 1839, warning that "black ascendancy" was the sole alternative to direct imperial rule. "A black oligarchy," minuted Henry Taylor, "will certainly oppress a white minority of the people, but it will not protect the population at large."[62] Thus, although there were assemblies, the essence of power remained firmly in the hands of the colonial governor and a small administration.

In the final colonial decades, models of representative and responsible government influenced imperial constitutional thought. Little beyond inertia slowed the gradually enlarging incorporation of the Afro-Caribbean majority into the structures of governance. The wave of rioting and disorder that swept the West Indies from 1935 to 1937 were a warning signal, sending shock waves as far as anglophone West Africa. The Moyne Commission appointed to investigate its causes, although it was unable to recommend universal suffrage, did call for an acceleration of political advance and public investment.

The colonial state succeeded in projecting a remarkably positive view of imperial society onto the Afro-Caribbean political elite that succeeded to power in the 1950s. In the words of a leading West Indian scholar, "Not the least ironic aspect of the Englishness of the West Indies was the fact that West Indians for so long preserved among themselves a Victorian Anglophilism, an almost imperialist chauvinism, and an uncritical loyalty to the Crown long after those attitudes had waned in Britain itself." This attachment to the imperial center was accompanied by an interpretation of its governance legacy that focused resolutely on the positive: "It was incorruptible, highly motivated, passionately conscious of duty and conduct . . . determinedly constitutionalist . . . [and] cared for civil liberties."[63]

One may discern several points of contrast with the African colonial state. Although the socioeconomic system, in its totality, perhaps exceeded in sheer brutality and harshness the exactions of Bula Matari during the eighteenth century, the process of extraction engaged the state itself less directly. A long time elapsed between the elimination of the most oppressive features of social relationships and production processes by abolition—though sharp inequalities of class and race remained—and the gaining of independence in the postwar period. Civil society deepened and extended; its racial compartmentalization blurred, and the state tradition as it was interpreted and absorbed more closely approximated the normative model of the liberal polity than did its African counterpart. Possibly the longer time period during which an associationally structured civil society could take form explains a part of the contrast. The much more compressed temporal frame of party, union, and other organizational life focused on the civic realm in Africa doubtless made easier the postcolonial projects of crushing autonomous associations, or forcing them to serve as simply ancillary instruments of political monopolies.[64] The unavoidable contrast with Haiti is instructive. A successful slave insurrection swept away the living inferno of the sugar-plantation society; building on the treacherous quicksand of this wholly negative societal and political tradition, a postliberation formula for governance remains as elusive as ever two centuries later.

The colonial state and its heritage in Asia varies far more widely than in the three categories considered so far, from the human tragedy of Cambodia or the self-encapsulated stagnation of Burma (Myanmar) to the developmental tigerhood of Taiwan, Singapore, Hong Kong, and

South Korea. There is no escaping separate consideration of the different colonial impacts.

THE JAPANESE AND RUSSIAN COLONIAL STATES

At first glance, the colonial impact in the former Japanese colonies seems to have been obliterated. In the Nanyo, where the weight of Japanese occupation was overpowering, its disappearance was most complete. Had World War II not intervened, the Pacific islands would almost certainly have been wholly absorbed, with the indigenous population overwhelmed by Japanese immigration. The ambiguously assimilative thrust of Japanese cultural policy could well have succeeded in "Japanizing" the Nanyo, remolding their population "into loyal, law-abiding subjects who could become almost, but not quite, Japanese."[65] But today in Micronesia few traces remain. As the masterful Peattie study concludes, "The islands contain no great imperial structures, no broad avenues of public parks to remind them, as the Taiwanese are reminded, of the order and efficiency brought by their former rulers; nor are they endowed as are the Koreans with a bitter energizing memory of the savage violation of their national soul . . . for most Micronesians the 'meaning' of the Japanese colonial presence has been written in foam: a dazzling incursion on their shores that has now all but evaporated."[66]

In Korea, the relentless interwar campaign to impose the Japanese language and efface symbols of historical self provoked a powerful assertion of Korean nationalism, even if divided at the 38th parallel by the cold war. The removal of the large Japanese implantation in industry, commerce, and even landholding opened economic space for (in the south) a rapidly developing Korean capitalism. The systematic land registration of the Japanese administration facilitated the postwar land reforms in both Korea and Taiwan that provided a solid agrarian base for a dynamic accumulation without the blockages of a landlord-dominated rural sector. Even though the superstructure of the Japanese colonial state was swept away by Japanese defeat in World War II, a state tradition reemerged that shares with Japan a capacity to manage a state-led capitalist development, which by the 1970s had formidable momentum.[67] Finally, one may note that, although there was an element of assimilationist thought in Japanese colonial doctrine, Japanese culture sprang from the same regional civilization as the cultures of Korea and Taiwan. The national soul of Korea was violated, but not the entirety of its cultural heritage.

Only the future will permit us to take the measure of the colonial impact of the Russian state in the central Asian lands, where the original nature of its domination most clearly resembled the imperial. Here intervened the seven decades of state socialism, which in ideological intent, or perhaps pretension, pointed toward the egalitarian utopia of communism. Turkestan, in the five republics into which it was culturally reconstructed, was conceived in state ideology as a partnership in a nation-state of socialist construction. Thus, three ideas of state intermingled; the old empire-state of the Russian historical polity; the socialist commonwealth; and the nation-state, creating a newly imagined community of a "Soviet people." The disintegration of this multinational state in 1991 came when its Marxist-Leninist legitimating myth utterly lost credibility, baring the illusions of the Soviet nation-state. All that was left was the older empire-state, now repudiated by its non-Russian subjects.

PLURAL COLONIAL SOCIETIES: MALAYSIA AND FIJI

Malaysia and Fiji carried into sovereignty the legacy of a very distinctive colonial strategy. In both cases incorporation into the imperial realm was largely negotiated rather than forcibly imposed. Particularly in the Fiji case considerations of security, internal and external, led not just the European missionaries and planters established in the island but also the chiefs and their subjects to request annexation. Britain agreed only after a commission in 1874 ascertained that virtually all articulate segments of the populace desired colonial status.[68] In Malaysia the impetus to expand came more clearly from the subimperial center of British India; nonetheless, the sultans of the Malay states were confirmed in their rule and accorded a deference and status that went well beyond the consideration given to African chiefs under indirect-rule doctrines.

In both territories the colonial state—which developed a comprehensive administrative framework separate from the sultans and chiefs—derived most of its sustenance from commercial plantations or mines developed by immigrant capital (European, Chinese in Malaya, in later years Indian in Fiji). The colonial state used its capacities for hegemonic persuasion to help capital secure land or mineral rights; however, it was not willing to compromise its security by forcing a self-sufficient indigenous peasantry into plantation or mine labor. Instead it chose to foster (and partly organize) the importation of Chinese and Indian labor. Also, a vibrant mercantile sector arose, almost wholly drawn from the immigrant communities.

Thus, a racially segmented colonial society took form, with the indigenous ruling class comfortable in a respectable subordinate partnership, and the peasantry undisturbed in its social organization, cultural practices, and economic livelihood. As a formula for low-cost colonial domination with minimal coercion, this structure of rule remained stable even late in the global processes of decolonization. By this time the immigrant communities outnumbered the indigenous population, which nonetheless held to a vision of society that perceived differential rights and entitlements for "sons of the soil" and the immigrants. The British had acquired an implicit obligation to the immigrants in negotiating the imperial retreat; the postcolonial state had to accept them as citizens. The complex political formulas to accommodate this special form of cultural pluralism, at once asserting the equality of all citizens and conceding superior rights to sons of the soil, produce recurring tensions, yet they have permitted tolerable governance and (in Malaysia) an economic performance that any African state would envy.

INDONESIA

Postcolonial Indonesian history divides into two distinct periods: first, two decades of instability, economic dislocation, regional uprisings, and intensifying conflict between nationalists, Communists, and Muslim-oriented movements, complicated by cold war intrusions; then, since 1965, a quarter-century of stable rule, authoritarian yet moderately consensual, and economically effective. Between these two periods was the bitter confrontation of 1965, in which the Communists as an organized force were decimated, with tens of thousands massacred.[69]

But for the circumstances of its dissolution, the colonial state would doubtless have left a much larger imprint. The Japanese occupation from 1942 to 1945, accompanied by the internment of most Dutch residents, was a decisive rupture. The war of reconquest from 1945 to 1949, although Dutch forces seemed to hold the upper hand militarily, swam against the currents of colonial liquidation of the postwar world. The friction-laden relationship with the former colonizer led to the departure of the Dutch residents—two hundred thousand on the eve of World War II—and by various mechanisms the termination of the large Dutch holdings, which had returned to Dutch capital some $100 million yearly in the 1930s. The circumstances of independence more thoroughly shattered the social foundations of the colonial order in Indonesia than in any other Asian state save Vietnam.[70]

The foundational idea that this vast archipelago—thirteen thousand islands stretching 3,600 miles from east to west—holds a vocation of unity is an inverted legacy of the colonial state. The historical depth and penetration of Dutch rule varied considerably; where it was most superficial—Irian Jaya (New Guinea)—the Indonesian state has encountered evident difficulty in winning local legitimacy for its rule. In the one minuscule zone that was not part of the Dutch East Indies—East Timor—the 1975 annexation in the wake of Portuguese abandonment of its colonial holdings triggered armed resistance that has yet to be extinguished.

The zones of most intense colonial impact were initially the Ambonese and Moluccas (the "spice islands"), then Java and later scattered zones of either Dutch plantation development, or focused Christian mission activity, or both (the east coast of Sumatra, the Batak areas of highland Sumatra, and Makassar in northern Sulawesi). Dutch administrative practices played a major part in the dynamic of identity construction, especially through the classification of *adat* (customary law) zones, which became a basis for ethnic taxonomies.[71] Perhaps paradoxically, the ethnic conglomeration collectively represented as Ambonese, the most heavily victimized, even decimated, group in the early spice-trade days of the seventeenth century, eventually became the most loyal to the colonial connection, forming the backbone of the postwar Dutch colonial army and emigrating in large numbers to the Netherlands following independence.

The period of most direct and interventionist state policy bearing upon the peasantry—the era of the "cultures policy" from 1830 to 1870—was limited to Java, and it was supplanted by the "liberal policy" (1870–1900) and the "ethical policy" (after 1900). "Never," wrote Furnivall, "has any Government set itself so wholeheartedly and with such zeal and comprehensive thoroughness to building up the welfare of its subjects ... zeal for the well-being of the people was a condition of promotion, as any who were reluctant to interfere with native life were regarded with disfavour as 'weak and recalcitrant administrators.'"[72] Even though it was composed in the discourse of another age, we may retain from this passage a recognition that the harshest years of the colonial state were well removed from the contemporary era. Although Indonesia stood out in Asia—at least in the zones of maximal penetration—for the relative density of the imperial presence, even here the actual relationship with peasant communities was buffered and mediated by an indigenous bureaucracy.

Yet the contrast I now perceive between colonial state impacts in Indonesia and Africa is indisputably influenced by the relative developmental success of the former. In 1976 I taught in collaboration with Donald

Emmerson, an Indonesian specialist, a pair of courses systematically juxtaposing Zaire and Indonesia; at that time there appeared to be fruitful parallels in the relatively intense colonial impact, the dislocations of decolonization, and the wave of uprisings in both countries in the mid-1960s that brought to power centralizing military regimes claiming to construct a new political order. But since then Zaire has experienced unending crisis, political decay, and economic disintegration, while Indonesia has prospered more than we could have imagined possible. Thus, in retrospect I am far more drawn by a search for contrasts than an intuition of commonalities.[73]

INDOCHINA

Vietnam is the other Asian colonial experience where similarities with Africa seem substantial; Cambodia and especially Laos were much more thinly ruled by the French. The colonial state in Vietnam was a thoroughly implanted system of domination, as I argued earlier in this chapter. The intensity was especially great in Cochinchina, where conquest began in 1860 and where rule was most direct; the mandarin bureaucracy, subsequently co-opted and used in Annam and Tonkin, fled in the southern districts and was supplanted by a plethora of French administrators.[74] A region that had paid only 4 million francs to the Vietnamese court just prior to French occupation, found itself paying 16 million in taxes by 1873, then 32 million by 1883.[75] Mission action, which well predated colonial conquest and was one of its precipitants, had created a larger foothold in this Buddhist society than anywhere else in south Asia, and is an unobtrusive but valid measure of cultural impact.

So also is the particular form assumed by nationalist revolt. The emergence of the Vietnamese Communist Party, by the time of the 1930 peasant uprising, partly borrowed the discourse of revolutionary opposition in France itself. But the barriers blocking all routes leading out of colonial subordination also contributed to the ideological expression chosen by nationalism; for many, only a revolutionary rupture with the colonial state could provide the remedy for impasse, and Marxism-Leninism then seemed the privileged text of revolution. After nearly thirty years of savage warfare, with only brief interludes, first against the French then the Americans, Vietnam was finally master of its destiny in 1975, only to discover that Marxism-Leninism was yet another road to oblivion—or, in Cambodia, an even more radical design for total war against civil society, whose killing fields efface the colonial state in the collective subconscious with an even more destructive and vivid memory.

THE BRITISH RAJ AND POSTCOLONIAL INDIA

India was the most gigantic colonial undertaking in history, in its human dimensions, broader impact on the imperial phenomenon, and pivotal role in framing the decolonization process. Its scale and complexity, and the span of historical time covered, make the Indian comparison especially important. The Indian Civil Service (ICS) and the Colonial Service, which supplied most British-ruled territories in Africa, were entirely separate, but there was an important flow of men and ideas from the Indian colonial state to Africa; Lord Lugard and Lord Hailey were but two of many individuals singularly important in fashioning colonial doctrine. Although indirect rule per se was not applied in India, the structure of thought that gave birth to it arose there. So also did the "martial race" theory in military recruitment and the fascination with cultural classification (castes and languages).

The long, slow process of political reform in India was of decisive import for colonial Africa; it supplied an authoritative model of institutional change and an emergent statement of end goals. Over time, what was conceded to India could not be withheld from other imperial dependencies when the subject society was "ready." But introducing the notion of "readiness" for political advance implied an obligation to assist in the creation of these conditions.

The contrast in time frame, however, was dramatic. The Indian National Congress was created in 1885, the symbolic birth of a nationalism that eventually became anticolonial. The 1909 Morley-Minto reforms introduced an electoral principle on a significant scale for the first time, responding to Congress calls for "a system of government similar to that enjoyed by the self-governing members of the British Empire and a participation by them in the rights and responsibilities of the Empire on equal terms with those members."[76] In 1917, under the pressure of World War I and the need to sustain the critical Indian contribution to the war effort, the promise of dominion status was first made, eventually—after years of tortuous negotiations—leading to the 1935 Government of India Act. By these steps, the precedent was slowly set that the way followed by the white dominions would also open not just to the old plantation colonies, composed entirely of a population planted under British auspices and culturally anglicized, but also to territories populated by a subjugated other.

The directness of the impact of the colonial state was significantly less in India than in Africa. Even though British colonial administrations in Africa were far less dense than the Belgian or French, their staff ratios were still much higher than in India. For example, in Nigeria, for fewer than thirty million people there were, in 1945, 1,300 senior staff, as compared to the 4,800 British personnel in the Indian service in late colonial times for 350 million people. The availability of land revenue in India as a basic source of state revenue meant that the colonial state was never faced with the imperative directly to organize and channel indigenous labor. Head taxes in much of Africa were a novelty, and their collection frequently provoked unrest, even revolts. In India the colonial state represented itself as a force for lowering tax rates; by the late nineteenth century, land revenue averaged only 5 percent of the crop, well below its level in precolonial times, and far less than the fiscal incidence in much of rural Africa, as I argued in chapters 4 and 5.[77] In contrast to most African railways, there was little difficulty in recruiting without resort to conscription the labor needed to construct the 31,500-mile Indian rail network. Market forces in other domains sufficed to meet labor needs; opening a mine did not compel the administration to become a man-catching machine. Only in a few plantation areas—those for indigo in particular—did the Indian labor policies resemble the African.

In the slowly evolving state tradition a curious hybridization occurred. The elite ranks of the Indian Civil Service cultivated a self-image of disinterested service as a platonic "guardian class," supplying governance to a society too riven by its communal divisions to rule itself. Although claiming not to create or aggravate these cleavages, in the apt phrase of one astute analyst, they "nevertheless accepted the fact of such divisions with the air of a man struggling joyfully in the grip of a benevolent fate."[78] But the "thin white line" admitted its first Indian in 1871, and by the interwar period Indians were a significant minority. The first commissioning of an Indian in the army was in 1763, although the number of Indian officers remained low until the interwar period, and their incorporation was constrained by the unstated principle that no British officer could serve under an Indian; there were 1,500 Indian officers on the eve of the Second World War.[79]

In the long period after India's metamorphosis into a colonial state, the administrative services—especially the elite Indian Civil Service—developed an indisputable professionalization, sophistication, and proficiency that have no real counterpart in colonial Africa. As the servant of alien domination, the ics was perhaps less disinterested than its guardian ethos might pretend. But the venality that earlier attended British East India Company rule was largely expunged by the time Victoria was proclaimed empress of India in 1858, and the self-image of the ics as an elite cadre entirely committed to the service of the state, fully assimilated by its growing number of Indian members, was transferred essentially intact to the postcolonial polity.[80]

Meanwhile, the civil society that the British Raj had long asserted was not possible took form, and acquired voice: India "discovered itself," in the words of its independence charter by Jawaharlal Nehru.[81] Nationalism arose, although bifurcated by the simultaneous politicization of the Hindu-Muslim divide and the Muslim League's insistence on a "two-nation" concept of civil society. The guardian class by degrees had to accommodate itself to the voice of the subject. Its capacity to insulate itself from civil society, at least in the twentieth century, was far less than in the African colonial state; habits of responsiveness and growing elements of accountability percolated into the official mind.

Another contrast I find critical lies in cultural politics. Although the British Raj was generally untroubled by doubts as to the superior qualities of Western culture, the notion that it could be systematically imposed on the Indian subject was swept away by the great sepoy mutiny in 1857, which shook the imperial edifice to its foundations. In the evangelical fervor that welled up in Britain in the early nineteenth century, the view took hold that imperial obligation included a mission of gradual displacement of a backward Indian culture, including its essential religious foundations. "If they went slowly," writes the former colonial officer who became a chronicler of British rule, "it was not because they had any doubt that their own learning and religion were infinitely superior to those of the Hindus. . . . Almost everyone, however, believed that as education spread the obvious superiority of Christianity would be recognized and there would be wholesale conversion."[82] Dispensing of Western education became acknowledged as a state responsibility; its initial philosophy was stated in the oft-cited passage from Whig historian Lord Macaulay that "a single shelf of a good European library was worth all the native literature of India and Arabia."[83]

Social practices deemed abhorrent were prohibited—the immolation of widows among higher castes was proscribed in Bengal in 1829, and subsequently elsewhere. Although few would care to defend suttee as an emblem of cultural integrity, this kind of intervention in the years leading up to the mutiny permeated the social environment with apprehensions that Islam and Hinduism were under threat. The specific trigger was information that a new kind of cartridge was packed in a pork-based lard, and that in biting off the casing to load their weapons troops would be compelled to violate a religious taboo. An anonymous letter of protest from a group of soldiers conveyed the mood:

We will not give up our religion. We serve for honour and religion. . . . You are the masters of the country. The Lord Sahib has given orders . . . to all commanding officers to destroy the religion. We know this. . . . The senior officers have ordered rajas, noblemen, landowners, money-lenders and peasants all to eat together and English bread has been sent to them; this is well known. . . . Throughout the country, the wives of respectable men, in fact all classes of Hindus, on becoming widows are to be married again; this is known. Therefore we consider ourselves as killed.[84]

The lessons of this experience were etched deeply on the official mind. Hinduism, Islam, and (in Burma and Sri Lanka) Buddhism were not to be confronted. Christian mission activity was mainly confined to "tribal" zones outside the reach of the great religious traditions of Asia (Nagaland, the Karen areas of Burma), and ceased to loom as a cultural threat. The Indian classes most closely associated with the colonial state mastered the cultural language of the Raj, but they were not expected to surrender their private essences of identity. The germination of nationalism drew on an assertion of the culturo-religious heritage of south Asia, synthesizing the discourse of liberalism and self-government through which the colonial state and its imperial overruler had to be addressed, a text richly grounded in history. The ransom was partition, but the legacy was less severed from a rooting in the past than was the case in the postcolonial polity in Africa.

THE AMERICAN COLONIAL STATE

The Philippines were a unique colonial hybrid. Were one to search the colonial legacy through the prism of the Marcos martial-law years of 1972 to 1986, when a patrimonial autocracy closely resembling a number of contemporaneous African states imposed its rule, the temptation to discover common historical roots might arise. An unrewarding impulse: there seems little common ground between either the Spanish or the American colonial states and their African counterparts.

In the three centuries of Spanish rule (1565–1898), a colonial society startlingly different from that in Latin America took form in the Philippines. There was no real conquistador class, nor did there subsequently emerge a dominant creole group of Spanish descent. Highly decentralized and localized sociopolitical structures dominated, whose leading families became incorporated in a loose-knit Spanish system of rule.

Conquest was most thorough in the religious field; aside from the south-western areas, where petty states linked to a maritime Islamic world had emerged not long before colonial subjugation, evangelization proceeded quickly, and the friars were an important part of the Spanish presence. In 1850 the Spanish population was only five thousand, of whom nearly half were friars. The dominant social class were not creoles, as in Latin America, but *illustrados,* Filipino landholders whose ancestry often included some Spanish and Chinese genetic traces.[85]

The American colonial state, as I noted above, lacked a colonial doctrine applicable to territories as large and populous as the Philippines, a colonial official class, and—in less than two decades—any real desire to perpetuate its domination. The class structure created in the Spanish era remained intact and quickly found opportunities for political ascendancy within the loosely articulated hegemony of the American colonial state. A highly clientelistic pattern of political competition swiftly developed, assimilating the liberal discourse of the colonizer. The fluid, patronage-driven, and often venal structure of politics became well rooted in the colonial era, and it has remained the defining feature of the Filipino polity to this day.

OCEANIA

The extension of imperial rule to the scattered islands of Oceania occurred, as in Africa, during the final stages of global European expansion. In most cases the colonial presence was small, and the most important impact came through Christian mission activity. In some instances—Tahiti, Hawaii—the territories were totally incorporated into the metropolitan domain. New Caledonia, seized by France in 1853, became, like early Australia, a dumping ground for the state disciplinary machinery; from 1863 to 1897 some forty thousand prisoners were transported to the island, many of whom then settled and acquired land. Within three years of annexation the indigenous Kanacks had lost control of 90 percent of the land.[86] The discovery of huge nickel deposits in the 1870s transformed New Caledonia into a mining enterprise as well. The legacy was a society that had a numerical French majority but an indigenous nationalism that rejected the model of assimilation into the French Republic as an overseas department, which was the ultimate destiny of the smaller fragments of empire scattered around the globe (Martinique, Guadaloupe, Mayotte, Reunion, Tahiti).

Neither the logic nor the legacy of the African colonial state seems replicated in Oceania. In a handful of instances local societies were overwhelmed and incorporated, impossible in Africa. In the larger Melanesian islands—New Guinea most notably—nothing drove the colonial state into the systematic pattern of domination characterizing the African colonial state. Australia assumed control of British New Guinea in 1901 and added Papua as a League of Nations mandate after World War I. For a time there was an illusion that a plantation economy could be built from the coast inland, with ultimate absorption into Australia. Although no requirement of fiscal self-sufficiency was imposed, the Australian commitment was tiny before World War II (50,000 pounds yearly in the interwar period and a total revenue in 1939 of only 660,000 pounds to administer Papua New Guinea.) Administration of much of the hinterland was rudimentary until 1945. Thereafter significant development investment and social expenditure became available, but the colonial state impact on Papua New Guinea was far less dense than in Africa.[87] The postcolonial successor, in a case like Papua New Guinea, has sustained the constitutional framework of terminal colonial rule, but rests lightly on its complex and highly fragmented civil society.

THE COLONIAL INTERLUDE IN THE MIDDLE EAST

The final extension of the colonial system on the heels of World War I was into Arab lands stripped from the Ottoman state, a costly revival of imperial habits of yesteryear. As I noted earlier, suppression of the Iraqi uprisings of 1920 occasioned huge outlays and a large deployment of the Indian Army. By 1920 the French effort to impose its rule on Syria had already cost 1.2 billion francs, enough to provoke serious parliamentary resistance to pursuing Middle Eastern expansion.[88] To add insult to injury, the altered international normative order permitted only contingent occupation, in the form of the mandate system, rather than the customary annexation.

The British interest was largely strategic. Transjordan, separated from the Palestine mandate in 1922, was a Bedouin polity placed by the British under the Hashemite prince Abdullah, whose main instrument of rule was a British-officered gendarme force of 1,300 provided with an annual subsidy of 150,000 pounds.[89] The Palestine mandate was tormented from the outset by the contradictory objectives and expectations of the Arab population and promoters of a Jewish homeland. A more extensive establishment was required, but the utter inability of the British to broker or manage this deepening conflict made the mandate a morass: never fully dominated, it was finally just abandoned.

The French mandates were more seriously pursued, in part because once under even the mitigated sovereignty of the mandate, an obsessive preoccupation with precedents of political evolution that might extend to the Maghreb permeated the official mind. But by 1920, when the mandates were occupied, the French encountered in both Lebanon and Syria solidly established landowning and mercantile classes, as well as a swiftly congealing political consciousness embracing nationalism. Further, in contrast to the former Ottoman state, the French colonial administration was never acknowledged as legitimate. Nor were French economic interests capable of achieving dominant positions in the productive infrastructure. Despite the assiduous efforts to play sectarian politics (as with the Maronite alliance in Lebanon, and the Druze and Alawi against the Sunni majority in Syria), France was never able to construct a self-standing colonial state in the mandates, and it was driven out in World War II.[90]

DISTINCTIVE CHARACTERISTICS OF THE AFRICAN COLONIAL STATE

The modern colonial state wore many masks during its half-millennium of existence. Some had scowling features as intimidating to the subject as Bula Matari (like early Peru, Mexico, and Vietnam). Some were stern and distant in demeanor (like British India). Still others were almost featureless, so concealed behind the throne of the ostensible suzerain as to be unfathomable to the subject (as in the Persian Gulf sheikdoms). Let me suggest by way of conclusion seven salient characteristics of the African colonial state that I believe mark it as a distinctive species.

First, the impact of the dynamic of partition was singularly important. The imperial irruption into the African interior came suddenly, after 1875, and acquired formidable interactive momentum. The sheer number of colonial claimants redoubled the intensity of this dialectic: in most areas only two or three competitors were active in any one time or place, whereas in Africa there were six (Britain, France, Germany, Italy, the Belgian monarchy, and Portugal). The forces of conquest were under a pressure unusual in imperial annals to give muscular effect to the doctrine of effective occupation, exhumed and sanctified at the Berlin Congress. In the longer history of European subjugation of Asia and the Americas, imperial atavism was the twin brother of international anarchy. But the drama played itself out over much longer time frames; only in Africa were the occupying powers under the compelling, immediate

$\triangle$

requirement of confirming proprietary title by forcible demonstration of dominance.

Second, driven by this compelling necessity for rapid conquest, the interactive dilemmas of the hegemony and revenue imperatives made survival of the fledgling colonial states contingent on ruthless extractive action. The promoters of imperial expansion enjoyed only tenuous support from the parent states; for the most part, the future gains were speculative, and the immediate costs and risks real. Thus, the managers of the colonial states were required to find the resources to finance the consolidation of conquest within the subjugated societies. In the core areas of colonial expansion in Asia, peasant societies were long subordinated to social hierarchies and state systems with established, if perhaps extortionate, revenue systems; the British claim to have actually lowered taxation in India is doubtless well-founded in many areas (though probably not Bengal). In Africa, newly created colonial institutions required for survival the simultaneous imposition of authority, extraction of resources to pay for it, and invention of intermediary mechanisms to organize the collection of tribute. The combined logic of these imperatives produced the ruthless brutalities so widespread in the construction phase.

Third, both revenue and accumulation imperatives propelled the colonial state into an active role in forcing rural Africans into labor service. The imposition of head taxes had this objective as well as revenue generation. The basic necessities of the colonial state, and the initial public infrastructure, were often met by conscription: porters, road workers, construction teams for administrative stations. European mines and plantations, whose development was presumed to benefit colonial treasuries through customs on their exports, demanded an assured labor supply at wages few would accept voluntarily; this drew the colonial state into labor conscription. In this respect the African colonial state has companions, such as early Latin America and Vietnam. But in comparative terms the degree to which the logic of colonial state construction was rooted in the control, conscription, regulation, and use of African labor stands out.

Fourth, the sequencing of decolonization, the assimilation by the late colonial state of a welfare ideology as doctrine of legitimation, and the nature of its developmentalism produced a curious syndrome of citizen attitudes and expectations. Welfare, in the terminal colonial era, was bestowed from above in the characteristically paternalist mode: borrowing a John Ayoade expression, and mixing gender metaphors, the colonial polity became a "Mother Theresa" state. But at the same time the state remained external to the citizen, an alien and predatory other. Ayoade writes: "The inheritors of the postcolonial state [tried] to out-bid their colonial predecessors by exaggerating the benevolence of the state . . . encouraged the growth of public spending by emphasizing the benefits, rather than the costs, of the welfare state as if benefits are costless."[91] In the Nigerian case, the flow of oil revenues after independence permitted abolition of most forms of local taxation, a pattern not matched in most other African states. Oil was viewed as a "national cake," for whose slices contending private actors and groups engaged in relentless struggle.[92] Nearly everywhere the curious terminal colonial state blend of long-standing autocratic paternalism and a newfound social beneficence engendered a *mentalité des assistés* among the subjects.

Fifth, the technologies of dominance in the terminal period were far more advanced than earlier. The degree of sheer military supremacy from advances in weaponry affected the texture of domination. The ready availability of the punitive expedition as an auxiliary medium of administration and its frequent use—especially in the early period—reflected the magnitude of the military imbalance. Particularly after World War I, colonial states were somewhat constrained by the risk of provoking a rebellion on a scale they could not master on their own. But the everyday supremacy of colonial power was of exceptional weight. Its capacity for mobility and communication rapidly expanded; motor vehicles became available early in the colonial era, replacing the hammock, and the telegraph and radio tied the superstructure together into a grid of domination not available in earlier centuries.

Sixth, the creation of the African colonial state coincided with the historical zenith of virulent racism. The colonial construction of the African as savage other permeated all spheres of policy thought. Racism was always present in colonial encounters, to be sure; imperialism is the parent of race as an ideology of human difference. But the arrogance of race was never stronger than at the moment of colonial onslaught on Africa. African culture had no redeeming value; only a wholly new African might be worthy of the colonial order, tailored from imported cloth.

Seventh, the cultural project of the colonial state confronted societies not only subjected to a pervasive domination but—outside the Islamic zones—also lacking the insulation provided in Asia by the major religious systems. The remarkable expansion of Islam in sub-Saharan Africa during the colonial period partly reflects a search for a cultural shield that indigenous religions alone could not easily provide. In its initial colonial version, Christianity, writes Mbembe, in claiming a "civilizing mission," sought to "impose recognition of the west as the sole center of meaning, the unique location competent to engender a discourse on the human and the divine."[93] The struggle for hegemony is carried out as a contest for meanings, as well as through material forces. The colonial state was unsparing in its efforts—through the Christian missions, the educational systems, and language policies—to monopolize the production of meaning and thus the construction of culture. Christianity became contested terrain, a vehicle for reassertion of the indigenous through syncretization. When the battle was first joined, however, Bula Matari demanded unconditional-surrender terms of settlement, which went well beyond the imperial norm. △

No claim is made that the African colonial state is in all respects unique. In one or another of its aspects, similarities can be found elsewhere. But when we assemble its traits, examine its trajectory, and weave together the determinants of its structure and behavior, a singular historical personality looms before us.

—— *Chapter Nine* ——

THE AFTERLIFE OF THE AFRICAN COLONIAL STATE: CONCLUDING REFLECTIONS

The balance sheet of . . . the last quarter-century is globally negative.

—Zairian Prime Minister Mulumba Lukoji, 1991

No condition is permanent.

—African proverb

Nganyi wanyi wasungila? (Who will save me from this situation?)

—Zairian popular painting

I thank God through Jesus Christ our Lord. So then with the mind I myself serve the law of God; but with the flesh of the law of sin.

—Romans 7:25

IMAGES OF CRISIS

In about 1980 a new genre of popular painting emerged in Zaire, especially in Kisangani and Kananga. The tableaux, painted with small variations by a number of street artists, depicted a man facing an open-jawed crocodile on a river bank, a snarling lion advancing from the forest, and a venomous serpent descending on him from a tree overhead. In a number of versions the canvas is accompanied by a reference to Romans 7:25. In the interpretation of a Zairian sociologist, this suggests that the Zairian crisis is so savage and cruel for the poor that only by entrusting themselves to Jesus Christ can deliverance be found.[1] The serpent might be read as the harsh austerity measures imposed by the Western phalanx of international financial institutions, the crocodile as the oppressive and predatory state, and the lion as the forces of impoverishment unleashed by a shrinking economy.

Yet ambiguous hopes suggested by the proverbial promise that "no condition is permanent" stirred at the beginning of the 1990s. Could democratization bring deliverance? Tremors of a reawakened expectation of resurrection swept the continent. Another mirage? Or a new beginning, a second independence? Could purifying forces arising within civil society remake the state, purge it of its negative legacies?

Looking backward, we can see more clearly than in 1980 how large is the challenge. Displacement of incumbents too long in office and obsessed with a statecraft deploying dwindling resources to sustain their grip on a weakening center, however indispensable, is far from sufficient. Nothing less than a reinvention of the state is the task at hand.

State traditions do not yield easily, even to moments of enthusiasm as far-reaching as those firing the popular imagination since 1989. The past is all too prone to impose itself on the future. A genetic code for the new states of Africa was already imprinted on its embryo within the womb of the African colonial state. By way of conclusion, I wish to suggest some of physical attributes of the postcolonial state that reflect its ancestry.

BULA MATARI EMBEDDED

The metaphor of the embryo did not suggest itself at the moment of independence. Rather, the common imagery perceived a triumphant nationalism storming the citadels of colonialism, erecting from its rubble an entirely new political order. The nationalist antithesis to the colonial state, in driving the historical dialectic to a new and immensely promising stage, perhaps absorbed in the synthesis some of the building material from a delegitimated, defeated, and repudiated ancien régime. But the architecture of tomorrow was to give form and structure to the dreams of nationalist protest, not to manage an old order. After all, had not Bula Matari destroyed and swept away the precolonial state tradition?

But Bula Matari was a crusher of rocks. In ways that earlier chapters have examined, the colonial state during its phase of construction in most cases created entirely novel institutions of domination and rule. Although we commonly described the independent polities as "new states," in reality they were successors to the colonial regime, inheriting its structures, its quotidian routines and practices, and its more hidden normative theories of governance. Thus, everyday reason of state, as it imposed its logic on the new rulers, incorporated subliminal codes of operation bearing the imprint of their colonial predecessors.

The legacy of the colonial state, however, is far from the sole determinant of political system and process in the era of independence. New dimensions appeared in the physiognomy of power; novel strategies soon proved necessary to assure its reproduction and the survival of those that ruled it. To weigh the impact of the colonial state in the pervasive crisis of the postcolonial order that became evident in the 1980s, we need to consider as well the new logics that became interwoven with those embedded within state behavior as colonial legacy.

In a perhaps superficial sense, similarities in the signature of power were visible to the visitor to any government outpost. The state undertook relatively little new building construction in district capitals; the administrative cadres occupied the rambling beige blocks of the colonial state: unpretentious, but exuding authority. The chief executive officers, in most countries, appeared in public in uniform, redolent of the military origins of regional administration in colonial times. In sartorial language, the norm of anonymity of agency found expression; the interchangeable human instruments of a distant state, clothed in a mode exclusive to government agents, silently asserted an entitlement to command. The coinage might change (President Mobutu replacing the colonial territorial officer's uniform with the collarless suit of faintly Maoist derivation), but the currency was the same.

National capitals went upscale; the residences of the colonial governors were supplanted by more lavish presidential palaces, better communicating the dignity of full sovereignty. In the good years before the winds of change became a hurricane of economic disaster, the panoply of new ministries reflecting the substantial expansion in scale of the summit institutions often acquired large new blocks of administrative architecture, perhaps of functional rather than sumptuous design, but still in a self-consciously modern motif stating the ambition of progress.[2] Limousines in the land of the mammy-wagon; exotic uniforms for presidential guards; ceremonial celebration of authority: these were the symbolic representations of state as fount of power whose lineage in the colonial state was apparent.

The unconscious assumptions of the new governing elite were permeated with a sense of the natural rightness of their rule. Certainly the racial arrogance that characterized colonial attitudes toward the subject was gone; but "they staked their claims to leadership," writes Ajayi, "on their superior knowledge" of external models of rule and development, and "took for granted the masses' and the traditional elite's willingness to accept their leadership."[3] Confrontation of the colonial state with a catalogue of its iniquities had earned the right to succession; the elite's rule was justified by a schooled vision denied to the unlettered masses. The schoolroom, however, was the colonial state.

Important consequences flowed from these axioms. The vocation of domination, so central to the colonial state but often shaken by the nationalist challenge, had to be restored, even reinforced. The path was often ill-defined at the moment of independence; ideologies of development really took shape only after transfer of power.[4] But promises of a life more abundant had been made; their fulfillment clearly demanded a strong state, an uninhibited hegemony.

Further, the very success of nationalist struggle exposed possible fragilities of the state. Did its authority perhaps rest on a mystique of power associated with its alien character and the doctrines of racial superiority so long lodged in the official mind, even if no longer openly asserted: the terror of Bula Matari? Did the fierce electoral contests of the 1950s threaten to so weaken the winners that they could not exercise the power they had won? Did the newly politicized ethnic cleavages subvert the necessity unity of authority? There were many questions, whose answers inevitably called for strengthened and reasserted state authority.

Security preoccupations pointed in the same direction. The cage of colonial subjugation had since World War I isolated African territories from predators in the international arena. Newly won independence faced a sensed threat of subversion by the former colonial powers and the broader forces of imperialism. The competitive quest for clienteles by the cold war superpowers introduced other menaces. The rapid emergence of ideological divisions within the African community of states over conceptions of pan-Africanism, philosophies of development, and global alignments raised the specter, and sometimes reality, of internal opposition finding sanctuary and support in neighboring states. The slowly shrinking bastions of colonial resistance and racial supremacy resorted to strategies of destabilizing their African neighbors. Thus, security imperatives fused with the hegemonical instincts of the new ruling elite.

The fragile institutions of a constitutional democratic order hastily erected in the final days of the colonial era soon seemed an unaffordable luxury. Indeed, the very notion of constitutionalism was soon denatured. Mamadou Diouf provides a suggestive explanation:

The African constitutions imported from London, Paris or Washington became inverted versions of those after which they were modelled. The historical logic which led to the appearance of constitutionalism in Europe is a logic of resistance by civil society, the dominated vis-à-vis the dominators. The constitution serves to limit the power of the state and to guarantee the liberty of the citizen. In Africa it served to guarantee the authority of the state and the uncontrollable and uncontrolled exercise of power by the occupants of the state apparatus. And for this reason the constitution undergoes constant modifications. The legislative armature, the structures which are supposed to be the expression of civil society, is constantly subjected to the assaults of networks of kinship and clientele, accentuating the tradition of the subordination to the state which the colonial system inaugurated.[5]

The more enduring traditions of governance that characterized the colonial state reemerged, their relative eclipse at the moment of transition only temporary. The robust bureaucratic autocracy that was the true bequest of Bula Matari regained its ascendancy, under differing guises. The theory of the single-party regime as the authentic embodiment of the aspirations of nationalism achieved wide currency. Competitive parties were perhaps legitimate in class-ridden Western industrial societies, but Africa—ran the argument—did not have such social divisions. The only classlike cleavage was that separating the European superstructure of the colonial order from all sectors of African society. Thus, lacking any sociologically valid reason for existence, opposing parties inevitably fostered and exacerbated illegitimate lines of division: those rooted in religion or ethnicity. Further, political society had a finite store of policy energy; whatever was committed to competitive politics was necessarily subtracted from developmental action. The scarce and precious resources available to advance the project of national well-being required husbanding by the developmental state. Only a vigorous, forceful, authoritative state could fulfill the promises of independence. Where the single-party ruler faltered in his task, military intervention reproduced the colonial state legacy of autocracy in a different form.

The discourse of development that had been employed so freely by the colonial state in its terminal phases found new expression. Novel terminology was frequently added: various forms of socialism, for example. A much greater sense of urgency was certainly in the air. The colonial development plans widely adopted in the decolonization phase were replaced by five-year plans embracing ambitious goals and tracing captivating pathways to prosperity. The pace of expanding the most eagerly desired elements of the social infrastructure—schools and medical facilities—was redoubled.

The state, as theologian of development, appeared to speak a new language. But more closely examined, if not deconstructed, one might detect a subtext of continuity. "The colonial administration was a command administration; we now practice development administration," Senegalese Minister of the Interior Jean Colin told a colloquium of senior bureaucrats in 1987.[6] But "development" was a managerial art; the role of the administrator was "encadrement" of the populace, to secure compliance with the edicts through which development policy was transformed into administrative law.

Revenue requirements of the postcolonial state were sharply higher. The size of state bureaucracies rose rapidly. An expanded social infrastructure implied substantial operating outlays to staff and equip the many additional schools and clinics. Major public investment projects required heavy borrowing, with repayment obligations soon weighing heavily on the state budget.

Independence opened some new revenue sources, especially grants and loans from abroad. Most former colonizers provided reasonably generous aid. But extractive efforts could not be relaxed on the domestic front, and the tax impact in the first postcolonial decades replicated earlier patterns. The most vulnerable target for state fiscal action was the peasantry. The form of taxation might alter; the head tax had become much less important in the postwar years, although in most colonial states and their initial successors it was preserved. But the easiest target was the export crop, taxable in several ways: through an export tax; through a pricing policy exercised by means of a state marketing monopoly; through various deductions made in the payment to the farmer.[7] The postcolonial state followed in the footsteps of its predecessors by collecting relatively little revenue from the state-based dominant class and the mercantile sector, and half or more of peasant income.

In short, what Mbembe terms a *principe autoritaire* informed the inner ethos of the postcolonial state. In its pretension to serve as theologian of power for civil society, "the independent African state aspires to the exercise of a symbolic hegemony over indigenous societies signified by its claim to a monopoly of legitimate vision" of politics. With a disposition to violence and a propensity to arbitrary discipline of the subject reminiscent of the *indigénat*, the state, committed to a vocation of "modernizing the nation and civilizing the society," inflated notions of subversion and "threats to state security" to facilitate punishment of the dissident "with the judicial formalism characteristic of authoritarian regimes."[8]

THE INTEGRAL STATE

Soon after independence, reaching its zenith in the 1970s, a new vision of state began to emerge, even more far-reaching than Bula Matari: what we might term, borrowing from Coulon and Copans, the "integral state." The state, with enlarged ambitions of transforming society according to its blueprint, sought an enhanced hegemony, to render it more capable of acting directly on civil society. Copans interprets the developing ambitions of the Senegalese state in the 1970s in these terms:

> The objective of the dominant groups in the state apparatus is the control, the maintenance, the augmentation of surplus extraction. . . . The lesson of recent years is the following: the interests of the Senegalese state have won over our local private interests . . . this growing role of the state, rendered concrete through the remodelling and multiplication of institutions for control of the peasantry, leads to a new policy. The Senegalese state aims more and more at a direct administrative, ideological and political control over the dominated masses, be they urban or rural.[9]

By "integral state" I have in mind a design of perfected hegemony, whereby the state seeks to achieve unrestricted domination over civil society. Thus unfettered, the state is free to engage in rational pursuit of its design for the future and to reward the ruling class amply for its governance. The integral state requires not only the autonomy from civil society achieved through comprehensive instruments of political control but also a suzereignty, if not monopoly, extending over social and economic vectors of accumulation. As, in Weberian terms, a "compulsory association which organizes domination,"[10] the integral state, guided by an infallible rationality, supplies purposive rule driven by an inspirational charter for the future.

The integral state is of course a mere incubus, an image of absolute power etched in the minds of its promoters, managers, and beneficiaries. Even at its zenith the empirical state fell far short of its extravagant designs, a point to which I shall return. Yet the normative model had important consequences in the political formulas that were adopted; the ironies of history prescribe that their failure was of a scale commensurate with the exorbitant pretensions of the design.

Building on the exclusionary principle of the colonial state, the integral state sharpens the line between state and society by proposing a comprehensive apparatus of domination. The subject is a passive citizen, whose civic obligations are enacted through public rituals of allegiance: support marches, applause for leaders, unanimous plebiscite votes for the ruler. Civil society is organized into party-structured ancillary organizations, which are mechanisms of surveillance and control rather than participation and voice.

The idea of the integral state emerges clearly in Tanzania's failed venture in populist socialism. After the new vision of the polity found textual expression in the 1967 Arusha Declaration, a cascade of measures ensued to implement the imagined polity. Through nationalization and the creation of public enterprises, a state-run economy was constructed; Reginald Green, an expatriate adviser to the Tanzanian treasury, noted with satisfaction that by the mid-1970s 80 percent of the medium- and large-scale economic activity lay in the public sector, and that a comparable fraction of total investment occurred through this sector or its contractors—figures that exceeded those of Eastern Europe at a comparable period after the imposition of Stalinist socialism.[11] There followed the sweeping relocation of the rural population under the aegis of a "villagization" program, and the displacement of cooperatives by state marketing monopolies for all major agricultural crops. The discourse of President Julius Nyerere was socialism; the submerged script was the integral state.

Similar projects are encountered in various rhetorical guises across the continent during the 1960s and 1970s. "Agrarian revolution" and allied projects in Algeria in 1971; the delirious schemes of "cultural revolution" in Chad during the final stages of the Tombalbaye regime; the "hegemonical project" of Ahmadu Ahidjo in Cameroun, captured so well by Bayart;[12] the claims to miraculous powers of the Eyadema regime, eloquently portrayed by Toulabor.[13]

Zaire at the zenith of the Mobutu era, in the mid-1970s, serves as a paradigmatic example. The ruling party, created as a political monopoly, the Mouvement Populaire de la Révolution (MPR), was declared to be "the nation politically organized," which incorporated all Zairians at birth. All organs of the state were subordinated to the presidential will; by the 1974 constitution Mobutu in effect named all members of the party's political bureau, the ministers, the legislators, and the judges. "Unity of command" was resurrected as the core state principle, with a comprehensive centralization of all institutions. Customary chiefs were declared to be mere "politico-administrative" cadres, subject to bureaucratic transfer, simple central agents at the bottom of an integrated hierarchical ladder. The 30 November 1973 "Zairianization" measures transferred a vast swath of the economy to Zairian *acquéreurs* as presidential patrimony, followed by a 1974 "radicalization of the revolution" that for a brief period completed seizure of colonial enterprises. The entire agricultural sector was covered by a network of state marketing monopolies. Emblematic of the extravagant pretensions of the state in its "integral" moment was a brief period in 1974 when the press was forbidden to mention the name of any state official other than the president; they were identified only by their functions. The integral state, in this compelling imagery, was served by depersonalized, nameless human agents who were anonymous instruments of its hegemonical will.[14]

PATRIMONIAL AUTOCRACY

The logics of the colonial and integral states were crosscut by a third form of reason, which attached to the ruler rather than the state. The presidential forms that autocracy invariably assumed produced an inevitable disposition to lifetime incumbency. Until the era of democratization in the late 1980s rulers only rarely surrendered power voluntarily. But the normative codes of the colonial-integral state did not suffice to assure the security of the incumbent. Suppression of opposition parties and elimination of competitive elections could avert political succession by constitutional means, but coups and conspiracies remained ever-present possibilities. Nor did tables of administrative organization assure flows of empirical control congruent with the pictorial hierarchy of the graph. The perennity of personal rule required intermediaries: reliable clients through whom the levers of power could be operated. Abstract principles of administrative deontology were far from sufficient to assure the control and motivation of key state operatives; a much more personal system of rewards and punishments was indispensable. The formal Weberian traits evoked by the image of the integral state—impersonality of office, uniform application of rules, predictability of behavior, rationality of organizational structure—were interpenetrated by a radically different set of patrimonial practices.

In this prebendal dimension of state behavior, office is a personal favor of the ruler; the holder of a tributary prebend was expected to derive a "living" from the post, while faithfully executing the will of the ruler.[15] The control functions inhering in the allotted post come first; the officeholder must ensure that the writ of the ruler runs (or at least encounters no overt challenge) in his sphere of responsibility. Ideally, the client also accomplishes some of the formal goals of the office. In the process, public authority may be converted to private return. The office is always insecure; the struggle for place and preference is intense, and loyalty must be regularly reconfirmed. The officeholder manages the allotted domain through a subsidiary clientelistic network, permitted so long as it does not coalesce into a force challenging the ruler.

The personalization of the actual operation of the state operates in both directions. Civil society, confronting the seemingly hard outer shell of the state in its integral illusions, cannot easily approach it through collective action or by challenging its regulations. Only by dissolving into the myriad kinship and other clientelistic networks can the will of the state be deflected, can passageways through its arbitrary and inflexible regulatory maze be discovered. Changing a rule through voice is all but impossible; securing an exemption through favor or payment is daily bread.

Patrimonial management of power played relatively little part in the colonial state, particularly in its upper echelons.[16] The hierarchy and the discipline of the state apparatus were ultimately subject to the surveillance of the metropolitan overruler, and they generally sufficed to shape the behavior of state agents. At first, patrimonial practices in the postcolonial state were of modest scale. But a steady inflation of prebendal costs set in, and by the 1970s the amounts diverted from public treasuries to lubricate patrimonial machinery were very large—colossal in such cases as Nigeria and Zaire. Further, "rent-seeking" by state elites corroded policy calculus. "Public choice" theory was privatized.

The interlocking impasse in the political economy, once the magnitude of the developmental crisis was recognized in the 1980s, was profound. The colonial state had blocked the emergence of an autonomous African capitalist class, particularly in the countryside. The transmission of its institutional legacy to the postcolonial successor was amplified by the ideology of the integral state. In turn, rent-seeking and effective use of patrimonial management of power tied the ruling elite to a state sector that was paralyzing in its resource demands. The reform packages, heavily marked by the external design of the international financial institutions, have thus far made only limited headway in the project of supplanting this heritage with a liberal political economy.[17]

By the 1980s the contradictory logics of the integral state and patrimonial ruler, superposed on the base of the autocratic heritage of the colonial state, had all but totally subverted the African polity. For civil society a deepening cynicism set in; the new state was but a derelict reproduction of the old one, unable to perform its functions with the same competence. The permeability of the state—through personal affinity or impersonal purchase of favor—in some ways softened its harshness but also rendered its behavior odious. Just as the colonial subject was a stigmatized other for the colonial state, so the independent state became a predatory other for the citizen.

Large fractions of civil society responded by diverting their energies to economic and social activity in spheres beyond the reach of the state: the parallel economy.[18] In cases like Sierra Leone or Zaire, the burgeoning second economy all but swallowed up the official sphere. The relative profitability of the second economy reflected both the dereliction of the state—its declining ability to enforce its regulatory will—and the exorbitant costs of transactions operated through official channels, a reflection of the interactive effect of integral state and patrimonial ruler.

Pursuing the dream of the integral state burdened the polity, whatever its ideological orientation, with a vast panoply of state enterprises, most in deficit. The giant development projects that littered the landscape saddled the state with unpayable foreign debts; the impossibility of collection did not stop the creditors from baying mercilessly at the heels of the impoverished African polity. And state resources were fatally compromised by the spiraling costs of the patrimonial mode of the ruler reproducing his hold on office.

Stripped to its essentials, the heart of the African state crisis of the 1980s lies in this lethal combination of the colonial state heritage, the failed vision of the integral state, and the prebendal realities of political management. The remarkable surge of self-assertion by civil society up and down the continent in the swelling demand for democratization in the early 1990s can be best understood not as a mimetic response to global trends or melodramatic developments in Eastern Europe—although these had their impact—but rather as a cathartic reaction to an alienating state. It is immensely promising and deeply problematic. Can a new state be invented that sheds the debilitating traditions of the past?

The question is open, and will perhaps be answered in the final years of the century. History tells us that the patterns of the past remain embedded in the present. Can they be rewoven to permit the emergence of a new kind of polity, one that employs the discourse of democracy but connects itself to the deeper African cultural heritage? Perhaps not all at once; certainly not all the contemporary transitions to democracy will take root. But in the longer run an affirmative response to this momentous historical question is indispensable to designing, to claiming, to seizing a future beyond crisis and decline.

NOTES

Chapter 1: Bula Matari and the Contemporary African Crisis

1. See Daniel R. Headrick, *The Tools of Empire: Technology and Euro-pean Imperialism in the Nineteenth Century* (New York: Oxford Univer-sity Press, 1981), for a seminal study on the impact of the steamboat and arms technology in assuring military superiority for the European powers.

2. Lusibu Zala N'kanza, "The Social Origins of Political Underdevelopment in the ex-Belgian Congo (Zaire)," Ph.D. diss., Harvard University, 1976, 232–34, 390. Sigbert Axelson indicates that the term, with a somewhat different meaning, is in fact traceable to the sixteenth century; *Culture Confrontation in the Lower Congo* (Falkoping, Sweden: Gummessons, 1970), 203. For another history of the term, see F. F. Boutinck, "Les deux Boula Matari," *Etudes Congolaises* 13 (July 1969): 83–97.

3. Gabriel A. Almond, Marvin Chodorow, and Roy Harvey Pearce, eds., *Progress and Its Discontents* (Berkeley: University of California Press, 1982).

4. J. F. Ade Ajayi, "Expectations of Independence," *Daedalus* 111 (Spring 1982): 2–3.

5. Frantz Fanon, *Les damnés de la terre* (Paris: Maspero, 1963).

6. René Dumont, *L'Afrique Noire est mal partie* (Paris: Editions du Seuil, 1962).

7. Former economic adviser to Kwame Nkrumah and West Indian intellec-tual W. Arthur Lewis created a stir in 1965 when he published his devas-tating critique of the single-party state, *Politics in West Africa* (New

York: Oxford University Press, 1965), entitled "Beyond African Dictatorship" in the original serialized form.

8. Barbara Stallings, *Banker to the Third World: Latin America and U.S. Capital Markets, 1900–1986* (Berkeley: University of California Press, 1987), gives an excellent account of this dynamic, focusing on Latin America.

9. Especially influential were such works as Walter Rodney, *How Europe Underdeveloped Africa* (Washington: Howard University Press, 1972), and diverse studies by Samir Amin, such as *Le développement inégal* (Paris: Editions de Minuit, 1973). For an invaluable review of this field, see Frederick Cooper, "Africa and the World Economy," *African Studies Review* 24 (June/September 1981): 1–86.

10. Among those launching this debate were the editors of the Marxist journal *Review of African Political Economy,* which published a special issue on the state in Africa in 1976. For a review of the academic debate on state and class, see Crawford Young, "Nationalism, Ethnicity, and Class in Africa: A Retrospective," *Cahiers d'Etudes Africaines* 26, no. 3 (1986): 421–95.

11. Cited in Ajayi, "Expectations of Independence," 1.

12. Crawford Young, *Ideology and Development in Africa* (New Haven: Yale University Press, 1982), 6.

13. *Lagos Plan of Action for Economic Development of Africa, 1980–2000* (Addis Ababa: Organization of African Unity, 1980); World Bank, *Accelerated Development in Sub-Saharan Africa* (Washington: World Bank, 1981).

14. Ajayi, "Expectations of Independence," 6.

15. John A. Marcum, "Africa: A Continent Adrift," *Foreign Affairs* 68 (Fall 1989): 159.

16. Carl K. Eicher, "Africa's Food Crisis," *Foreign Affairs* 72 (Fall 1982): 151–74.

17. Michael Crowder, "Whose Dream Was It Anyway?: Twenty-Five Years of African Independence," *African Affairs* 88 (January 1987): 7–24.

18. Naomi Chazan, *An Anatomy of Ghanaian Politics: Managing Political Recession, 1969–1982* (Boulder: Westview Press, 1982), 334–35.

19. Robert H. Jackson and Carl G. Rosberg, "Why Africa's Weak States Persist: The Empirical and the Juridical in Statehood," *World Politics* 35 (October 1982): 1–24.

20. John A. A. Ayoade, "States without Citizens: An Emerging African Phenomenon," in Donald Rothchild and Naomi Chazan, eds., *The Precarious Balance: State and Society in Africa* (Boulder: Westview Press, 1988), 100–18.

21. Achille Mbembe, *Afriques indociles: Christianisme, pouvoir et Etat en société postcoloniale* (Paris: Karthala, 1988), 148–49.

22. Jean-François Bayart, *L'Etat en Afrique: La politique du ventre* (Paris: Fayard, 1989), 314–15.

23. Ayi Kwei Armah, *The Beautyful Ones Are Not Yet Born* (London: Heinemann, 1968).

24. Ngugi wa Thiong'o, *Petals of Blood* (New York: E. P. Dutton, 1978).

25. Okot p'Bitek, *Song of Prisoner,* quoted in Richard Sandbrook, *The Politics of Africa's Economic Stagnation* (Cambridge: Cambridge University Press, 1985), 1.

26. Pierre Ryckmans, *Dominer pour servir* (Brussels: Edition Universelle, 1948).

27. Patrick Chabal, ed., *Political Domination in Africa: Reflection on the Limits of Power* (New York: Cambridge University Press, 1986), 13.

28. David B. Abernethy, "Bureaucratic Growth and Economic Decline in Sub-Saharan Africa," annual meeting, African Studies Association, Boston, 1983.

29. Nazih N. M. Ayubi, "Bureaucratic Inflation and Administrative Inefficiency: The Deadlock in Egyptian Administration," *Middle Eastern Studies* 18 (July 1982): 286–99.

30. Abernethy, "Bureaucratic Growth."

31. Alex Radian, *Resource Mobilization in Poor Countries: Implementing Tax Policies* (New Brunswick, N.J.: Transaction Books, 1980), 5–11.

32. Abernethy, "Bureaucratic Growth." See also Larry Diamond, "Class Formation in the Swollen African State," *Journal of Modern African Studies* 25, no. 4 (1987): 567–96.

33. Reginald Herbert Green, "'A Time of Struggle': Exogenous Shocks, Structural Transformation, and Crisis in Tanzania," *Millenium* 10 (Spring 1981): 29–41.

34. Lual Deng, "Economic Recovery Program: An Overview of the Adjustment Experiences in Africa in the 1980s," Seminar on Economic Reform and Liberalization, Nairobi, September 1988.

35. *West Africa* (1–7 May 1989): 684. On this point I am also indebted to Robert West, personal communication. West has assembled detailed data validating the point. Not all African states had large security forces or outlays; the aggregate figures are influenced by states like Libya, Egypt, Ethiopia, Angola, and South Africa, which were especially profligate by choice or necessity in military expenditures. For most states, the economic crisis has compelled compression of security budgets.

36. Lester B. Pearson, *Partners in Development* (New York: Praeger, 1969), 345, quoted in World Bank, *Toward Sustained Development in Sub-Saharan Africa: A Joint Program of Action* (Washington: World Bank, 1984), 14.

37. This viewpoint is advanced by Andrew M. Kamarck, "The Resources of Tropical Africa," *Daedalus* 111 (Spring 1982): 149–64.

38. The initial World Bank report on the African economic crisis, the "Berg

report," *Accelerated Development in Sub-Saharan Africa: An Agenda for Action* (Washington: World Bank, 1981), disputed African claims that declining terms of trade were a major cause of the continent's distress. However, *Sustained Development* and subsequent World Bank reports concede the importance of this factor for the recent period.

39. Joseph Hanlon, *Beggar Your Neighbours: Apartheid Power in Southern Africa* (Bloomington: Indiana University Press, 1986).

40. For an invaluable overview of the literature relative to the state in Africa, see the review essay by John Lonsdale, "States and Social Processes in Africa: A Historiographical Survey," *African Studies Review* 24 (June/September 1981): 139–226.

41. Crawford Young and Thomas Turner, *The Rise and Decline of the Zairian State* (Madison: University of Wisconsin Press, 1985).

42. Albert O. Hirschman, *Exit, Voice, and Loyalty: Response to Decline in Firms, Organizations, and States* (Cambridge: Harvard University Press, 1970).

43. Quoted in Albert O. Hirschman, *The Passions and the Interests: Political Arguments for Capitalism before Its Triumph* (Princeton: Princeton University Press, 1977), 17.

44. Albert O. Hirschman, *Development Projects Observed* (Washington: Brookings Institution, 1967).

Chapter 2: On the State

1. Clifford Geertz, *Negara: The Theatre State in Nineteenth-Century Bali* (Princeton: Princeton University Press, 1980), 121.

2. See for example David Easton, *A Systems Analysis of Political Life* (New York: John Wiley, 1965).

3. Peter B. Evans, Dietrich Rueschemeyer, and Theda Skocpol, eds., *Bringing the State Back In* (New York: Cambridge University Press, 1985). Skocpol played a major role in redirecting analytical attention to the state through her influential earlier work, *States and Social Revolutions* (Cambridge: Cambridge University Press, 1979).

4. Michael Bratton enters an eloquent plea in this sense in "Beyond the State: Civil Society and Associational Life in Africa," *World Politics* 41 (April 1989): 407–30. See also Jean-François Bayart, *L'Etat en Afrique: La politique du ventre* (Paris: Fayart, 1989), and Achille Mbembe, *Afriques indociles: Christianisme, pouvoir et Etat en société postcoloniale* (Paris, Karthela, 1988), focusing on modes of popular action; Joel Migdal, *Strong Societies and Weak States: State-Society Relations and State Capabilities in the Third World* (Princeton: Princeton University Press, 1988); and Donald Rothchild and Naomi Chazan, eds., *The Precarious Balance: State and Society in Africa* (Boulder: Westview Press, 1988).

5. On the rationality of the state, as for many other dimensions, our intel-

lectual debt to Max Weber is extensive. See especially Max Weber, *Economy and Society,* edited by Guenther Roth and Claus Wittich (Berkeley: University of California Press, 1978). For an excellent treatment of the rationality issue in Weber, see Rogers Brubaker, *The Limits of Rationality: An Essay on the Social and Moral Thought of Max Weber* (London: Allen and Unwin, 1984).

6. Works undertaking such a task that I have found particularly valuable, in addition to those already cited, include Gianfranco Poggi, *The Development of the Modern State: A Sociological Introduction* (Stanford: Stanford University Press, 1978); Anthony Giddens, *A Contemporary Critique of Historical Materialism: Power, Property, and the State* (Berkeley: University of California Press, 1981), and *The Nation-State and Violence* (Berkeley: University of California Press, 1987); Robert Fossaert, *Les états* (Paris: Editions du Seuil, 1981); Bertrand Badie and Pierre Birnbaum, *Sociologie de l'état* (Paris: Bernard Grasset, 1979); "The State," *Daedalus* 108 (Fall 1979); John H. Herz, *The Nation-State and the Crisis of World Politics* (New York: David McKay, 1976); Roger King, *The State in Modern Society* (Chatham, N.J.: Chatham House Publishers, 1986); Henri Lefebvre, *De l'état* (Paris: Union Générale des Editions, 1976); Eric A. Nordlinger, *On the Autonomy of the Democratic State* (Cambridge: Harvard University Press, 1981); Robert A. Solo, *The Positive State* (Cincinnati: South-Western Publishing Co., 1982); Martin Carnoy, *The State and Political Theory* (Princeton: Princeton University Press, 1984); Gregor McLennan, David Heald, and Stuart Hall, eds., *The Idea of the Modern State* (Philadelphia: Open University Press, 1984); David Held et al., eds., *States and Societies* (New York: New York University Press, 1983); Philip G. Cerney, *The Changing Architecture of Politics: Structure, Agency, and the Future of the State* (London: Sage Publications, 1990).

7. On the emergence of the state, see Henry J. M. Claessen and Peter Skalnik, eds., *The Early State* (The Hague: Mouton, 1978); Lawrence Krader, *Formation of the State* (Englewood Cliffs, N.J.: Prentice-Hall, 1968); Elmer R. Service, *Origins of the State and Civilization* (New York: W. W. Norton, 1975); Michael Mann, *The Sources of Social Power,* vol. 1, *Authority of Power from the Beginning to A.D. 1760* (Cambridge: Cambridge University Press, 1986).

8. See especially Reinhard Bendix, *Kings or People: Power and the Mandate to Rule* (Berkeley: University of California Press, 1978).

9. Amid a vast literature, I find especially valuable Marshall G. S. Hodgson, *The Venture of Islam* (Chicago: University of Chicago Press, 1974), 3 vols.; on the Ottoman variant, I find particularly useful Stanford Shaw, *History of the Ottoman Empire and Modern Turkey* (Cambridge: Cambridge University Press, 1976), 2 vols. For a point of entry into the recent wave of scholarship on the Islamic state, triggered by the Iranian Revolution and

the attendant resurrection of integralist visions of Islam, see Mohammed Panahi, "Theory and Application of Islamic Economy: A Case Study of Iran," Ph.D. diss., University of Wisconsin–Madison, 1987.

10. S. J. Tambiah, *World Conqueror and World Renouncer* (Cambridge: Cambridge University Press, 1976); Melford E. Spiro, *Buddhism and Society* (New York: Harper and Row, 1970).

11. Immanuel C. Y. Hsu, *The Rise of Modern China,* 3d ed. (New York: Oxford University Press, 1983); Jacques Gernet, *A History of Chinese Civilization,* trans. J. R. Foster (Cambridge: Cambridge University Press, 1982).

12. Geertz, *Negara.*

13. S. N. Eisenstadt, *The Political Systems of Empires: The Rise and Fall of the Historical Bureaucratic Societies* (New York: Free Press, 1969); Michael W. Doyle, *Empires* (Ithaca: Cornell University Press, 1986).

14. See the splendid review article by John Lonsdale, "States and Social Processes in Africa: A Historiographical Survey," *African Studies Review* 24 (June/September 1981): 139–226.

15. See the classic etymological exploration by H. C. Dowdall, "The Word 'State,'" *Law Quarterly Review* 39 (January 1923): 98–125.

16. Michael Oakeshott, "The Vocabulary of a Modern European State," *Political Studies* 23 (September–October 1975): 319.

17. Particularly helpful references include Perry Anderson, *Lineages of the Absolute State* (London: NLB, 1974); Heinz Lubasz, ed., *The Development of the Modern State* (New York: Macmillan, 1964); J. N. Shennan, *The Origins of the Modern European State, 1450–1725* (London: Hutchison University Library, 1974); Charles Tilly, ed., *The Formation of National States in Western Europe* (Princeton: Princeton University Press, 1973).

18. On the evolution of the philosophical underpinnings of the modern state, see especially Aryeh Botwinick, *Epic Political Theorists and the Conceptualization of the State* (Washington: University Press of America, 1982); Alexandre Passerin d'Entrêves, *The Notion of the State* (Oxford: Clarendon Press, 1967); Kenneth H. F. Dyson, *The State Tradition in Western Europe* (New York: Oxford University Press, 1980).

19. Carl J. Friedrich, *Constitutional Government and Democracy: Theory and Practice in Europe and America,* rev. ed. (Boston: Ginn, 1950).

20. J. P. Nettl, "The State as a Conceptual Variable," *World Politics* 20, no. 4 (1968): 567. This influential article was in many respects the most important precursor of the reawakened interest in the state.

21. Particularly useful on this point are Hedley Bull and Adam Watson, eds., *The Expansion of International Society* (Oxford: Clarendon Press, 1984); Robert A. Klein, *Sovereign Equality among States: The History of an Idea* (Toronto: University of Toronto Press, 1974); Martin Wight, *Systems of*

States (Leicester: Leicester University Press, 1977); Hedley Bull, *The Anarchical Society* (New York: Columbia University Press, 1977).

22. On the international jurisprudence of the state, useful treatises include J. L. Brierly, *The Law of Nations,* 6th ed. (New York: Oxford University Press, 1963); Antonio Cassese, *International Law in a Divided World* (Oxford: Clarendon Press, 1986); Hans Kelsen, *General Theory of Law and State,* trans. Anders Weberg (New York: Russell, 1961); Charles de Visscher, *Theory and Reality in Public International Law,* rev. ed., trans. P. E. Corbett (Princeton: Princeton University Press, 1968). Some international legal theorists suggest that a whole new system of international law is coming into being, based on the different normative orientations of the newly independent states, which Cassese labels "the U.N. Charter system," as contrasted to the "Westphalian system." See also Michael Donelan, ed., *The Reason of States: A Study in International Political Theory* (London: George Allen and Unwin, 1978).

23. Guillermo A. O'Donnell, *Modernization and Bureaucratic-Authoritarianism: Studies in South American Politics* (Berkeley: Institute of International Studies, University of California, 1973); David Collier, ed., *The New Authoritarianism in Latin America* (Princeton: Princeton University Press, 1979).

24. "Lectures on the Philosophy of World History," reprinted in Held et al., *States and Societies,* 94–95. On the Hegelian notion of the state, see Z. A. Pelczynski, ed., *The State and Civil Society: Studies in Hegel's Political Philosophy* (Cambridge: Cambridge University Press, 1984); Shlomo Aveneri, *Hegel's Theory of the Modern State* (Cambridge: Cambridge University Press, 1972).

25. Dyson, *The State Tradition in Western Europe,* 3.

26. There was an active debate in Marxist scholarship, especially during the 1970s, on the "relative autonomy" of the capitalist state. Most completely developed in the rather abstruse "structuralism" of Louis Althusser and Nicos Poulantzas, this strand of Marxism argued that the capitalist state needed to both appear and act with some autonomy from the hegemonic class to sustain state legitimacy and to ensure the long-term viability of capitalism. Whether the relative autonomy is exercised for more effective class rule, more efficient performance of the accumulation function, or to conceal class struggle, the state remains chained to the curiously functionalist axioms of the paradigm, and the scope of its role as actor must always remain circumscribed. For valuable reviews of diverse strands of Marxist theory concerning the state, see Carnoy, *The State and Political Theory;* Bob Jessop, *Theories of the State* (New York: New York University Press, 1983); and David Gold, C. Lo, and Erick O. Wright, "Recent Developments in Marxist Theories of the State," *Monthly Review* 18, nos. 5 and 6 (1975): 29–43, 36–51.

27. Friedrich Meinecke, *Machiavellism,* trans. Douglas Scott (New Haven: Yale University Press, 1957).
28. Mann, *A History of Power.*
29. Eli F. Heckscher, *Mercantilism* (London: George Allen and Unwin, 1934), 1:22.
30. Giddens, *The Nation-State and Violence,* 20–21.
31. Badie and Birnbaum, *Sociologie de l'Etat,* 27–37.
32. Weber, "Politics as a Vocation," 79. For fuller exposition of Weberian theories of the rational state, see Weber, *Economy and Society,* 1:212–301.
33. See especially Margaret Levi, *Of Rule and Revenue* (Berkeley: University of California Press, 1988). In the African realm, application of rational-choice behavior to state behavior is particularly associated with Robert H. Bates, *Markets and States in Tropical Africa* (Berkeley: University of California Press, 1981), and *Essays on the Political Economy of Rural Africa* (Berkeley: University of California Press, 1983).
34. The "new institutionalism" seeks to temper the individualist predisposition of rational-choice theory with an institutionalist focus. See Elinor Ostrom, "Rational Choice Theory and Institutional Analysis: Toward Complementarity," *American Political Science Review* 85, no. 1 (1991): 237–43; James G. March and John P. Olsen, *Rediscovering Institutions: The Organizational Basis of Politics* (New York: Free Press, 1989); Walter W. Powell and Paul J. DiMaggio, *The New Institutionalism in Organizational Analysis* (Chicago: University of Chicago Press, 1991).
35. On the idea of sovereignty, see F. H. Hinsley, *Sovereignty* (London: C. A. Watts, 1966); Bertrand de Jouvenal, *Sovereignty: An Inquiry into the Political Good* (Cambridge: Cambridge University Press, 1957); Passerin d'Entrêves, *The Notion of the State.*
36. Morton H. Fried, "State: The Institution," *International Encyclopedia of the Social Sciences* (New York: Macmillan, 1968), 15:143–50.
37. Watkins, "State: The Concept," 15:153.
38. Andrew Vincent, *Theories of the State* (Oxford: Basil Blackwell, 1987), 218.
39. Giddens, *A Contemporary Critique,* 4.
40. Michel Foucault, "Power, Sovereignty, and Discipline," in Held et al., *States and Societies,* 312. Law, adds Foucault, as discourse of state effaces "the domination intrinsic to power in order to present the latter . . . on the one hand, as the legitimate rights of sovereignty, and on the other, as the legal obligation to obey it."
41. Evans et al., *Bringing the State Back In,* 350.
42. Poggi, *The Development of the Modern State,* 6–7.
43. For a discussion on this point, see Kenneth Waltz, *Theory of International Politics* (Reading, Mass.: Addison-Wesley, 1979).
44. Vincent, *Theories of the State,* 6.

45. Timothy Mitchell, "The Limits of the State: Beyond Statist Approaches and their Critics," *American Political Science Review* 85, no. 1 (1991): 81.

46. Graham Allison, *Essence of Decision: Explaining the Cuban Missile Crisis* (Boston: Little, Brown, 1979).

47. Michael G. Schatzberg, *The Dialectics of Oppression in Zaire* (Bloomington: Indiana University Press, 1988), 5.

48. Cerny, *The Changing Architecture of Politics,* is an excellent effort to unite structure and agency in a single framework.

49. Giddens, *A Contemporary Critique,* 32–68.

50. Mitchell, "Limits of the State," 95.

51. Cerny, *The Architect of Power,* 32.

52. Nicos Poulantzas, *Classes in Contemporary Capitalism* (London: New Left Books, 1975), 25.

53. T. H. Marshall, *Class, Citizenship, and Social Development* (New York: Doubleday, 1964), 92.

54. Mbembe, *Afriques indociles,* 148.

55. "Civil society," on close inspection, is a complex and contested notion, like "state." Paradoxically, the term had experienced a long eclipse— since the mid-nineteenth century, argues its most influential contemporary student, John Keane. Like state as concept, civil society reappeared in everyday discourse in the 1980s, powerfully fueled by its appropriation by the East European intelligentsia as a lexical challenge to decaying state socialism. I return to an extended discussion of the concept, which also became central to the discourse of democratization in Africa in the later 1980s, in chapter 7. For a particularly valuable discussion, see John Keane, ed., *Civil Society and the State: New European Perspectives* (London: Verso, 1988).

56. Dyson, *The State Tradition,* 206–08.

57. Giddens, *A Contemporary Critique,* 3–4.

58. R. Y. Jennings, *The Acquisition of Territory in International Law* (Manchester: Manchester University Press, 1963), 2.

59. Jean Bodin, *Six Books of the Commonwealth,* trans. M. J. Tooley (Oxford: Basil Blackwell, 1955), 25.

60. de Jouvenal, *Sovereignty,* 170.

61. Klein, *Sovereign Equality among Nations.*

62. James Mayall, "International Society and International Theory," in Michael Donelan, ed., *The Reason of States: A Study in International Political Theory* (London: George Allen and Unwin, 1978), 130–31.

63. de Visscher, *Theory and Reality in Public International Law,* 89–90.

64. Ibid.

65. Kelsen, *General Theory of Law and State,* 242.

66. Giddens, *The Nation-State and Violence,* 9–17.

67. Kelsen, *General Theory of Law and State,* 140.

68. Cited in Dyson, *The State Tradition,* 108.

69. On this pivotal notion, I find especially valuable Benedict Anderson, *Imagined Communities: Reflections on the Origin and Spread of Nationalism* (London: Verso, 1983); John Armstrong, *Nations before Nationalism* (Chapel Hill: University of North Carolina Press, 1982); John Breuilly, *Nationalism and the State* (Manchester: Manchester University Press, 1982); Hans Kohn, *The Idea of Nationalism* (New York: Macmillan, 1943); Carleton R. Hayes, *The Historical Evolution of Modern Nationalism* (New York: Richard R. Smith, 1931); Rupert Emerson, *From Empire to Nation* (Cambridge: Harvard University Press, 1960); Anthony D. Smith, *Theories of Nationalism* (New York: Harper and Row, 1971); Ernest Gellner, *Nations and Nationalism* (Ithaca, N.Y.: Cornell University Press, 1983); Hugh Seton-Watson, *Nations and States* (Boulder: Westview Press, 1977); Eric Hobsbawm, *Nations and Nationalism Since 1780: Programme, Myth, Reality* (Cambridge: Cambridge University Press, 1990).

70. Z. A. Pelczynski, "Nation, Civil Society, State: Hegelian Sources of the Marxian Non-Theory of Nationality," in Pelczynski, ed., *The State and Civil Society,* 262–78.

71. The collapse of state socialism and the attendant breakup of the Soviet Union, Yugoslavia, and Czechoslovakia reintroduced a more cultural concept of "nation," endowing the state with a vocation of homogenization, a doctrine that in its extreme form leads to "ethnic cleansing." Such excesses are partly a consequence of the "nationality policy" developed by Lenin and Stalin to manage multicultural realities; the impact of the new dynamic introduced in 1991 may well alter the content of the "nation-state" equation. See various contributions in the special issue on "Reconstructing Nations and States," *Daedalus* 122 (Summer 1993).

72. I rely here on the image of the international order constructed by Bull, *The Anarchical Society.*

73. Charles Tilly, "Reflections on the History of European State-Making," in Tilly, ed., *The Formation of National States in Western Europe* (Princeton: Princeton University Press, 1975), 3–83.

74. Michael Howard, "War and the Nation-State," *Daedalus* 108 (Fall 1979): 101–10.

75. See the important work by Stephen D. Krasner, *Defending the National Interest: Raw Materials Investments and U.S. Foreign Policy* (Princeton: Princeton University Press, 1978).

76. See the stimulating exploration of the symbolizing of the state in Harold D. Lasswell, *The Signature of Power* (New Brunswick: Transaction Books, 1979).

77. Murray J. Edelman, *Constructing the Political Spectacle* (Chicago: University of Chicago Press, 1988).

78. Geertz, *Negara,* 13.

79. Goran Therborn, *What Does the Ruling Class Do When It Rules?: State*

Apparatuses and State Power under Feudalism, Capitalism, and Socialism (London: NLB, 1978).

80. One can find exceptions to this proposition, in the form of small and marginal groups whose dissidence in delimited fields is accepted: the Jehovah's Witnesses spring to mind. A degree of tolerance, for liberal states, is possible because such groups are exceptional and do not challenge the overall hegemony of the state.

81. David Bayley, "The Police and Political Development in Europe," in Tilly, ed., *The Formation of National States,* 328–79.

82. To borrow the keywords of the imaginative analysis of the functions of power in Michel Foucault, *Discipline and Punish* (New York: Random House, 1978).

83. Sheldon S. Wolin, *Politics and Vision: Continuity and Innovation in Western Political Thought* (Boston: Little, Brown, 1960), 265–66.

84. Nordlinger, *Autonomy of the Democratic State,* 19–20.

85. Giddens, *The Nation-State and Violence,* 293.

86. Among other sources developing this metaphor, see Talcott Parsons, "Some Reflections on the Place of Force in Social Process," in Harry Eckstein, ed., *Internal War* (New York: Free Press of Glencoe, 1964), 33–70.

87. Paul Veyne, *Le pain et le cirque: Sociologie historique d'un pluralisme politique* (Paris: Editions du Seuil, 1976.

88. See the veritable explosion of comparative works capturing this trend; for example, Giovanni Sartori, *The Theory of Democracy Revisited* (Chatham, N.J.: Chatham House Publishers, 1987); Guillermo O'Donnell, Philippe C. Schmitter, and Laurence Whitehead, eds., *Transitions from Authoritarian Rule* (Baltimore: Johns Hopkins University Press, 1986), 5 vols.; Larry Diamond, Juan J. Linz, and Seymour Martin Lipset, *Democracy in Developing Countries* (Boulder: Lynne Riener, 1988), 4 vols; Dov Ronen, ed., *Democracy and Pluralism in Africa* (Boulder: Lynne Riener, 1986); Peter Anyang' Nyong'o, ed., *Popular Struggles for Democracy in Africa* (London: Zed Books Ltd., 1987); Walter Oyugi, E. S. Atieno Odhiambo, Michael Chege, and Afrika K. Gitonga, eds., *Democratic Theory and Practice in Africa* (Portsmouth, N.H.: Heinemann, 1988).

89. Levi, *Of Rule and Revenue,* 1–2.

90. John F. Witte, *The Politics and Development of the Federal Income Tax* (Madison: University of Wisconsin Press, 1985).

91. Levi, *Of Rule and Revenue,* 23.

92. James O'Connor, *The Fiscal Crisis of the State* (New York: St. Martin's Press, 1973).

93. Carnoy, *The State and Political Theory,* 134.

94. Adam Przeworski and Michael Wallerstein, "Structural Dependence of the State on Capital," *American Political Science Review* 82 (March 1988): 13.

95. W. Howard Wriggins, *The Ruler's Imperative: Strategies for Political*

Survival in Asia and Africa (New York: Columbia University Press, 1969), 12.

96. Levi, *Of Rule and Revenue;* Nordlinger, *On the Autonomy of the Democratic State.*

Chapter 3: The Nature and Genesis of the Colonial State

1. Henry C. Morris, *The History of Colonization from the Earliest Times to the Present Day* (New York: Macmillan, 1900), 2 vols. The problematic of the Morris work is set by the new role perceived for the United States as blessed with a colonial future.

2. For the anatomy of the security logic governing Roman imperial expansion, rule, and defense, see the imaginative reconstruction in Edward N. Luttwak, *The Grand Strategy of the Roman Empire* (Baltimore: Johns Hopkins University Press, 1976).

3. Paul Veyne, *Le pain et le cirque: Sociologie historique d'un pluralisme politique* (Paris: Editions du Seuil, 1976).

4. For the shrewd insights of a conquered Greek co-opted into the upper echelons of Roman society, see Polybius, *On Roman Imperialism,* trans. Evelyn S. Shuckburgh (South Bend: Regnery/Gateway, 1980).

5. I am indebted to G. W. Bowersock of the Institute for Advanced Study at Princeton for helpful guidance on Rome as a colonial power. I have also found useful E. Badian, *Roman Imperialism in the Late Republic* (Oxford: Basil Blackwell, 1968); Peter Garnsey and Richard Saller, *The Roman Empire: Economy, Society, and Culture* (Berkeley: University of California Press, 1987).

6. The structural and doctrinal concepts of the Ottoman state are described well in Stanford Shaw, *History of the Ottoman Empire and Modern Turkey* (Cambridge: Cambridge University Press, 1976), 2 vols.

7. On this issue, see C. P. Fitzgerald, *The Southern Expansion of the Chinese People* (London: Barrie and Jenkins, 1972).

8. I am indebted to Brian Digre, research assistant at the Woodrow Wilson International Center for Scholars, for his excellent work on this theme. Irish history specialists Tome Garvin and James Donnelly also provided helpful guidance. Useful sources include Francis Godwin James, *Ireland in the Empire, 1688–1770: A History of Ireland from the Williamite Wars to the Eve of the American Revolution* (Cambridge: Harvard University Press, 1973); J. F. Lydon, *The Lordship of Ireland in the Middle Ages* (Toronto: University of Toronto Press, 1972); J. C. Beckett, *The Making of Modern Ireland, 1603–1923* (New York: Knopf, 1966); Robert Dudley Edwards, *Ireland in the Age of the Tudors* (London: Croon Helm, 1977); Eric Strauss, *Irish Nationalism and British Democracy* (New York: Columbia University Press, 1951); Tom Garvin, *The Evolution of Irish Nationalist Politics* (Dublin: Gill and Macmillan, 1981).

9. Frederic C. Lane, *Venice: A Maritime Republic* (Baltimore: Johns Hopkins University Press, 1973).

10. C. R. Boxer, *The Portuguese Sea-Borne Empire, 1415–1825* (London: Hutchison, 1969), 21–23.

11. Ibid., 93–94.

12. Charles Boxer, *Portuguese Society in the Tropics: The Municipal Councils of Goa, Macao, Bahia, and Luanda, 1510–1800* (Madison: University of Wisconsin Press, 1985), 42–43.

13. H. B. Johnson, "The Portuguese Settlement of Brazil, 1500–1800," in Leslie Bethell, ed., *The Cambridge History of Latin America: Colonial Latin America* (Cambridge: Cambridge University Press, 1984), 1:269.

14. Recent research shows that Indian slavery remained significant longer than was once believed. Although legislation forbidding enslavement of Indians existed from 1570 on, they remained a substantial though decreasing fraction of the sugar-plantation slave-labor force from 1580 to 1650. In frontier regions like Parana, and during the early period of Sao Paulo's development, Indian servitude continued much longer, lightly disguised as *administrado* status but differing little from slavery. See the excellent study by Stuart B. Schwartz, *Slaves, Peasants, and Rebels* (Urbana: University of Illinois Press, 1992), 110–12, 147–48, and his earlier seminal article, "Indian Labor and New World Plantations: European Demands and Indian Responses in Northeastern Brazil," *American Historical Review* 83 (February 1978): 43–79. See also Alida C. Metcalf, *Family and Frontier in Colonial Brazil: Santana de Parnaiba, 1580–1822* (Berkeley: University of California Press, 1992).

15. Boxer, *The Portuguese Sea-Borne Empire*, 103–04.

16. Johnson, "The Portuguese Settlement of Brazil," 286.

17. On the early colonial state in Brazil, see Johnson, "The Portuguese Settlement of Brazil"; Fernando Uricoechea, *The Patrimonial Foundations of the Brazilian Bureaucratic State* (Berkeley: University of California Press, 1980).

18. On medieval Spain and the reconquista, see Thomas F. Glick, *Islamic and Christian Spain in the Early Middle Ages* (Princeton: Princeton University Press, 1979); J. H. Elliott, *Imperial Spain, 1469–1716* (New York: St. Martin's Press, 1964).

19. J. A. Fernandez-Santamaria, *The State, War, and Peace: Spanish Political Thought in the Renaissance, 1516–1559* (Cambridge: Cambridge University Press, 1977); Colin M. MacLachlan, *Spain's Empire in the New World: The Role of Ideas in Institutional and Social Change* (Berkeley: University of California Press, 1988).

20. Elliott, *Imperial Spain*, 80–87.

21. Fernandes-Santamaria, *The State, War, and Peace*, 6.

22. Jacques LaFaye, *Les conquistadores* (Paris: Editions de Seuil, 1964);

J. H. Elliott, "The Spanish Conquest and Settlement of America," in Bethel, ed., *Cambridge History of Latin America*, 1:149–206.

23. Steve J. Stern, *Peru's Indian Peoples and the Challenge of Spanish Conquest* (Madison: University of Wisconsin Press, 1982), 80. This masterful monograph is an invaluable source of insight into the early Spanish colonial state.

24. Claudio Veliz, *The Centralist Tradition in Latin America* (Princeton: Princeton University Press, 1980), 43.

25. James Lang, *Commerce and Conquest: Spain and England in the Americas* (New York: Academic Press, 1975), 7.

26. This extraordinary text, prepared by royal jurists in 1514, veiled an act of brutal aggression in a curious cloak of theological and juridical formalism. The Spanish conquerers, in full knightly regalia, read the proclamation to an assembled Indian community, doubtless uncomprehending, prior to seizing and enslaving them. After giving a brief history of humanity, they announced the appearance of Christ, which they followed with a narrative of the apostolic succession leading to the papal gift of sovereignty in the Indies. The juridical foundations thus laid, the Indians were summoned to accept Christ's kingdom, failing which dire consequences awaited them: "But if you do not [acknowledge Christianity], and wickedly and intentionally delay to do so, I certify to you that, with the help of God, we shall forcibly enter into your country and shall make war against you in all ways and manners that we can, and shall subject you to the yoke and obedience of the Church and of their Highnesses; we shall take you and your wives and your children, and shall make slaves of them as their Highnesses may command; and we shall take away your goods, and we shall do all the harm and damage that we can as to vassals who do not obey and refuse to receive their Lord, and resist and contradict him." (Tzvetan Todorov, *The Conquest of America: The Question of the Other,* trans. Richard Howard [New York: Harper and Row, 1984], 147.) This extreme doctrine did not long stand alone; in 1530 King Charles issued a contrary edict: "No one must dare to enslave any Indian, neither in war nor in peace time, nor must he keep any Indian enslaved on the pretext of having acquired him through a just war, or . . . purchase or barter . . . even if these Indians be considered as slaves by the natives." Other protective decrees followed, most notably the 1542 New Laws of the Indies, but some time passed before the practice of enslaving Indians, through whatever artifice, was eliminated. (Ibid., 161–67).

27. J. H. Parry, *The Spanish Theory of Empire in the Sixteenth Century* (Cambridge: Cambridge University Press, 1940), 27–43.

28. Elliott, "The Spanish Conquest and Settlement," 202.

29. Philip D. Curtin, *The Rise and Fall of the Plantation Complex: Essays in Atlantic History* (Cambridge: Cambridge University Press, 1990), 63–

64. Edmund S. Morgan, *American Slavery, American Freedom: The Ordeal of Colonial Virginia* (New York: W. W. Norton, 1975), 7, advances the figure of eight million as the pre-Columbian population of Hispaniola, of whom only two hundred remained by 1552.

30. Stern, *Peru's Indian Peoples.*

31. William B. Taylor, *Drinking, Homicide, and Rebellion in a Colonial Mexican Village* (Stanford: Stanford University Press, 1979), 170. Stern, *Peru's Indian Peoples,* also provides interesting insight into the scale of Indian-initiated litigation in local Spanish colonial courts.

32. Orlando Patterson, *Slavery and Social Death: A Comparative Study* (Cambridge: Harvard University Press, 1982).

33. Leslie B. Rout, *The African Experience in Spanish America* (Cambridge: Cambridge University Press, 1976).

34. Elliott, *Imperial Spain,* 279–81 and passim.

35. See, for example, the interesting detail on debates leading to the "planting of the western plantations" in Tudor England in Morgan, *American Slavery, American Freedom,* 7–43.

36. On the formation of the Dutch state in comparative perspective, see Hugh Seton-Watson, *Nations and States* (Boulder: Westview Press, 1977).

37. George Masselman, *The Cradle of Colonialism* (New Haven: Yale University Press, 1963), 455.

38. Philip Woodruff [Mason], *The Men Who Ruled India* (London: Jonathan Cape, 1953), 1:19–20.

39. Ibid., 33–36.

40. Ibid., 67–68.

41. See the excellent history of the Indian Army by Philip Mason, *A Matter of Honour* (New York: Holt, Rinehart, and Winston, 1974).

42. D. A. Low, *Lion Rampant: Essays in the Study of British Imperialism* (London: Frank Cass, 1973), 41.

43. Woodruff, *The Men Who Ruled India,* 1:133–50.

44. On the early phase of English West Indian colonial history, see Sidney W. Mintz, *Sweetness and Power: The Place of Sugar in Modern History* (New York: Viking, 1985); Richard S. Dunn, *Sugar and Slaves: The Rise of the Planter Class in the English West Indies, 1624–1713* (Chapel Hill: University of North Carolina Press, 1972).

45. Quoted in Klaus E. Knorr, *British Colonial Theories, 1570–1850* (Toronto: University of Toronto Press, 1944), 42.

46. Lang, *Commerce and Conquest,* 112.

47. Cited in Howard Robinson, *The Development of the British Empire* (Boston: Houghton Mifflin Company, 1922), 37–38.

48. Morgan, *American Slavery, American Freedom,* 144–45.

49. See ibid. for exhaustive detail on the complex relationships with the small-scale Indian political units encountered in Virginia.

50. Eric R. Wolf, *Europe and the People without History* (Berkeley: University of California Press), 158–94. See also the fascinating analysis of Indian, French, and British relationships in the inner frontier at a time when no group had the capacity or the interest to impose full hegemony on the others in Richard White, *The Middle Ground: Indians, Empires, and Republics in the Great Lakes Region, 1650–1815* (Cambridge: Cambridge University Press, 1991).

51. Morgan, *American Slavery, American Freedom,* 193.

52. Ibid., 108–30.

53. Lang, *Commerce and Conquest,* 113–27.

54. Winthrop S. Hudson, *Religion in America,* 3d ed. (New York: Charles Scribner's Sons, 1981), 13.

55. Morgan, *American Slavery, American Freedom,* 193.

56. The issue of parliamentary sovereignty over the colonies, posed by the series of revenue acts in the 1760s, raised in the eyes of colonial civil societies fundamental issues of constitutional theory. The doctrine they used as a frame of reference, which dates from Calvin's Case in 1606, asserted that England and Scotland were joined through the crown but retained separate legal personalities. This constitutional theory served as authoritative reference for colonial public law; thus, while the sovereignty of the royal writ was acknowledged, the right of British Parliament to share in that sovereignty through unilateral imposition of legislation was contested. For details, see Harvey Wheeler, "Constitutionalism," in Fred I. Greenstein and Nelson W. Polsby, eds., *Handbook of Political Science* (Reading, Mass.: Addison-Wesley, 1975), 5:54–57.

57. Lang, *Commerce and Conquest,* 235.

58. I am indebted to Bernard Bailyn for valuable orientation on the thirteen colonies as colonial states. Other sources I have found helpful include R. C. Simmons, *The American Colonies from Settlement to Independence* (New York: W. W. Norton, 1976); Kenneth Robinson and Frederick Madden, *Essays in Imperial Government* (Oxford: Basil Blackwell, 1963); Peter Marshall and Glynn Williams, eds., *The British Atlantic Empire before the American Revolution* (London: Frank Cass, 1980).

59. Ronald Kent Richardson, *Moral Imperium: Afro-Caribbeans and the Transformation of British Rule, 1776–1838* (New York: Greenwood Press, 1987). Virginia and the Carolinas, with large slave populations by 1700, bore some demographic resemblance to the West Indian colonies. However, with Virginia as model, a firm alliance was welded between the emergent landed gentry and the impoverished segment of the white population, which permitted the remarkable contradiction of a generation of eloquent republican leaders who were the architects of the American Republic but were in their private lives large-scale slave owners. Morgan, *American Slavery, American Freedom* gives an insightful exploration of this profound paradox.

60. Dunn, *Sugar and Slaves;* Gordon K. Lewis, *The Growth of the Modern West Indies* (New York: Monthly Review Press, 1968).

61. On the Pombal era, see Dauril Alden, *Royal Government in Colonial Brazil: With Special Reference to the Administration of Lavradio, Viceroy, 1769–1779* (Berkeley: University of California Press, 1968).

62. On the Bourbon reforms in colonial Spanish America, see John Lynch, *Spanish Colonial Administration, 1782–1810: The Intendant System in the Viceroyalty of the Rio de la Plata* (London: Athlone, 1958); Karen Spalding, *Essays on the Political, Economic, and Social History of Colonial Latin America* (Newark: University of Delaware Latin American Studies Program, Occasional Papers and Monographs 3, 1982); John Leddy Phelan, *The People and the King: The Communero Revolution in Colombia, 1781* (Madison: University of Wisconsin Press, 1978); Mark Burkholder and Lyman L. Johnson, *Colonial Latin America* (New York: Oxford University Press, 1990).

63. I am endebted to Steve J. Stern for insisting on the importance of this period of intense imperial rivalry.

64. Cited in Knorr, *British Colonial Theories,* 188.

65. From the pen of Charles Davenant, quoted in ibid., 106.

66. Leonard Binder et al., *Crisis and Sequences in Political Development* (Princeton: Princeton University Press, 1971); Gabriel A. Almond and G. Bingham Powell, *Comparative Politics: A Developmental Approach* (Boston: Little, Brown, 1966). Indeed, one might argue that the paroxysm of imperial expansion further deepened the structures of the modern state; Mamadou Diouf, personal communication.

67. For an overall treatment of this theme in broad historical perspective, see William H. McNeill, *The Pursuit of Power: Technology, Armed Force, and Society since A.D. 1000* (Chicago: University of Chicago Press, 1982).

68. See the excellent examination of the technologies of conquest in Daniel R. Headrick, *The Tools of Empire: Technology and European Imperialism in the Nineteenth Century* (New York: Oxford University Press, 1981).

Chapter 4: Constructing Bula Matari

1. Daniel R. Headrick, *The Tools of Empire: Technology and European Imperialism in the Nineteenth Century* (New York: Oxford University Press, 1981), 118.

2. G. N. Sanderson, "The Nile Basin and the Eastern Horn, 1870–1908," in Roland Oliver and G. N. Sanderson, eds., *The Cambridge History of Africa* (Cambridge: Cambridge University Press, 1985), 6:625.

3. This gave rise to the epigraph to this chapter, cited in Gabriel Warburg, *The Sudan under Wingate: Administration in the Anglo-Egyptian Sudan, 1899–1916* (London: Frank Cass, 1971), 4.

4. Jean Stengers, "The Congo Free State and the Belgian Congo before 1914," in J. H. Gann and Peter Duignan, eds., *Colonialism in Africa, 1870–1960* (Cambridge: Cambridge University Press, 1969), 1:265.

5. For basic chronicles of the Pan-African idea, see Vincent Bakpetu Thompson, *Africa and Unity: The Evolution of Pan-Africanism* (London: Longman, 1969), and Colin Legum, *Pan-Africanism: A Short Political Guide* (London: Pall Mall, 1962).

6. Douglas Johnson, "The Maghrib," in John E. Flint, ed., *The Cambridge History of Africa* (Cambridge: Cambridge University Press, 1976), 5:104–20; Stephen H. Roberts, *The History of French Colonial Policy, 1870–1925* (London: P. S. King, 1929), 177–87.

7. For detail, see Mamadou Diouf, "Le Kayoor au XIXe siècle et la conquête coloniale," thèse de 3e cycle, Université de Paris I, 1980; Boubacar Barry, *La Sénégambie du XVe au XIXe siècle: Traite negrière, Islam et conquête coloniale* (Paris: L'Harmattan, 1988); Iba Der Thiam, "Evolution politique et syndicale du Sénégal colonial de 1840 à 1936," thèse de Doctorat d'Etat, Université de Paris I, 1983, 8 vols.

8. On nineteenth-century Sierra Leone, see the comprehensive work by Christopher Fyfe, *A History of Sierra Leone* (London: Oxford University Press, 1962).

9. For detail on this period, W. E. F. Ward, *A History of Ghana,* 2d ed. (London: George Allen and Unwin, 1958), remains useful.

10. Gerald J. Bender, *Angola under the Portuguese: The Myth and the Reality* (London: Heinemann, 1978), lays particular stress on the *degradado* element in sustaining a larger European population in Angola than in other imperial outposts during the nineteenth century; the perceived success of the "Australian model" gave this mechanism of strengthening imperial control renewed importance. See also Allen F. Isaacman, *Mozambique: The Africanization of a European Institution: The Zambezi Prazos, 1750–1902* (Madison: University of Wisconsin Press, 1972); James Duffy, *Portuguese Africa* (Cambridge: Harvard University Press, 1959); David Birmingham and Phyllis M. Martin, eds., *History of Central Africa* (London: Longman, 1983), 2 vols; Joseph Miller, *Way of Death: Merchant Capitalism and the Slave Trade* (Madison: University of Wisconsin Press, 1988).

11. Quoted in Wolfgang J. Mommsen, *Theories of Imperialism* (New York: Random House, 1980), 22.

12. Reliable summaries of this period may be found in Donald Denoon, *Southern Africa since 1800* (New York: Praeger, 1972), and J. D. Omer-Cooper, "Colonial South Africa and Its Frontiers," in Flint, ed., *Cambridge History of Africa,* 5:353–92.

13. Diouf, "Le Kajoor," 239–317.

14. J. D. Hargreaves, "The Making of the Boundaries: Focus on West Africa," in A. I. Asiwaju, ed., *Partitioned Africans: Ethnic Relations across*

Africa's International Boundaries, 1884–1984 (London: C. Hurst, 1984), 19–27.

15. For telling critiques, see Mommsen, *Theories of Imperialism;* D. J. Fieldhouse, *Economies and Empire, 1830–1914* (London: Weidenfeld and Nicolson, 1973); A. G. Hopkins, *An Economic History of West Africa* (New York: Columbia University Press, 1973); Benjamin J. Cohen, *The Question of Imperialism* (New York: Basic Books, 1973).

16. The Duke of Brabant to De Jonghe d'Ardoye, 23 March 1859, quoted in H. L. Wesseling, "The Impact of Dutch Colonialism on European Imperialism," typescript, 1980.

17. Paul Kennedy, *The Rise and Fall of the Great Powers: Economic Change and Military Conflict from 1500 to 2000* (New York: Vintage Books, 1987), 155.

18. Reference is made to various reports in the 1 G series in the Archives Nationales du Sénégal (hereafter ANS), formerly the archival center for Afrique Occidentale Française.

19. Charles Wilson, *The History of Unilever* (London: Cassell, 1954), 2 vols.

20. ANS, 1 G 50, Mission du Haut Niger, 1880.

21. On colonial Congo missions, see especially Ruth M. Slade, *English-Speaking Missions in the Congo Independent State, 1878–1908* (Brussels: Académie Royale des Sciences Coloniales, 1959). On Uganda, see John V. Taylor, *The Growth of the Church in Buganda* (London: SCM Press, 1958), and Roland Oliver, *The Missionary Factor in East Africa* (London: Longmans, 1952). For an overview, see Kenneth Scott Latourette, "The Spread of Christianity: British and German Missions in Africa," in Prosser Gifford and Wm. Roger Louis, eds., *Britain and Germany in Africa* (New Haven: Yale University Press, 1967).

22. For detail on the crystallization of a potent colonial party in France, see Raoul Girardet, *L'idée coloniale en France de 1871 à 1962* (Paris: La Table Ronde, 1972); Stuart Michael Persell, *The French Colonial Lobby, 1889–1938* (Stanford: Hoover Institution Press, 1983); Raymond Betts, *Tricouleur: The French Overseas Empire* (London: Gordon and Cremondesi, 1978).

23. Ottavio Barie, "Italian Imperialism: The First Stage," *Journal of Italian History* 2 (Winter 1979): 531–65.

24. J. R. Seeley, *The Expansion of England* (Chicago: University of Chicago Press, 1971), 36. First published 1881, it sold eighty thousand copies in its first two years, a fair measure of its resonance as a tract for the times. One should note that Seeley was not an imperial chauvinist like Charles Dilkey but was viewed as a voice of moderation. The expansion of England advocated by Seeley envisaged above all settlement colonies; India he viewed with some ambivalence. On the one hand, he warned that "when the State advances beyond the limits of the nationality, its power becomes precarious and artificial . . . the chances are

311

that it will there meet with other nationalities which it cannot destroy or completely drive out, even if it succeeds in conquering them. When this happens, it has a great and permanent difficulty to contend with." Ibid., 40.

25. ANS, 1 G 70 (17), Mission de l'Ambassadeur de Timboktou, 1885–1886.

26. Cited in A. S. Kanya-Forstner, *The Conquest of the Western Sudan: A Study in French Military Imperialism* (Cambridge: Cambridge University Press, 1969).

27. Ibid., 175.

28. John Marlowe, *Cecil Rhodes: The Anatomy of Empire* (London: Paul Elek, 1972), 64–65.

29. Quoted in Henry S. Wilson, *The Imperial Experience in Sub-Saharan Africa since 1870* (Minneapolis: University of Minnesota Press, 1977), 84.

30. Ibid., 85.

31. John E. Flint, *Sir George Goldie and the Making of Nigeria* (London: Oxford University Press, 1960), 53–55.

32. Wilson, *The Imperial Experience in Sub-Saharan Africa,* 82–87.

33. Henry M. Stanley, *The Congo and the Founding of Its Free State* (London: Sampson, Low, Marston, Searle, and Rivington, 1885), 2:379–80.

34. ANS, 1 G 92, Lt. Reichenberg Mission dans le Bambouck, 1887–1888.

35. Quoted in Anthony Thrall Sullivan, *Thomas-Robert Bugeaud: France and Algeria, 1784–1849: Politics, Power, and the Good Society* (Hamden, Conn.: Archon Books, 1983), 124–25.

36. For graphic descriptions, see Robin Bidwell, *Morocco under Colonial Rule* (London: Frank Cass, 1973). The organization of these sham battles, which permitted the "defeated" clan to retain its sense of honor, reflected a subjugation strategy far removed from the sanguinary scorched-earth conquest of Bugeaud; Marshal Hubert Lyautey invoked the slogan, "Force must be demonstrated in order to avoid its use." Ibid., 13.

37. Tekena N. Tamuno, *The Evolution of the Nigerian State: The Southern Phase, 1898–1914* (London: Longman, 1972), 53.

38. Quoted in Wilson, *The Imperial Experience,* 94.

39. R. Y. Jennings, *The Acquisition of Territory in International Law* (Manchester: Manchester University Press, 1963), 2.

40. Ibid., 53–54.

41. Louis, for example, argues that the Berlin Congress had far more narrow purposes than designing partition; in its own terms, this argument is persuasive, but the symbolic importance of the Berlin Congress in establishing a diplomatic framework for subsequent division of African territory remains central, and the key role of the doctrine of effective occupation, explicitly enunciated at Berlin, indisputable. See Wm. Roger Louis, "The Berlin Congo Conference," in Prosser Gifford

and Wm. Roger Louis, eds., *France and Britain in Africa: Imperial Rivalry and Colonial Rule* (New Haven: Yale University Press, 1971), 167–220.

42. Fyfe, *A History of Sierra Leone,* 410 and passim, for details of London's sporadic grants to Sierra Leone. Occasional small infusions were also needed for the Gambia and the Gold Coast in this period.

43. D. K. Fieldhouse, *Economics and Empire, 1830–1914* (London: Weidenfeld and Nicolson, 1973), 135–44.

44. As characterized by Colonial Minister Albert Decrais in the parliamentary debates on the proposed law in 1899; *Annales de la Chambre des Députés: Débats Parlementaires.* Sess. Extraordinaire 1899, 11 December, 378–84, 2454–62.

45. Roberts, *The History of French Colonial Policy,* 625–28.

46. Curiously, both the Belgian state and civil society subscribed to the view that large metropolitan sacrifices had been made in support of the prodigious colony; see the intriguing calculations by Jean Stengers, *Combien le Congo a-t-il coute à la Belgique* (Brussels: Academie Royale des Sciences d'Outre-Mer, Sci. Mor. et Pol., N.S., T. XI, fasc. 1, 1957).

47. Lisa Anderson, *The State and Social Transformation in Tunisia and Libya, 1830–1980* (Princeton: Princeton University Press, 1986); Stephen H. Longrigg, *A Short History of Eritrea* (Oxford: Clarendon Press, 1945). The charter company that governed Somalia from 1889 to 1904 required an annual Italian subsidy. By the close of World War I, 75 percent of Somalia's colonial revenue came from Italy. Robert L. Hess, *Italian Colonialism in Somalia* (Chicago: University of Chicago Press, 1966), 118 and passim.

48. Jules Harmand, *Domination et colonisation,* cited in Roberts, *The History of French Colonial Policy,* 29.

49. For the emergence and development of these ideas, see Philip D. Curtin, *The Image of Africa: British Ideas and Action, 1780–1850* (Madison: University of Wisconsin Press, 1964); William B. Cohen, *The French Encounter with Africans: White Response to Blacks, 1530–1880* (Bloomington: Indiana University Press, 1980).

50. G. N. Sanderson, "The European Partition of Africa: Origins and Dynamics," in Fage and Oliver, eds., *Cambridge History of Africa,* 6:156.

51. Cited in Louis, "The Berlin Congo Conference," 188.

52. See the engaging essay on this theme by Henri Brunschwig, "Anglophobia and French African Policy," in Gifford and Louis, eds., *France and Britain in Africa,* 3–34.

53. Sanderson, "The Nile Basin," 599–622.

54. See, among other sources, Robert I. Rotberg and Ali A. Mazrui, *Protest and Power in Black Africa* (New York: Oxford University Press, 1970); on the Rhodesian uprisings, T. O. Ranger, *Revolt in Southern Rhodesia, 1896–1897* (Evanston: Northwestern University Press, 1967); on the

Sierra Leone hut-tax war, Arthur Abraham, *Mende Government and Politics under Colonial Rule* (Freetown: Sierra Leone University Press, 1978).

55. I. M. Lewis, *The Modern History of Somaliland: From Nation to State* (New York: Frederick A. Praeger, 1965), 65–85.

56. Warburg, *The Sudan under Wingate.*

57. L. H. Gann and Peter Duignan, *The Rulers of Belgian Africa, 1884–1914* (Princeton: Princeton University Press, 1979), 100.

58. Wilson, *The Imperial Experience,* 113.

59. Timothy C. Weiskel, *French Colonial Rule and the Baule Peoples: Resistance and Collaboration, 1880–1911* (Oxford: Clarendon Press, 1980), 86.

60. G. Angoulvant, *La pacification de la Côte d'Ivoire* (Paris: Larose, 1916), quoted in Jean Suret-Canale, *Afrique noire: L'ère coloniale, 1900–1945* (Paris: Editions Sociales, 1964), 63.

61. James F. Searing, "Accommodation and Resistance: Chiefs, Muslim Leaders, and Politicians in Colonial Senegal, 1890–1934," Ph.D. diss., Princeton University, 1985, 127–51. Lisa Anderson, *The State and Social Transformation,* argues that the contrast between the relatively stable and integrated relationship between the state and civil society in contemporary Tunisia, as compared to Libya, is explicable in terms of the texture of the colonial pattern of rule.

62. Settler land appetites were insatiable; settlers not only demanded large and virtually free servings but also believed they were entitled to start-up costs. For example, in Algeria during this period settlers came into possession of 2,720,000 hectares of the best land, while Algerians were crowded into 7,812,100 hectares of often very marginal and arid holdings. Robert Aron, *Les origines de la guerre d'Algérie* (Paris: Fayard, 1982), 224.

63. Kenneth J. Perkins, *Qaids, Captains, and Colons: French Military Administration in the Colonial Maghrib, 1844–1934* (New York: Africana Publishing Company, 1981), 20. Their paternalism was clearly placed within a hegemonical ethos; as Perkins observes, "Circumstances in the 1830s and 1840s had given rise to the conviction that only superior force could induce the Algerians to conform to French designs for their welfare. . . . Many administrators shared the beliefs of two of their number that 'the Christian can remain just toward the Muslim only on the condition that he is stronger' and that 'the Arabs do not understand good will among those who direct them; they accept only force.'" Ibid., 151.

64. Flint, *Sir George Goldie.*

65. Fieldhouse, *Economics and Empire,* 364–82.

66. On the early phases of the British South Africa Company, see John S. Galbraith, *Crown and Charter: The Early Years of the British South*

Africa Company (Berkeley: University of California Press, 1974). For
evidence of the scale of BSAC stripping of assets and extortion of labor
from Africans within its reach, see Charles van Onselen, *Chibaro: African Mine Labour in Southern Rhodesia, 1900–1930* (London: Pluto
Press, 1976).

67. The most detailed study of the concessionary regime is Robert Harms,
    "Abir: The Rise and Fall of a Rubber Empire," M.A. diss., University of
    Wisconsin—Madison, 1973.

68. Samir Amin and Catherine Coquery-Vidrovitch, *Histoire économique
    du Congo 1880–1968* (Paris: Editions Anthropos, 1969), 40–51.

69. Yarisse Zoctizoum, *Histoire de la Centrafrique: Violence du développe-
    ment, domination et inégalités* (Paris: L'Harmattan, 1983), 1:63.

70. On this issue, see Cynthia H. Enloe, *Ethnic Soldiers: State Security in
    Divided Societies* (Athens: University of Georgia Press, 1980).

71. Abraham, *Mende Government and Politics,* 119.

72. Lt. Col. Charles Mangin, *La Force Noire* (Paris: Librairie Hachette,
    1910), 233–34.

73. On the early years of the Force Publique, see Bryant P. Shaw, *"Force
    Publique, Force Unique:* The Military in the Belgian Congo, 1914–
    1939," Ph.D. diss., University of Wisconsin—Madison, 1984; Deuxième
    Section de l'Etat-Major de la Force Publique, *La Force Publique de sa
    naissance à 1914* (Brussels: Académie Royale des Sciences d'Outre-
    Mer, Sci. Mor. et Pol., T. XXVII, 1952); Gann and Duignan, *The Rulers of
    Belgian Africa, 1884–1914,* 52–83.

74. W. G. Clarence-Smith, "Capital Accumulation and Class Formation in
    Angola," in Birmingham and Martin, eds., *History of Central Africa,*
    2:172–73.

75. Hess, *Italian Colonialism,* 109–10.

76. Gann and Duignan, *The Rulers of Belgian Africa,* 100.

77. I. F. Nicholson, *The Administration of Nigeria, 1900–1960: Men, Meth-
    ods, and Myths* (Oxford: Clarendon Press, 1969); Michael Crowder,
    West Africa under Colonial Rule (London: Hutchinson, 1968), 198–216.

78. Amin and Coquery-Vidrovitch, *Histoire économique du Congo,* 40–51.

79. M. W. Daly, *British Administration and the Northern Sudan, 1917–
    1924: The Governor-Generalship of Sir Lee Stack in the Sudan* (Leiden:
    Nederlands Institut voor het Nabije Oosten, 1980), 17.

80. Amin and Coquery-Vidrovitch, *Histoire économique du Congo,* 26.

81. Captain S. D. Vallier, *L'organisation militaire du Congo français* (Paris:
    Henri Charles Laranzelles, 1908), cited in Pierre Philippe Rey, *Colo-
    nialisme, néo-colonialisme et transition au capitalisme: Exemple de la
    "Comilog" au Congo-Brazzaville* (Paris: François Maspero, 1971), 323–
    24.

82. The unusual Bugandan pattern is the object of an especially rich litera-
    ture; see especially D. Anthony Low and R. Cranford Pratt, *Buganda*

and British Overrule (London: Oxford University Press, 1960); Low, *Religion and Society in Buganda, 1875–1900* (Kampala: East African Institute of Social Research, 1957); David Apter, *The Political Kingdom in Uganda* (Princeton: Princeton University Press, 1961); Martin Southwold, *Bureaucracy and Chiefship in Buganda* (Kampala: East African Institute of Social Research, 1961); C. C. Wrigley, "The Christian Revolution in Buganda," *Comparative Studies in Society and History* 2, no. 1 (1959): 33–48; John A. Rowe, "Revolution in Buganda, 1856–1900, Part 1," Ph.D. diss., University of Wisconsin, 1966; Lloyd A. Fallers, ed., *The King's Men* (London: Oxford University Press, 1964); Crawford Young, "Buganda," in René Lemarchand, ed., *African Kingships in Perspective: Political Change and Modernization in Monarchical Settings* (London: Frank Cass, 1977), 193–235; Semaula Kiwanuku, *A History of Buganda from the Foundation of the Kingdom to 1900* (New York: Africana Publishing Corporation, 1972).

83. Abdoulaye-Bara Diop, *La société wolof: Tradition et changement: Les systèmes d'inégalité et de domination* (Paris: Editions Karthala, 1981); Searing, "Accommodation and Resistance."

84. Quoted in Ruth Slade, *King Leopold's Congo* (New York: Oxford University Press, 1962), 150.

85. T. O. Beidelman, *Colonial Evangelism: A Socio-Historical Study of an East African Mission at the Grassroots* (Bloomington: Indiana University Press, 1982), 6.

86. David D. Laitin, *Hegemony and Culture: Politics and Religious Change among the Yoruba* (Chicago: Chicago University Press, 1986).

87. John V. Taylor, *The Growth of the Church in Buganda* (London: SCM Press, 1958), provides evidence of the extraordinary speed of Christian conversion in the 1890s.

88. Cited in Beidelman, *Colonial Evangelism,* 128.

89. See Barbara A. Yates, "The Missions and Educational Development in Belgian Africa, 1876–1908," Ph.D. diss., Columbia University, 1967.

90. Shlomo Avineri, *Hegel's Theory of the Modern State* (Cambridge University Press, 1973), 147.

91. The central role of Islam as an ideological shelter and basis for resistance in West Africa is given convincing development in the fine study by Barry, *La Sénégambie du XVe au XIXe siècle.*

92. Warburg, *The Sudan under Wingate,* 95.

93. For some detail, see J. S. Trimingham, *Islam in the Sudan* (New York: Barnes and Noble, 1949). One of the two leading Khatmiyya figures in the early years of British rule became a CBE, the other a KCMG and KCVO.

94. Cited in Daly, *British Administration and the Northern Sudan,* 17.

95. Paul Marty, *Etudes sur l'Islam au Sénégal* (Paris: Ernest Leroux, 1917), 1:10.

96. For exhaustive detail on Catholic mission relations with the colonial administration during this period, see Joseph-Roger de Benoist, *Eglise et pouvoir colonial au Soudan Français: Administrateurs et missionaires dans la Boucle du Niger, 1885–1945* (Paris: Editions Karthala, 1987).

97. Cited in Marty, *Etudes sur l'Islam au Sénégal,* 208. See also Christian Coulon, *Le marabout et le prince: Islam et pouvoir au Sénégal* (Paris: Editions A. Pedone, 1981); Lucy C. Behrman, *Muslim Brotherhoods and Politics in Senegal* (Cambridge: Harvard University Press, 1970); Donal B. Cruise O'Brien, *The Mourides of Senegal* (Oxford: Clarendon Press, 1971).

98. Finn Fuglestad, *A History of Niger, 1850–1960* (Cambridge: Cambridge University Press, 1983), provides some detail.

99. On the rigorous efforts to encapsulate and isolate the small Muslim communities in east central Zaire that took root only a few years before colonial penetration, see Crawford Young, "Islam in the Congo," in William Kritzeck and William Lewis, eds., *Islam in Africa* (New York: Van Nostrand, 1970), 250–69.

100. The most thorough study is by the distinguished Belgian colonial historian Jean Stengers, *Belgique et Congo: Elaboration de la Charte Coloniale* (Brussels: La Renaissance du Livre, 1963).

101. For a brief overview of the development of this form, see Sir Alan Burns, *In Defence of Colonies* (London: George Allen and Unwin, 1957), 54–71; see also Lord Hailey, *An African Survey,* rev. ed. (London: Oxford University Press, 1957).

102. Napolean III created a Ministry of Algeria and Colonies in 1858, but this ephemeral ministry was abolished in 1860.

103. Girardet, *L'idée coloniale en France,* 83.

104. Suret-Canale, *Afrique noire,* 93–95.

105. Martin Chanock, *Law, Custom, and Social Order: The Colonial Experience in Malawi and Zambia* (Cambridge: Cambridge University Press, 1985), 47.

106. Fuglestad, *A History of Niger,* 81.

107. ANS, 17 G 55 (17), Indigénat, contains a legislative history of the code and correspondence from the early 1920s concerning its possible reform.

108. This is the central argument of Betts, *Tricouleur.*

109. See for example, Maurice Delafosse, *Haut-Sénégal-Niger* (Paris: G.-P. Maisonneuve et Larose, 1972, first published 1912), or Marty, *Etudes sur l'Islam.*

110. Examples include Georges Vanderkerken, *Les sociétés bantus du Congo Belge* (Brussels: Etablissements Emile Bruylant, 1920); E. Torday and T. A. Joyce, *Notes ethnographiques sur les populations habitant les bassins du Kasai et du Kwango Oriental* (Brussels: Ministry of Colonies, 1922).

111. Sir Harry Johnston, who served in Uganda and Nyasaland, wrote an early compendium on Uganda, *The Uganda Protectorate* (London: Hutchinson, 1904), 2 vols.

112. Samuel Johnson, *A History of the Yorubas from the Earliest Times to the Beginning of the British Protectorate,* ed. O. Johnson (Lagos: CMS [Nigeria] Bookshops, 1956, first published 1897); Sir Apolo Kagwa, *The Customs of the Baganda,* ed. Mary Mandelbaum Edel, trans. Ernest Kalibala (New York: Columbia University Press, 1934).

113. For detail on the scope of these requisitions and their impact, see Fuglestad, *A History of Niger;* Stephen Baier, *An Economic History of Central Niger* (Oxford: Clarendon Press, 1981).

114. Anderson makes this argument central to her interpretation of the character of the postcolonial Tunisian state in *The State and Social Transformation in Tunisia and Libya.*

115. Adele Smith Simmons, *Modern Mauritius: The Politics of Decolonization* (Bloomington: Indiana University Press, 1982).

116. Anne Phillips, *The Enigma of Colonialism: British Policy in West Africa* (Bloomington: Indiana University Press, 1989), 10–14 and passim.

117. Quoted in C. C. Wrigley, "Kenya: The Patterns of Economic Life, 1902–1945," in Vincent Harlow and E. M. Chilver, eds., *History of East Africa* (Oxford: Clarendon Press, 1965), 2:213.

118. Shula Marks, "Southern and Central Africa, 1886–1910," in Oliver and Sanderson, eds., *Cambridge History of Africa,* 6:491.

119. Roberts, *The History of French Colonial Policy,* 83–88.

120. I am indebted to Ammar Bouhouche for stressing in his critical comments on my manuscript the importance of the intra-European conflicts in the early days, which perhaps peaked during the wave of anti-Semitism that swept France in the 1890s and culminated in the "Dreyfuss affair."

121. For thorough detail on the development of the Creole community and its Freetown political role in the nineteenth century, see Fyfe, *A History of Sierra Leone.*

122. G. Wesley Johnson, *The Emergence of Black Politics in Senegal: The Struggle for Power in the Four Communes, 1900–1920* (Stanford: Stanford University Press, 1971); Searing, "Accommodation and Resistance." Encyclopedic detail is available in the four-thousand-page dissertation by Thiam, "Evolution politique du Sénégal."

123. For detailed discussion, see Charles-André Julien, *Histoire de l'Algérie contemporaine,* 2d ed. (Paris: Presses Universitaires de France, 1979).

124. William B. Cohen, *Rulers of Empire: The French Colonial Service in Africa* (Stanford: Hoover Institution Press, 1971), 57–83.

125. Julien, *Histoire de l'Algérie contemporaine,* 2d ed., 1:77–98.

126. For evidence, see Baier, *An Economic History of Central Niger,* 23–24. In Abomey and some surrounding states, the emergence of palm-oil

exports in the nineteenth century produced a set of slave-worked royal plantations for its production; Patrick Manning, *Slavery, Colonialism, and Economic Growth in Dahomey, 1640–1960* (Cambridge: Cambridge University Press, 1982), 54–55.

127. Slade, *King Leopold's Congo,* 102–03.
128. Robert L. Tignor, *Modernization and British Colonial Rule in Egypt, 1882–1914* (Princeton: Princeton University Press, 1966), 48–93.
129. Anderson, *The State and Social Transformation,* 39–42.
130. Warburg, *The Sudan under Wingate,* 52–58.
131. Fyfe, *A History of Sierra Leone,* 404.
132. This is the basis for the theory of an "African mode of production," once advanced by Catherine Coquery-Vidrovitch but since abandoned; see Bogumil Jewsiewicki and J. Letourneau, eds., *Mode of Production: The Challenge of Africa* (Ste. Foy, Quebec: SAFI, 1985).
133. Indeed, Heussler argues that in the British case the source of recruitment for the colonial service as it became professionalized yielded officers with Oxbridge generalist backgrounds and upper-class, even aristocratic, antecedents. For the typical new recruit, "modern industrialisation and urbanisation were anathema to him, as were the *nouveaux riches* who epitomized these trends. He cared little for money as such; he preferred the country to the city, and was usually happy in an exclusively male society." Building capitalism would be too vulgar an enterprise to engage the energies of such scions of the squirearchy. Robert Heussler, *Yesterday's Rulers* (Syracuse, N.Y.: Syracuse University Press, 1963), 104. Furse, the principal recruiting officer for most of the colonial era, makes clear in his autobiographical reflections the criteria he used. He relied primarily on his personal intuition about character: confidence, cheerfulness, active bodily habits, a passion for physical games, presence, discipline. "For natives," writes Furse, "have exceptional powers of intuitive operation. Like children, they instinctively 'size up' the man they are dealing with; and this they do very quickly, and generally with accuracy. White officers of the right stamp win their confidence to a remarkable extent; but the best technical advice is thrown away if they do not regard the giver of it as . . . 'a chief in his own country.'" Major Sir Ralph Furse, *Aucuparius: Recollections of a Recruiting Officer* (London: Oxford University Press, 1962), 142. Mastery of the principles of a liberal economy was not among the requisite traits. The French colonial service was professionalized after World War I. The entrants were predominantly from an upper-middle-class background, schooled to be sure in *mise en valeur* doctrines but above all pledged, as the oath of entry to the colonial school phrased it, to devote their lives "to the service of the Empire, for the grandeur of France, and the development of our civilisation." Cohen, *Rulers of Empire,* 148. The Belgian colonial service came closest to pursuing a con-

scious mandate to develop capitalism, partly through the interest of its agents; with an early mandatory retirement age of 55, many wanted to position themselves for postretirement employment by one of the large colonial corporations.

134. Rey, *Colonialisme, néo-colonialisme et transition au capitalisme*, 322.

135. Weiskel, *French Colonial Rule*, 184.

136. Abraham, *Mende Government and Politics*, 133–34. His forebodings were indeed correct; imposition of this tax engulfed Sierra Leone in a wave of rebellion, beginning with Bai Bureh in Temneland, then sweeping much of the Mende zone, which took far more than the Frontier Police to repress.

137. Searing, "Accommodation and Resistance," 243.

138. Suret-Canale describes the process well: "The *cercle* commandant places upon the chiefs responsibility for implementing . . . administrative exactions: so much the worse if the task is impossible. It is the chief who will go to prison or be stripped of office, if the tax . . . is not collected, if the road is poorly maintained, if food demanded is not furnished . . . if recruits for forced labor or the army are not supplied. He must fend for himself, while the administrator keeps a clean conscience regarding the means utilized. The chief may dirty his hands if necessary; the commandant prefers to know nothing about it." Suret-Canale, *Afrique noire*, 410.

139. Christian Roche, *Histoire de la Casamance: Conquête et résistance, 1850–1920* (Paris: Karthala, 1985, first published 1976), 356. This work provides a comprehensive account of the resistance encountered by the French administration in lower Casamance, especially among the Diola.

140. Fuglestad, *A History of Niger*, 91.

141. Rey, *Colonialisme, néo-colonialisme et transition au capitalisme*, 329–41.

142. A. J. Wauters, *L'Etat Indépendant du Congo* (Brussels: Librairie Falk Fils, 1899), 348.

143. Lonsdale, "The European Scramble," 756.

144. Babacar Fall, "Le travail forcé en Afrique Occidentale Française, 1900–1946: Cas du Sénégal, de la Guinée et du Soudan," thèse de doctorat du 3e cycle, University of Dakar, 1984, 63–67.

145. Mohammed Mbodj, "Un exemple d'économie coloniale: Le Sine-Saloum (Senegal) de 1887 à 1940: Cultures arachidières et mutations sociales," thèse de doctorat d'Etat, Université de Paris VII, 1978, 205.

146. For detail, see Baier, *An Economic History of Central Niger*, 82–103.

147. Patrick Manning, *Slavery, Colonialism, and Economic Growth in Dahomey, 1640–1980* (Cambridge: Cambridge University Press, 1982), 171.

148. For evidence, see Barry, *La Sénégambie;* Baier, *An Economic History of Central Niger.*

149. Diouf, "Le Kayoor," 360–96; Mbodj, "Un exemple de l'économie coloniale," 260–61; Coulon, *Le marabout et le prince,* 54–72.
150. C. C. Wrigley, *Crops and Wealth in Uganda* (Kampala: East African Institute of Social Research, 1959), 14–15. See also the excellent analysis of the imposition of a cotton economy by the colonial state in Joan Vincent, *Teso in Transformation: The Political Economy of Peasant and Class in Eastern Africa* (Berkeley: University of California Press, 1982).
151. Kanya-Forstner, *The Conquest of the Western Sudan,* 59–84.
152. Headrick, *The Tools of Empire,* 180–90.
153. René J. Cornet, *La bataille du rail* (Brussels: Editions L. Cuypers, 1947).
154. Pierre Joye and Rosina Lewin, *Les trusts au Congo* (Brussels: Société Populaire d'Editions, 1961), 295.
155. France, Gouvernement Général de l'Afrique Occidentale Française, *Budget Général Exercise 1914,* 6.
156. Tignor, *Modernization and British Colonial Rule in Egypt,* 214–48.
157. Neal Ascherson, *The King Incorporated* (London: George Allen and Unwin, 1963), 241. Leopold's personal take was estimated by a contemporary source at 2.9 million pounds, a sum usefully compared to the annual Congo budget at the time of about 1.4 million pounds.
158. Warburg, *The Sudan under Wingate,* 51.
159. Richard L. Roberts, *Warriors, Merchants, and Slaves: The State and the Economy in the Middle Niger Valley, 1700–1914* (Stanford: Stanford University Press, 1987), 174.
160. Ibid., 177.
161. Ibid., 182.
162. Frederick Cooper, *From Slaves to Squatters: Plantation Labor and Agriculture in Zanzibar and Coastal Kenya, 1890–1925* (New Haven: Yale University Press, 1980), 2–3.
163. John M. Carlund, "Public Expenditure and Development in a Crown Colony: The Colonial Office, Sir Walter Egerton, and Southern Nigeria, 1900–1912," *Albion* 112 (Winter 1980): 380.
164. Bruce Berman, "Structure and Process in the Bureaucratic States of Colonial Africa," *Development and Change* 11 (April 1984): 161–63.
165. B. R. Tomlinson, *The Political Economy of the Raj, 1914–1947: The Economics of Decolonization in India* (London: Macmillan, 1979).

Chapter 5: The Colonial State Institutionalized

1. Paul Salkin, *L'Afrique Centrale dans cent ans* (Paris: Payot, 1926).
2. Jacques Berque, *French North Africa. The Maghrib Between Two World Wars* (New York: Frederick A. Praeger, 1962), 70.
3. Bruce Marshall, *The French Colonial Myth and Constitution-Making in the Fourth Republic* (New Haven: Yale University Press, 1973), 45.

4. Ronald Robinson and John Gallagher, *Africa and the Victorians: The Climax of Imperialism* (New York: St. Martin's Press, 1961), launched the thesis that the seizure of Egypt by Britain was the catalytic event whose final consequence was the dialectic of partition.

5. Berque, *French North Africa,* 99–100.

6. B. R. Tomlinson, *The Political Economy of the Raj, 1914–1947: The Economics of Decolonization in India* (London: Macmillan, 1979), 106–07. Although Britain paid a good part of the charges, the Indian colonial state was forced to absorb a significant fraction of the costs of the imperial war effort.

7. D. C. Dorward, "British West Africa and Liberia," in A. D. Roberts, ed., *Cambridge History of Africa* (Cambridge: Cambridge University Press, 1986), 7:424.

8. John McCracken, "British Central Africa," and Andrew Roberts, "East Africa," in ibid., 624, 667.

9. Leland Conley Barrows, "L'influence des conquêtes algériennes et coloniales sur l'armée française, 1830–1919: Une mise au point préliminaire, *Le Mois en Afrique* 16 (December 1981–January 1982): 109.

10. Jean Suret-Canale, *Afrique Noire: L'ère coloniale, 1900–1945* (Paris: Editions Sociales, 1964), 176–82.

11. Ibid.

12. Finn Fuglestad, *A History of Niger, 1850–1960* (Cambridge: Cambridge University Press, 1983), 100–01.

13. Joseph-Roger de Benoist, *Eglise et pouvoir colonial au Soudan francais: Administrateurs et missionnaires dans la Boucle du Niger (1885–1945)* (Paris: Karthala, 1987), 245.

14. Charles-Robert Ageron, *Les algériens musulmans et la France (1817–1919)* (Paris: Presses Universitaires de France, 1968), 2:1159.

15. Charles-Robert Ageron, *Histoire de l'Algérie contemporaine,* 2d ed. (Paris: Presses Universitaires de France, 1979), 2:254–66. Among Algerian military personnel, 25,711 were killed and 72,035 wounded.

16. Wilson testified in 1920 to the Senate Committee on Foreign Relations: "When I gave utterance to those words [that all nations had a right to self-determination], I said them without the knowledge that nationalities existed, which are coming to us day after day. . . . You do not know and cannot appreciate the anxieties that I have experienced as a result of many millions of people having their hopes raised by what I have said." Quoted in Alfred Cobban, *The Nation State and National Self-Determination* (New York: Thomas Y. Crowell, 1970), 64–65.

17. Maynard W. Swanson, "South-West Africa in Trust, 1915–1939," in Prosser Gifford and Wm. Roger Louis, eds., *Britain and Germany in Africa: Imperial Rivalry and Colonial Rule* (New Haven: Yale University Press, 1967), 640.

18. Quoted in B. T. G. Chidzero, *Tanganyika and International Trusteeship* (London: Oxford University Press, 1961), 2.

19. In the words of a chronicler of the colonial congresses in Belgium, held in 1920, 1926, 1930, and 1935 during the interwar period, their labors were devoted to "humanitarian and civilizing problems, economic questions, and administrative methods." P. Coppens, "Les Congrès Coloniaux Nationaux," in Académie Royale des Sciences d'Outre Mer, *Livre Blanc: Apport scientifique de la Belgique au développement de l'Afrique centrale* (Brussels: 1962), 1:4.

20. William B. Cohen, *Rulers of Empire: The French Colonial Service in Africa* (Stanford: Hoover Institution, 1971), 84–107.

21. Major Sir Ralph Furse, *Aucuparius: Recollections of a Recruiting Officer* (London: Oxford University Press, 1962), 221.

22. Robert Heussler, *Yesterday's Rulers,* (Syracuse, N.Y.: Syracuse University Press, 1963), 50.

23. de Benoist, *Eglise et pouvoir colonial,* 355.

24. A. H. M. Kirk-Greene, "The Thin White Line: The Size of the British Colonial Service in Africa," *African Affairs* 79 (January 1980): 42, 44.

25. Hubert Deschamps, "French Policy in Africa between the World Wars," in Prosser Gifford and Wm. Roger Louis, eds., *France and Britain in Africa: Imperial Rivalry and Colonial Rule* (New Haven: Yale University Press, 1971), 569.

26. Jeremy White, *Central Administration in Nigeria, 1914–1948,* (Dublin: Irish University Press, 1981), 79.

27. Lord Hailey, *Native Administration in the British African Territories* (London: His Majesty's Stationery Office, 1950), 1:212.

28. Or, as Karen Fields puts it, the formalization of "custom"—that "museum display we gaze at in much ethnographic writing"—permitted the colonial state to congeal politics as administration; *Revival and Rebellion in Colonial Central Africa* (Princeton: Princeton University Press, 1985), 64–65.

29. For evidence of the progressive transformation of chiefs in East Africa into de facto civil servants, see Audrey Richards, ed., *East African Chiefs: A Study of Political Development in Some Uganda and Tanganyika Tribes* (London: Faber and Faber, 1959).

30. Suret-Canale, *Afrique Noire,* 407.

31. Robin Bidwell, *Morocco under Colonial Rule* (London: Frank Cass, 1973), 16. Lyautey added that the very essence of the protectorate concept was "control," as opposed to the "direct administration" formula.

32. Lisa Anderson, *The State and Social Transformation in Tunisia and Libya, 1830–1980* (Princeton: Princeton University Press, 1986). Anderson argues that the particular texture to colonial hegemony in Tunisia, beyond its simple role of domination, supported the crystallization

of a civil society whose emergence dates from Ottoman times, which helps explain the relative stability of the postcolonial state and society.

33. Fuglestad, *A History of Niger,* 115.

34. For exhaustive detail, see Charles-André Julien, *Histoire de l'Algérie contemporaine* (Paris: Presses Universitaires de France, 1979, first published 1964), 2 vols. For a more succinct argument, see Ian Lusstick, *State-Building Failure in British Ireland and French Algeria* (Berkeley: Institute of International Studies, University of California at Berkeley, 1985).

35. Ministry of Colonies, Kingdom of Belgium, *Recueil à l'usage des fonctionnaires et des agents du Service territorial au Congo Belge,* 5th ed. (Brussels: M. Weissenbruch, 1930), 8–9.

36. For valuable monographs capturing the local dynamic of the colonial state in interaction with African kingdoms subjected to its rule, see Jan Vansina, *The Children of Woot: A History of the Kuba Peoples* (Madison: University of Wisconsin Press, 1978); Catharine Newbury, *The Cohesion of Oppression* (New York: Columbia University Press, 1989); Edouard Bustin, *Lunda under Belgian Rule: The Politics of Ethnicity* (Cambridge: Harvard University Press, 1975).

37. The basic public-law text supplying an exegesis of this legislation is J. Magotte, *Les circonscriptions indigènes* (La Louvière: Imprimerie Louvieroise, n.d. (1952).

38. Roger Anstey, *King Leopold's Legacy* (London: Oxford University Press, 1966), 68.

39. Andrew Roberts, "Portuguese Africa," in Roberts, ed., *The Cambridge History of Africa,* 7:501.

40. A. James Gregor, *The Ideology of Fascism: The Rationale of Totalitarianism* (New York: Free Press, 1969), 172; see also Denis Mack Smith, *Italy: Modern History* (Ann Arbor: University of Michigan Press, 1959).

41. Anderson, *The State and Social Transformation,* 207–08.

42. Stephen H. Longrigg, *A Short History of Eritrea* (Westport, Conn.: Greenwood Publishers, 1954, first published 1945), 132.

43. Tony Hodges, *Western Sahara: The Roots of a Desert War* (Westport, Conn.: Lawrence Hill, 1983), 55–67.

44. *Recueil à l'usage des fonctionnaires,* 119–20. Like the French indigénat code, this central provision is reinforced by an extended listing of other acts of *lèse-majesté* that make the subject liable to summary punishment: defacing a symbol of the state (flag-burning and related acts); circulating rumors; refusal to furnish information; impeding state transport; failure to respond to a summons, among other infractions.

45. Ibid., 134–35.

46. Ibid., 141.

47. Ibid.

48. ANS, 17 G 55 (17), Indigénat, Letter of Lieutenant Governor of Guinea to AOF Governor-General, 10 February 1925.
49. ANS, 17 G 97 (17), Réforme de l'indigénat. Documentation fourni par Labouret en prévision d'une campagne contre l'indigénat. Letter from Lieutenant Governor, Ivory Coast, to AOF Governor-General, 13 April 1937.
50. de Benoist, *Eglise et pouvoir colonial,* 253.
51. *Recueil à l'usage des fonctionnaires,* 57–58.
52. For extensive detail, see de Benoist, *Eglise et pouvoir colonial,* 369–462. This episode illustrated other kinds of divisions within the colonial bureaucracy, which seem of particular intensity in the French case. Governor-General Jules Brévié, obsessed with the risk of a major uprising, denounced Governor François Reste of the Ivory Coast in a 16 November 1934 dispatch to the minister of colonies as culpable of an "inconceivable submission" to the Catholic missions. A local administrator, Pierre Adam, wrote a coded letter to Brévié in which he denounced Reste as a "salaud," a "dangerous man" who had become "mentally unstable." The missions believed themselves victims of Freemason conspiracy, grounded in fabricated allegations of imminent uprising. Henri Carbou, an inspector at Ougadougou, wrote a private letter to the governor in 1936 claiming that the White Fathers "are the masters. Myself, I can do nothing to defend the Mossi; *I am afraid of the Mission* (I underline this stupefying confession). I can not speak freely, for the Fathers have established an espionage system . . . by means of their catechumens." ANS, 17 G 249, Evénement de Dedougou, Situation politique en Côte d'Ivoire, 1934–1938.
53. Bruce Fetter, "L'Union Minière du Haut-Katanga, 1920–1940: La naissance d'une sous-culture totalitaire," *Cahiers du CEDAF* 6 (1973): 38.
54. Mary Douglas, *The Lele of the Kasai* (London: Oxford University Press, 1963), 259. Her remarks are generally applicable in the Belgian Congo, where the triple alliance was particularly salient.
55. I am grateful to Catherine Boone for the citation, and the observation in her comments on an earlier paper on this subject.
56. White, *Central Administration in Nigeria,* 231.
57. Wolfe W. Schmokel, *Dream of Empire: German Colonialism, 1919–1945* (New Haven: Yale University Press, 1964).
58. Julien, *Histoire de l'Algérie contemporaine,* 2:348–61.
59. I am indebted to Valerie Mitchell for sharing some of the evidence and conclusions in her 1992 Howard University dissertation on the Garvey impact on Senegal.
60. ANS, 17 G 53 (17), Propagande révolutionnaire et communiste, Circular of Governor-General to Lieutenant Governors concerning the decree of 27 March regulating the press, 8 May 1928.

61. In a few cases, another supervising ministry; for example, the Foreign Office for Sudan, the Foreign Ministry for Tunisia and Morocco, the Interior Ministry for Algeria. "Colonial ministry" is employed generically to refer to all metropolitan government departments responsible for monitoring the exercise of colonial authority.

62. Bernard Lanne, "Le Tchad pendant la Guerre (1939–1945)," in Charles-Robert Ageron, ed., *Les chemins de la décolonisation de l'empire française, 1936–1956* (Paris: Editions du CNRS, 1986), 440.

63. For a valuable overview of the African colonial governors, see L. H. Gann and Peter Duignan, eds., *African Proconsuls: European Governors in Africa* (New York: Free Press, 1978).

64. E. A. Brett, *Colonialism and Underdevelopment in East Africa: The Politics of "Economic Change," 1919–1939* (London: Heinemann, 1973), 60. One should add that some 170 members asked at least one question.

65. Hailey, *Native Administration,* 1:211.

66. For detailed recapitulation of the Blum-Violette proposals and other interwar reform efforts, see the admirable study by Julien, *Histoire de l'Algérie contemporaine,* 2.

67. Hailey, *Native Administration,* 5:79.

68. Tomlinson, *The Political Economy of the Raj,* 111.

69. Raoul Girardet, *L'idée coloniale en France de 1871 à 1962* (Paris: La Table Ronde, 1972), 112.

70. *Congo, 1885–1960: Positions socialistes* (Brussels: Institut Vandervelde, n.d. [1961?]).

71. Cited in James S. Coleman, *Nigeria: Background to Nationalism* (Berkeley: University of California Press, 1958), 156.

72. Ibid.

73. Mauritius represents an interesting special case. By the interwar period the colonial state faced not only a clamorous Franco-Mauritian settler group but also articulate Afro-Mauritians (Creoles) and an emergent Indo-Mauritian professional and political class. The elected Port Louis Urban Council was a major battleground, and the Legislative Council much less an administrative creature than elsewhere in interwar Africa. See Adele Smith Simmons, *Modern Mauritius: The Politics of Decolonization* (Bloomington: Indiana University Press, 1982).

74. For an elaboration of the "good government" notion, see J. M. Lee, *Colonial Development and Good Government* (Oxford: Clarendon Press, 1967).

75. Brett, *Colonialism and Underdevelopment,* 50–51.

76. Sir F. D. Lugard, *The Dual Mandate in British Tropical Africa* (Edinburgh: Blackwood, 1922), 5.

77. Jorge Ameal, quoted in James Duffy, *Portuguese Africa* (Cambridge: Harvard University Press, 1959), 270.

78. Louis Franck, *Le Congo Belge* (Brussels: La Renaissance du Livre, 1930), 1:282. On this point, see the insightful analysis of Michael G. Schatzberg, *The Dialectics of Oppression in Zaire* (Bloomington: Indiana University Press, 1988), 84–88.

79. Albert Sarraut, *Grandeur et servitude coloniales,* cited in Bruce Marshall, *The French Colonial Myth and Constitution-Making in the Fourth Republic* (New Haven: Yale University Press, 1973), 46.

80. The mise en valeur theme runs through his magnum opus, *Le Congo Belge.*

81. Julien, *Histoire de l'Algérie contemporaine,* 2:412–18.

82. Cited in Lord Hailey, *An African Survey: A Study of Problems Arising in Africa South of the Sahara,* rev. ed. (London: Oxford University Press, 1957), 190.

83. Duffy, *Portuguese Africa,* 270.

84. Ibid.

85. Smith, *Italy,* 448, 461.

86. Grover Clark, *The Balance Sheets of Imperialism* (New York: Columbia University Press, 1936).

87. Constant Southworth, *The French Colonial Venture* (New York: Arno Press, 1977, first published 1931).

88. Jacques Marseille, *Empire colonial et capitalisme français: Histoire d'un divorce* (Paris: A. Michel, 1984).

89. Coleman, *Nigeria,* 126.

90. Jan Vansina, "Deep-Down Time: Political Tradition in Central Africa," *History in Africa* 16 (1989): 344.

91. Julien, *Histoire de l'Algérie contemporaine,* 2:201–23.

92. Ralph A. Austen and Rita Hendricks, "Equatorial Africa under Colonial Rule," in David Birmingham and Phyllis M. Martin, eds., *History of Central Africa* (London: Longman, 1983), 2:64.

93. Stephen H. Roberts, *The History of French Colonial Policy, 1870–1925* (London: P. S. King, 1925), 311.

94. George Bennett, "Settlers and Politics in Kenya," in Vincent Harlow and E. M. Chilver, eds., *History of East Africa* (Oxford: Clarendon Press, 1965), 295–96.

95. The treatment of these issues by Coleman, *Nigeria,* 113–66, remains of exemplary clarity and incisiveness.

96. According to Joseph-Roger de Benoist, in Ageron, ed., *Les chemins de la décolonisation,* 556.

97. Brian Weinstein, "Governor-General Félix Eboué (1884–1944)," in Gann and Duignan, eds., *African Proconsuls,* 157–84.

98. Aimée Houemavo, "La politique économique coloniale au Dahomey (entre les deux guerres) et ses implications sociales," mémoire de maitrise, Département d'Histoire, Faculté des Lettres et Sciences Humaines, Université de Dakar, 1984, 52–53.

99. Peter Duignan, "Sir Robert Coryndon (1970–1925)," in Gann and Duignan, eds., *African Proconsuls,* 312–52.

100. Vali Jamal, "Taxation and Inequality in Uganda, 1900–1964," *Journal of Economic History* 38 (June 1978): 418–38.

101. E. H. Winter, *Bwamba Economy: The Development of a Primitive Subsistence Economy in Uganda* (Kampala: East African Institute of Social Research, 1955), 34–36.

102. For these figures, and many others, see Julien, *Histoire de l'Algérie contemporaine,* 2 and passim.

103. Houemavo, "La politique économique coloniale," 68.

104. Hailey, *An African Survey,* 1363–64.

105. Babacar Fall, "Le travail forcé au Sénégal, 1900–1946," memoire de maitrise, Département d'Histoire, Faculté des Lettres et Sciences Humaines, Université de Dakar, 1977, 98.

106. Ibid., 99.

107. Babacar Fall provides a comprehensive catalogue of the ways and means of financing colonial infrastructure through forced labor in his excellent dissertation, "Le travail forcé en Afrique Occidentale Française, 1900–1946," thèse de doctorat de 3e cycle, Département d'Histoire, Faculté des Lettres et Sciences Humaines, Université de Dakar, 1984.

108. René Lemarchand, "The Politics of Sara Ethnicity: A Note on the Origins of the Civil War in Chad," *Cahiers d'Etudes Africaines* 20, no. 4 (1980): 453–54.

109. Bakonzi Agayo, "The Gold Mines of Kilo-Moto in Northeastern Zaire, 1905–1960," Ph.D. diss., University of Wisconsin—Madison, 1982.

110. Jean-Philippe Peemans, "Capital Accumulation in the Congo under Colonialism: The Role of the State," in L. H. Gann and Peter Duignan, eds., *Colonialism in Africa, 1870–1960* (Cambridge: Cambridge University Press, 1975), 4:176.

111. Ibid., 180.

112. Crawford Young, *Politics in the Congo: Decolonization and Independence* (Princeton: Princeton University Press, 1965), 206.

113. Cited in ibid., 16. Lippens added later that same year that every official should be "penetrated with the idea that his reason for existence is to favor and develop our occupation and that this duty consists of supporting every enterprise." (Ibid.)

114. Cited in Duffy, *Portuguese Africa,* 318.

115. W. C. Clarence-Smith, *Slaves, Peasants, and Capitalists in Southern Angola, 1840–1926* (Cambridge: Cambridge University Press, 1979).

116. Peemans, "Capital Accumulation in the Congo," 175.

117. Mulambu Muvulya, "Le régime des cultures obligatoires et le radicalisme rural au Zaire (1917–1960)," thèse de doctorat, Université Libre de Bruxelles, 1974, 96.

118. Ibid., 102.
119. Goran Hyden, *Beyond Ujamaa in Tanzania: Underdevelopment and an Uncaptured Peasantry* (Berkeley: University of California Press, 1980).
120. Jack Wayne, "Structural Contradictions of the Colonial State: The Case of Tanganyika in the Early Years," Department of Sociology, University of Toronto, Working Paper No. 23, 1981, 22–23.

Chapter 6: Toward African Independence

1. R. D. Pearce, *The Turning Point in Africa: British Colonial Policy, 1938–1948* (London: Frank Cass, 1982), 23.
2. William B. Cohen, *Rulers of Empire: The French Colonial Service in Africa* (Stanford: Hoover Institution Press, 1971), 167.
3. This speech, entitled "Vers l'avenir," and his other official addresses are gathered in Pierre Ryckmans, *Etapes et jalons* (Brussels: Ferdinand Larcier, 1946).
4. For interesting insights into the importance then attached by France to averting Libyan independence as a single state, see Pierre Guillen, "Une ménace pour l'Afrique française: Le débat international sur le statut des anciennes colonies italiennes," in Charles-Robert Ageron, ed., *Les chemins de la décolonisation de l'empire français, 1936–1956* (Paris: Editions du CNRS, 1986), 69–81.
5. Henry S. Wilson, *The Imperial Experience in Sub-Saharan Africa since 1870* (Minneapolis: University of Minnesota Press, 1977), 275.
6. This commitment was opposed in some influential colonial circles, whose spokesman was Archbishop de Hemptinne of Elisabethville. The archbishop, a convinced apostle of Latin Europe as sole repository of "civilization," felt that, with the defeat of France and Belgium, the war was only among Germans, Anglo-Saxons, Bolsheviks, and Asiatics, and that the colonial Congo, as an outpost of Latin Europe, had no interest in the war's outcome. For an engaging account, see Denis Denuit, *Le Congo champion de la Belgique en guerre* (Brussels: Editions Frans van Belle, n.d. [1946?]). The moment of confusion ensuing from the German sweep across Belgium was also marked by a short-lived military intervention led by Emile Janssens, later commander of the Force Publique, who was to acquire great notoriety at the time of independence.
7. Monsignor de Hemptinne, quoted in O.-P. Gilbert, *L'empire du silence* (Brussels: Editions du Peuple, 1947), 23–29.
8. Antoine Rubbens, in *Dettes de guerre* (Elisabethville: Editions de l'Essor du Congo, 1945), 191.
9. Pearce, *The Turning Point in Africa,* 29.
10. On the American impact on British colonial policy, see Wm. Roger Louis and Ronald Robinson, "The United States and the Liquidation of British Empire in Tropical Africa, 1941–1951," in Gifford and Louis, eds., *The*

Transfer of Power in Africa: Decolonization, 1940–1960 (New Haven: Yale University Press, 1982), 31–56.

11. See, for example, the essays by Pierre Ryckmans, dispatched to New York to defend the Belgian colonial dossier at the United Nations after completion of a decade of service as Congo Governor-General in 1946, *Dominer pour servir* (Brussels: L'Edition Universelle, 1948). The colonial powers, Ryckmans observes, were the real losers at San Francisco (ibid., 20). See also the apprehensive juridical commentary by O. Louwers, *L'Article 73 de la Charte et l'anticolonialisme de l'Organisation des Nations Unies* (Brussels: Académie Royale des Sciences d'Outre-Mer, 1952).

12. The contrasting doctrines of international law embodied in the Westphalian and U.N. Charter traditions form the basis for the elegant treatise by Antonio Cassese, *International Law in a Divided World* (Oxford: Clarendon Press, 1986).

13. Former Leopoldville Province Governor Alain Stenmans, personal communication.

14. F. van Langenhove, "Factors of Decolonization," *Civilisations* 2 (1961): 401–23.

15. On the Cameroon, see especially Georges Chaffard, *Les carnets secrets de la décolonisation* (Paris: Calmann-Levy, 1965); Richard Joseph, *Radical Nationalism in the Cameroon: Social Origins of the UPC Rebellion* (Oxford: Clarendon Press, 1977); on the "Mau Mau" in Kenya, see Carl G. Rosberg and John Nottingham, *The Myth of Mau Mau: Nationalism in Kenya* (London: Pall Mall, 1965).

16. For detail, see Jean-Philippe Peemans, "Capital Accumulation in the Congo under Colonialism: The Role of the State," in Peter Duignan and L. H. Gann, eds., *Colonialism in Africa, 1870–1960* (Cambridge: Cambridge University Press, 1978), 4:165–212.

17. Economic motivations played some part as well, and they are given particular stress in the analysis by Kenneth Maxwell, "Portugal and Africa: The Last Empire," in Gifford and Louis, eds., *The Transfer of Power,* 337–86.

18. Cecil Hurst in a study in the 1920s of the emerging Commonwealth regards it as a single political conglomerate: "The British Empire is a strange complex. It is a heterogeneous collection of separate entities, and yet it is a political unit. It is wholly unprecedented; it has no written constitution; it is of quite recent growth; and its development has been amazingly rapid." Cecil J. B. Hurst et al., *Great Britain and the Dominions* (Chicago: University of Chicago Press, 1928), 3. The continued existence of an Imperial Defence Committee, implying a unified security system, and the seeming obligation of the dominions to join at once in World War I, sustained the ambiguities, which were clarified only with

the accession of India to the Commonwealth, pursuing a foreign policy largely at variance with Britain and other members.

19. J. M. Lee and Martin Petter, *The Colonial Office, War, and Development Policy* (London: Maurice Temple Smith, 1982), 244.

20. For a somewhat idyllic account of this process by a former leading colonial official, see Sir Alan Burns, *In Defence of Colonies* (London: George Allen and Unwin, 1957), 57–71.

21. Quoted in John D. Hargreaves, *The End of Colonial Rule in West Africa* (London: Macmillan, 1979), 28.

22. Of the vast literature on this topic, I find particularly helpful Ageron, *Les chemins de la décolonisation;* Joseph-Roger de Benoist, *La balkanisation de l'Afrique Occidentale Française* (Dakar: Nouvelles Editions Africaines, 1979); D. Bruce Marshall, *The French Colonial Myth and Constitution-Making in the Fourth Republic* (New Haven: Yale University Press, 1973); the essays by Yves Person, Henri Brunschwig, and Elikia M'Bokolo in Gifford and Louis, eds., *The Transfer of Power in Africa;* Prosser Gifford and Wm. Roger Louis, eds., *Decolonization and African Independence: The Transfers of Power, 1960–1980* (New Haven: Yale University Press, 1988).

23. Paul Iscart, "L'élaboration de la Constitution de l'Union Française: Les Assemblées Constituantes et le problème colonial," in Ageron, ed., *Les chemins de la décolonisation,* 19.

24. In AOF indigenous citizens numbered only ninety thousand in 1938, over half originaires, with a mere five thousand in AEF.

25. Elikia M'Bokolo, "French Colonial Policy in Equatorial Africa," in Gifford and Louis, eds., *The Transfer of Power in Africa,* 206.

26. Ibid., 207.

27. Charles-André Julien, *Histoire de l'Algérie contemporaine,* 2d ed. (Paris: Presses Universitaires de France, 1979), 2:547–78; Lucile Rabearimana, "Les malgaches et l'idée d'indépendance de 1945 à 1956," in Ageron, ed. *Les chemins de la décolonisation,* 263–74. According to Ageron, newly available archival evidence demonstrates that the actual death toll was eleven thousand, rather than the figure of sixty thousand to ninety thousand widely cited in studies of the uprising.

28. de Benoist, editor of an influential Catholic weekly in Dakar during this period, provides ample evidence in his detailed and authoritative study, *La balkanisation de l'Afrique Occidentale Française.*

29. Antoine Omari, "Le rôle civilisateur de Léopold II," *La Voix du Congolais* (December 1949), 461–63, cited in Jean Stengers, "Precipitous Decolonization: The Belgian Congo," in Gifford and Louis, eds., *The Transfer of Power in Africa,* 318–19. Even in 1956 the manuscript by Patrice Lumumba echoes in less extravagant form some of these sentiments, a posture that cannot be entirely explained by prudent concern for the

colonial censors; *Le Congo, terre d'avenir, est-il menacé?* (Brussels: Office de Publicité, 1961).

30. For details, see Crawford Young, *Politics in the Congo* (Princeton: Princeton University Press, 1965), 33–105.

31. Of a vast literature, particular mention should be made of the splendid documentary analyses by the collaborators of the Centre de Recherche et d'Information Socio-Politiques, *Congo 1959* (Brussels: Centre de Recherche et d'Information Socio-Politiques, 1960), and J. Gérard-Libois and Benoit Verhaegen, *Congo 1960* (Brussels: Centre de Recherche et d'Information Socio-Politiques, 1961); the transcripts of Belgian radio debates on these events more than a decade later by leading participants, Pierre de Vos, *La décolonisation: Les événements du Congo de 1959 à 1967* (Brussels: Editions ABC, 1975); and the excellent monograph by René Lemarchand, *Political Awakening in the Congo: The Politics of Fragmentation* (Berkeley: University of California Press, 1964).

32. Tony Hodges, *Western Sahara: The Roots of a Desert War* (Westport, Conn.: Lawrence Hill, 1983), 122.

33. Ibrahima K. Sundiata, "The Roots of African Despotism: The Question of Political Culture," *African Studies Review* 31 (April 1988): 33–47.

34. Pearce, *The Turning Point in Africa,* 42–67.

35. Ibid., 132–57.

36. C. A. G. Wallis, *Report of an Inquiry into African Local Government in the Protectorate of Uganda* (Entebbe: Government Printer, 1953), 13–14.

37. To recapture the flavor of these views, see for example Pierre Houart, *La pénétration communiste au Congo* (Brussels: Centre de Documentation Internationale, 1960).

38. For one account of the nature of the French military response, see George A. Kelly, *Lost Soldiers: The French Army and Empire in Crisis, 1947–1962* (Cambridge: MIT Press, 1965).

39. Peter Woodward, "The South in Sudanese Politics, 1946–1956," *Middle Eastern Studies* 16 (October 1980): 178–92.

40. Ronald Robinson, "Sir Andrew Cohen: Proconsul of African Nationalism (1909–1968)," in L. H. Gann and Peter Duignan, eds., *African Proconsuls: European Governors in Africa* (New York: Free Press, 1978), 356. On this topic, see also Lee and Petter, *The Colonial Office, War, and Development Policy,* and Pearce, *The Turning Point in Africa.*

41. See the account by Sir Andrew Cohen, *British Policy in Changing Africa* (Evanston: Northwestern University Press, 1959); as assistant under-secretary for Africa during these years, Cohen played a central role in policy definition.

42. Robinson, "Sir Andrew Cohen," 360.

43. A number of these are collected in Arthur Creech-Jones, *New Fabian Colonial Essays* (New York: Praeger, 1959).

44. A puppet sultan, Ben Arafa, was placed on the throne by the French, but his credibility was nil.
45. Julien, *Histoire de l'Algérie contemporaine,* 612. On the 1947 statute and its sabotage, see also Tayeb Chenntouf, "L'assemblée algérienne et l'application des réformes prévues par le statut du 20 septembre 1947," in Ageron, ed., *Les chemins de la décolonisation,* 367–75.
46. On the army role in Algeria, see Kelly, *Lost Soldiers.* On terminal colonial politics in the Maghrib, see among other sources Roger le Tourneau, *Evolution politique de l'Afrique du Nord musulmane, 1920–1961* (Paris: Librairie Armand Colin, 1962); Clement Henry Moore, *Politics in North Africa* (Boston: Little, Brown, 1970); Moore, "The Maghrib," in Michael Crowder, ed., *Cambridge History of Africa* (Cambridge: Cambridge University Press, 1984), 8:564–610; Jean-Claude Vatin, *Algérie: Politique, histoire et société* (Paris: Fondation National des Sciences Politiques, 1974); Michael Clark, *Algeria in Turmoil* (London: Thames and Hudson, 1960).
47. On this process, see Joseph Roger de Benoist, *L'Afrique Occidentale Française de la Conférence de Brazzaville (1944) à l'indépendance (1960)* (Dakar: Nouvelles Editions Africaines, 1982).
48. Stengers, "Precipitous Decolonization," 333.
49. For his detailed chronicle, see W. J. Ganshof van der Meersch, *Fin de la souveraineté belge au Congo* (Brussels: Institut Royal des Relations Internationales, 1963).
50. For an example of this brief, see Burns, *In Defence of Colonies.*
51. In the preface to his edited volume, *Les chemins de la décolonisation,* 10.
52. Cited in Gerard-Libois and Verhaegen, *Congo 1960,* 1:106.
53. See the insightful analysis by Anthony Low, "The End of the British Empire in Africa," in Gifford and Louis eds., *Decolonization and African Independence,* 33–72.
54. Tony Killick, *Development Economics in Action* (London: Heinemann, 1978), 24.
55. John D. Hargreaves, *The End of Colonial Rule in West Africa* (London: Macmillan, 1979), 41.
56. Jean Stengers, "La Belgique et le Congo," in *Histoire de la Belgique contemporaine* (Brussels: La Renaissance du Livre, 1974).
57. Julien, *Histoire de l'Algérie contemporaine,* 535.
58. Crawford Young, Neal Sherman, and Tim Rose, *Cooperatives and Development: Agricultural Politics in Ghana and Uganda* (Madison: University of Wisconsin Press, 1981), 165.
59. Colonial Annual Reports, Nigeria.
60. Lord Hailey, *An African Survey. A Study of Problems Arising South of the Sahara,* rev. ed. (London: Oxford University Press, 1957), 1323–37.
61. Ibid., 1339.

62. This argument is persuasively documented by Lisa Anderson, *The State and Social Transformation in Tunisia and Libya, 1830–1980* (Princeton: Princeton University Press, 1980).

63. For evidence supportive of such an interpretation, see the excellent dissertation by John Stephen Morrison, "Developmental Optimism and State Failure in Africa: How to Understand Botswana's Relative Success," Ph.D. diss., University of Wisconsin—Madison, 1987. Other favorable factors, such as an exceptionally fortunate revenue situation, also enter the picture.

Chapter 7: The Ambiguous Challenge of Civil Society

1. The signal importance of the vocabulary of contestation was a significant theme in the excellent papers presented to a conference on Relationships between the State and Civil Society in Africa and Eastern Europe organized by Bogumil Jewsiewicki and Prosser Gifford at Bellagio, Italy, in February 1990. Implicit in the term *civil society* was a vocation of empowerment against the totalitarian state. The term had fallen into discredit in Western analysis but was revalidated as a vocabulary of challenge to a form of rule that blocked the emergence of a "normal" relationship between state and society.

2. Organized by Naomi Chazan and John Harbeson at the Harry S Truman Institute of the Hebrew University of Jerusalem in January 1992. Chazan, Harbeson, and Donald Rothchild are organizing the publication of a selection of the papers from this conference, forthcoming in 1994 from Lynne Reinner.

3. A larger array of antecedents could be mentioned. For excellent recent treatments of the origins and content of the civil-society notion, see John Keane, ed., *Civil Society and the State: New European Perspectives* (London: Verso, 1988), and Adam Seligman, *The Idea of Civil Society* (New York: Free Press, 1992).

4. John Locke, *Two Treatises of Civil Government* (London: J. M. Dent and Sons, 1955), 160.

5. Z. A. Pelczynski, "Introduction: The Significance of Hegel's Separation of the State and Civil Society," in Pelczynski, ed., *The State and Civil Society: Studies in Hegel's Political Philosophy* (Cambridge: Cambridge University Press, 1984). The Hegelian rendering of "civil society" reflected the influence of eighteenth-century French physiocrats; Patrick Riley, personal communication.

6. Schlomo Avineri, *Hegel's Theory of the Modern State* (Cambridge: Cambridge University Press, 1972), 147.

7. Keane, *Civil Society and the State,* 50; Seligman, *The Idea of Civil Society,* 45.

8. Martin Carnoy, *The State and Political Theory* (Princeton: Princeton University Press, 1984), 70.

9. Jean-François Bayart, "Civil Society in Africa," in Patrick Chabal, ed., *Political Domination in Africa: Reflections on the Limits of Power* (Cambridge: Cambridge University Press, 1986), 111–14. At the 1992 Jerusalem conference on civil society in Africa, Bayart indicated that this essay no longer reflected well his views on the issue (partly because of an inadequate translation of his text). The vulgarization of the term in journalistic writing has corroded its meanings and devalued its utility. In his magnum opus *L'Etat en Afrique* (Paris: Fayard, 1989), Bayart abandons the expression *civil society.*

10. Robert Fossaert, *La Société: Les Etats* (Paris: Editions du Seuil, 1981), 5:146.

11. Bayart, "Civil Society in Africa," 112–13.

12. Michael Bratton, "Beyond the State: Civil Society and Associational Life in Africa," *World Politics* 41 (April 1989): 417, quoting Alfred Stepan, *Rethinking Military Politics: Brazil and the Southern Cone* (Princeton: Princeton University Press, 1988), 3–4. A more elaborate view of "civil society" is found in Bratton's paper, "Civil Society and Political Transition in Africa," International Conference on Civil Society in Africa, Jerusalem, 5–10 January 1992.

13. Joel D. Barkan, Michael L. McNulty, and M. A. O. Ayeni, "'Hometown' Voluntary Associations and the Emergence of Civil Society in Western Nigeria," *Journal of Modern African Studies* 29, no. 3 (1991): 457.

14. Naomi Chazan, "The Dynamics of Civil Society in Africa," International Conference on Civil Society in Africa, Jerusalem, 5–10 January 1992.

15. Patrick Chabal, "Introduction," in Chabal, ed., *Political Domination in Africa,* 15.

16. To borrow the familiar triptych from Albert O. Hirschman, *Exit, Voice, and Loyalty: Responses to Decline in Firms, Organizations, and States* (Cambridge: Harvard University Press, 1970).

17. Jan Vansina, *Paths in the Rainforests: Toward a History of Political Tradition in Equatorial Africa* (Madison: University of Wisconsin Press, 1990), 259.

18. W. E. Abraham, *The Mind of Africa* (Chicago: University of Chicago Press, 1962), 75, quoted in Fred M. Hayward, "Introduction," in Hayward, ed., *Elections in Independent Africa* (Boulder: Westview Press, 1987), 5.

19. I draw here upon a remarkably evocative presentation of "Swazi nation" by Gloria Mwamba in a colloquium delivered to the African Studies Program, University of Wisconsin—Madison, "The Kingdom of Swaziland: Swazi Culture and the King," April 1992, illustrated with scenes from the coronation of the new Ngwenyama.

20. One may note the contrast between the autocracy of Bula Matari, which sought comprehensive hegemony through complete subjugation and exclusion of African society, and the totalitarian mode of rule in the former Soviet bloc, which aspired to absorb civil society completely in the socialist state. This contrast notwithstanding, it is striking that the reappearance of the term *civil society* occurs above all in Eastern Europe and Africa.

21. V. Y. Mudimbe, *The Invention of Africa: Gnosis, Philosophy, and the Orders of Knowledge* (Bloomington: Indiana University Press, 1988), 1.

22. William B. Cohen, *The French Encounter with Africans: White Response to Blacks, 1530–1880* (Bloomington: Indiana University Press, 1980), 68.

23. L. Moutoulle, *Politique sociale de l'Union Minière du Haut-Katanga* (Brussels: ARSOM, Sci. Mor. et Pol., T. 14, fasc. 3, 1946), 5–6, 15.

24. Henrika Kuklick, *The Imperial Bureaucrat: The Colonial Administrative Service in the Gold Coast, 1920–1959* (Stanford: Stanford University Press, 1979), 43.

25. Quoted in Jeremy White, *Central Administration in Nigeria, 1914–1948* (Dublin: Irish Academic Press, 1981), 216–17.

26. This nationalist version of history is ably presented by a large number of contributors to volume 7 of the UNESCO *General History of Africa;* A. Adu Boahen, ed., *Africa under Colonial Domination, 1880–1935* (Berkeley: University of California Press, 1985).

27. James F. Searing, "Accommodation and Resistance: Chiefs, Muslim Leaders and Politicians in Colonial Senegal, 1890–1934," Ph.D. diss., Princeton University, 1985, 528.

28. J. Berque, "Politics and Nationalism in the Maghrib and the Sahara, 1919–1935," in Boahen, ed., *Africa under Colonial Domination,* 613.

29. Quoted in Michael Clark, *Algeria in Turmoil* (London: Thames and Hudson, 1960), 17.

30. Searing, "Accommodation and Resistance," 467–73.

31. This group is given superb treatment in Joseph Miller's masterful study, *Way of Death: Merchant Capitalism and the Slave Trade* (Madison: University of Wisconsin Press, 1988).

32. David W. Robinson, "La mise en place d'une 'hégémonie' coloniale au Sénégal," *Historiens-Géographes du Sénégal* 3 (April 1988): 2.

33. *Dettes de guerre* (Elisabethville: Editions de l'Essor du Congo, 1945), 128–29.

34. Patrice Lumumba, *Le Congo, terre d'avenir, est-il menacé?* (Brussels: Office de Publicité, 1961). On Lumumba and the context of this publication, see the carefully balanced and thoroughly documented political biography by Jean-Claude Willame, *Patrice Lumumba: La crise congolaise révisitée* (Paris: Karthala, 1990).

35. A. Adu Boahen, "Africa and the Colonial Challenge," in Boahen, ed., *Africa under Colonial Domination,* 4.

36. Amid the vast literature spawned by these macrosocial phenomena, one benefits from the series of critical review essays commissioned by the Social Science Research Council. See in particular Allen Isaacman, "Peasants and Rural Social Protest in Africa," *African Studies Review* 23 (September 1990): 1–120; Bill Freund, "Labor and Labor History in Africa: A Review of the Literature," *African Studies Review* 27 (June 1984): 1–58; Sara Berry, "The Food Crisis and Agrarian Change in Africa: A Review Essay," *African Studies Review* 27 (June 1984): 59–112; Frederick Cooper, "Africa and the World Economy," *African Studies Review* 24 (June/September 1981): 1–86; Crawford Young, "Nationalism, Ethnicity, and Class: A Retrospective," *Cahiers d'Etudes Africaines* 26 (1986): 421–95.

37. P. C. Lloyd, *Africa in Social Change* (Harmondsworth: Penguin, 1967), 306.

38. Georges Balandier, "La situation coloniale: approche théorique," *Cahiers Internationaux de Sociologie* 11, no. 44 (1951): 44–79.

39. Julius K. Nyerere, *Ujamaa: Essays on Socialism* (Oxford: Oxford University Press, 1968), 11.

40. This was long a theme in labor sociology; for an influential example, see Walter Elkan, *Migrants and Proletarians* (London: Oxford University Press, 1960).

41. Bruce Fetter, "L'Union Minière du Haut-Katanga, 1920–1940: La naissance d'une sous-culture totalitaire," *Cahiers du CEDAF,* 6 (1973); Charles van Onselen, *Chibaro: African Mine Labour in Southern Rhodesia* (London: Pluto Press, 1976).

42. Ousmane Sembene, *God's Bits of Wood* (New York: Doubleday Anchor Books, 1962).

43. Isaacman, "Peasants and Social Protest," 2.

44. On some of the local household accumulation imperatives, see the elegant study by Sara S. Berry, *Fathers Work for Their Sons: Accumulation, Mobility, and Class Formation in an Extended Yoruba Community* (Berkeley: University of California Press, 1985).

45. This argument is developed in ingenious fashion by Goran Hyden, *Beyond Ujamaa in Tanzania: Underdevelopment and an Uncaptured Peasantry* (Berkeley: University of California Press, 1980).

46. Isaacman, "Peasants and Social Protest."

47. James C. Scott, *Domination and the Arts of Resistance: Hidden Transcripts* (New Haven: Yale University Press, 1990).

48. Stephen Feierman, *Peasant Intellectuals: Anthropology and History in Northern Tanzania* (Madison: University of Wisconsin Press, 1990).

49. Amilcar Cabral, *Revolution in Guinea: An African People's Struggle: Selected Texts* (New York: Monthly Review Press, 1969).

50. Quoted in Basil Davidson, *The Black Man's Burden: Africa and the Curse of the Nation-State* (New York: Random House, 1992), 107–08.

51. The literature on this theme is now abundant; a particularly useful example is Jane L. Parpart and Kathleen Staudt, eds., *Women and the State in Africa* (Boulder: Lynne Rienner, 1990). Female prime ministers first appeared in Rwanda and Burundi in the early 1990s.

52. Patrick Harries, "Exclusion, Classification, and Internal Colonialism: The Emergence of Ethnicity among the Tsonga-Speakers of South Africa," in Leroy Vail, ed., *The Creation of Tribalism in Southern Africa* (Berkeley: University of California Press, 1989), 90.

53. Raymond Apthorpe, "Does Tribalism Really Matter?" *Transition* 7 (1968): 18.

54. Johannes Fabian, *Language and Colonial Power* (Berkeley: University of California Press, 1986), 71.

55. George W. Stocking, "Maclay, Kubary, Malinowski: Archetypes from the Dreamtime of Anthropology," in Stocking, ed., *Colonial Situations: Essays on the Contextualization of Ethnographic Knowledge* (Madison: University of Wisconsin Press, 1991), 68.

56. The term comes from the influential, "constructivist" reading of nationalism by Benedict Anderson, *Imagined Communities: Reflections on the Origin and Spread of Nationalism* (London: Verso, 1983).

57. For detail, see Nelson Kasfir, *The Shrinking Political Arena: Participation and Ethnicity in African Politics, with a Case Study of Uganda* (Berkeley: University of California Press, 1975); Crawford Young, *The Politics of Cultural Pluralism* (Madison: University of Wisconsin Press, 1976). In a forthcoming study by an Acholi historian, further detail is provided on the role of a contingent of rulers identified by the British and established as a hereditary oligarchy; Amii Omara-Otunnu, *Conflict, Coexistence, and Inequality in the Nile Basin, c. 1850–1960: The Case of Acholi.*

58. Brian Siegel, "The 'Wild' and 'Lazy' Lambas: Ethnic Stereotypes on the Central African Copperbelt," in Vail, ed., *The Creation of Tribalism,* 350–71.

59. P. Mercier, "Remarques sur la signification du 'tribalisme' actuel en Afrique noire," *Cahiers Internationaux de Sociologie* 31 (1960): 61–80; Immanuel M. Wallerstein, "Ethnicity and National Integration in West Africa," *Cahiers d'Etudes Africaines* 3 (1960): 129–39; J. Clyde Mitchell, *The Kalela Dance: Aspects of Social Relationships among Urban Africans in Northern Rhodesia* (Manchester: Manchester University Press, 1956); A. L. Epstein, *Politics in an Urban African Community* (Manchester: Manchester University Press, 1958).

60. David B. Abernethy, *The Political Dilemma of Popular Education* (Stanford: Stanford University Press, 1969), 108.

61. Harold R. Isaacs, *Idols of the Tribe: Group Identity and Political Change* (New York: Harper and Row, 1975), 1.

62. Cited in Robin Bidwell, *Morocco under Colonial Rule* (London: Frank Cass, 1973). Bidwell provides an excellent recapitulation of Berber policy. See also Ernest Gellner and Charles Micaud, eds., *Arabs and Berbers: From Tribe to Nation in North Africa* (Lexington, Mass.: D. C. Heath, 1972).

63. Bidwell, *Morocco under French Rule,* 56. For an explanation of the tendency toward expansion of Arabic culture in Morocco, see Crawford Young, *The Politics of Cultural Pluralism* (Madison: University of Wisconsin Press, 1976), 413–19.

64. Thomas Hodgkin, *Nationalism in Colonial Africa* (London: F. Muller, 1956).

65. For detail on Uganda, see especially the valuable study of the potent Bugisu Cooperative Union by Stephen G. Bunker, *Peasants against the State: The Politics of Market Control in Bugisu* (Urbana: University of Illinois Press, 1987). See also Crawford Young, Neal Sherman, and Tim Rose, *Cooperatives and Development: Agricultural Politics in Ghana and Uganda* (Madison: University of Wisconsin Press, 1981).

66. Rupert Emerson, *From Empire to Nation: The Rise to Self-Assertion of African and Asian Peoples* (Cambridge: Harvard University Press, 1960), 378–79.

67. Cheikh Anta Diop, *Nations nègres et culture* (Paris: Présence Africaine, 1965).

68. Léopold S. Senghor, *African Socialism: A Report to the Constitutive Congress of the Party of the African Federation* (London: Pall Mall, 1964); Aimé Cesaire, *Cahier d'un retour au pays natal* (Paris: Présence Africaine, 1958).

69. See especially Frantz Fanon, *Les damnés de la terre* (Paris: Maspero, 1963); *Peau noire, masques blancs* (Paris: Editions du Seuil, 1952).

70. A generation of scholars saw in political parties not only the instrument of liberation but also the very essence of African society, the key to any political sociology of change dynamics in Africa. Of a vast literature, see especially Thomas Hodgkin, *African Political Parties* (Harmondsworth: Penguin, 1961); James S. Coleman and Carl G. Rosberg, eds., *Political Parties and National Integration in Tropical Africa* (Berkeley: University of California Press, 1964); Ruth S. Morganthau, *Political Parties in French-Speaking West Africa* (Oxford: Clarendon Press, 1964); Immanuel M. Wallerstein, *Africa: The Politics of Independence: An Interpretation of Modern African History* (New York: Vintage, 1961); Aristide R. Zolberg, *Creating Political Order: The Party-States of West Africa* (Chicago: Rand McNally, 1966).

71. Davidson, *The Black Man's Burden,* 108–09; the material in quotation marks is from Hodgkin, *African Political Parties,* 139.

72. But see the arresting study by Norma Krieger, *Zimbabwe's Guerrilla*

War: Peasant Voices (Cambridge: Cambridge University Press, 1992), which documents a more ambivalent and troubled relationship between guerrilla fighters and their peasant base than is commonly assumed.

73. Patrick Manning, *Slavery, Colonialism, and Economic Growth in Dahomey, 1640–1960* (Cambridge: Cambridge University Press, 1982).

74. The most thorough study of the final years of the AOF federation is Joseph-Roger de Benoist, *La balkanisation de l'Afrique Occidentale Française* (Dakar: Nouvelles Editions Africaines, 1979).

75. Davidson, *The Black Man's Burden*, 162–63.

76. Basil Davidson, "The Challenge of Comparative Analysis: Anti-Imperialist Nationalism in Africa and Europe," paper presented at the Conference on Relationships between the State and Civil Society in Africa and Eastern Europe, Bellagio, Italy, February 1989, 7–8.

77. Peter Ekeh, "Colonialism and the Two Publics in Africa: A Theoretical Statement," *Comparative Studies in Society and History* 17, no. 1 (1975): 91–112.

78. Jan Vansina, "A Past for the Future?" *Dalhousie Review* 68, nos. 1–2 (1989): 21–23.

Chapter 8: The Imperial Legacy and State Traditions

1. On Japanese colonial rule, see especially Ramon H. Myers and Mark R. Peattie, eds., *The Japanese Colonial Empire, 1895–1945* (Princeton: Princeton University Press, 1984); Mark R. Peattie, *Nanyo: The Rise and Fall of the Japanese in Micronesia, 1885–1945* (Honolulu: University of Hawaii Press, 1988).

2. David Laitin, "The National Uprisings in the Soviet Union," *World Politics* 44 (1991): 139–77. Laitin's imprudent prophecy in this article of the Soviet Union's resilience and capacity for survival was overtaken by events even before the appearance of the article, but his historical analysis remains insightful.

3. Klaus E. Knorr, *British Colonial Theories, 1570–1850* (Toronto: University of Toronto Press, 1944), clearly shows that changing patterns of imperial thought, in spite of the defection of the American colonies, were steadfast in the conviction that the colonies had to remain tied to the realm.

4. Peggy K. Liss, *Atlantic Empires: The Network of Trade and Revolution, 1713–1826* (Baltimore: Johns Hopkins University Press, 1983).

5. Ernest S. Dodge, *Islands and Empires: Western Impact on the Pacific and East Asia* (Minneapolis: University of Minnesota Press, 1976).

6. See the thorough history of the Indian Army by Philip Mason, *A Matter of Honour* (New York: Holt, Rinehart, and Winston, 1974).

7. Jorge I. Dominguez, *Insurrection or Loyalty: The Breakdown of the Spanish American Empire* (Cambridge: Harvard University Press, 1980).

8. Gwendolyn Midlo Hall, *Social Control in Slave Plantation Societies: A Comparison of St. Domingue and Cuba* (Baltimore: Johns Hopkins University Press, 1971).

9. J. H. Elliott, *Imperial Spain, 1469–1716* (New York: St. Martin's Press, 1964).

10. Stuart B. Schwartz, *Sovereignty and Society in Colonial Brazil: The High Court of Bahia and Its Judges, 1609–1751* (Berkeley: University of California Press, 1973), xvi. See also Dauril Alden, *Royal Government in Colonial Brazil: With Special Reference to the Administration of Lavradio, Viceroy, 1769–1779* (Berkeley: University of California Press, 1968).

11. Roman Szporluk, "The Imperial Legacy and the Soviet Nationalities Problem," in Lubomyr Hajda and Mark Beissinger, eds., *The Nationalities Factor in Soviet Politics and Society* (Boulder: Westview Press, 1990), 2.

12. Edward Chen, "The Attempt to Integrate the Empire: Legal Perspectives," Roman H. Myers and Mark R. Peattie, eds., *The Japanese Colonial Empire, 1895–1945* (Princeton: Princeton University Press, 1984), 240–74.

13. Fascinating documentation is provided in the draft manuscript by Louise Young, "Mobilizing for Empire: Japan and Manchukuo, 1931–1945."

14. Cited in Raoul Girardet, *L'idée coloniale en France de 1871 à 1962* (Paris: La Table Ronde, 1972), 83.

15. Max Savelle, *Empires to Nations: Expansion in America, 1713–1824* (Minneapolis: University of Minnesota Press, 1974), 224.

16. The term *creole* is burdened with several contrastive meanings. In Spanish America creoles were persons of Spanish ancestry born in the Americas. In the Caribbean a creole was a person of color, of mixed (usually European and African) ancestry. In Sierre Leone creoles were African freed slaves, from England, Nova Scotia, or captured on the high seas, deposited in Freetown. Linguistically, a creole is a new language born of the encounter between two disparate speech codes.

17. Dominguez, *Insurrection or Loyalty,* 82–113.

18. The wave of centralizing reforms in the later eighteenth century aimed at "a unitary state in which all the resources of Spain's diverse and far-flung dominions could be mobilized to defend the monarch," breaking with earlier concepts of imperial federation. Crucial to this strategy was a veritable peninsular reconquest of the Americas by displacing creoles in the audiencias, where they were quite numerous. Creole nomination or purchase of high office was to be limited to relatively remote areas not threatened by Britain (Chile, Charcas, Guadalajara), and creoles were to be removed from critical areas like Santo Domingo, Bogota, or Mexico. Instead, office for creoles would be open in Spain itself, which, joined

with increased use of Spaniards in the Americas, would "bring the two together in friendship and unity, and make of them a single nation, for every creole who is brought to Spain will be hostage to ensure that those lands remain subject to your Majesty's mild rule." Quoted from a 1762 court position paper, cited in John Leddy Phelan, *The People and the King: The Communero Revolution in Columbia, 1781* (Madison: University of Wisconsin Press, 1978), 3, 11.

19. Ibid., 149–50.
20. Michael E. Robinson, "Colonial Publication Policy and the Korean Nationalist Movement," in Myers and Peattie, eds., *The Japanese Colonial Empire,* 329–31.
21. Raymond Carr, *Puerto Rico: A Colonial Experiment* (New York: Vintage Books, 1984), 42.
22. Mark R. Peattie, "Introduction," in Myers and Peattie, eds., *The Japanese Colonial Empire,* 30.
23. Young, *Mobilizing for Empire.*
24. George Masselman, *The Cradle of Colonialism* (New Haven: Yale University Press, 1963), 466.
25. Richard Robison, *Indonesia: The Rise of Capital* (North Sydney: Allen and Unwin, 1986), 5–6.
26. H. L. Wesseling, "The Impact of European Imperialism on Dutch Colonialism," paper presented to Social Science Seminar on Comparative Colonialism, Institute for Advanced Study, Princeton, November 1980, 12.
27. Ann Stoler, *Capitalism and Confrontation in Sumatra's Plantation Belt, 1870–1979* (New Haven: Yale University Press, 1985), 25; see also Anne Booth, "The Burden of Taxation in Colonial Indonesia," *Journal of Southeast Asian Studies* 11 (March 1980): 91–109; Robert van Neil, "The Effect of Export Cultivation in Nineteenth-Century Java," *Modern Asian Studies* 15, no. 1 (1981): 25–58.
28. Sir Edward Blunt, *The I.C.S.: The Indian Civil Service* (London: Faber and Faber, 1937), 123.
29. B. R. Tomlinson, *The Political Economy of the Raj, 1914–1947: The Economics of Decolonization in India* (London: Macmillan, 1979), 28.
30. Ibid., 108–17.
31. For detail, see D. J. Fieldhouse, *Economics and Empire, 1830–1914* (London: Weidenfeld and Nicolson, 1973), 213–23. In 1828 opium constituted $11.2 million of $20.3 million worth of Indian exports to China.
32. Daniel R. Headrick, *The Tools of Empire: Technology and European Imperialism in the Nineteenth Century* (New York: Oxford University Press, 1981), 43–54.
33. Joseph Buttinger, *Vietnam: A Dragon Embattled* (New York: Frederick A. Praeger, 1967), 104.
34. David P. Chandler, *A History of Cambodia* (Boulder: Westview Press, 1983), 153–54.

35. Martin J. Murray, *The Development of Capitalism in Colonial Indochina (1870–1940)* (Berkeley: University of California Press, 1980); Jacques Marseille, *Empire coloniale et capitalisme français* (Paris: Editions Albini Michel, 1984).

36. Cited in Sidney W. Mintz, *Sweetness and Power: The Place of Sugar in Modern History* (New York: Viking, 1985), 184.

37. James Lang, *Commerce and Conquest: Spain and England in the Americas* (New York: Academic Press, 1975), 47–67.

38. J. H. Elliott, *Imperial Spain, 1469–1716* (New York: St. Martin's Press, 1964), 173–90.

39. J. H. Elliott, *The Old World and the New, 1492–1650* (Cambridge: Cambridge University Press, 1970), 84–87.

40. Murdo J. Macleod, "Aspects of the Internal Economy of Colonial Spanish America: Labour, Taxation, Distribution, and Exchange," in Leslie Bethell, ed., *The Cambridge History of Latin America: Colonial Latin America* (Cambridge: Cambridge University Press, 1984), 2:249 (and passim for details on colonial fiscal policy generally).

41. Details on Brazilian revenue generation may be found in Alden, *Royal Government in Colonial Brazil.*

42. For detail on colonial mining in Spanish America, see Peter Bakewell, "Mining in Spanish America," in Bethell, ed., *Colonial Latin America,* 2:105–52.

43. This was doubtless the largest colonial public investment anywhere, requiring subsidy only in the first years. Headrick, *Tools of Empire,* 180–90.

44. J. P. Nettl, "The State as a Conceptual Variable," *World Politics* 20, no. 4 (1968): 559–92.

45. Although the reconquista was a source of early Spanish ideas about organizing the American realm, there were also important contrasts. The occupation of southern Spain was an exercise in expropriating and excluding much of the conquered population (Moors and Jews), while in the Americas Indians were to be included—both because their labor and tribute was crucial tó the viability of the enterprise and because evangelization was fundamental to imperial legitimacy. I am grateful to Steve Stern for stressing this difference in his comments on the manuscript.

46. Wesseling, "The Impact of European Imperialism."

47. Theodore Friend, *Between Two Empires* (New Haven: Yale University Press, 1963), 35.

48. Peattie, "Introduction," in Myers and Peattie, eds., *The Japanese Colonial Empire,* 5.

49. See especially Marc Raeff, *Understanding Imperial Russia: State and Society in the Old Regime* (New York: Columbia University Press, 1984); Hugh Seton-Watson, *The Russian Empire, 1801–1917* (Oxford: Clarendon Press, 1967); John A. Armstrong, *The European Administrative Elite* (Princeton: Princeton University Press, 1973).

50. Richard S. Dunn, *Sugar and Slaves: The Rise of the Planter Class in the English West Indies, 1624–1713* (London: W. W. Norton, 1972).

51. Martin J. Murray, *The Development of Capitalism in Colonial Indonesia (1870–1940)* (Berkeley: University of California Press, 1980), 20.

52. I do not consider here as a separate issue the relationship between indigenous peoples and colonial states identified with immigrant settler populations, in recent times often characterized as "internal colonialism." This term achieved visibility with its use in Michael Hechter, *Internal Colonialism: The Celtic Fringe in British National Development, 1536–1966* (London: Routledge and Kegan Paul, 1975). Although Hechter has abandoned this framework as paradigm, others find it useful as a vehicle for analyzing the situation of native peoples in the Americas, Arctic groups in Russia, and indigenous communities in Australasia. Whatever perspective one adopts with respect to the internal-colonialism proposition, contemporary Canada, Russia, and the United States are not colonial states in the sense used in this study, analogous to British India or the Belgian Congo.

53. Stephen Saunders Webb, *The Governors-General: The English Army and the Definition of the Empire, 1569–1681* (Chapel Hill: University of North Carolina Press, 1979), 39.

54. Ibid., 438.

55. Sir Charles Lucas, ed., *Lord Durham's Report on the Affairs of British North America* (Oxford: Clarendon Press, 1912), 1:26, 28.

56. Knorr, *British Colonial Theories*, 234.

57. For a lucid rendering of the convict origins of the Australian settlements, and their legacy, see Robert Hughes, *The Fatal Shore* (New York: Knopf, 1986).

58. The phrase comes from Francis G. Hutchins, *The Illusion of Permanence: British Imperialism in India* (Princeton: Princeton University Press, 1967).

59. Jacques Lafaye, *Quetzalcoatl and Guadalupe: The Formation of Mexican National Consciousness, 1531–1813* (Chicago: University of Chicago Press, 1976). I am grateful to Professor Lafaye for a number of illuminating conversations concerning the Spanish colonial state during our joint sojourn at the Institute for Advanced Study in Princeton in 1980 and 1981.

60. Philip D. Curtin, *The Atlantic Slave Trade: A Census* (Madison: University of Wisconsin Press, 1969).

61. Quoted in Eric Williams, *History of the People of Trinidad and Tobago* (New York: Frederic A. Praeger, 1962), 86.

62. Gordon K. Lewis, *The Growth of the Modern West Indies* (New York: Monthly Review Press, 1968), 109.

63. Ibid., 71, 115.

64. I am indebted to John Stephens and Evelyn Stephens for this observa-

tion, and for their critical reading of the paper that served as forerunner to this book.

65. Mark R. Peattie, *Nanyo: The Rise and Fall of the Japanese in Micronesia, 1885–1945* (Honolulu: University of Hawaii Press, 1988), 104.

66. Ibid., 316.

67. Influential recent works seeking an explanation for the phenomenal pace of economic expansion in South Korea and Taiwan in recent years include Robert Wade, *Governing the Market: Economic Theory and the Role of Government in East Asian Industrialization* (Princeton: Princeton University Press, 1990), and Alice Amsden, *Asia's Next Giant: South Korea and Late Industrialization* (New York: Oxford University Press, 1989). Although these interpretations do not stress the colonial impact, it did not have the negative consequences so visible in Africa.

68. Dodge, *Islands and Empires,* 173–74.

69. For an account, see Rex Mortimer, *Indonesian Communism under Sukarno: Ideology and Politics, 1959–1965* (Ithaca, N.Y.: Cornell University Press, 1974). Mortimer estimates the number slaughtered at between half a million and one million.

70. Herbert Feith, *The Decline of Constitutional Democracy in Indonesia* (Ithaca, N.Y.: Cornell University Press, 1962), 1–2.

71. On Indonesian ethnic issues, see Crawford Young, *The Politics of Cultural Pluralism* (Madison: University of Wisconsin Press, 1976), 327–72.

72. J. S. Furnivall, *Colonial Policy and Practice* (Cambridge: Cambridge University Press, 1948), 256, quoting from his 1939 book, *Netherlands Indies.*

73. In comparing popular art in the two countries at that time, a jarring contrast was even then visible. Zairian popular art was far more pessimistic, viewing the past as a series of tragic episodes: the slave trade, the coming of Bula Matari, the oppressiveness of the colonial order, the disappointments of independence. See Crawford Young, "Painting the Burden of the Past," in Bogumil Jewsiewicki, ed., *Art Pictural Zairois* (Quebec City: Editions du Septentrion, 1992), 117–38.

74. Milton E. Osborne, *The French Presence in Cochinchina and Cambodia: Rule and Response (1859–1905)* (Ithaca, N.Y.: Cornell University Press, 1969).

75. Buttinger, *Vietnam,* 124.

76. A 1908 Congress resolution, cited in V. P. Menon, *The Transfer of Power in India* (Princeton: Princeton University Press, 1957), 11.

77. Philip Woodruff [Mason], *The Men Who Ruled India: The Guardians* (London: Jonathan Cape, 1954), 2:158.

78. P. Hardy, *The Muslims of British India* (Cambridge: Cambridge University Press, 1972), 134.

79. Philip Mason, *A Matter of Honour* (New York: Holt, Rinehart, and Winston, 1974); Stephen Cohen, *The Indian Army* (Berkeley: University of California Press, 1971).

80. I am grateful to Atul Kohli for insisting on this contrast in his comments on an earlier paper on this subject. The resiliency of this ethos of professionalism doubtless explains the greater resistance of the ICS successor, the Indian Administrative Service, to the pressures for penetration of clientelistic norms and behavior. See also Ralph Braibanti, ed., *Asian Bureaucratic Systems Emergent from the British Imperial Tradition* (Durham: Duke University Press, 1986).

81. Jawaharlal Nehru, *The Discovery of India* (New York: Meridian Books, 1946).

82. Woodruff, *The Men Who Ruled India,* 1:242.

83. E. L. Woodward, *The Age of Reform, 1815–1870* (Oxford: Clarendon Press, 1954), 390.

84. Mason, *A Matter of Honour,* 273.

85. I am particularly indebted, for a synthesis of historical material on the Philippines, to Mohammed Kismadi, Indonesian journalist, intellectual, and quondam doctoral candidate, who served as my research assistant for a year and had lived in the Philippines for several years. For an overview of the Spanish impact, the admirable monograph by John Leddy Phelan, *The Hispanization of the Philippines* (Madison: University of Wisconsin Press, 1959), remains an invaluable source.

86. Dodge, *Islands and Empires,* 171.

87. James Griffith, Hank Nelson, and Stewart Firth, *Papua New Guinea: A Political History* (Richmond, Australia: Heinemann Educational Australia, 1979); J. A. Ballard, ed., *Policy-Making in a New State: Papua New Guinea, 1972–1977* (St. Lucia: University of Queensland Press, 1981).

88. Christopher M. Andrew and A. S. Kanya-Forstner, *The Climax of French Imperial Expansion, 1914–1924* (Stanford: Stanford University Press, 1981), 216–36.

89. Mary C. Wilson, *King Abdullah, Britain, and the Making of Jordan* (Cambridge: Cambridge University Press, 1987).

90. I am grateful to Brian Digre for his assistance in synthesizing the secondary literature concerning the French mandates. See especially, on Syria, Philip S. Khoury, *Syria and the French Mandate: The Politics of Arab Nationalism, 1920–1945* (Princeton: Princeton University Press, 1987).

91. John A. A. Ayoade, "States without Citizens: An Emerging African Phenomenon," in Donald Rothchild and Naomi Chazan, eds., *The Precarious Balance: State and Society in Africa* (Boulder: Westview Press, 1988), 100–04. On the "Mother Theresa" state, see also Jane L. Guyer, "Representation without Taxation: An Essay on Democracy in Rural Nigeria, 1952–1960," *African Studies Review* 35 (April 1992): 41–79.

92. Kohli was again helpful in suggesting a contrast between the evolution of

welfare and development concepts as state tasks in India and Nigeria; personal communication.

93. Achille Mbembe, *Afriques indociles: Christianisme, pouvoir et Etat en société postcoloniale* (Paris: Karthala, 1988), 39.

Chapter 9: The Afterlife of the African Colonial State

1. T. K. Biayi, "L'impasse de crise zairoise et la peinture populaire urbaine, 1970–1985," paper presented at conference on Popular Urban Painting from Zaire: History and Politics, Social Knowledge and Poetics, Woodrow Wilson International Center for Scholars, June 1987. Recourse to the religious realm as an autonomous zone of retreat, resistance, and salvation is a common popular response to the years of distress and decline for most Africans; see also Achille Mbembe, *Afriques indociles: Christianisme, pouvoir et Etat en société postcoloniale* (Paris: Karthala, 1988).

2. The symbolic role of architecture as a discourse of power is engagingly examined in Harold D. Lasswell, *The Signature of Power* (New Brunswick, N.J.: Transaction Books, 1979).

3. J. F. Ade Ajayi, "Expectations of Independence," *Daedalus* 111 (Spring 1982): 2.

4. Crawford Young, *Ideology and Development in Africa* (New Haven: Yale University Press, 1982).

5. Mamadou Diouf, personal communication.

6. This statement summarized the essence of an address opening a colloquium on administrative ethos in Dakar, Senegal, in December 1987, organized by Professor Jacques Nzouankeu.

7. For some evidence, see Robert Bates, *Markets and States in Rural Africa* (Berkeley: University of California Press, 1981), and Crawford Young, Neal Sherman, and Tim Rose, *Cooperatives and Development: Agricultural Politics in Ghana and Uganda* (Madison: University of Wisconsin Press, 1981).

8. Mbembe, *Afriques indociles*, 128–43.

9. J. Copans, *Les marabouts et l'arachide: La confrèrie mouride et les paysans du Sénégal* (Paris: Editions le Sycamore, 1980), 248; see also Christian Coulon, *Le marabout et le prince: Islam et pouvoir au Sénégal* (Paris: Editions A. Pedone, 1981), 289.

10. Max Weber, "Politics as a Vocation," reprinted in H. H. Gerth and C. Wright Mills, eds., *From Max Weber: Essays in Sociology* (New York: Oxford University Press, 1958), 82–83.

11. Young, *Ideology and Development in Africa*, 106.

12. Jean-François Bayart, *L'Etat au Cameroun* (Paris: Presses de la Fondation Nationale des Sciences Politiques, 1979).

13. Comi M. Toulabor, *Le Togo sous Eyadema* (Paris: Karthala, 1986).

14. For analysis of the Mobutu regime in this period, see Thomas Callaghy, *The State-Society Struggle: Zaire in Comparative Perspective* (New York: Columbia University Press, 1984), and Crawford Young and Thomas Turner, *The Rise and Decline of the Zairian State* (Madison: University of Wisconsin Press, 1985).

15. This notion finds elegant elaboration in Richard Joseph, *Democracy and Prebendal Politics in Nigeria* (Cambridge: Cambridge University Press, 1987). See also Robert H. Jackson and Carl G. Rosberg, *Personal Rule in Black Africa* (Berkeley: University of California Press, 1982).

16. There was a fair amount of peculation at the "Native Administration" level, whose operation prefigured the patrimonial politics of the postcolonial era. For examples, see Gavin Kitching, *Class and Economic Change in Kenya: The Making of an African Petite-Bourgeoisie* (New Haven: Yale University Press, 1980).

17. I acknowledge the insightful comments of Mamadou Diouf on an earlier paper developing some of the themes of this work. "The impossibility (or difficulty) in the development of capitalism is structural," Diouf writes, "and is linked to these state institutions and apparatus which have not undergone major modification at the moment of independence." Personal communication.

18. For two excellent case studies, see Janet MacGaffey, *The Real Economy of Zaire: The Contribution of Smuggling and Other Unofficial Activities to National Wealth* (Philadelphia: University of Pennsylvania Press, 1991), and William Reno, "Who Really Rules Sierra Leone? Informal Markets and the Ironies of Reform," Ph.D. diss., University of Wisconsin—Madison, 1991.

INDEX

Abernethy, David B.: on ethnicity, 235
Absolutism: state, 15–16
Accumulation: economic management, 39, 40; link to revenue, 133–38; development, 215–17; ingredients of, 255–56
Adedeji, Adebayo (director of U.N. Economic Commission), 4
Afrikaners: ancestors, 81
Afrique Occidental Française (AOF), 88
Agriculture: importance to state, 133, 134; taxes, 172, 214; export markets, 179; post–World War II demands, 213
AIDS, 8
Ajayi, J. F. Ade (Jacob), 4; on new African elites, 284
Algeria, 80, 206; importance of settlers, 161–62; post–World War II, 190; arms availability, 203
Amin, Idi, 9, 41
Anglo-Belgium Indian Rubber Co., 104
Angola: relation with South Africa, 9; slave trade, 81
Angoulvant, Gabriel (governor-

general of Nigeria): on head tax, 127–28; military effort from colonial states, 144; on population, 169
Anthropology, colonial, 233–34
Anti-imperialism, 187
Apthorpe, Raymond: on tribes, 233
Autocracy: African external and internal, 118–22; loss by colonial state, 204–8; beginnings with colonial state, 247–49; one-party system, 285–86
Awolowo, Obafemi (Nigerian leader), 231
Ayoade, John: on postcolonial state evolution, 5

Badie, Bertrand: on state functions, 20
Balandier, Georges: on Europeans and Africans, 229
Baudouin (King of Belgium), 207
Bayart, Jean-François: on African state, 5; on civil society, 221
Belgium: Bula Matari, 1–2, 3; colonial hegemony, 100; charter companies,